LARSON'S BOOK OF CULTS

LARSON'S
BOOK OF

Bob Larson

Tyndale House Publishers, Inc., Wheaton, Illinois

I would like to extend a special thanks to Gretchen
and Robert Passantino, for their expert advice and
review of the original manuscript.

Scripture references are taken from the *King
James Version* of the Bible, unless otherwise
indicated.

First printing, September 1982
Library of Congress Catalog Number 82-60018
ISBN 0-8423-2104-7

Contents

Pseudo-Christian Cults

Personality Cults

Occult/Mystical Cults

AN INTRODUCTION TO THE CULTS

1

Drinking at the Fountain

It was only five-thirty in the morning, but this author had already been up over an hour. Most people rise early in Banaras, India, the Hindu "holy city." Each day, more than one-half million begin springing from bed long before sunrise. Their trek to the shores of the river Ganges must be completed before the tip of that glowing orb lifts above the eastern horizon.

Most of them carry buckets or vials — some kind of container — to ferry Ganges water back to their homes. The Ganges provides thousands of Banaras residents with their only source of drink and bathing. Never mind that its putrid flow is spiked with human excrement and the carcasses of dead cattle. When its journey begins, high in the Himalayas, Ganges water may be pristine. But by the time this most sacred river in all Hinduism reaches the plains of Banaras, its translucent stream has turned into a murky green soup of sewage.

Devout Hindus hurry toward the Ganges as vendors of various religious accessories vie for their attention. They offer a wide assortment of pious wares. The most popular is a small garland of flowers costing more than these poor people can easily afford. But gaining the favor of the mother goddess of the Ganges is worth almost any price. To the non-Hindu it probably seems absurd. If that small string of petals were to festoon the buyer's neck or grace his home with fragrance, the expenditure might be considered a reasonable investment. But instead of having some personal value, this small garland is taken to the Ganges and placed in its current to float downstream.

This wasn't the first time the author had witnessed the daily Banaras ritual of sunworship. Ten years earlier the mist of the Ganges dawn had beckoned these curious eyes. At that same time a decade ago, halfway across the Indian subcontinent, a musical group known as the Beatles had also traveled to this land of fables and fakirs. Their journey had taken them to Rishikesh where they chose to meditate at the feet of a bearded swami named Maharishi Mahesh Yogi.

In 1968 the Beatles proclaimed that Transcendental Meditation was the answer to all mankind's distress. Though the advice sounded strange to most Westerners, it wasn't the first time that the "virtues" of Hinduism had been exported beyond the shores of India. Long before the current invasion of mysticism took root in the philosophically sterile milieu of twentieth century science and technology, the Eastern perspective was hailed as a superior world-view. In 1893 the Parliament of World Religions, held in Chicago, felt the first surge of what was to become a transcendental tidal wave. In praise of the Hinduistic concept of God, theosophists and *swamis* echoed the endorsement of nineteenth century luminaries, Emerson and Thoreau. (On the shores of Walden Pond, the latter had pored over pages of the *Bhagavad-Gita*.)

American Protestantism was jolted by the message of delegates to the Parliament who declared, "All is one. Man is divine. God is not out there, he is within every man." A seed had been planted and the pluralism of republican democracy insured that it would grow wherever non-Christian thinking predominated. Mysticism flourished in the fifties beatnik culture of Jack Kerouac, Allen Ginsberg, Herman Hesse, and Alan Watts. With the advent of the flower-powered sixties, psychedelia fostered "religious" experiences that paralleled the introspection of Thoreau and the mystical vision in the *Tibetan Book of the Dead*.

The next step came in the late sixties. Young pop fans who had screamed their lungs breathless at the beguiling Fab Four in Shea Stadium, now heard their music idols singing "I am he as you are he as you are me and we are all together" (from "The Walrus"). What did the Beatles mean? Alan Watts and crew smiled knowingly as the Liverpool Foursome went on to sing of "Instant Karma." It was left to George Harrison, after the group split, to erase all doubts about pop music's role in promoting Eastern religions when "My Sweet Lord" chanted praises to the Hindu pantheon.

As preparations were being made for a short boat trip down the Ganges, this author nostalgically surveyed how much Western culture had changed in those ten years. *Yoga, mantras,* and *gurus* had become as American as the proverbial apple pie. And it all began in Banaras. Here was the fountain of all Hinduism (and just up the road a few miles at Sarnath, the birthplace of Buddha and his "enlightenment"). As the boatsman leaned against his oars to propel the rickety craft upstream, the first rays of the "sun-god" streaked above the Earth's rim.

Devout Hindus streamed down the *ghats* (steps) leading to the water's edge. Small canopies sheltered stationary swamis who watched over the personal belongings of their devotional clients. Watches, exterior clothing, and hand-carried items were placed at their feet for safe-keeping while the devotees stripped to the bare essentials and launched out waist-deep into the waters. Worshipers clasped their hands in gestures of prayer as the ritual of dipping and bathing began. Some chanted mantras of praise to the Lord Sun. Others drank profusely from the river. On the banks the more energetic contorted their limbs in yogic postures. Those who arrived early were collecting their containers of Ganges water for the walk home.

Every few feet on the bank a *lingam* (a three foot high, Hindu phallic symbol of fertility) rose above the *ghats*. The eye of a Westerner couldn't miss either this erotic symbol or the huge culvert pouring refuse into the stream near the spot where thousands performed their ceremonies. To remind these devotees that this outlet dispensed all the sewage of Banaras' 800,000 souls would have been a futile warning. The Ganges is a god, and god is pure and "holy" no matter what the cholera statistics say to the contrary.

Further upstream the boat passes near the burning *ghats,* the site where devout Hindus are cremated. Every orthodox Hindu wants to die in Banaras. Legend has it that doing so circumvents the endless cycle of reincarnation. Those whose bodies are burned in the "holy city" are freed from transmigrations and are absorbed directly into the Brahman Absolute. Only victims of smallpox and other contagious diseases are exempted. Fanatical Hindus fear that germs may be reincarnated ancestors; they thus avoid cremation the one time it would be medically advisable. In those cases, the bodies are thrown into the Ganges to pollute its waters in a deathly manner.

Having navigated the two-mile stretch of river rimmed with *ghats,* the oarsman steered toward the original point of departure. For this author, the boat ride was a microcosmic reminder of how scenes so familiar a decade earlier were now less shocking to the Western mind. Ten years ago these same scenes would have produced a case of culture shock. This time, it all seemed so familiar. What had changed? Banaras appeared no different with its millennia-old religious rituals. What made Banaras seem less exotic was the extensive incursion such beliefs and practices had made on Western values and lifestyles.

As the boat touched shore amidst a flotilla of garlands offered to appease the Ganges goddess, a wail of grief pierced the still, morning air. Not far away, an Indian woman writhed in agony at the feet of a six-foot-tall stone idol — Hanuman, the monkey-god. Half human with a monkey's head, the lifeless statue was oblivious to the penitent's desperate pleas. Though her god failed to respond, she persisted in her cry for assistance, pressing herself against its cold, limestone legs.

The cause of her desperation was undiscernible to one who couldn't speak Hindi. Even her fellow citizens paid little attention to her hysterical plight. Perhaps their subservience to the fatalistic philosophy of Hinduism dulled their ability to empathize. After all, whatever the source of her distress, the law of *karma* is immutable. If she were suffering, so be it. The will of the gods and the consequences of reaping have no ultimate remedy in this life, or the next. Even Hanuman surely knew that.

Though her tongue was impossible to translate, the grief of her spirit spoke a universal language. As with millions of Americans trapped in the bondage of cults, her petition for help went unheeded. Hinduism, the mother faith of many cults, had no spiritual nourishment to offer her pleading soul. In a word-picture this hungering Indian woman epitomized what the faith of the East has done to the hope of the West.

What struck this author as most ironic, was the date of this tragic April morning scene. As the pathetic woman sought the assistance of a mongrelized demigod to relieve her crushing burden, it just happened to be Easter Sunday. All around the world, millions of Christians were reaffirming the glorious news, "He is risen!" If this woman could have comprehended those three words in English, this author would have rushed to her side with the message of hope in Christ. And if the reader had witnessed the same scene, his desire to share the message of Jesus would undoubtedly have been just as urgent.

Are we also aware that many others involved in cults languish in the same predicament? They kneel at the feet of Joseph Smith, Mary Baker Eddy, Charles and Myrtle Fillmore, Bhagwan Shree Rajneesh, Charles Taze Russell, L. Ron Hubbard, Herbert W. Armstrong, Meher Baba, and scores of others who claim (or claimed) to possess the answer to life's search for truth. Do the unheard and unanswered cries of today's cult adherents stir our spirits with compassion and love?

This book is the most exhausting, challenging, and compelling task this author has ever attempted. During long nights of burning midnight oil and consuming inexhaustible hours of intensive investigation, the plaintive wail of that Indian woman has been a haunting reminder of the urgency of this mission. It is for her, and for the sake of those who share her slavery, that this book has been carefully researched and prayerfully written.

2

Dismantling the Myth

The swamis are coming from India, and they're taking away the flock. They're speaking of religion as dealing with the interior of life and not about dogmatic formulae and ritual requirements. — Joseph Campbell, author of *The Masks of God* and professor of literature at Sarah Lawrence College.

Such is the way one writer described the current voguish interest in Eastern mysticism. Most Westerners don't seem to care that the Oriental system of faith is based on a tenuous, mystical foundation. The manner in which cults of the East present a veiled explanation of truth, is apparently of no more concern to the modern mind than whether Joseph Smith (Mormonism's founder) really did discover golden plates buried in Palmyra, New York, or whether Victor Wierwille (guiding force of The Way) actually heard the voice of God. As a result, 20 million Americans involved in cults have placed their hope in belief structures with tenets based on mixtures of fact and fantasy.

It matters little to the mystic whether his system of worship is historically accurate. If Krishna's discourses with Arjuna in the *Bhagavad-Gita* are mere legends, pointing out this fact is dismissed with a shrug. Expediency is what counts. Consequently, the historic validation of an empty tomb and a blood-stained cross has little meaning to the mystic's mind. Whether Calvary and the Resurrection actually took place seems less important to the false religionist than what he sees as the allegorical grandeur of the story.

But truth *does* matter! When the legendary accounts which comprise the superstructure of mystical philosophy have collapsed, the child of God must be ready to offer the disillusioned an objectively valid response to the "whys" of life. When the myths have been shattered, the Bible-based Christian should be in a position to defend the claims of Jesus' divinity. "Be ready always to give an answer to every man that asketh a reason of the hope that is in you," the Apostle Peter urged (1 Pet. 3:15). This book has been written to help provide that answer. The reader whose faith is experientially rooted in the living Logos will find on these pages a concrete intellectual rationale for pointing the cultist to the historical Christ.

American soil has been the foremost battleground in the war of the cults versus Christianity. It's ironic this struggle has occurred here. Both the devout and the deists who settled this land were committed to a transcendent faith which recognized a personal God based on the Judeo-Christian model. However, a careful study of America's past reveals that even those early years of settling and exploration were influenced by the breeze that became the tumultuous gale of twentieth century cultism. The promise of free exercise of religion which originally lured people to this land also fostered utopian, communal, and apocalyptic dreams. The American vision has always been enamored with idealistic answers promising a simplistic and sacred explanation for life's purpose. This philosophy of "Manifest Destiny" has been most evident in times of cultural transition such as the Armageddon-crazed days of the industrial revolution. Today's cult invasion is the cultural extension of this uniquely American attitude.

Established religion, the legitimizer of the status quo, suffers today from the moral vacuum created in part by technology's triumph. In this setting, the myth of the cults helps to steady men's nerves and placate their fears. Exploring psychic inner space and conducting mythic ceremonies seem to reinforce each man's worth in the computer age. The ritualism and imagery of our twentieth century cultic myths (whether they are a Mormon's proxy baptism or the promise of astral travel held forth by ECKANKAR advocates) awaken a sense of awe about man's relationship to the world around him. Most of all, the mythology of the cults reveals to the "faithful" where they belong in the scheme of the universe. From birth to death the cultist is guided by his myth with an assurance that each step fits into the divine order.

Souls for whom Christ shed his blood deserve more of a spiritually fulfilling answer than that which is provided by modern myths. The author of this book bears a solemn obligation. If Jehovah's Witnesses really do have inside information about the world's end, and if Scientology really can extinguish our hang-ups from past lives, you, the reader, have a right to know. If Moon is the Messiah or if Baha'u'llah was the Christ, then no personal prejudice should stand in the way of proclaiming these facts. But if these spiritual leaders and philosophers are in error, then every person whose life this book touches deserves to know the unvarnished truth.

The reader also has a right to know that the theological perspective of this volume is committed to an evangelical Christian stance. This author has not been commissioned by any church or denomination. No official communion of any theological persuasion has given instructions to dismantle a particular philosophy held dear by any cult group or leader. Orthodox, Protestant, and Reformation presuppositions alone provide the frame of reference for the analysis of each cult. Two basic theological principles guide this study: (1) Jesus Christ is fully God, from eternity past to eternity future (Col. 2:10); and (2) obedience to the command that Christians are to, "Abhor that which is evil; cleave to that which is good" (Rom. 12:9).

This book is not intended to be a sociological or theological treatise. Its purpose is to aid and inform the average person whose friends or loved ones are involved in cult activities. *Larson's Book of Cults* is also intended to prepare the layman who dreads the intrusion of the canvassing cultist knocking on his door. Each commentary is intended to be practical, embellished with the author's personal experiences confronting the cults. It also includes the insights gained from travels to over seventy countries (including many weeks of research in Indian and Asian societies).

Why is the myth of the cults so attractive to modern man? Is the recent explosion of cult activity indicative of societal or spiritual factors? Has America's proclivity for "inventive" solutions caused her to turn Eastward? Is it the fault of science for heralding the advance of problem-solving by microprocessors? Can the innate spiritual hunger in man's heart be blamed for pursuing escapist solutions to desperate dilemmas? Or has mankind entered an age in which conflicting supernatural forces tug at his allegiance in one final bid for control of civilization before its last gasp?

The secular behaviorist would probably choose one or more of the above explanations while the evangelical Christian would, in all likelihood, check off all five. There are other causes one might add to this list. In his book, *Those Curious New Cults,* author William Petersen includes: (1) disillusionment with American political life; (2) dehumanization by science; (3) advent of the drug culture; (4) future fright (fear of nuclear or environmental cataclysms); (5) breakdown of the family; (6) popular culture (music and literature); (7) psychology and the occult (Jung to Joseph Rhine); (8) decline of the church; and (9) the ecology crisis.

Because of these and other reasons, an estimated 1,500 to 3,000 cult groups flourish in North American society. Their adherents range from thousands to small bands of disciples numbering a few hundred or less. Membership is divided between established cults with reasonably respectable followings (e.g. Mormonism, Christian Science, Unity) and New Age Cults. The latter believe that man's evolutionary spiritual ascent will reach fruition in a new-dawning era of utopian goals of spiritual brotherhood and peace. All cults have one thing in common. They consider the claims of Christ to be optional, not essential to salvation.

Idealistic young people whose quest for spiritual identity supersedes their desire for materialistic comfort, are ripe for exploitation by cultic myths. The promise of psychic enhancement and raised consciousness has a powerful sway over the naive and unsuspecting. Adolescents who want to intellectually short-circuit the agonizing process of maturation can be easily victimized by a myth which offers a painless way of ignoring the discomfort of learning life's lessons the hard way. New Age Cults are particularly adept at beckoning the lonely and confused to step over the threshold of an altered perception of reality. All the answers to mankind's great questions are dismissed by merging one's ego into the common good of the cult's vision for the future. The myth they offer is no passing fad. Their vision of remaking the world will endure even after the most optimistic predictions of a Rev. Moon have been proven false.

The mythology of cult teaching presents a formidable challenge to society. Secularists who once said, "It can't happen to my kids," have had their illusions shattered. Instead of reaching out to meet the needs of a searching generation, they have offered the solutions of governmental control or remedial deprogramming. Interference by the State in matters of religious conviction is a specter that could haunt religious freedom for years to come. Legislated regulations aimed at bizarre groups could one day be turned into edicts which would hinder legitimate alternative expressions of faith. Recent clashes between humanists and evangelicals illustrate all too succinctly that antireligionists would not hesitate to use any lawful power to thwart the concerns of born-again believers. "Today the Moonies, tomorrow the Pentecostals" may be a slogan of alarm worth heeding.

Those whose responsibility it would be to establish religious norms might well someday officially repudiate the Bible in favor of atheism. What then? Temporarily stemming the tide of cult brainwashing probably appeals to evangelicals, especially those whose children have become cult converts. But undermining First Amendment rights to achieve momentary suppression of an undesirable belief system might eventually invite suppression of biblically orthodox groups.

The plight of parents whose offspring have been

unfairly captivated by mind-bending cults is a genuine
concern of everyone, especially jurists. There is no way
to calculate the emotional grief of a mother and father
who suddenly find a family member undergoing a
complete personality transformation. What is a parent to
do when his own child sees him as an instrument of Satan
and refuses to answer calls or letters? For some,
deprogramming, forceable kidnapping, and "coercive
dissuasion," seem to be their last hope.

For fees upwards of $10,000 they enlist the services of a
"professional" such as Ted Patrick ("Black Lightning"),
who will abduct the cult adherent and sequester him in a
motel room where his cult beliefs are persistently
challenged. Patrick, whose activities have earned him
frequent brushes with the law, claims to have
deconverted more than 1,600 young people. Such
conduct raises serious questions about violating the law
to prevent so-called "greater injury" to one's mind and
beliefs. It would appear that the First Amendment
guarantees the right of any person to believe what he
wishes. Patrick argues that certain cults have so
perfected their recruitment techniques that their victims
are effectively denied the privilege of free moral choice.
Whether fighting fire with fire is justifiable, considering
the circumstances, is a major question facing those
concerned with protecting religious freedoms.

Most Christians would oppose violating an individual's
will and integrity to free him from any kind of
enslavement. They would argue that it is only the truth of
Christ that makes any man free (John 8:32) and that
violence should not answer violence. In analyzing this
phenomenon, the Spiritual Counterfeit Project newsletter
concluded, "We are convinced that the insidious
infringements of personality which are involved in cultic
manipulation of commitment should not remain totally
beyond the reach of society and its sanctions. Since one
of the key techniques of coercive persuasion is to isolate
the perspective convert from any influence which might
challenge or disrupt the belief-system, we believe that a
person who has been subjected to such techniques
should have an opportunity to evaluate his or her
commitment and beliefs free from the self-reinforcing
context of cult involvement with its propaganda, fear,

guilt, and harassment." The S.C.P. recommends "reality testing" applied through the authority of the government "by means of conservatorship proceedings or some acceptable substitute."

Even if a morally and legally acceptable method to extract cult members is found, the fundamental issue of countering cult evangelism still needs to be addressed. The appalling number of cult devotees who have left evangelical ranks poses a crucial question. How well is the Church training its members to understand the foundation of their beliefs? Countering the cult invasion requires that Christians be properly grounded in the biblical science of apologetics. Believers may need to be reminded that they have a sacred responsibility to "contend for the faith which was once delivered unto the saints" (Jude 3).

The prolific growth of the cults is not likely to recede anytime soon. As Dr. Walter Martin points out, Christians cannot sit back passively and assume that those teachers who are not of God will eventually fade away. Some who adopt this passive attitude cite Gamaliel's advice to the Jewish council (Acts 5:33-39) as their theological pretext. When Gamaliel advised his brethren not to oppose the apostles lest they also oppose God, his counsel was directed toward a consideration of anti-Christian persecution. Thus Gamaliel's proposition cannot be used to justify a failure to counter false doctrines. Adopting such an attitude would be to concede Godly origin to the successes of major world religions which oppose Christian beliefs. To "just preach the Gospel" and leave the cults to "hang themselves when they get enough rope" would be to confine the Great Commission to non-cult evangelism.

If Christians are to confidently challenge the cults, they must be spiritually prepared. "Judgment must begin at the house of God" (1 Pet. 4:17) and confronting the myth of the cults also means the Church first has to purge its own ranks. Doing so requires facing some serious, introspective questions. What about the excessive authority conceded to Christian leaders who command large followings? How much attention is being paid to encouraging strong family units where young people find secure parental relationships that are too strong for cult authoritarianism to crack? Do laymen need carefully to weigh in the light of Scripture the pronouncements of their respected leaders? (Even the Apostle Paul acknowledged the necessity of such checks and balances in Acts 17:11.) Should the Church be reminded of the supernatural gifts and spiritual spontaneity which characterized its early growth and is now indicative of what sometimes attracts youth to cults? To dismiss the success of aberrant beliefs with the excuse that Satan has blinded the eyes of cultists could be a way of ignoring the fact that the true Church is also at fault.

The Apostle Paul's love for the Church caused him to do more than merely issue a warning about "grievous wolves." His command to defend diligently the cause of Christ ushered forth day and night "with tears" (Acts 20:28-31). Paul's impassioned appeal, coupled with Christ's advance notice ("Behold, I have told you before," Matt. 24:25), leaves some churches in the embarrassing position of having abdicated the throne of dominion over men's souls to the more energetic cult groups.

Sound theology, doctrinal purity, and aggressive evangelistic techniques do not provide the whole answer to thwarting cultic expansion. Christians are not only known by their adherence to lofty ethics rooted in biblical theology. John 13:34, 35 reminds believers that love is the mark of discipleship. And love for one's neighbor is the distinguishing characteristic of one's love for God. Such is the message of the Good Samaritan parable of Luke 10:30-35. A personal anecdote from the author may emphasize this fact in a practical manner.

Just a few paragraphs prior to penning this very page, there was a knock at the door of my cabin. (Most of my writing is done at a mountain retreat where there are no phones or visitors to interfere.) It was pouring rain outside, and two drenched Japanese-American girls named Harriet and Ellen were seeking entrance. Once inside, they explained to my wife and me that the friends they were with had slid off a muddy road and wrecked their car. They asked for a ride to a nearby lodge where they could call a tow truck. No writer appreciates an interruption. However, there was no choice but to render them immediate assistance in their distress.

The two girls were soaking wet and covered with mud. Needless to say, my vehicle suffered the consequences! To make matters worse, on the way to the lodge the heater fan conked out and the knob to the defroster fell off. It was as if one irritation after another was being heaped upon me to exacerbate the situation. After phoning for a wrecker, the girls asked me for another ride to the place where they had joined their friends and left their car — a half hour's drive away. There was no questioning that these young ladies needed my help. What concerned me was that their plight had interfered with what appeared to be a more important spiritual responsibility — writing this book.

On the way to retrieving their automobile, the conversation centered on the weather and how the accident occurred. Finally, Ellen asked what I did for a living. That led to a lengthy explanation regarding my personal faith in Christ, something neither girl seemed to understand.

"Where do you attend church?" I asked.

"We're Buddhists," they replied.

Suddenly, I knew why God had allowed this interruption. What I had considered an irritating infringement of my time was God's way of reminding me that this book was not as important as showing God's love and helping someone in need.

The devout Buddhist beliefs of Harriet and Ellen soon collided with my scriptural insistence that Christ is the only means of salvation. When we reached their car, Ellen's parting words climaxed the episode.

"Well, I guess we won't really know who's right until we're both dead," she concluded.

"But if Jesus was correct," I answered, "it will be a little too late for you to find out."

As I drove off, the Holy Spirit impressed upon me an important lesson. God loves mankind so much that he is willing to provide shelter and kindness even to those who reject his Son. My knowledge of the cults, particularly Buddhism, would probably have enabled me to argue effectively on an intellectual level with Harriet and Ellen. But God was more concerned about my extending a Samaritan act of love than my winning a theological debate in the defense of truth.

When I arrived back at the cabin I was prepared to pursue this book with new resolve and enthusiasm. Most importantly, I felt the need to do something more than just issue a warning about the dangers of cults. Dismantling the myth of the cults is not only the work of biblical apologetics, it is also a labor of love.

3

A Sociological Perspective on Cults

What is a cult? An adequate definition evades most people. *Webster's New Collegiate Dictionary* (1981) states that a cult represents a religious body that is "unorthodox or spurious." It also cites the wider perimeter of "devotion to a great person, idea, or thing," a frame of reference to which this book in part ascribes. To understand the technical and inherent implications of the word "cult," its sociological perimeters need to be explored. Before doing that, the theological considerations of this book need to be restated.

The sociological considerations of cult activity must mirror the standard that Christ is the source of determining error and truth. Thus, any group which intentionally manipulates its language to mimic evangelical beliefs must have its semantic distortions exposed. Any cult which places itself in opposition to historic Christianity should not be allowed to hide behind a cloak of religious good will or misleading terminology.

Do false belief systems deserve credit for their good works? Many cults have made significant contributions to the social welfare of humanity. In some instances cult leaders are sincerely concerned about meeting the spiritual needs of seeking souls. Even though this book recognizes positive elements in certain cults, it must not be forgotten that the Bible requires reproof and rebuke of any teaching which exalts itself against the necessity of salvation through Christ (2 Tim. 4:2). According to scriptural criteria, any false teacher is a "deceitful worker" (2 Cor. 11:13) who is an enemy "of the cross of Christ" (Phil. 3:18). Gratuitous words in recognition of positive values should not be mistaken for any endorsement of what the Bible calls "doctrines of devils" (1 Tim. 4:1).

With the biblical standards of cultic evaluation established, we now consider the question, "What is a cult?" It would be impossible in any treatment of this subject to consider all contingent factors. The listing of cults which appears later in the book is not intended to be exhaustive or definitively categoric. Each group will be classified according to the primary focus of its teachings. Thus, even established world religions which do not bear the sociological earmarks of a cult will be included because of their departure from Christian theology.

Apart from theological considerations, what classifies a certain group as a "cult"? The designation obviously requires a subjective value judgment. Many respectable groups that are admired by society (e.g. Mormons, Bahais) were considered repugnant and persecuted during their formation. In the sociological sense, who is to say which of today's non-traditional eccentrics will be considered socially acceptable in years to come? In Dr. Walter Martin's book *The Kingdom of the Cults,* Dr. Charles Braden is quoted as saying: "A cult . . . is any religious group which differs significantly in some one or more respects as to belief or practice from those religious groups which are regarded as the normative expression of religion in our total culture."

Ronald Enroth points out that the origin of the word "cult" can be traced to the Latin "cultus" which "connotes all that is involved in worship-ritual, emotion, liturgy, and attitude." Cultic philosophy is diverse, ranging from the rigidly aesthetic to the sexually permissive. Though adherents may exhibit certain typical motivational characteristics, attitudes vary from selfish narcissism to abandonment of the ego for communal welfare.

These are things which most cults share in common: (1) a centralized authority which tightly structures both philosophy and lifestyle; (2) a "we" versus "they" complex, pitting the supposed superior insights of the group against a hostile outside culture; (3) a commitment for each member to intensively proselytize the unconverted; and (4) an entrenched isolationism that divorces the devotee from the realities of the world at large.

In the beginning many such groups displayed sincere expressions of a humble desire to better society and follow God's will. At some point the founder's teachings were codified into an organized system of revelational authority. Allegiance to the founder's ideals became absolute prerequisites. What may have been one man's honest opinion was presented as having the weight of divine endorsement. If such a transformation takes place while the leader is still alive, he usually claims supernatural certification for his beliefs. What then develops is a "type of institutional dogmatism and a pronounced intolerance for any position but their own," according to Dr. Walter Martin.

The person who seeks out a cult or is ensnared by cult propaganda also fits a composite psychological profile. Conventional solutions and institutions may have struck him as being sterile or unfulfilling. He is looking for an affirming community with which he can identify. Such a group will be all the more appealing if it offers a single, idealistic principle around which his entire life can revolve. In a society which is biblically illiterate, the deception of cults is particularly enticing if they claim to have "restored" certain truths which have been lost or undiscovered.

Cults generally attract prospects with an outpouring of attention and affection, the so-called "love-bombing" technique. Feeling, not doctrine, is the lure. In fact, the belief structure is seldom mentioned in the beginning. Cult leaders know that once an initiate has been reconditioned to accept their particular world-view, and as soon as he feels a sense of meaningful belonging, his mind will be ready to accept any teaching, including a belief that the leader represents God.

When the recruit's mind shifts into neutral, the period of intensive indoctrination begins. The effectiveness of this tactic is often enhanced by sensory deprivation, extreme amounts of physical activity coupled with fatigue, severance of all ties with family and friends, and the forsaking of all belongings and material possessions. In a short time, the initiate becomes emotionally and spiritually dependent on the cult for decisions, direction and even the physical necessities of life. The outside world appears more and more threatening. Finally, his mind "snaps" and "the sudden, drastic alteration of personality in all its many forms" takes place.

Approval, acceptance, belonging, authority — all those things that were missing are supplied by the cult. Motivation is generated by rewards for excessive zeal. Critical thinking is discouraged and corporate identification with some larger-than-life mission (as conveyed by the leader) causes the member to equate what is good for the cult as being good for him. Young adult cult recruits are the least likely to consider thoughts of abandoning the group. Severing the cult-fostered dependency would mean having to cope with hardships and to fend for themselves in a hostile world. Any consideration of leaving immediately conjures guilt feelings of forsaking God's calling, falling into Satan's hands, or even worse, risking the wrath and judgment of God.

These profiles will not always be apparent with all cults or all adherents. One group may practice economic exploitation while another allows its members to maintain a lifestyle which is financially independent from the cult. Certain cults entice members who are curious about their secret doctrines while others openly evangelize by public propagation of their beliefs (though few cults qualify for this category). Most groups generally adhere to one or more of the characteristics that have been described.

The term "cult" as used in this book is generally understood to have a negative connotation which indicates morally reprehensible practices or beliefs which significantly depart from historic Christianity. However, no chapter is intended to ridicule any particular organization. Our main concern is with truth as it is biblically defined and with sound ethics as they are taught in Scripture. A cult may offend in one area without erring in another. For example, Mormonism maintains high ethical values while promoting tenets which are contrary to the Bible. Thus, Mormonism is classified as a cult because of its teachings while a group such as The Children of God are considered cultic because both their doctrines and ethics are unscriptural.

As an evangelical perspective, this book is concerned with any cult practice that insults human integrity or violates the sovereignty of the will. But an even more pertinent criterion concerns the Christian. Whether a belief system conforms to Scripture or the extent to which it departs from biblical precepts is the ultimate gauge for truth and error. As Ronald Enroth warns in *The Lure of the Cults,* any deviation from orthodoxy must be carefully considered with "spiritual discernment...lest the definition net be cast too widely."

Just what are the scriptural perimeters beyond which no religious group may lay claim to biblical orthodoxy?

4

A Christian Perspective on Cults

Because Christians believe that each person has been created by God with intrinsic human worth, they oppose any form of social bondage. This ideal alone places the Church in opposition to most cults. But there are certain morally conscious cults which also have high ethical values. These groups would oppose the dehumanizing practices of other groups with whom they are categorically lumped. Jehovah's Witnesses might justifiably be offended because they are included under the same heading as Children of God disciples. That's why it is so important for the reader to understand that from a Christian standpoint, any cult classification has to be made according to biblical criteria. As Dr. Walter Martin has observed, "A person can be morally good, but if he sets his face against Jesus, his fruit is corrupt."

Whether or not a particular religious group claims to be Christian is not a prime consideration. They may quote the Bible profusely and covet the endorsement of Christ for their efforts. But the premises of this book are based on two contingent factors which evaluate whether a group is cultic: (1) if they ignore or purposely omit central

Apostolic doctrines; or (2) if they hold to beliefs which are distinctly opposite to orthodox Christianity. Deviation from either criterion prohibits their inclusion in the Christian community.

The good works and apparent beneficial effects of their belief system are inconsequential considerations. Healing, for example, cannot validate the biblical credibility of a cult's doctrines. The miracles of Pharaoh's magicians (as recorded in Exodus 7) illustrate that the supernatural is an arena where both Godly and demonic powers operate. Only those with true scriptural discernment will be able to know whether good or evil can be credited as the source of any teaching. Jesus pointed out that apparent authority over evil spirits would not qualify one for entrance into heaven if the exorcist operated under a system of false doctrine (Matt. 7:21-23).

What perplexes many Christians is that the cultists they confront often seem to voice harmony with evangelical positions. They quote the Bible, profess devout reverence for Christ, and use the same familiar evangelical clichés. What the bewildered Christian fails to understand is that the cultist redefines orthodox terminology to suit his own belief system. In such a case, the cult adherent should be forced to assume an intellectually honest stance with reference to indispensable Bible doctrines. Only then will his perfidy of language be revealed for its malicious intent. Such individuals need to be clearly warned they are "handling the word of God deceitfully" (2 Cor. 4:2), an act which insures their own destruction (2 Pet. 3:16).

If a religious group is to be evaluated according to biblical criteria, what areas of doctrine are vital for consideration? Exclusivity, elitism, misplaced authority, and eschatological error are all cult characteristics. But these distinctives are not germane to determining orthodoxy. The basic fault of cults is that they demote God, devalue Christ, deify man, deny sin, and denigrate Scripture. Therefore, correct theology regarding all of the following Bible doctrines is necessary to be in accordance with historic Christianity.

1. The attributes of God
2. The Person of Christ

3. The nature of man
4. The requirements of atonement
5. The source of revelation

In the next chapter the faulty theological concepts of cults will be compared with Church doctrines which have endured and been affirmed throughout the ages. One intent of this book is to rekindle an interest in the fundamental doctrines of Christianity. The Apostle Peter warned that false teachers would invade the body of Christ (2 Pet. 2:1). But those who propagate "damnable heresies" will not go undetected where believers are thoroughly entrenched in biblical theology.

The major section of this book will give the reader a brief but comprehensive appraisal of those cults which are most threatening to the Church of Jesus Christ. This book is primarily written for the nonprofessional who wants to know where a certain cult originated, how it developed historically, the nature of its main teachings, and its relationship to biblical truth. Though some cults exhibit an arrogant air of superiority, care has been taken not to counter this attitude with a spirit of antagonism. The unlimited grace of God which the Apostle John so eloquently described (1 John 2:2) is extended to all who have not experienced salvation by grace, including the cultist. The cult adherent may wonder why the evangelical would dare to dispute his beliefs since they are presumed to be the "restored" or "revealed" truths of God. But such a response must be met with love that remembers that, except for God's intervention, the reader might also be ensnared in the same spiritual bondage.

Not everyone who reads this book will immediately become a missionary to counter the cults. But the knowledge on these pages will hopefully result in a prepared vessel whom the Lord can use when an appropriate opportunity presents itself. Some may choose to actively invade Satan's kingdom, being filled with the Spirit and determined to dismantle the myth that holds millions in spiritual servitude. Others will reach out with new love and empathy for those who sorrow because a family member has joined a cult. Still others may sense the need for rehabilitative follow-up programs which will minister to the emotional needs of those who have been ravaged by cult ideology. Any one of these fruits will make this book worth its investment of time and energy. May God show you, the reader, what part you should play in helping to destroy the myth of the cults.

5

Biblical Theology and the Cults

It has already been stated that the intent of this book is to avoid the approach of a weighty theological treatise. This does not mean that the author and publisher consider theology to be unimportant. In fact, the lack of sound biblical theology in our culture has resulted in a post-Christian era which enhances the myth of the cults. However, in the interest of compiling an easy-to-read guide of modern cults we have avoided the appearance of a treatment intended for the clergy alone. It is the man in the pew who most desperately needs clear guidelines to combat the cult invasion.

In the last chapter we cited five basic areas of doctrine where truth may be distinguished from error. Before embarking on an analysis of the cults that are a concern to this study, we will first delineate the position of historic Christianity regarding these five doctrines. A general synopsis will also be presented illustrating the typical cult response to these beliefs.

It should be noted that a prospectus this brief could not possibly present the belief of every major cult in respect to each doctrine. Only the most prevalent cult beliefs will be cited. In other words, a general, not definitive, cult view of major Christian doctrines is our concern. This will be of value in illustrating the basic philosophical system of the cultic myths. Any student of the cults recognizes immediately that within certain aberrational groupings there is a striking harmony in the way all false belief systems view truth. This is to be expected because all ideologies which are contrary to Scripture originated from the same source — Satan.

This brief theological survey was not constructed to precipitate a quarrel with any particular cult. It is the source (Satan) of all antichrist systems who is the Christian's real enemy. Those who expound erroneous doctrines may be sincere but misguided individuals. The purpose of the following outline is to determine the scriptural conformity of doctrines, not the motivational integrity of individuals.

There will be three divisions to each doctrine included in this analysis:

1. A statement regarding the historic Christian position will introduce each doctrinal section. Though this declaration will not be completely comprehensive, it will allow the reader to have at his fingertips a capsule summary of the basic biblical belief.
2. A list of five Scriptures supporting the biblical doctrine will provide corroborating evidence. In most cases, dozens of biblical references could have been cited, but for the purpose of brevity these five should suffice.
3. An example of three distinct cultic viewpoints on each doctrine will be presented. In some cases, there are many cultic variations but space limitations require condensing cult doctrines into these three categories. The cults listed as holding these teachings are representational examples only, not a complete catalogue of all cults adhering to such views.

Please note that all scriptural references are from the *King James Version* since this version is the one most frequently quoted (and misquoted) by cultists.

GOD

Christian Theology. Both the Old and New Testament proclaim the triune nature of God — Father, Son, and Holy

Spirit. They are co-equal, co-existent, and co-eternal, three Persons of the same Substance (John 1:1-3; 14:26). God is a personality who can speak and create and who possesses a mind and will (Gen. 1:1, 26; Jer. 29:11; Ezek. 18:30). God's character is eternal (1 Tim. 1:17), omnipotent (Rev. 19:6), omnipresent (Psa. 139:7-12), omniscient (Rom. 11:33), perfect (Deut. 32:4), and holy (1 Pet. 1:16).

Supportive Scriptures
1. 1 Cor. 8:6 — "...there is but one God, the Father, of whom are all things...."
2. Isa. 43:10 — "...before me there was no God formed, neither shall there be after me."
3. Exod. 3:14 — "And God said unto Moses, I AM THAT I AM...."
4. 1 Tim. 2:5 — "For there is one God...."
5. Psa. 90:2 — "...from everlasting to everlasting, thou art God."

Cult Doctrine
1. Impersonal, unknowable essence (Hinduism, Bahaism).
2. Divine idea, principle, or example (Christian Science, Unity).
3. Non-trinitarianism (Jehovah's Witnesses, The Way).

CHRIST

Christian Theology. The Apostles' Creed states: "Conceived by the Holy Ghost, born of the Virgin Mary, suffered under Pontius Pilate, died and was buried; He descended into Hell; the third day He arose from the dead; He ascended into Heaven and sitteth on the right hand of God the Father Almighty; from thence He shall come to judge the quick and the dead." Jesus Christ is the second Person of the Trinity, the eternally Begotten Son of God who became flesh and is now our "great high priest, that is passed into the heavens...[who] was in all points tempted like as we are, yet without sin" (Heb. 4:14, 15).

Supportive Scriptures
1. John 1:1, 3 — "In the beginning was the Word, and the Word was with God, and the Word was God....All

things were made by him; and without him was not any
thing made...."
2. John 1:14 — "And the Word was made flesh and dwelt
among us, (and we beheld his glory, the glory as of the
only begotten of the Father)...."
3. 1 John 4:3 — "...every spirit that confesseth not that
Jesus Christ is come in the flesh is not of God; and this
is the spirit of antichrist...."
4. Eph. 1:21 — "Far above all principality, and power, and
might, and dominion, and every name that is
named...."
5. Col. 2:9 — "For in him dwelleth all the fulness of the
Godhead bodily...."

Cult Doctrine
1. Merely a human being without divinity who attained
"Christ Consciousness" (The Church Universal and
Triumphant, The International Community of Christ).
2. Created being (Mormonism, Jehovah's Witnesses).
3. One of many *avatars* or revelations of God (Hinduism,
Divine Light Mission).

MAN

Christian Theology. God created man in his own image
(Gen. 1:26), perfect and without sin so that he could know
and love God. Man is the highest distinction of God's
creative genius, separate from him, made "a little lower
than the angels" (Psa. 8:5) with dominion over all the earth
(Gen. 1:28). In Eden, man fell by disobedience;
henceforth all men are conceived in sin with a depraved
nature destined for damnation unless they are spiritually
reborn (John 3:3).

Supportive Scriptures
1. Jer. 17:9 — "The heart is deceitful above all things, and
desperately wicked...."
2. Rom. 5:12 — "...by one man sin entered into the
world, and death by sin;...all have sinned."
3. Rom. 5:19 — "For as by one man's disobedience many
were made sinners...."
4. Psa. 51:5 — "...in sin did my mother conceive me."
5. Rom. 1:21 — "...their foolish heart was darkened."

Cult Doctrine
1. Divine, an emanation of the infinite Impersonal (Theosophy, Rosicrucianism).
2. Sinful but capable of attaining the same "Christ Consciousness" that Jesus did (Church Universal and Triumphant, Holy Order of MANS).
3. Destined to be a god (Mormonism, Worldwide Church of God).

ATONEMENT

Christian Theology. The Old Testament sacrifices foreshadowed the Lamb of God, "slain from the foundation of the world" (Rev. 13:8), whose shed blood would be the final sacrifice and cleansing for sin (1 John 1:7). Man, whose sinful rebellion has separated him from God, can now have "peace through the blood of his cross" (Col. 1:20) and be "reconciled" to God (2 Cor. 5:19) because of his vicarious, substitutionary death.

Supportive Scriptures
1. 1 Pet. 2:24 — "Who his own self bare our sins in his own body on the tree...."
2. Rom. 5:8 — "...while we were yet sinners, Christ died for us."
3. Acts 4:12 — "Neither is there salvation in any other: for there is none other name under heaven given among men, whereby we must be saved."
4. Heb. 9:22 — "...without shedding of blood is no remission."
5. 1 John 1:9 — "If we confess our sins, he is faithful and just to forgive us our sins, and to cleanse us from all unrighteousness."

Cult Doctrine
1. Good works and beneficent deeds will cause one to achieve at-one-ment with God (Unity, Bahaism).
2. Reincarnation will fulfill the law of karma. (Scientology, Krishna Consciousness).
3. Universalism; all will eventually be saved (Mormonism, Christian Science).

REVELATION

Christian Theology. The Word of God in scriptural canon is inspired (God-breathed), inerrant, complete (Rev. 22:18, 19), and the only infallible rule of faith. It reveals the origin and destiny of all things; records God's dealings with mankind in the past, present, and future; and focuses on the Person and work of Jesus Christ. The Bible inspires faith (Rom. 10:17) and will make men "wise unto salvation" (2 Tim. 3:15).

Supportive Scriptures
1. 2 Tim. 3:16 — "All scripture is given by inspiration of God, and is profitable for doctrine, for reproof, for correction, for instruction in righteousness."
2. 2 Pet. 1:21 — ". . . holy men of God spake as they were moved by the Holy Ghost."
3. Psa. 119:105 — "Thy word is a lamp unto my feet, and a light unto my path."
4. Isa. 40:8 — ". . . the word of our God shall stand for ever."
5. Heb. 4:12 — "For the word of God is quick, and powerful, and sharper than any two-edged sword . . . and is a discerner of the thoughts and intents of the heart."

Cult Doctrine
1. The Bible needs additional subjective or written revelation for our age (Mormonism, The Walk).
2. The Word of God needs to be properly translated with accompanying explanations (Jehovah's Witnesses, The Way).
3. The Bible is one of many equally divine, sacred books (Unity, Bahaism).

AN INTRODUCTION
TO CULT CONCEPTS

6

Understanding Cult Concepts

It's a lyric from a Ray Charles soul-song of the late fifties: "Tell me what'd I say?" But it also expresses the sentiment of Western man in the late twentieth century who finds himself wondering about his own language. Every day, millions of North Americans use words with a commonplace frequency that were unknown utterances scarcely a decade ago: yoga, TM, karma, Zen, nirvana, mantra, guru, just to name a few. In addition, words with ill-defined meanings are bantered about in casual conversation: mysticism, transcendentalism, reincarnation, meditation, god-realization.

What's going on? In brief, the way Westerners talk is being influenced by the way they live. The Judeo-Christian heritage may officially sanction society's institutions, but its concepts of God and reality rooted in objective revelation mean little to the average person. The world-view held by most is subtly embedded with a distinctly Eastern mode of interpreting man's relationship to God and the material universe. America's monetary system proclaims, "In God We Trust," but its spiritual consciousness bears the inscription, "Mystery Babylon."

The whorish faith of Revelation's false religious system is no distant projection awaiting some distinctive prophetic fulfillment. Its ideology is already in our midst, merely awaiting the final unveiling of the Antichrist. Meanwhile, the words of man's mouth are preparing his mind for the domination of the Lawless One's totalitarian regime.

Words can do all that? Absolutely! Just think for a moment how often you hear someone calmly discuss his astrology sign or speak about yoga exercises and meditation. Cocktail conversations explore the merits of psychic power. "Human potential," "transpersonal," "holistic," "actualization," "higher consciousness," and many other terms of communication say more about what man really believes than any statistic about church attendance could reveal. And underlying all this are some basic presuppositions about the faith and hope that compels the man on the street.

Whether he wears a three-piece, pin-striped suit or a sweatshirt and sneakers, the modern religionist (whose thinking has been affected by Eastern cults) has much in common with his fellow citizens. His belief system may be summarized as follows: This material existence is not the Ultimate Reality. Spirit transcends the baser realm experienced by the objective senses, and enlightenment may only be realized intuitionally. Feeling is more important than knowing. Being is of more value than doing. God is not a personal, transcendent deity before whom one is morally accountable. He'll not be found by looking out there. Inside of man dwells the divine essence, and introspection is the way to discover truth. Once one discovers the inner potential for spiritual power and knowledge, there is no longer any need to be bound by the outmoded ideas of heaven and hell, judgment, sin and salvation. God is, after all, one's own cosmic consciousness, a Presence pervading all life. And communion with him is not the result of a reasoned search for hope in Someone. Subjectivism is the pathway to peace, and the solution to all problems is to deny they exist.

This categoric appraisal of the modern mind describes a majority of those who would nominally call themselves "Christians." These same individuals probably would hesitate if asked to supply a precise definition for words like mysticism, self-deification, and pantheism. Like a dry sponge, the Western mind, drained of spiritual moisture by the desert of scientific rationalism, now soaks up the "wisdom" of the East. As a result, many "Christians" pay lip service to the church of their choice while philosophically adhering to an occult/mystical/Hinduistic/Buddhist/Taoist/spiritualist concept of life.

The most elemental fact of man's existence is his search for God. Theology, which combines the Greek words *theos* (God) and *logos* (word), literally means "words describing the nature of God." Even the atheist, by this definition, has a theology. Though most people might feel inadequate to explain their personal beliefs, given the opportunity, they eventually articulate a belief system that is based on either the Good News of Jesus or the precepts of Mystery Babylon. When espousing the latter, they implicitly reject the orthodox ("correct belief") scriptural interpretations of historic Christianity.

Christianity is not based upon some relativistic impression of reality. It is rooted in the teachings of Jesus and the doctrines of the Apostles, those who were privileged to sit at his feet and hear directly his words of life. Never once did they suggest that Christ had secretly given them access to divine mysteries that could only be discovered by a tedious search of esoteric truth. Peter, Paul, James, and John openly declared what they had received. Their message is based on the authority of the Old Testament and the Apostolic office conferred upon them by the Lord. Not one of them claimed any private understanding of Jesus' teachings apart from the scrutiny of the other eleven.

The cults, no matter how diverse their origins, display a remarkable conformity of ideology. Considering that the source of cultic knowledge is the *gnosis* of Eden's serpent, the Bible-believing Christian is not surprised to observe such harmony. But all true believers, likewise, have a uniformity of doctrine that transcends all cultural and convictional barriers, such as the Bible's presentation of the origin and existence of life, and the eternal struggle between good and evil based on the perpetual conflict between God and Satan. Sin and rebellion began in the heart of Lucifer (Isa. 14, Ezek. 28), and their ultimate defeat (Gen. 3:14, 15) and dissolution (Rev. 20) are a certainty. The conclusion of God's pronouncements have been settled (Psa. 119), and the source of a correct

world-view must be based on the authority of Scripture
(2 Tim. 3:16).

Christianity in the West may have felt it was impervious
to any incursion of the devilish doctrines of the Eastern
mindset. But during the last century "certain men crept in
unawares...denying the only Lord God...Jesus Christ"
(Jude 4). Very subtly, the language of the mystic has
influenced the way in which contemporary man's
theology perceives the goal of peace with God and
eternal life. It would be impossible in a book of this scope
to include every religious term that pervades our speech.
This section will, however, analyze three of the most
common words condensing the essence of today's
spiritual outlook: enlightenment, meditation, and
reincarnation.

7

Enlightenment

No matter what name it goes by, the goal is the same. It may be called "heightened awareness," "*nirvana,*" "*satori,*" "transcendental bliss," "god-realization," "expanded consciousness," "altered perception of reality," or "cosmic consciousness." The discipline may be yoga, Zen, asceticism, or meditation. And the religious frame of reference may be Buddhism, Unity, Hinduism, Theosophy, or Scientology. When all of the semantic externals are stripped away, whatever remains is the nebulous goal of "enlightenment." How is it achieved, and what separates it from biblical Christianity?

The first step toward enlightenment, in the mystical sense of the word, is the negation of one's rational faculties. Man's mind is an obstacle on the pathway to a higher consciousness. Truth is not perceived to be an absolute of objective revelation. Its reality must be experienced pragmatically by psychic or suprarational input. Logic plays no part in finally determining that enlightenment has been achieved. This author has debated many cultists who affirm the authority of their messianic leader. When pressed to explain how they decided to follow a man as god, the answer is the same: "I just know."

The subjectivized experience offered by many cult captains, whether it be the "knowledge" of Guru Maharaj Ji or the *shakipat* of Muktananda Paramahansa, forms its own proof. When no rational attempt is made to judge intuitional experiences by objective standards, the enlightened cult member fails to ask, "Is it right?" He only concludes, "It works," and that is enough.

Some mystics would even admit that their altered perception of reality might be fantasized or hallucinogenic. That probability doesn't matter to them. It's most frustrating, however, to debate a devotee of cosmic consciousness and try to proceed to a logical conclusion, only to have him roll his eyes back in his head and trance-out! When he returns from his momentary trip, he dons a sweet smile declaring, "Try it, you'll like it," dismissing any further intelligent conversation. When thinking has been replaced by feeling, the sea of subjectivism swallows up any effort to distinguish between reality and illusion.

While Christians may share glowing testimonies of conversion experiences, Hebrews 11 clearly designates the believer's life as one of faith. This transforming confidence in God is based on the objective criteria of his promises as revealed in the written Word. Jesus Christ declared that the basis of eternal life is knowing God (John 17:3). Christians have a personal, conscious relationship with their Lord, one that combines the emotional dynamics of the new birth with the intellectual capacity to understand God's character by his creation (Rom. 1:20). Man's faith does not rely upon some empirical foundation of truth which is being psychically communicated. The "power of God" as revealed in the miracles of the historical Christ offers far more hope than the mythology of the mystic (1 Cor. 2:5).

After the rational mental processes have been negated, the mystic next pursues enlightenment by seeking to release his spirit from the limitations of the body. One intention of enlightenment is "to be at one with the universe." However, the "subtle" or "material" body clouds spiritual perception by its attachment to the world of senses. The mystic may release his spirit by yoga exercises or by astral projection. Once the shell of flesh is left behind, time and space have no boundaries, giving spiritual entities (demons) the opportunity to guide the "true self" as it searches for the essence of life out of the body.

The enlightenment resulting from shedding the bondage of the physical body is generally a perception of self-deification. This exaltation of the ego leads many to conclude that they are indwelt with a "Christ-consciousness," or even that they are God. In the monist view, such a conclusion is perfectly logical because the Creator and the created are all one of the same essence. When enlightenment has been experienced in this manner, God is reduced to an impersonal principle. Gone is any concept of judgment and moral accountability. One's own enlightened self becomes the arbiter of all actions and the gauge of all truth.

All procedures leading to enlightenment and all cultic systems achieving their own illumination must operate on these propositions: (1) the mind and the body inhibit the attainment of truth by their confining sensory capacity, (2) a universal unity of spirit pervades the universe, which essence includes the nature of God and the souls of men, and (3) time, space, and matter are all illusory, therefore ignorant of good, with sin being a figment of the mind and not a state of conduct.

Jesus was interrogated by the Jewish leaders of his day (John 5) who demanded to know the authority by which he healed and forgave sins. Christ did not lure them down the road of speculative spiritual introspection. Instead, he offered himself and his words as the basis for determining the validity of his actions. Jesus did not dispel their skepticism by suggesting they sit by a riverbank and think deep thoughts about the cosmos. "He that heareth [exercises objective mental comprehension] my words [which contain guiding spiritual truth] and believeth [compelling the intellect by faith] on him that hath sent me, hath everlasting life," Jesus declared (John 5:24).

Instead of dispensing enlightenment, Jesus offers the light of his life. The Apostle John declared that Jesus is ". . . the true light which lighteth every man." Why, then, do some men prefer the glimmer of a self-described state of higher consciousness to the penetrating glare of moral purity offered by the Lord? John tells us, ". . . that light is come into the world, and men loved darkness rather than light because their deeds were evil." At last, we see the real reason behind the mystic's search for spiritual illumination. It is not truly the radiance of God he seeks, but rather, shelter from the penetrating searchlight of God's Holy Spirit. And the enlightenment upon which he stumbles is the false glow of one whom the Bible depicts as a deceiving "angel of light" — the devil (2 Cor. 11:14).

8

Reincarnation

"Say a prayer to your higher self and Almighty God. Your mental body will leave your physical body and come back down in the life having the answers to the questions you have posed."

This monologue was delivered by a psychiatrist who practices "past-lives therapy." His patient wanted to know why she was blind in one eye. Under a hypnotic state she supposedly regressed in time and saw herself in New York. Her mental journey had taken her back to 1943 when she found herself in the body of another person hurling a bottle at her lover's face. As the psychiatrist moved her forward in time, she once again saw her boyfriend, this time with a patch over his eye. Now, she was ready to return to her body. The answer was plain. She had committed a sin of violence in her last reincarnation, and in this life she had to be punished in order to work out her *karma.* What lesson had she learned? "My higher self says I must learn to control myself in this life," she replied to the psychiatrist.

This story is true. Whether the facts are accurate is open to question. The only certainty is that practitioners of "past-lives therapy" have their calendars full of appointments. It seems in our age of stress and tension, there are those who eschew any thought of assuming personal responsibility for the consequences of their conduct. It's much easier to blame everything on a former existence. Hindus have been doing it for centuries. Now, many Westerners are following the same karmic path of fatalism. Belief in reincarnation is on the rise, and the classic inquiry, "Who *am* I?" has been replaced by the puzzling question, "Who *was* I?"

With the shift away from ecclesiastical directives and moral absolutism, our society has a desperate need to explain the nature of its existence. Historically, the declension from faith to hedonism has not always resulted in atheism. Generally, man seeks for something that will satisfy the spiritual vacuum left by the denial of God as a guiding force in his life. The growth of interest in occult phenomena illustrates that Western man has traded his unbelief for a new system of order and meaning. Astrology, psychic predictions, and parapsychological investigations are pillars of this new "religious" system, with reincarnation as a major part of its foundation.

Belief in reincarnation has reached a level of respectability. Those who talk about past lives are no longer considered odd. Films such as *The Reincarnation of Peter Proud* and *Heaven Can Wait* have focused attention on reincarnation, along with the best-seller *Jonathan Livingston Seagull*. Back in the fifties, another book, *The Search for Bridey Murphy,* told the story of Virginia Tighe, a thirty-three-year-old housewife who under hypnosis assumed the personality of what was thought to be a nineteenth-century Irish woman. Virginia spoke with an Irish brogue and described in detail a land she supposedly had never seen. After millions had swallowed the tale, investigators discovered that Mrs. Tighe had a grandmother who spoke Gaelic and had given Virginia history books about Ireland to read as a child.

Virginia seems undaunted and professes to maintain her beliefs in reincarnation. Recently she was a guest on the set of the film *Audrey Rose,* adapted from the novel by Frank De Felitta. After hearing his six-year-old child play the piano as an accomplished musician, when, in fact, he had never taken lessons, De Felitta investigated Hindu texts on reincarnation and explored the writings of Edgar

Cayce (discussed later in this book). The child explained that his fingers had moved spontaneously without any conscious effort. De Felitta took this to mean his son was the reincarnation of a great musician.

A variety of cults consider reincarnation to be an essential aspect of their teachings. Scientology proposes to remove the traumas of past lives by the use of a device called an E-meter. Almost all of the important Eastern cults base their quest for higher consciousness on the premise of reincarnation. Other groups espousing this belief include Rosicrucianism, Unity School of Christianity, Hare Krishna, Theosophy, and Urantia. But belief in reincarnation itself is not confined to exotic cults. More than 60 percent of Americans consider human events experienced in the past and passed on to future lives to be a reasonable probability.

The word "reincarnation" takes its root from the word "incarnation," *in carnis* (Latin), which means "in the flesh." Reincarnation refers to the cyclical evolution of each man's soul as it passes into another body after death. The process continues until the soul has reached a state of perfection and merges back with its source. In the theory of reincarnation, the soul can only inhabit another *human* body. Transmigration, the Hindu doctrine from which reincarnation originated, teaches that each successive cycle may result in the soul incorporating itself in organic or inorganic life, meaning anything from a chicken to a rock. The choice depends upon the karma accumulated by the soul in its previous reincarnations. Western advocates of "rebirthing" have generally emphasized reincarnation rather than transmigration, knowing that the principles of the latter might be rejected by the more educated adherent. The average American would not necessarily be offended by the possibility of reincarnating as a respectable human being, but the thought of coming back as a pig or a bug is hardly enticing.

The doctrine of karma has found suprisingly easy acceptance among Westerners. (Since the chapter on Hinduism deals extensively with this concept, it will not be thoroughly analyzed here.) In the earliest Hindu texts karma connoted an act of ritual significance. In later writings it was modified to illustrate how events in this life affect the quality of life in the next incarnation. Eventually, karma came to represent the immutable law of sowing and reaping, with pronounced punishment in future lives as a purification from evil in this life. It was hoped that this refining process would permit the soul to be worthy of reabsorption into the Universal Soul from which it came. In India, the teaching of karma justified the prejudices of the developing social strata, resulting in the infamous caste system. The Untouchable had no hope of bettering his lot. His miserable destiny had been predetermined by a former existence. Likewise, the priestly Brahmin class saw no need to extend acts of kindness to the less fortunate. To do so would interfere with the karma of those beneath them and bring disrespect upon the privileges of their class, a status which they deserved because of their conduct in previous reincarnations.

The Indian subcontinent is not entirely responsible for promoting the theory of reincarnation. Gnostic cults of the first century and early challengers to the new Christian faith flirted with the idea. They had taken their cue from the philosopher Plato, who put forward the concept of dualism which had also been discussed by earlier Greek philosophers. Plato viewed the spirit as a positive entity encased in the evil "prison house" of the body. Therefore, man's spirit longs to be free from its captor and to return to its Source, fading into the nebulous consciousness of the Universal Soul.

Spiritualism's resurgence in the 1800s formally introduced reincarnation to Westerners. The foremost twentieth-century advocate was Edgar Cayce (discussed later in this book). Cayce, who had a church-oriented background, was at first hesitant to adopt the belief. However, his spiritual teacher, Arthur Lammers, convinced Cayce that reincarnation was an evolutionary process by which one could attain the perfection of Christ. Lammers insisted that Jesus taught reincarnation to his disciples, but the belief had been deliberately omitted as Bible translations passed from one language to another. Eventually Cayce came to believe that phrases refuting reincarnation such as "resurrection of the dead" and "last judgment day" were "meant to be understood symbolically rather than literally." In the end, Edgar Cayce ridiculed the idea that Christ was "offering a hit-or-miss, one-chance-only hope of survival...."

Today's foremost secular "expert" on reincarnation is Dr. Ian Stevenson. A Montreal-born psychiatrist, Stevenson became interested in reincarnation while serving as chairman of the Department of Psychiatry at the University of Virginia School of Medicine. He has carefully documented 1,800 actual cases of reincarnation, each of which he has attempted to deduce with logical explanations. While most of these stories have been labeled as fraudulent or resulting from parapsychological phenomena, Stevenson remains intrigued by those examples which appear to be legitimate. He theorizes that mental stress in this life could be alleviated if the traumas of previous existences could be identified. (He sounds very much like a Scientologist.) He even goes so far as to suggest that parents who believe in reincarnation have a head start on child-rearing. By accepting the fact that the baby had a history before conception, the child will be given greater respect as an individual, and that, he says, ". . . could greatly reduce parental guilt."

Why have teachings about reincarnation been received so readily? On the surface, some of its claims do sound reasonable to those not grounded in biblical theology. First of all, since every man senses his own sinfulness outside of Christ, he must have a way to cope with the burden of unrighteousness. Reincarnation promises an eventual freedom from the confines of moral guilt. It also provides a future opportunity to finish every worthy goal in this life which remains uncompleted at death. The talented achiever may be convinced that any application of his skills will come to fruition in the next life, if not this one.

Above all, reincarnation seeks to provide the ultimate answer for understanding suffering and injustice. As Robert Morey points out in his book, *Reincarnation and Christianity,* "The ancient philosophers used the theory of karmic reincarnation to explain away such things as birth defects, physical handicaps, low I.Q.'s, retardation, personality traits, etc., because they had no knowledge of genetics or the DNA code. They assumed that all babies should normally be born in perfect health and that all birth defects had a mystical or religious explanation, thus giving a mystical quality to an obviously genetic problem."

Morey goes on to point out that since the "mentally and

physically handicapped are receiving the karma they deserve, they have been left to suffer...." What Morey so clearly illustrates is that the explanation of reincarnation only perpetuates the problem. Is it any wonder that health care and social services are seldom seen in the East, except where Christian missionaries have brought a healing hand? To be a Good Samaritan, according to reincarnation, would only interfere with the divine order of karmic punishment.

Apart from any appraisal of reincarnation in the light of scriptural scrutiny, mere logic dismisses most of its claims. If successive lives are designed to bring about moral refinement, then what good does it do to be punished for something you can't remember having done? Since a finite number of souls is assumed to exist as an extension of the Universal Soul, with some of them being purified and reabsorbed, then why is the world population increasing? The global birth rate obviously exceeds the death rate, so where do all those newly reincarnated souls come from? (Some reincarnationists tenuously argue that this discrepancy is made up by the addition of souls from other planets.) If the essence of karma is to rid humanity of its selfish desires, then shouldn't there be a noticeable improvement in human nature after all the millenia of reincarnations? If those such as the Marquis de Sade and Attila the Hun were on an evolutionary moral ascent, then why do we still have the Hitlers and Charles Mansons?

Above all, it seems obvious that belief in reincarnation virtually removes any incentive to excel morally, since there will always be a second chance. One needs only glimpse at the lands where karmic philosophy and theories of transmigration have held sway for centuries to see the subhuman view of life fostered by these teachings. If suffering is the result of sin in other peoples' lives, then what recompense is there for the pain endured by malformed children whose broken limbs were deliberately twisted to make them more useful to professional begging syndicates? Why lift a man from the gutter to clean his sores and feed his belly, if some impersonal, unforgiving law of retribution is perpetuating his hunger? What eventual economic and social price will the West pay someday when it reaps the whirlwind of its fascination with the essence of karmic thought in reincarnation? Will we, too, create a generation callously indifferent to human misery, because all concepts of ultimate accountability have been swept from our culture and replaced by the philosophy, "I'll do better the next time around"?

Unexplainable cases of cognition and other phenomena which seem to support reincarnation continue to baffle those who seek to determine scientifically the validity of claims regarding past lives. In the strictest sense, there is no objective way to verify or deny such occurrences. Some tales of former existences are obviously fraudulent. People with low self-esteem have been known to invent marvelous stories in which they were persons of power, beauty, and nobility in another age. But what about those cases where an individual recounts in precise detail a number of verified facts concerning another place or time about which he presumably knew nothing?

Intuitive recall ("deja vu," as it is commonly known) is the experience of having done something or having been somewhere before. Could this explain the phenomenon of reincarnation? It should be noted that the human subconscious mind contains an incalculable record of sights and sounds, most of which have long since been forgotten. Movies, TV programs, photographs, songs, and literature may all provide bits and pieces from which the mind composes the image of a person or place, creating the feeling that it all happened in precisely the same way at some other time in the past. Even though the person or place may not be consciously recalled, the mind may have been imprinted with the memory of an instance with striking similarity. Some psychologists have also speculated that cases of deja vu result when the experiential and memory functions of the brain go slightly out of phase. In this case, one really *has* been there before — a split second earlier.

Spontaneous recall, the memory a child may have concerning a previous life, is often intriguing, but seldom verifiable. Most cases reported by researchers such as Dr. Stevenson (mentioned earlier), involve children raised in cultures with a predisposition to belief in reincarnation. Considering the vivid imagination of most youngsters, it would take little parental encouragement to spin a tale of fascinating proportions. The resulting doting attention would enable even a child's mind to construct a very believable scenario.

What about the girl's case at the beginning of this discussion? Did hypnotism actually regress her to another life in New York circa 1943? Hypnosis is an unreliable technique to judge qualitatively. Deeply imbedded memories may surface which seem to validate reincarnation. A good novel or an impressive film, long since forgotten, may set the stage for a compelling story the hypnotist accepts as a first-person account. Under hypnosis, the subject has a susceptible tendency to be suggestively guided by the hypnotist, who may bring forth information that he in part has unwittingly planted. In summary, hypnosis is hardly a reliable investigative tool to probe the proofs of reincarnation.

The greatest danger in using hypnosis to verify reincarnation is the subject's spiritually vulnerable condition, in which a trance-state could be manipulated by demonic forces. The information about another life being impressed upon the mind may come from an alien spiritual source. Since these beings have existed far back beyond the span of recorded history, they could easily construct a verifiable time, person, and place, because they were there! Such a case would indeed seem legitimate, since the demon could supernaturally provide any date necessary apparently to confirm a previous existence. And the individual in question could honestly claim to have had no means of secretly or unwittingly obtaining such information. People may be led to assume that since the facts are correct, the phenomenon verifies reincarnation. But confirming a particular circumstance does not automatically verify that it actually took place. If the source of the information is evil, and if the application is unbiblical, nothing is proved except that Satan is able supernaturally to manipulate one's consciousness. The spiritual source of reincarnation episodes needs to be tested (1 John 4:1), and the accuracy of the facts in question must be verified.

In spite of reincarnation's unconcealable ethical and spiritual inconsistencies, advocates seek to buttress their claims by quoting Scripture. While acknowledging that the Bible does not explicitly endorse reincarnation, they do cite a few verses which appear to support their theories. These references are listed below, along with the orthodox perspective on each passage.

1. Matt. 14:2 — His critics may have suggested that Jesus was a reincarnation of John the Baptist, but the Bible doesn't endorse their claim. Even by the tenets of reincarnation such a proposition would not have been possible, since Jesus was a grown adult when John was beheaded.

2. John 8:58 — If Jesus had actually suggested he was a reincarnation of Abraham, the Jews would have dismissed him as a lunatic. They tried to kill Christ because they knew that his claim to be the "I Am" before Abraham was an assertion of his eternally preexistent diety.

3. Heb. 7:1-4 — Melchizedek is merely presented as a type of Christ, whose priesthood is a point of comparison with that of Jesus. Even if one accepts Melchizedek as a theophany (Old Testament appearance of Christ), which this author does not, such a conclusion would still not endorse a belief in reincarnation.

4. Matt. 11:14 — To say that John the Baptist was a reincarnation of Elijah is to ignore his own answer to those who raised this possibility. "I am not," he emphatically declared (John 1:21). Luke plainly records that it was in the "spirit and power," the *style* of Elijah's ministry, that John came (Luke 1:17).

5. John 3:1-8 — Jesus clearly indicates in this passage that he is speaking of a spiritual, not natural birth. The emphasis is upon God's requirement for entrance into his Kingdom, not a succession of cyclic rebirths on a journey to nirvana.

In contrast to the attempt made by reincarnationists to justify their beliefs by quoting certain Scriptures, the Bible is filled with proof texts which deal a fatal blow to any hopes of an evolving soul. Here are some passages which may be cited to refute reincarnation.

1. Phil. 1:21 — "For to me to live is Christ and to die is gain." The "gain" by death of which the Apostle Paul speaks, expresses his longing to be immediately "with Christ."

2. 2 Cor. 5:8 — "We are confident and willing rather to be absent from the body, and to be present with the

Lord." To leave this body is to be instantly in the presence of Jesus, not floating around the realms of the spirit world waiting in line for another body to inhabit.

3. Acts 7:59 — "...Stephen, calling upon God, and saying, Lord Jesus, receive my spirit." While being stoned, Stephen beheld Christ awaiting him in glory upon the moment of his death, without having to perfect his karma through any further lives.

4. Luke 23:43 — "Jesus said, Verily I say unto thee, Today shalt thou be with me in paradise." The thief on the cross received the promise of paradise that very day, instead of a lecture on how he'd be punished in the next life for the sins leading to his crucifixion.

5. Acts 17:31 — "Because he hath appointed a day, in which he will judge the world in righteousness...." How could the certainty of God's judgment be specified by an appointed day if varying numbers of reincarnations would be necessary for each person before all mankind could be perfected?

6. Eccles. 12:7 — "Then shall the dust return to earth as it was: and the spirit shall return unto God who gave it." Solomon in his wisdom declared that the destination of man's spirit is not another body, but an appearance before God to be judged.

7. 1 John 3:2 — "...but we know that, when he shall appear, we shall be like him; for we shall see him as he is." The expectation of every Christian is to be like Christ in the resurrection, instead of acquiring multiple identities through a series of reincarnations.

8. Rev. 3:21 — "To him that overcometh will I grant to sit with me in my throne...." The redeemed of Christ look forward at death to being joined with Christ, reigning with him instead of being indistinguishably absorbed into an impersonal essence.

9. John 9:1-3 — "And as Jesus passed by, he saw a man which was blind from his birth. And his disciples asked him, saying, Master, who did sin, this man, or his parents, that he was born blind? Jesus answered, Neither hath this man sinned, nor his parents: but that the works of God should be made manifest in him." When the disciples echoed a popular notion similar to the principles of karma, Jesus succinctly stated that the child's blindness since birth was in no way associated with either his moral conduct or that of his parents.

These Scriptures indicate that reincarnation and the Bible are mutually exclusive. No false claim of countless opportunities of reformation can stand alongside the finished work of Christ's redemption. The sacrifice of Christ on the cross and the shedding of his blood cannot be compatible with a system of belief that denies his atonement. The law of karma inhibits any choice of the will to determine a life of obedience to God's plan. It is a selfish concept that sees no merit in sacrifice for the welfare of others, and only despair and resignation, not hope, are its result. Reincarnation offers no loving God, no forgiving grace, and robs the Almighty of his attribute of mercy.

The Apostle Paul told Timothy (1 Tim. 4:1) to avoid any doctrine which comes of demonic inspiration. Reincarnation surely qualifies in this regard, for it seeks to replace the hope of the Christian faith — the resurrection. Paul's great treatise on the resurrection found in 1 Corinthians 15 states without compromise, "If Christ be not raised, your faith is in vain" (v. 17). It is no wonder that a fatalistic gloom permeates any religious system that upholds reincarnation. As Paul put it, "If in this life only we have faith in Christ, we are of all men most miserable" (v. 19). It is the promise of eternal life with Jesus immediately beyond the grave that brings worth and meaning to serving Christ in this life.

Daniel foreshadowed the hope of Christ's victory over death (Dan. 12:2) by reminding the reader that either "shame" or "everlasting life" await all who die. Jesus affirmed the same alternatives in John 3:36, and offered the proof of his own body to substantiate his promise. He invited Thomas to place a hand in his side (John 20:27) and challenged his disciples to touch him, to feel his flesh and bones (Luke 24:39). Such infallible proofs were witnessed by hundreds of his followers over a period of forty days, removing any doubts that he had conquered man's last enemy. Instead of directing them to prepare for successive reincarnations, Jesus instructed them to prepare for the day when they too would be raised from the dead to be with him forever! (1 Thess. 4:17).

9

Meditation

Meditation is one of the most misunderstood words in the vocabulary of cults. The average noncultist is put off by shaven heads, secret ceremonies, and mind control. But meditation has such a harmless ring to it. After all, the Bible encourages meditation. So, whatever other practices of cults may raise eyebrows, meditation is seen as possibly beneficial and certainly not dangerous. Such a conclusion is erroneous. In fact, of all the techniques facilitating the goals of cult philosophy, meditation probably ends up being the one practice that is the most spiritually devastating. Meditation isn't a neutral indulgence. Its benefits or damage depend on why and how one meditates.

Though the Western world has rediscovered the phenomenon of a contemplative life, meditation is as old as the Hindu Vedic scriptures and the Book of Joshua. "This book of the law shall not depart out of thy mouth; but thou shalt meditate therein day and night . . ." the Word of God declares (Joshua 1:8). Since the words "meditate" or "meditation" appear twenty times in the Old and New Testaments, it is unquestionable that the lost art of biblical meditation is strongly endorsed in Scripture. What, then, makes it different from the procedures recommended by TM and other Eastern cults?

The "how" of mystical meditation involves a process of shutting down the mind. While the Bible emphasizes the importance of knowledge as a key to communion with God, the mystic wishes to pacify the will and ego until they no longer function actively. Christianity teaches that the channel of the mind represents one avenue by which God reveals his laws and love. The Creator has gifted man with the capacity of reason, which plays an important role in discerning the will and ways of the Lord. Eastern mysticism considers the mind to be an enemy of the spirit. Therefore, it must be set aside by techniques which cause it to cease functioning.

This assault on the mind may involve a physical or verbal means of stilling its processes. Fasting, posturing positions, long periods of silence, and repetitive *mantras* are just a few of the techniques employed. The mantra is the most popular and frequently used method. By repeatedly chanting a word or syllable over and over, the neurosensory faculties of the body become fatigued and shut down. This psychophysiological phenomenon can be illustrated by noticing, when entering a room with a foul odor, that the smell gradually becomes indistinguishable. In a similar manner, repeating a word over and over causes the meditator to lose touch with the objective meaning of the word. For example, saying the word "chair" in a repetitious fashion for fifteen minutes may actually render the mind incapable of consciously comprehending the relationship between what becomes a nonsensical sound and a material object on which one sits, a "chair." If the mantra is based on the name of a pagan deity or spiritual principle, an even more powerful and dangerous effect takes place that may actually induce a tranced-out state of altered consciousness.

The "why" of mystical meditation is predicated on the goal of god-realization and the merging of one's consciousness with the Universal Mind. Once the mind has been emptied of any awareness regarding the objective, external world, the meditator becomes conscious of what appears to be a unifying oneness of reality. In such a condition, mystical meditators often report a state of joy, peace, and indescribable bliss. If the meditator has previously been coached in a system of religious philosophy by which he can interpret the experience, he readily identifies it as achieving union with Ultimate Reality.

What really happens? The intensity of the experience may trigger biological responses similar to the effect drugs have when creating illusionary experiences. It might be that demonic beings seize upon the opportunity of an emptied, unguarded, and defenseless mind to create spiritistic hallucinations. On the other hand, the dormant powers of the human spirit may suddenly be unleashed. Whatever triggers the reaction, this much is certain. The mystical meditator should not be deceived into thinking that he has communed with the Lord. At best, he has only come face to face with his own alter ego, which the Bible declares to be "desperately wicked" (Jer. 17:9, 10). At worst, he could have left his mind and body to an evil invasion by spirit-beings associated with the particular discipline employed.

Is there any place for meditation in the life of a Christian? Yes, if the "hows" and "whys" conform to biblical standards. The child of God has no need to twist his limbs or to sit in any particular position in order to properly meditate. There is no virtue in slowing one's pulse, closing one's eyes, or being certain that unrestrictive clothing allows one to properly relax. The Christian meditator is not trying to empty his mind. Instead, he seeks to fill it with the knowledge of God. Psalm 119 speaks of meditating "all the day" with "understanding" (vv. 97-99). There is no suggestion here of any rigidly ascetic discipline, but rather a natural flow of constant concentration on the things of the Lord throughout the waking hours — working, walking, driving, eating, and talking.

Christians approach meditation differently from the mystics because they believe that the intellect was ordained of God to be a recipient of his truth. God who is infinite and beyond our complete understanding has graciously condescended to express himself through the human communicative skill of language. The Living Word became the written Word that we might comprehend enough of his ways to appropriate salvation through his Son. Our relationship to God is based on the experience of his presence, and the understanding of his Word by which we properly evaluate the subjective dimensions of conversion.

The root word of "meditation" implies a ruminating process of slowly digesting God's truths. It involves concentrative, directive thought that ponders the laws, works, precepts, word, and person of God. "Meditate on him," is the message of Scripture. The meditation of man's soul is to be "acceptable in the sight of the Lord," not predicated on some glassy-eyed encounter with an overactive ego. In short, meditation is prayer and communication with the Lord of the Universe, not the worked-up state of hyperventilation found in some cults.

Biblical meditation is not formless and aimless. It is the natural process of being constantly absorbed by God's life and love. And it means setting aside the mundane things of this world to concentrate on the Kingdom of God. Mystical meditation worships the self as a divine inner manifestation of god. Biblical meditation reaches outward to a transcendent God who lifts us above our sinful inner nature to fellowship with him through the blood of his Son. The Christian who meditates according to the scriptural pattern finds his mind "renewed" (Rom. 12:2). Unlike the mystic whose deepest thoughts lead to darkness, the believer who actively thinks upon those things which are of a "good report" (Phil. 4:8) finds comfort and direction for the activities of life.

CULTIC ROOTS
IN WORLD RELIGIONS

10

Prologue

The superstructure of modern cultism is built upon the foundation of past religious speculations. As Solomon expressed it, "There is no new thing under the sun. . . . is there any thing whereof it may be said, See, this is new? it hath been already of old time, which was before us" (Eccles. 1:9, 10). While each cult claims to have newly revealed truth, most are syncretistic coalescences of beliefs borrowed from the religious systems which have superseded them.

Modern cults often borrow bits and pieces from each other (est from Mind Dynamics, and Lifespring from est). Others trace their lineage directly to the classic religions of man (Hare Krishna to Hinduism, and Black Muslims to Islam). Even when a cult may not have an obvious link with a major religious system, the inherent nature of its teachings indicates roots in a faith of the past. When the Christian Scientist denies the existence of matter, he owes a debt of gratitude to the Hindu philosophers who expounded the concept of *maya* (referring to the illusory nature of the material world). The karate student may only be interested in perfecting physical prowess, but the martial art he practices could not have existed without the enlightenment of Buddha and the *satori* of certain Zen masters. Each guru imported to our shores, from Yogi Bhajan to Muktananda Paramahansa, only echoes the variation of a theme developed millenia ago.

For these reasons, it is important to understand the current proliferation of cults in the perspective of their spiritual heritage. Only by understanding a doctrine in its original form are we able to distinguish the subtleties of its contemporary variations. And by observing how much knowledge today's cultists have borrowed from ancient teachers and sages, we can determine more easily the commonality of cultic inspiration. Understanding the eclectic inclinations of cult systems may lead one to conclude that some kind of masterminded conspiracy is underfoot.

Why is it so many cults deny the existence of evil, the personality of God, and the necessity of an atoning Savior? Why do they gravitate so often to reincarnation, astrology, and other occult practices? Why is there such reverence for the *man* Jesus, but no recognition of his sinless deity? And why is the Bible quoted so often, but at the same time denied the importance of its validity? Is there something or someone behind it all?

The evangelical Christian answers a resounding, "Yes!" He has not forgotten Lucifer's first rebellious challenge to the Lord, "I will be like the Most High!" Since Satan is by nature a destroyer and not a creator, he is handicapped by his own evil attributes. That's why there is so little originality in false teachings. The devil can only mimic God by taking what is true and twisting it just enough to produce an erroneous facsimile of reality. By studying the major religions of the world we uncover the essence of this diabolical error. As we enter the center of the spider's web, we can then trace from this focal point the vast network of "new" spiritual disciplines mushrooming into existence.

11

Hinduism

"Truth is one. They call him by different names,"
proclaim the *Vedas,* most sacred of all Hindu texts. In a
nutshell, that is the essence of Hinduism, the most
absorptive, assimilative, and perhaps oldest false religion
of mankind. In fact, the revered sage Mahatma ("Great
Soul") Gandhi once wrote: "A man may not believe in
God and still call himself a Hindu."

To know Hinduism, one must first understand the Indian
culture and history. Unlike most religions which have an
ecclesiastical order and hierarchical governing body,
Hinduism might be viewed as religious anarchy in action.
But what would be viewed as a weakness by other
devotional structures is seen as a source of durability by
the Hindu. Time is on his side. Since the Aryan
Indo-Europeans stormed into the subcontinent from the
north in 1500 B.C., Hinduism has grown in zeal and
numbers. Even though its rituals and beliefs are
inextricably interwoven with the Indian social fabric, its
amalgamating tentacles have reached out beyond 570
million Indian devotees to the shores of North America.

The term "Hinduism" is derived from the Sanskrit word
Sindhu or *Indus* (ocean or river), a geographical instead
of theological designation first used by the Persian

invaders. This origin underscores the importance of understanding Indian history, which is divided into four periods. The first is called pre-Vedic and dates back beyond three millenia. Known as Dravidians, the earliest settlers of the Indian Peninsula were animistic. Local deities were worshiped in a fashion resembling witchcraft.

The Aryan conquerors brought their own gods, such as Soma, deity of the hallucinogenic soma plant. The *Vedas* ("wise sayings" or "knowledge") dominated the religious philosophy of this second period. Originally, these texts were orally preserved, but by 1000 B.C. were collected into written form (such as the ten-volume set of 1,028 hymns and prayers known as the *Rig Veda*). The extreme polytheistic nature of Hinduism developed during this time. (Hinduism proverbially has 33 million gods, although the number is a metaphorical allusion to the seemingly infinite array of deities and is not intended to be a definitive numerical designation.)

It was during this second historical period that the caste system began developing. Castes were originally an outgrowth of vocational classifications: *Brahmins* were priests and scholars; *Kshatriyas* the rulers and soldiers; *Vaishyas* the merchants and farmers; *Sudras* the peasants and servants. In later centuries, this class division was presumed to be a justification for the doctrines of karma and reincarnation (to be discussed later). One's caste became fixed at birth and was so immutable that a Brahmin dying of thirst would not take water from a Sudra lest he be polluted.

Eventually, a social mosiac of 3,000 subcastes developed with those known as Untouchables at the bottom of the list. Untouchables were seen as virtually inhuman and good only to clean dirt, excrement, and blood. Though Gandhi and other reformers persuaded the Indian Parliament to outlaw Untouchability in its 1949 Constitution, it still remains a hallowed tradition in the villages where most Indians live. There, endogamy, marriage only within one's caste, is a socially enforced practice. While other castes may not share the degradation of the Untouchables, they are intimidated with the knowledge that they were created from the feet of Brahma while the Brahmins sprang from Brahma's face.

About 600 B.C. the third (Upanishadic) period dawned on India. The *Upanishads* transformed the dominant religious outlook from a positive view of fulfillment to an escapist outlook seeking release from life. In the *Rig Veda* the old Vedic gods were merely finite superhumans who indulged in licentiousness and debauchery. The *Artharvaveda* emphasized themes of exorcism and spellcasting in its 6,000 verses. In contrast, the 108 poems of the *Upanishads* (which means "sitting at the feet of" and conjures images of sages instructing disciples) synthesized what would become the basic doctrines of Hinduism.

Hinduism had always been a grass-roots religion of the masses, but the *Upanishads* developed it into a monistic, philosophic faith. Life was seen as an endless cycle of the soul's transmigration (*samasara*). Escaping the retributive law of karma and achieving liberation (*moksha/mukti*) from the wheel of life would occur only when the *atman* (individual soul), would be identified with and absorbed by the Universal Soul (Brahman). This establishment of a religious world-view known as Brahmanism was the beginning of modern Hinduism as it is known today. Its two basic theological premises are rooted in pantheism (the belief that God is at one with and pervasive in all created matter) and monism (the idea that "all is one," the universe exists as a unitary principle).

The final period of Hinduism's development occurred after the beginning of the Christian era, when the Vedantic literature became the dominant scriptures. Under the leadership of the philosopher Shankara, who expounded the theory of *maya* (all matter and reality is illusory), Hinduism enjoyed a "revival" from the corrupt and sterile forms that had developed. Self renunciation and moral duty (*dharma*) became a pathway to freedom from the self and inclusion in the impersonal One (*nirvana,* a heavenly state).

Maya, in all its ramifications, is the explanation the Westerner is given when he sees the suffering and poverty of India. This author has walked the streets of Indian cities where millions sleep on sidewalks and naked children bathe in gutters. Even as a writer, words seem inadequate to describe the sight of lepers and the congenitally deformed banging on the taxi window to beg for "buckshesh" (handouts), and wretched waifs with crippled bodies rummaging through garbage for morsels of food.

The Hindu has inoculated himself against any empathy for his fellow man. All of the universe is *lila,* God's cosmic game. And pain and pleasure are not absolutes but an illusion. The suffering one sees is not real, it is *maya* and therefore unworthy of any efforts to alleviate. Furthermore, to extend kindness to those who are less fortunate would be to disobey the law of karma. That poor creature is suffering because of his sins in a past life and lending any assistance to his state would violate the sacred principle of divine vengeance.

It might appear to the reader as though Hinduism is a religion too complex to explain in terms of basic presuppositions. As one writer stated, "It rejects nothing. It is all comprehensive, all tolerant, all compliant." Still, there are some common denominators in Hinduism's past and present.

All Hindus do share the same basic scriptural foundation. Granted, certain sects may emphasize one school of literature over another, but the *Vedas* and *Upanishads* remain supreme. (Other revered scriptures include the *Mahabharata, Brahmans, Sutras, Ramayana, Aranyakas,* and the *Brahma-Sutra.*) The most popular Hindu writing is the portion of the Indian epic, the *Mahabharata,* known as the *Bhagavad-Gita,* "Song of the Lord." It might well be called the "Bible" of India. (This volume will be discussed in more detail in the analysis of Hare Krishna later in the book.) The *Gita's* message centers on developing indifference to desire, pleasure, and pain. Its message of "salvation" is found in Krishna's words, "Whoever surrenders to me is not destroyed."

Hindus also share a similar view of God, man, and their relationship to each other. At the heart of Hinduism is a monotheistic conundrum which views reality as being of one essence, but also insists that it has many forms or expressions (polytheism). The human soul (atman) is divine and yearns for union with Brahma. This Brahma-atman unity produces an illuminating, mystical experience. In this state, the self or ego is dissolved, extinguished by the oneness of God. Since man is ultimately god, and sin is merely an illusion, moral guilt and final judgment for one's conduct are moot concepts.

The divisions of Hinduism are more devotional than theological. One's favorite deity tends to classify the school of thought and form of ritual to which one ascribes. Brahma is the Creator (*Brahma* is the masculine form of *Brahman* which is neuter), *Vishnu* is the Preserver, and *Shiva* (sometimes spelled *Siva*) is the Destroyer. These three comprise the Hindu Trinity. Though there are hundreds of deities with whom the Hindu is usually familiar, it is Vishnu and Shiva who elicit the most devotion. Followers of these gods are divided into Vaishnavites and Shaivites. Vaishnavites generally concentrate their attention on one of Vishnu's ten incarnations (i.e. *Rama, Krishna, Buddha,* and *Kalkin* who is yet to appear). As the Vedic sun-god, Vishnu's popularity was based on his power to reincarnate. The Symbionese Liberation Army, associated with the Patty Hearst kidnapping and sixties radicalism in the U.S., chose as its symbol the seven-headed cobra, a manifestation of Vishnu as *Sesha* the serpent king. Shiva, however, attracts the most attention and devotion. The multiplicity of characters he assumes in Indian folklore has enhanced his popularity. A study of his disguises and forms says much about the essence of Hinduism. Here are some examples: *Bhairava* — the patricidal god of terror using his father's skull for a bowl; *Ardhanarisvara* — an androgynous, hermaphroditic sexual image; *Nataraja* — lord of the dance with four arms. Shiva wanders naked about the countryside on his white bull *Nandi,* overindulging in drugs, and encouraging starvation and self-mutilation. The innermost sanctuaries of Shiva temples always feature a *lingam,* the stylized erect phallus which symbolizes his rampant sexuality.

On a moral scale, his (female) consorts assume no better role. *Shakti,* for example, encourages orgies, temple prostitution, and annual sacrifices. She is also credited with originating *sutee,* the sacrifice of widows throwing themselves into the fire of their husband's funeral pyre. (This practice was opposed by the nineteenth century reformer Rammohun Roy, but still continues today in remote areas.) But it is Shakti's manifestation as *Kali* that presents her most sinister and bloodthirsty image.

Idols of Kali show her standing on a beheaded body, wearing a necklace of human skulls. This author has personally witnessed animal sacrifices at Kali temples.

When the priests were questioned as to the bloody overtones of a god trampling corpses, they replied that the image of Kali portrays a "dualistic perspective of illusion and reality." Philosophy aside, even today there are a reported 100 human sacrifice murders every year in India, all in honor of Kali.

To fully comprehend the philosophical structure of Hinduism, one must first understand the concepts of karma, reincarnation, and the doctrine of *avatars.*

Karma is "an inexorable law of retributive justice...an internal law of nature independent of...the gods." Unlike the sowing and reaping law of Galatians 6:7, karma has no final judgment. Its consequences are felt in this life, and the next, and so on. Every act in this life influences the fate of the immortal soul's next incarnation. The wealthy and healthy are viewed as having accumulated good karma in a previous life while the less fortunate are seen as getting their just reward for past sins. In other words, sin and punishment are mathematically adjusted on a divine scale.

In the system of karma, there is no forgiving Savior to redeem the consequences of one's deeds. The action of karma keeps moving onward, adding good or evil to its credit in a merciless manner. Though all Hindus seek *moksha,* liberation from the bondage of karma, most resign themselves to the fact that they may need to be reborn millions of times to accomplish the feat. Evangelical Christians may find karma a difficult belief to understand since they are accustomed to the idea that, although each man is accountable to God, he can also become a new, forgiven creation in this life (2 Cor. 5:17). (John 9:1-3 is the most direct biblical account refuting karma: Jesus pointed out that a certain man's blindness did not result from sins in a previous existence.)

The doctrine of reincarnation, which influences so many New Age cults, is an integral belief of Hinduism. Though an earlier chapter covered the subject exhaustively, a few comments are in order at this point. Whereas the Christian anticipates a resurrection of his body, the Hindu views his physical nature as the source of his soul's bondage. Even animals are subject to the cycles of rebirth known as *samsara.* The Bible teaches that each human maintains his personal identity throughout all eternity. In Hinduism, the consciousness of each individual is irrelevant since he might come back after death as a monkey or goat or even a plant (in extreme Hinduistic views).

In spite of attempts to cite biblical pretexts supporting reincarnation (i.e. the Transfiguration in Matthew 17 and Jesus' statement in John 8:58 "...before Abraham was, I am"), Hebrews 9:27 explicitly states that all men die once. In contrast to reincarnation's uncertain game of chance with life, in John 5:28, 29 Jesus indicated but two destinations for living souls: "the resurrection of life," and "the resurrection of judgment." The basis for the theory of reincarnation is that man can eventually work out his own salvation, contrary to the Christian doctrine of grace. In addition, it marks a fundamental difference in the view of creation. Hinduism sees each soul as but a portion of the First Cause with only legendary explanations as to how each being came into its original state of existence. This is a sharp contrast to the Genesis account of man's origin as occurring from a divine act of creation by a purposeful God possessing a moral will.

Since the doctrines of karma and reincarnation leave man in a somewhat hopeless state, victimized by the forces of cosmic chance, the Hindu philosophers needed to inject some ray of hope. The impact of Christianity forced Hinduism to come up with some method of illustrating the personality of an impersonal god and thus show the way, to avoid endless transmigrations. The theistic branch of Hinduism made the Unknowable God more approachable by suggesting that he would occasionally incarnate in some illusory form visible to man. Such a god-man is called an *avatar*. This event is not a constant occurrence, but only takes place once for each age when man is in desperate need of such assistance.

Krishnaites cite the *Bhagavad-Gita* as the best example of God incarnating in flesh, though twenty-one other examples are also mentioned in the epic. Unlike Christ who came to earth to be an eternal Savior by dying once for the sins of men (Heb. 10:10-12), the Hindu avatar must return again and again to show men the way to God. The god Vishnu, whose job it is to sustain the universe, takes human birth in the form of *Narayana,* the seed of all avatars. Of this belief the *Srimad Bhagavata* states, "As countless rivers are born from an ocean that never goes dry, so countless are the descents of the lord."

Below the rank of major incarnations (Krishna, Rama, et al.) there are "minor rays from the supreme radiance," partial or lesser avatars. *Swamis* are learned, usually celebate, monks who follow the ascetic road to God. *Sadhus* are the less educated "holy men" who seek spiritual merit by meandering restlessly (and often naked with cow dung in their hair) across India. A step up the Hinduistic ladder is the guru, a religious teacher who has mastered the path of yoga. He may be a Perfect Master, a *satguru* capable of transmitting instantaneous enlightenment and thus leading disciples directly to god-realization.

The avatar, on the other hand, is a human object of veneration and worship. He is supposed to possess supernatural powers (*siddhis*) and is said to be totally merged with God. His incarnation is seen as an act of love since he is totally enlightened. Thus, he has no karmic unfinished business to settle on earth, which would require his return. An avatar may show human emotion, since he is in a body, but his spiritual perception is supposed to be beyond the *maya* of time and space.

Hinduism has no single system of salvation. Instead, the philosophy of *yoga* ("union with God") offers four different pathways to God, depending on the disposition of the seeker. *Bhakti Yoga* ("the way of devotion") is the most popular god-road in India. Love toward god is expressed by devotion to a guru who is the embodiment of divine grace. This way may also involve the recitation of god-name mantras. *Karma Yoga* ("the way of service") generally appeals to more active individuals who are willing to perform ceremonies diligently, make pilgrimages, and carry out actions of good work. *Jnana Yoga* ("the way of knowledge") requires that one seek out sadhus and gurus and also explore the sacred Hindu scriptures. By knowledge the seeker comes to realize the divine nature of his atman. *Raja Yoga* ("the way of contemplation") inculcates meditation techniques that are known as the "royal road." The devotee must learn to discipline his body and mind to achieve *samadhi,* union with the Absolute.

On a practical level of daily life, these disciplines involve an endless array of idolatrous ceremonies and rituals. Deities kept in the home must be "awakened," "fed," "washed," and "put to sleep each night." These

acts of *puja* ("worship") are followed with exacting detail.
There are temples to visit, offerings (money, flowers, fruit)
to deposit, and pilgrimages to make. Every devout Hindu
hopes at least once in his life to visit the "holy city" of
Banaras, or the sacred source of the Ganges at Gaumukh,
high in the Himalayas. He may settle for some major
festival like the famous Car Festival of Jugannath in Puri,
where devotees suicidally throw themselves in front of a
huge chariot bearing a deity's image. Despite the lofty
philosophical ideals of Hinduism, its effect can be seen in
the more bizarre outgrowths inherent in this ancient faith.

In some villages, temples care for and feed sacred rats
at a cost of $4,000 a year. Such vermin dispose of 15
percent of India's grain. The cobra, which is also
worshiped, kills 20,000 Indians each year. Females, which
Hindu legends relegate to a decidedly inferior state, are
so despised that some Indian mothers deliberately
strangle their girl babies. Sadhus, in the name of religious
devotion, have been known to sit on a bed of nails and not
speak for years, grow their hair into seven-foot braids,
stand on a leg like a stork for months, or hold an arm
outstretched until it has atrophied.

But sacred cows get the most publicity — all 159 million
of them, which is 20 percent of the world's total. (Since the
cow is believed to be the mother-goddess of life, its urine
is drunk to purify the soul.) They freely roam the streets of
urban centers like Bombay and Calcutta, depositing dung
everywhere. Aged holy cows are even provided with rest
homes called *gosadans*. This author once observed two
Indian women fighting over a pile of warm fresh cow
manure. A swami nearby explained their zeal by
declaring, "Since the cow is a god, the cow is holy.
Therefore whatever comes out of the cow is also holy."

These and other less desirable aspects of Hinduism
have sparked momentarily effective reform movements.
The most successful was that of Buddha, who developed
the Hindu ideal of *ahimsa* (nonviolence to all living things)
into a social creed. (Buddhism will be discussed in more
detail in the next chapter.) The Jains, led by the sixth
century ascetic Mahavira, enforced the command against
killing to such an extent that present-day followers of this
sect still avoid even swatting a fly.

Jains strain the water they drink, sweep the path in front
of them lest they step on an ant, and sometimes go on

death-defying fasts as the ultimate way to avoid destroying any life-form. Mahavira proclaimed that spiritual truth could be found in the "three jewels" of Right Faith, Right Knowledge, and Right Living. In pursuit of these goals, Jain monks never bathe, brush their teeth, or sleep on a bed. With such a rigidly ascetic view of life it is little wonder that Mahavira's disciples today number little more than a million worldwide.

The other major reform movement in Hinduism's history was the fifteenth century upheaval of Sikhism brought about by the guru Nanak. Disavowing castes and idolatry, he grafted Islamic ideals onto a Hinduistic system of salvation-by-works, to which he added the grace of god (whom he called Sat Nam, "True Name"). The *Granth,* a collection of poems and prayers from the first four Sikh gurus, is Sikhdom's Bible and is literally worshiped as a symbolic guru. Sikhism eventually turned into a militant brotherhood marked by five "K's": *kes,* long hair; *kangha,* comb; *kacha,* short pants; *kara,* iron bracelet; *kirpan,* sword. It is said that if a Sikh ever draws his sword, its blade must draw blood, even if it is his own. Sikhism remains a vital faith for eight million Indians and more than 200,000 Americans (to be discussed later in reference to Yogi Bhajan).

The final reform movement that needs consideration is the Vedanta movement organized in the 1800s by Swami Vivekananda. India's conquest by England created a Hindu Renaissance in response to the incursion of an alien culture and religion. Vivekananda, a disciple of Sri Ramakrishna, insisted that man's greatest good was to express his humanity. In 1893, he created a sensation by addressing the Parliament of Religions in Chicago. His emphasis was on the unity of all religions with special importance placed on promoting Vedantic Hinduism with missionary fervor.

With nearly 100,000 spiritually curious young Americans flocking to India's shores each year, the exportation of Hinduistic variants will likely continue. Hinduism apparently has little about which to worry. Governmental policies in India render it a virtual state-religion, thwarting Christian missionary efforts. As the West embarks upon a post-Christian pilgrimage, Hinduism may continue to look ever more attractive in spite of its inconsistencies and abject failures to alleviate human misery in its own motherland. Kipling's dictum suggesting that East and West were diametric opposites which would never meet, may prove to be a hollow prophecy that could not have predicted spiritually bankrupt Occidentals looking for hope in the ancient Indus valley.

Founder: No founder or exact date of origin is known. The precepts of Hinduism go back at least 4,000 or more years and have evolved over the millenia without a codified form.

Text: Hindu scriptures: *Vedas, Upanishads* and other *Sruti* (canonical revealed scriptures) plus the *Smriti* (traditional, semicanonical writings).

Symbol: What has become known in the twentieth century as the Nazi Swastika. Originally it denoted the duality of the universe and implied good luck.

Appeal: Most religious systems (excepting Christianity) may promote an inclusive viewpoint but ultimately require adherence to specific beliefs which set them apart from other devotional structures. Hinduism is an all-encompassing faith that strives to adopt any other doctrines into its own interpretation and frame of reference. In the words of Radha Krishna, "While fixed intellectual beliefs mark off one religion from another, Hinduism sets itself no such limits." Its doctrines of karma and reincarnation insure even the most evil men that there will be a second chance to progress upward spiritually.

Purpose: Each soul is an immortal part of the Universal Soul from which it came. Re-emergence into the Impersonal Absolute is the goal of each living creature. One must therefore choose the system of god-realization that will most expediently avoid the cycles of rebirth (reincarnation), and permit him to achieve oneness with God.

Errors: The polytheistic and idolatrous practices of Hinduism are pagan forms of worship which constitute collusion with demonic forces. Karma's system of salvation-by-conduct is contrary to the biblical doctrine of salvation by the sole grace of God. The Hindu cannot acknowledge his need of a Savior without repudiating his entire belief system. As Vivekananda said, "It is a sin to call a person a sinner." The Hindu strives to attain purity by becoming a god, instead of having his sins washed away by the imputed righteousness of a transcendant, personal God. Christ cannot be accepted as an incarnation of Vishnu or Krishna. (In the *Bhagavad-Gita,* chapter 10, Krishna declares, "I am the prince of demons.") Romans 1 denounces those who worship the creation rather than the Creator. In this respect, consider this quote from the *Vedas:* "Worship, O Cow, to thy tail-hair, and to thy hooves, and to thy form."

Background Sources: *Great Religions of the World,* 1971, National Geographic Society, pp. 34-76; *Eastern Religions in the Electric Age,* 1969, John Garabedian and Orde Coombs, Tempo Books; *Religions of the World,* 1965, Barnes & Noble, Inc.; *Cults, World Religions and You,* 1980, Kenneth Boa, Victor Books, Wheaton, IL; *The Encyclopedia of American Religions,* 1978, J. Gordon Melton, McGrath Publishing Company, Wilmington, NC; *Time,* 3/11/74, p. 6; *Ibid.,* 3/16/81; *Newsweek,* 6/4/79, p. 50; *Ibid.,* 4/1/79, p. 68; *Ibid.,* 5/4/81, p. 89; *East West Journal,* 2/78; *Ibid.,* 7/78, p. 49; *Hamilton Spectator,* 3/6/80.

Address/Location: The entire nation of India and smaller representations in Asia and the West.

12

Buddhism
(Theravada/Mahayana/Tibetan/Zen)

If consumer laws of full disclosure were applied to the
"sale" of religions, Buddhism would probably be left on
the shelf. Many Westerners who reject the complexities
and sophistication of modern life have investigated the
ancient faith of India and Asia. They wrongly assume that
the mystical road laid out by Gautama Buddha is a
simplified path to truth. In fact, Buddhism is perhaps the
most complex and paradoxical of all Eastern religions.
Buddha's Eightfold Path to *nirvana* is an intricate system
of rules and regulations that can require a lifetime to
master.

Buddha was born in 563 B.C. in the small town of Lumbini
near Nepal's border with India. The accounts given of his
life are filled with facts and fables which are impossible to
verify historically. As a result, the reader should be aware
that the following information obtained from Buddhist
tradition is partly legendary. Maya, Buddha's mother, was
the wife of a ruler from the Kshatriya caste. One night she
dreamed that a white elephant had a sexual relationship
with her. Shortly thereafter, she found herself pregnant
and bore a son whom she named Siddhartha, who was to
become Gautama Buddha. Gautama was Buddha's family

name. The name Buddha means "enlightened one." He is also known as Shakyamuni, referring to the Kingdom of Shakya in which he was born. Sometimes, devotees call him *Tathagata* (Truth-Winner) or *Bhagara* (Lord).

Buddha was born a prince and during his formative years knew only the confines of palace pleasures. When he needed cheering, his father, Suddhodana, would summon 40,000 dancing girls. At the age of sixteen Buddha married the princess Yasodharma who bore him a son named Rahula. Everything in his aristocratic surroundings went smoothly until his early twenties. Though forbidden to roam the countryside, he left the palace grounds one day and was abruptly confronted with the realities of life.

Buddha witnessed a scene which shattered the illusions of his princely perception. A gnarled and bent old man was soliciting for alms. This was Buddha's first encounter with poverty and the frailty of human existence. On other journeys beyond the palace walls he was confronted with death and disease. But the day he met a shaven, ascetic monk had the most effect upon him. The religious devotion of this monk was a sharp contrast to the leisure and wealth he had known. From that point onward, Buddha found his life unfulfilling. Finally, on his twenty-ninth birthday, he left his wife and child behind in order that he might seek the peace of nirvana and discover the cause of all suffering.

Buddha began his search by studying with two yoga masters. Unsatisfied with this approach, he turned to extreme asceticism. Sometimes he would stand without sitting for weeks. At times his diet consisted of a single grain of rice each day. In desperation he even tried eating his own excrement. One night on his thirty-fifth birthday, as a full moon shined above, he sat down under a pipal tree in a forest near Buddh Gaya. Buddha declared, "Until I have attained understanding, I will not rise from here." That night he entered a trance state and according to legend, remembered his previous incarnations. His "divine eye" was quickened, and he was able at last to extinguish all his ignorance and desires.

When he arose from the foot of the *Bodhi* ("wisdom") tree, Siddhartha had become Buddha. Life's problems were no longer an enigma to him. In a sermon at the nearby deer park he revealed his "truth" to five disciples. "Birth is sorrow, age is sorrow, and death is sorrow," he told them. Suffering, he explained, is the result of man's desire to seek pleasure in the existence of this life. Grief can only be excluded when a man ends all his cravings. Buddha's discovery may be summarized in these three premises: (1) existence is suffering; (2) desire causes suffering; and (3) ridding all desire ends suffering. These precepts led to a fourth conclusion: desire can be eradicated by following what Buddha called the Eightfold Path. Buddha's spiritual insights became known as the Four Noble Truths, a so-called Middle Way between asceticism and hedonism.

During Buddha's time, Northeast India was embroiled in religious and political ferment. The parochial philosophy of the Brahmanistic Hindu leaders had disenchanted the masses. In this spiritual vacuum, religious sects and charismatic leaders abounded. But Buddha was different. He dared to question the authority of the *Vedic* scriptures and advocated abolishing both the caste system and the priesthood. He also wanted to do away with prayers and ritual. Buddha even suggested that the concept of God be abolished. For the next forty-five years of his life (he died at eighty from dysentery), Buddha traveled, begging for food and setting up communities to further his teachings. With missionary zeal he commissioned his followers: "Go ye now out of compassion for the world and preach the doctrine which is glorious."

Buddha's *dharma* ("way" or "doctrine" or literally, "work" — *dhamma* in the Pali language which he spoke) was aimed at ending the cycle of suffering in successive transmigrations. (He had borrowed Hinduism's concepts of *karma* and reincarnation.) Escape from the sorrow of existence would be possible by reaching nirvana, a condition of infinite bliss likened to an extinguished flame. Nirvana, meaning "blow out," would be the result of reaching a state where all desire is eradicated. Though local deities could be petitioned for immediate benefits, no god could facilitate the search for nirvana's enlightenment. Only the Eightfold Path would lead to this exalted spiritual realm.

The eight steps to salvation in Buddha's system are as

follows: (1) Right Belief — correctly understanding the Four Noble Truths free of illusion and superstition; (2) Right Resolve — maintaining pure motives; (3) Right Speech — speaking truthfully; (4) Right Conduct — living peacefully and honestly; (5) Right Livelihood — choosing an occupation that harms no one; (6) Right Effort — seeking knowledge with self-control; (7) Right Thought — keeping an active self-critical mind; and (8) Right Concentration — practicing meditation and Raja Yoga with earnest zeal.

Such high ideals were intended to dissolve the illusion of self and free one from the wheel of existence. Buddha taught that self-effort is the key to understanding the truth. According to a pamphlet published by the Buddhist Church of America, patience and perseverance matter more than "the blood of crucifixion, [God] sacrificing his own being" on the cross. God "is not a Creator...does not judge or punish...is not transcendent" and is not a deity of "fear and mercy."

Buddha was indifferent to the question of man's origin and refused to recognize any supernatural authority in the cosmos. Man is the center of the Buddhist universe, and only what he does matters. Heaven or hell are *conditions* of feeling and emotion, not loci. No eschatological scheme is speculated, and no reason is offered for the reality of death and sin. Self-control, not the remission of sin, is its central doctrine. In Buddha's own words, "Seek in the impersonal for the eternal man, and having sought him out, look inward — thou art Buddha."

Buddhism appears to be a simple system of belief. But in fact, it is one of the most complex of all Oriental faiths. In addition to the Four Noble Truths and the Eightfold Path, the following practices and doctrines are considered essential to attaining Buddhahood:

1. The state of *Arahatship* (being worthy) contains thirty-seven precepts to be followed by the devout Buddhist. Twenty-nine of these are in addition to requirements of the Eightfold Path.
2. Five obstacles hinder one's approach to enlightenment — sloth, pride, malice, lust, and doubt.
3. Three refuges must be affirmed by all who belong to the *Sangha* (brotherhood of monks): refuge in Buddha, the dharma, and the Sangha. They also must adhere to

227 regulations which, among other things, forbid them to touch a woman (even their mother) or drink unstrained water (lest they kill any living thing).

4. Man has no soul but rather exists in Five Conditions: body, feeling, ideas, will, and pure consciousness.

5. Ten Commandments are propagated, the last five of which apply only to the Sangha. These "shalt nots" include: killing, stealing, adultery, lying, drinking intoxicating liquors, eating after midday, being present at any dramatic or musical performance, applying personal adornment or perfume, sleeping on a comfortable bed, and owning silver or gold.

6. Three Principles guide the Buddhist in his search for nirvana. The First Principle designates thirty-one planes of existence, from Higher Spiritual Beings on down through humans and lower Beings-in-Torment (who endure an existence similar to Purgatory). The Second Principle teaches that one's karma determines his spiritual plane, though progression and retrogression are constant throughout successive transmigrations. Finally, the Third Principle, promises "complete awareness" by practicing contemplation. The one who achieves this state is supposed to become immune to all feeling and emotion, including hate and love. Four progressive stages of awareness await the seeker: *Sotapatti Magga, Sakadagami Magga, Anagami Magga,* and *Arahatta Magga.* Some Buddhists believe that an individual who has attained *Sotapatti Magga* can no longer "kill, seduce...utter falsehood, take drugs...make evil utterances or have bad thoughts."

For generations after his death, Buddha's teachings were orally communicated. In 245 B.C., a council of monks was held to decree the sacred teachings in written form. They drew up a three-part document in the Pali language which became known as the *Tripitaka* ("Three Baskets of Law"). Kasyapa, an original disciple of Buddha, was credited as the source of the *Abidharma Pitaka,* a basic interpretation of Buddha's message. The *Vinaya Pitaka,* containing rules for the monastic life and the Ten Commandments mentioned above, was the work of another disciple named Upali. The third "basket," or *Sutta Pitaka,* expounds Buddha's sermons and parables.

During the so-called "Indian Empire" of the ruler Asoka, Buddhism spread rapidly throughout India and Asia. After Asoka's death, Buddhism split into two main schools, one liberal and the other conservative. The latter became known as *Theravada* ("The Way of the Elders" — also sometimes called *Hinayana,* "The Lesser Vehicle"), based on the writings of an early disciple of Buddha named Sariputra. Theravada Buddhism emphasized monastic life as the pathway to nirvana and became entrenched in Burma, Sri Lanka, Cambodia, and Thailand. The canon of the *Tripitaka* became its main source of doctrine. Hinduism, which had become an abstract faith for many Indians, experienced a revival during the first century A.D., Gupta dynasty. It was at this time that *Mahayana* ("The Greater Vehicle") Buddhism emerged. This more liberal school is prevalent in China, Korea, Japan, Tibet, Indonesia, Nepal, and Vietnam. Mahayana Buddhism is more of a cult religion utilizing incense, magic, and occult rituals. Buddha figures are objects of deified worship. (Standing, Buddha symbolizes compassion. Sitting, he signifies serenity.) The Mahayana Buddhist does not strive to become a saint (*arhat*). More than anything he desires to be a *bodhisattva* — one who attains the supreme perfection of Buddhahood but denies his entry into nirvana to return and help mortals on their spiritual pilgrimage in this life.

Theravada (the way of the few) and Mahayana (the way of many) are so distinct in their beliefs and practices that they almost represent two entirely different religions. The godless, virtually atheistic system of Theravada is worlds apart from the Mahayana school with its polytheistic legends of gods and goddesses. The essence of Mahayana is faith in the divinity of Buddha (and a line of *bodhisattvas*). Theravada pursues the more theologically abstract goal of nirvana.

A minor variant, *tantric* Buddhism, borrowed the Hindu belief in *Shakti* sexual power and developed a cult devoted to idols and magic. The union of the individual with the divine is accomplished by ritual sexual intercourse. Coitus is said to combine the opposite forces of the universe (positive masculine and negative feminine) resulting in the cohabitant's ability to perform supernatural acts.

With a quarter-billion adherents, Buddhism is the world's fourth major religion (behind Christianity, Islam, and Hinduism). Its numbers in North America, estimated between 100,000–200,000 (excluding Nichiren Shoshu — discussed later in the book), are growing rapidly. The image of saffron robes and begging bowls may be foreign to the Western mind, but the concept of joining a cosmic flow to abolish the ego goes down well in an age that has turned inward. Those who look Eastward for spiritual answers may find Christianity's promise of heaven less attractive than Buddhism's mystical, impenetrable "truths." To a drug-saturated generation, problem-solving by constructive action appears less desirable than the subjective quest for nirvana.

Archaeologists recently recovered a huge sandstone casket in the ruins of an ancient city near Kapilvastu, India. The inscription on the coffin indicates that the contents are the mortal remains of Buddha. "Be a lamp unto yourself," the sage declared before his death. This instruction sharply contrasts with the biblical claim to such guidance (Psa. 119:105). Buddha's wisdom, backed by the evidence of his own decayed body, seems far less credible than the Word of God which bears the authority of Christ's empty tomb. Whether the Good News of Jesus will prevail over the introspective appeal of Buddha is a fundamental choice that may well determine the spiritual direction of Western culture.

TIBETAN BUDDHISM

Padina Sambhava, a famed pagan exorcist, introduced Buddhism to Tibet in A.D. 747. His reputation so impressed the king, that the entire land soon was following his blend of Hindu/Buddhist beliefs mingled with spells and secretive *tantric* ceremonies. Devotees preceded acts of sexual union with the ritualistic consumption of wine, meat, fish, and parched grains. They instituted a priesthood of *lamas* ("superior ones") and designed prayer wheels with inscribed litanies.

Mantras and *mandalas,* mystic diagrams, were also adopted. The former (to be discussed in more detail in the analysis of TM) was believed to possess a sound able to induce transcendent experiences. *Mandalas,* circular cosmograms of the universe, were also used as an aid in worship. (The center of the *mandala* was thought to be a focal point of the universe.) Adherents of Tibetan Buddhism were taught that merely glimpsing a *mandala* could start one on the road to nirvana. They also developed the legend of *Shambhala,* an imaginary kingdom of enlightened citizens. This central Asian civilization was said to be the spiritual inspiration of the entire world. Their "warriors" were people of compassion and awareness who still serve as models of Tibetan Buddhist aspirations.

In 1951 Chinese Communist soldiers invaded the mountaintop kingdom of Tibet. At that time, the Dalai Lama (his Buddhist name is Tenzin Gyatso, meaning "radiant oceans of wisdom") was worshiped by his 6 million fellow Buddhist citizens as a god-king. Tibetans bowed before the sight of his portrait and prostrated themselves outside his 1,300-year-old Jokka Temple. The Dalai Lama finally fled the Communists in 1959, taking 110,000 refugees with him. He settled in Dharamsala, India, vowing he'd return someday to his native land. In 1981 he returned for a brief but triumphant visit, celebrating new freedoms the government had granted his monks.

The advent of Buddhism in Tibet was so successful that by the time of the Communist invasion, as many as 10,000 monks studied at one monastery. Neighboring kingdoms in Nepal, Sikkim, and Bhutan also felt the Buddhist influence. Because of Tibet's isolation and inaccessibility, some Buddhist scholars believe it has preserved the purist form of Buddhism. Devout Tibetan Buddhists insist they are custodians of the correct traditions and esoteric teachings of the Indian saints and sages.

A major Tibetan Buddhist text, *The Tibetan Book of the Dead* (or *Bardo Thodal*) has had great influence among America's youth. The volume is an occult guide to aid one's traverse through the existence of *bardo,* the dreamlike realm between death and reincarnation. In the sixties, some who experimented with LSD reported hallucinogenic visions paralleling experiences in *The Book of the Dead,* stirring Western interest in this exotic faith. Tibetan Buddhists believe that the demons, spirits, and powers of witchcraft encountered in *The Book* are real forces to be avoided and appeased.

The theory of reincarnated lamas (*bodhisattvas*) came to prominence in the fifteenth century. According to this doctrine, the soul of a dead lama passes to a newborn boy. The current Dalai Lama, the fourteenth incarnation in Tibetan Buddhism's line of spiritual succession, was chosen at age two after oracles were consulted. Marks found on his shoulders (said to be remnants of a deity's two extra arms) established the proof required to designate his office. The young lad also had to correctly identify the crown of his predecessor from among five examples.

The Dalai Lama has toured the West, has had glowing praise from the press and gratuitous plaudits from ecumenical religious leaders. He disarms reporters by insisting, "I'm just a humble monk." However, he did consent to performing the *Kalachakra* ceremony on a recent trip to the U.S. Participants were promised instant enlightenment and Buddhahood after completing "only" seven future rebirths. The essence of Tibetan Buddhist philosophy is expressed in the Dalai Lama's view of life: "If the situation can be fixed, there is nothing to worry about. If it can't be fixed, there is nothing to worry about. After all, things are due to past karma."

Such views are of crucial concern to American evangelicals who lament Buddhism's growing foothold in North America. The first Western Buddhist University has been established in Boulder, Colorado. Led by Chogyam Trungpa Rinpoche, a forty-two-year-old Tibetan exile, the Naropa Institute has effectively introduced *tantric* teachings in the West. The institution boasts thousands of summer students and a distinguished faculty including poet Allen Ginsberg and theologian Harvey Cox. Rinpoche, who is believed to be an incarnation of a revered monk, has developed an enticing curriculum which includes an array of mystical and spiritualistic disciplines.

This author had the opportunity to witness a Naropa-sponsored ceremony held on the University of Colorado campus. Fifteen hundred students (many of them having graduate status) paid eight dollars each to witness the Tibetan Buddhist Vajra Crown Ceremony. His Holiness, Gyalwa Karmapa, was introduced as an incarnation in a lineage of *bodhisattvas*. As one having attained Buddhahood, he claimed the ability to transmit spontaneous spiritual insight. He was ushered to a ten-foot-high throne that had been constructed for the occasion. The ritual he performed consisted of his holding a black hat over his head for two minutes and forty-eight seconds! Nearly every one in the highly-educated audience was overwhelmed at the sight of such a "holy" and "enlightened" man.

Former Christian missionaries to Tibet report that Tibetan Buddhism is the most openly occultic of all non-Christian world religions. Even the monks themselves make no pretense about their consorting with demonic demigods. This acknowledgment emphasizes the irony that this sect of Buddhism should gain such a powerful influence in a Christianized land. Devotees in the homeland of the Dalai Lama have kept his bedroom untouched since the day he fled, awaiting his return. Perhaps the demonic forces behind Tibetan Buddhism have deliberately prolonged his exile as a means of exporting this ancient, shamanistic faith.

ZEN BUDDHISM

"What is the sound of one hand clapping?" Most people would easily recognize this riddle without knowing either its purpose or source. This conundrum and 1,700 others like it are known as *koans,* paradoxical questions concerning imponderable thoughts. The perplexity posed by the *koan* is designed to lead the mind toward intuitive truth. In the world of Zen, logic and reason are taboo. As one Zen practitioner put it, "Be nothing, think nothing." Zen may be defined as concentration with an empty mind.

The ancient sage, Bodhidharma, who is generally credited as being the founder of Zen practices, studied Buddhism in India for over forty years. He returned to China and encouraged the ruling Emperor Wu to adopt the technique he had developed known as "wall meditation." To prove his diligence at Zen, Bodhidharma sat in a cave while staring at a wall for nine years. He eventually lost the use of his legs through atrophy and even had to cut off his eyelids so he could sustain open-eye meditation.

Nearly seven centuries later, two Japanese Buddhists

developed what were to become the two prominent schools of Zen: Eisai originated the *Rinzai* sect in 1191 and Dogen initiated the *Soto* sect in 1227. Both disciplines strived to achieve the same goal of enlightenment, though Soto claimed it must be gradually attained while Rinzai insisted it could come as a flash of insight.

The *koan* is but one of several terms distinctive to the nomenclature of Zen. *Bodhi, satori, mondo,* and *zazen* are other words describing Zen concepts. *Bodhi* refers to the "awakening" of introspective truth. Buddhism has traditionally held that *bodhi* could only be possible after many lives. Zen purports to offer *bodhi* here and now, perhaps today or at least in several years. Experiencing the immediate perception of truth is known as *satori,* a condition in which the meditator realizes all reality as one (pantheism). In such a state, there is no such thing as right or wrong, only subjective reality pervades the consciousness. Alan Watts, the late writer and mystic, described the state of *satori* this way: ". . . at this moment [the universe] is so completely right as to need no explanation or justification beyond what it simply is."

Though Zen offers enlightenment more quickly than traditional Buddhism, achieving *satori* is no easy task. Zen is an arduous training of the mind with *koans* and *zazen* (seated meditation). The *roshi* (Zen master) invites the initiate to enter a *zendo* (meditation hall) where an altar and idol of Buddha is the focal point. Practicing *zazen* in the proper manner may require at least two three-hour periods each day. Hallucinogenic visions and demonic apparitions are common occurrences to persistent Zen meditators. A thick pillow is the only comfort provided, and correct physical posture is crucial. The back must be kept perfectly erect to be certain the ears, shoulders, and navel are in proper alignment. The teeth are to be firmly closed and the eyes have to be left open at all times. During *zazen,* the meditator is instructed to free his mind of all earthly attachments and think of "neither good, nor evil."

A pool, a rock, a flower — any object can be used to focus one's attention. The *roshi* may verbally assault the student with *mondos,* a series of rapid questions. Chief of these is the *koan* (discussed earlier). Abstract paradoxes are presented to boggle the meditator's mind.

Contradictory and confused statements are posed so that he delves more deeply inward to fathom truth. If he dozes, the master may subject him to shouts and painful blows from a *keisaku* ("warning stick"). Such rigorous self-discipline accompanied by unanswerable questions is intended to trigger a newly conditioned view of reality. Ironically, in the words of Dr. T. Susuki, a foremost Western Zen master, "Zen teaches nothing."

While the precepts of Zen may not be based on specific theological doctrines, the inherent Buddhist world-view which results from *zazen* causes the meditator to see himself as an integrated part of the Whole. Buddhism presupposes that only one essence exists and that we are all somehow part of this one essence (monism). This teaching is contrary to the Christian assertion that the Eternal One (God) created the world and man out of nothing. Thus, no part of this material existence is part of God. There is an eternal distinction between the Creator and the created. The inherent contradictory nature of the anecdotal *koan* conditions the devotee to reject reason and logic and instead rely on mystical experience to test truth. Zen is ultimately an egocentric search for subjective authority while inherently denying any objective authority for morality.

Since Zen has no God, even the priests have no role of intercession for sin. There is no speculation on the nature of creation nor the future of an afterlife, since everything considered important is embodied in the experience of the moment. Zen adherents consider their practices to be the quintessential essence of Buddhism, liberating the devotee from all life's miseries. Christians may see *satori* as a false perception of spiritual insight. But many young Americans who have experimented with its rigorous spiritual disciplines are obviously fascinated with the idea of Zen's narcissistic non-answers.

Founder: Sidhartha Gautama, born 563 B.C., Lumbini, Nepal. Died 483 B.C., Kapilvastu, India.

Text: *Tripitaka* Canon divided into the *Abidharma Pitaka,* the *Vinaya Pitaka* and the *Sutta Pitaka*.

Symbols: Figure of Buddha standing with one arm raised, seated in a lotus position, or reclining.

Appeal: Truth is said to have a subjective quality that can only be experienced, not objectively communicated. Buddhism is attractive to those who find objective belief systems to be sterile and devoid of spontaneous reality. Concepts of moral accountability in an afterlife are replaced with a passive approach to traditional religious issues. Enlightenment promises a state of bliss beyond human comprehension.

Purpose: The Eightfold Path promises to rid followers of mankind's four basic evils — sensuality, the desire to perpetuate one's own existence, wrong belief, and ignorance. Those who attain Buddhahood will entertain only pure thoughts and be indifferent to wealth, pain, and pleasure. In brief, the goal is maximum well-being with a minimum of active effort.

Error: The original ethical ideals of Buddha degenerated into a system of theological dogmas with Buddha as god and nirvana as a post-mortem heaven. Idolatrous sects which advocate demonic ceremonialism and the propitiation of spirits constitute a form of witchcraft which is scripturally forbidden (Deut. 18). The greatest commandment of Jesus to love one's neighbor unselfishly (Matt. 22:35-39) contrasts sharply with the introspective egocentricity of Buddhism which has produced social indifference in the lands it has dominated. Scripture presents an orderly universe under the control of a sovereign God. Buddhists see karmic chance as life's only guiding force and make no attempt to explain the nature and origin of sin.

Background Sources: *Occult Shock and Psychic Forces,* 1980, Wilson and Wildon, Master Books, San Diego, CA; *Kingdom of the Cults,* 1977, Walter Martin, Bethany Fellowship, Minneapolis, MN; *Eastern Religions in the Electric Age,* 1969, John Garabedian and Orde Coombs, Tempo Books, New York, NY; *Great Religions of the World,* 1971, National Geographic Society; *The Encyclopedia of American Religions,* 1978, J. Gordon Melton, McGrath Publishing Co., Wilmington, NC; *The Mystical Maze,* 1976, Pat Means, Campus Crusade for Christ; *Religions of the World,* 1965, Barnes and Noble, Inc., New York, NY; *Cults, World Religions and You,* 1980, Kenneth Boa, Victor Books, Wheaton, IL; miscellaneous:

Naropa Institute promotional literature; *To The Point International,* 11/1/76, p. 46; *Ibid.,* 3/7/77, p. 10; *Newsweek,* 8/18/80, p. 52; *Time,* 2/14/77, p. 86; *Ibid.,* 7/27/81, p. 71; *The Denver Post,* 3/11/72, p. 8; *Ibid.,* 10/18/74, p. 6BB; *Ibid.,* 8/8/75; *Ibid.,* 6/11/76, p. 7BB; *Ibid.,* 9/3/76, p. 2BB; *Ibid.,* 7/16/76, p. 7BB; *Ibid.,* 8/20/76, p. 5BB, *Ibid.,* 8/14/81, p. 26; "Is There a God?" — pamphlet published by the Buddhist Church of America.

Address/Location: Buddhism is the dominant religion in many Asian countries. In the U.S. there are Buddhist churches and meditation centers in most large cities. Naropa Institute, 1111 Pearl St., Boulder, CO 80302.

13

Taoism

What do acupuncture and the martial arts have in common? Both practices view the body as a microcosmic organism that needs to be balanced with the macrocosm of the universe in order to achieve physical well-being. Both are also rooted in an Oriental philosophy that teaches a duality of equilibrium known as *yin* and *yang*. Taoism, the root of this theory, has been the victim of official governmental persecution in its homeland of China. But while the Communist rulers seek to stamp out this ancient faith, Westerners increasingly look to it as an antidote in a neurotic, materialistic age. Taoism (pronounced dow-ism) is not a major world religion. But its teachings influence so many modern cults that a brief survey of its precepts is essential.

Lao-tse was born in South China in 604 B.C. His name, meaning "wise old child," was derived from the legend that he was born an old man. He was an archivist who wearied of political life and dropped out of society. For decades he lived in a hut on the slope of a mountain. It was there, at eighty years of age, he wrote the Bible of

Taoism, *Tao Teh Ching.* The 5,000-word volume discussed the nature of life in relationship to its harmony with the universe. Tao means "way" and Teh denotes "virtue." Thus, the book came to be known as "the way of virtue," or simply the Tao ("the way").

Chuang Tzu, a third century B.C. Chinese philosopher, spread the teachings of Lao-tse. Chuang believed the *Tao Teh Ching* was the source of all wisdom and the solution to all life's problems. Though Taoism originally ignored a Creator-God, the principle of the Tao eventually was equated with a God-concept. "Before the Heaven and Earth existed, there was something nebulous...I do not know its name and I address it as Tao," Lao-tse wrote.

The Tao is considered to be eternal and all-pervasive. Taoism teaches that when events and things are allowed to exist in natural harmony with the macrocosmic forces, peace will result. The wise man is supposed to order his life according to the Tao, living passively in tune with the universe. The basic doctrines of Taoism are summarized in practical form as the so-called Three Jewels: compassion, moderation, and humility. Goodness, simplicity, gentleness, and purity are also virtues Taoism seeks to inculcate.

The most important aspect of Taoistic philosophy to consider when discussing modern cults is the dualistic view of opposites known as *yin* and *yang.* These two essences are said to symbolize the complementary nature of all forces in the universe which seem to be diametric. Yang is the positive force of good, light, life, and masculinity. Yin is the negative essence of evil, death, and femininity. All matter is said to contain both yin and yang, and orderly affairs are possible only when these two qualities exist in a state of proper equilibrium. When they are unbalanced, the rhythm of nature is disturbed with strife, resulting in conflict. Like water molds itself to a container, man must learn to balance his yin and yang to live in harmony with the Tao, returning good for evil and overcoming strength with weakness.

In time, the doctrines of Taoism were transmuted into a ritualistic superstitious system with the *Tao Teh Ching* as a source of magical incantations. Lao-tse was deified and worshiped with offerings of sacrifices. His disciples claimed power over nature and became soothsayers and exorcists. The idealism of early Taoistic speculation evolved into a folk religion emphasized by placating demons with gifts in order to insure a safe passage on earth.

Taoism has some similarities with Buddhism. Like the teachings of Siddhartha, classical Taoism insisted that the intellect could not comprehend the unknowable. Understanding is not derived from knowledge or theory but by comprehending what is obvious. The belief in an impersonal principle that sustains life is not unlike Buddhism's atheistic approach to morality. In fact, Japanese Zen has been strongly influenced by Taoism. Many New Age cults are founded on a philosophy combining the principles of Buddhism and Taoism in a syncretistic manner.

Books and university courses based on the "Tao of physics" suggest that the principles of Taoism are scientifically verifiable. As researchers delve more deeply into subatomic physics, they discover phenomena appearing to suggest a certain kind of duality (e.g., protons and electrons, matter and antimatter). Most scientists would contend that such findings are coincidental and bear no relationship to the wider philosophical speculation of the yin/yang theory.

The very fact that an integration of the pure science of physics and the essentially occult hypotheses of Taoism would actually be considered by the intelligentsia, is an interesting commentary on the Western mind. Historically, scientific research has been of prime concern to Occidental nations because their religious traditions have been founded on Christian beliefs. Explorers, inventors, and scientists concluded that since God is an orderly, sovereign Creator, his cosmos is also fashioned in a precise manner which invites systematic investigation. The scientific method of inquiry which brought mankind such marvelous technological advances would not likely have evolved in a Taoist setting. Objective verification has been the foundation of Western science while subjective experience and mysticism have been the cornerstones of Eastern philosophy. During the last several decades Eastern thought has turned to objective verification of subjective mystical experience while Western thought has become increasingly more subjective and mystical. If it becomes acceptable for the West to combine science and subjectivism, then testing for truth will become meaningless and the door will be opened for unrestrained occultic experiences, all supposedly condoned by the "objective" judgment of science.

The "Star Wars" movie epics, including *The Empire Strikes Back,* have been profoundly influenced by Taoistic philosophy. In conceptualizing "The Force," producer George Lucas has borrowed heavily from the hypothesis of a primordial, universal energy flow that is neither good nor evil. Since the motive of the individual determines the moral nature of the force (e.g., Luke Skywalker uses "The Force" for good and Darth Vader uses it for evil), it thus possesses a duality whose positive and negative components are equivalent.

This is, of course, not compatible with biblical theology which sees God as the omnipotent source of all that is good. Satan, the Scriptures declare, was created by God and therefore has limitations on both his authority and power. As the source of all evil, the devil opposes the work of God, but he is not an equalizing, harmonizing opposite.

The idea of "The Force" is from a concept found in Chinese philosophy which envisions *ch'i* (or *ki*) as a basic flow of energy sustaining all life. *Ch'i* (pronounced kēy) embodies the characteristics of the Tao, possessing a dual nature of yin and yang. In the martial arts, one's equilibrium with the Tao is established when *ch'i* flows through the body and is extended to disable one's opponent. Acupuncture views physiological health as an evidence of properly balanced yin and yang. If either essence is out of equilibrium, disease and illness result. Restoring health necessitates a disruption of the flow of yin and yang by applying a "counter-irritant" (an acupuncture needle). Once the equilibrium has been re-established, the Tao of *ch'i* can flow freely through one's body bringing healing. Even *yoga* has incorporated the Taoistic premise of *ch'i,* the force, as a sustainer of life and physical prowess. The *chakras* of yoga must be carefully aligned so that the body resides harmoniously with the Tao (though this term is not generally referred to by yogis).

This brief survey could not possibly explore all the ramifications of Taoist philosophy as it effects modern thought. Yoga and the martial arts will be discussed later

64869

in the book and the reader will then see how the
principles of Taoism are so crucial to the undergirding
philosophy of these practices.

Evangelicals may conclude that Lao-tse might have
stumbled upon a basic non-Christian perception of reality
that to one degree or another has found its way into all
false Eastern religious systems. Taoism's insistence upon
having discovered "the way" certainly collides with the
contention of Jesus in John 14:6 that he is the Way. As the
Western world gradually shifts its footing from the
objective knowledge of revealed truth to the subjective
interpretation of perceived truth, the reader should note
carefully the results of this shift in science, religion, and
culture. Bodhidharma's years in that cave and Lao-tse's
hermitage in his hut may portend a Western trend toward
reflective isolation that will bring about a retreat from
societal and scientific progress.

Founder: Lao-tse, a contemporary of Confucius, born 604
B.C., in South China and died 517 B.C., though accounts
report he was never seen again after departing from his
mountain hut. Some scholars insist he was a legendary
figure and doubt he ever existed.

Text: *Tao Teh Ching,* a 5,000-word book written in
seclusion by Lao-tse.

Symbol: The Tao. See chapter on the Martial Arts for a
detailed description.

Appeal: Ecological concern about the despoiling of
Earth's environment makes Taoism's appeal to abide
peacefully with nature very attractive to the young.
Technology has alienated man from nature and in
contrast, Taoism promotes a veneration of primordial
life-giving forces.

Purpose: "The Great Tao flows everywhere," wrote
Lao-tse. One should not attempt to decipher its origin or
nature but merely adapt to its flow. The *Tao Teh Ching*
states, "To yield is to be preserved whole. To be bent is to
become straight." Taoism is an anti-intellectual faith that
elevates contemplative thought on abiding with nature's
apparent laws, rather than inquiring to comprehend the
structure of these principles. "Abide by the effect, and

do not seek to discover the nature of the cause," might be the Taoist's creed.

Errors: Pure, classical Taoism is atheistic and borders on being pantheistic. Modern Taoism is polytheistic and idolatrous, and involves consultation with familiar spirits. It falls under the indictment of Romans 1:25 by worshiping the supposed creation-principle of the Tao more than the personal Creator-God of Scripture. The contemplative life of virtue and gentleness may appear to be ethically valid but it fails to deal with the sin-nature of man (1 John 1:8), and offers no remedy to restore man's fellowship with God. Respecting the laws of nature should be an outgrowth of man's stewardship of dominion over Earth, not a form of religious devotion.

Background Sources: *Cults, World Religions, and You,* 1980, Kenneth Boa, Victor Books, Wheaton, IL; *Eastern Religions in the Electric Age,* 1969, John Garabedian and Orde Coombs, Tempo Books, New York, NY; *Religions of the World,* 1965, Barnes and Noble, New York, NY; *Two Be One,* 1978, Ernest H. J. Steed, Logos International, Plainfield, NJ.

Address/Location: Before the Communist takeover, one out of every eleven Chinese was a Taoist, primarily of the polytheistic/animistic variety. Its practice has diminished in China but still continues fervently in Chinese societies of Asia and Southeast Asia. Taoism is not an organized religion in the U.S., but its philosophical principles are found in many Eastern-oriented cults.

14

Islam
(Including Sufism and Black Muslims)

"There is no god but God, and Muhammad is the Messenger of God." Those thirteen words comprise the Muslim (or Moslem — "one who submits") *Shahada* (confession of faith). Five times a day the devout, from sheiks to camel drivers, respond to the *muezzins* (callers to prayer) and bow toward Mecca. Some Muslims display a round spot on their foreheads, an indelible souvenir memorializing the thousands of times they have touched the ground in respect to the Prophet's command.

The Christian is taught to thank God for his blessings and to petition him for divine favor. Not so with the Muslim. His passive fatalism will not permit him to seek spiritual merit or to desire material provisions. Islam means "submission," and that definition is the sum of a Muslim's faith. *Inshallah* — "if God wills" —is the byword of Arabic conversation. In *umma* (the world community of Islam), faithful Muslims view every event, the fortuitous and accidental, as an expression of Allah's divine will.

Separating Islam from its Arabic cultural heritage is impossible. More than a religion, it is an all-encompassing way of life with its own jurisprudence system and traditional honor code. It is an intolerant faith that has impeded progress and repressed women. Perhaps this is because the Muslim tends to see the world in black and white. There are only two classes of people: *Dar ul-Islam,* those who have submitted, and *Dar ul-harb,* those who resist. The latter are fair game for missionary efforts, financial pressure (e.g. the oil embargo), the "sword of Allah" in a *jihad* ("holy war"), or whatever measures are necessary to bring them under the authority of Islam.

Today, the crescent and star of Islam fly on the flag over a half-dozen nations. Adopting the evangelism techniques of Christianity, Muslims have broken out of their mud huts and desert terrain to confront the world with the message of Muhammad. Saudi Arabia has even financed a communications satellite to beam the Koran's precepts. Since October 1973 when Egyptian soldiers stormed the Suez and the oil embargo brought the West to its knees, the cry "Allahu Akbar!" ("God is great") has been heard with new fervor.

Islam began with the mystic visions of a nondescript camel driver named Ubu'l-Kassim (who became known as Muhammad). For six months he had been in solitary meditation in a cave at the foot of Mount Hira near Mecca. Had he not married a widow named Khadijah, fifteen years his senior, he might have spent his life on caravan journeys. Khadijah's wealth gave Ubu'l-Kassim the time he needed for ascetic reflection.

Muhammad was born in A.D. 570 in Mecca. He was yet a baby when his father died, and his mother passed away when he was six. Abu-Talib, an uncle, raised the young lad and took him on lengthy trips to Egypt and throughout the Near East. During these travels Muhammad engaged in lively conversations with Jews and Christians. From these encounters he learned the theological concepts that were later to influence his teachings.

In Muhammad's time, the Arabian peninsula was populated by wandering tribes which practiced various forms of polytheistic idolatry. The pantheon of deities they worshiped included angels, demons *(djinn),* and a supreme god known as Allah. Ubu'-Kassin seemed an unlikely challenger to confront such a firmly entrenched animistic religious system. He was afflicted by a strange disorder that caused him to foam at the mouth and fall into unconscious trances. Christians might well wonder in retrospect whether such phenomena reflect the symptoms of demonic possession as represented in the Bible. Muhammad himself questioned whether the seizures were divine or devilish, but his wife encouraged him to ignore any such considerations.

According to Islamic tradition, at forty years of age he entered the Hira cave and was confronted by a being who identified himself as the angel Gabriel. "Proclaim," Gabriel declared, choking Muhammad into submission. "Proclaim in the name of the Lord the Creator who created man from a clot of blood." During periodic return visits to Hira, the frequency of revelations increased. What he saw and heard was summarized in what became Islam's sacred book, the Koran (*Qur'an,* "recitation"). Over a twenty-two-year period, Muhammad memorized all 78,000 words of the Koran's 114 chapters and transmitted its teachings orally (he was illiterate).

Its message encountered stiff resistance from the pagan populace. Wealth and material gain were their "gods," and Muhammad (which means "the Praised One") insisted they share their wealth with the poor in exchange for the promise of a glorious afterlife. The God about whom he preached was a transcendent being who was both lawgiver and divine arbiter. Muhammad's theology proclaimed a Day of Judgment with severe punishment for the unbeliever. This harsh warning of accountability was contrasted with a sensual heaven where green meadows, rivers of wine, and beautiful virgins awaited the faithful.

Few converts accepted this message in the beginning because his denunciation of idol worship threatened the livelihood of Meccan businessmen. Those who followed Muhammad were stoned and beaten. In A.D. 622, he received a vision warning of mortal danger. His escape toward the oasis of Yathrib, 250 miles away, became known as the *Hegira* ("migration" or "flight"). This event marks the beginning of the Moslem era. Later, the name Yathrib was changed to Madinat al-Nabi (Medina), the "city of the prophet," second only to Mecca as a Muslim spiritual center.

To raise funds for his spiritual quest, Muhammad sanctioned plundering expeditions that raided caravans. Even during his native land's traditional month of peace, his followers mercilessly attacked innocent citizens. During this time when Muhammad ruled as a king and prophet, he forged the Islamic concept of the *jihad* ("exertion"), the "holy war" which advocates military ventures in God's name. Those who die in battle are promised immediate transition into Paradise. In A.D. 628, Muhammad led a force of 10,000 men toward Mecca and in a bloodless coup gained control of the city. Within ten years of his Hegira, all Arabia was under his control.

Not long after his triumphal entry into Mecca, Muhammad died in A.D. 632. One of his early disciples, Abu Bakr, was chosen as a successor, establishing the system of religious leaders known as *caliphs.* Filled with religious zeal, Muslim armies spread the message of Islam to India, across North Africa, and into Spain. Had it not been for the Battle of Tours in A.D. 732, all Europe might have succumbed to the message of the Koran. A capital was established in Bagdad, and the *caliph* who ruled from there was the most powerful man on earth and headed a regime spanning three continents.

The Islamic empire was to last for a thousand years. Arabs developed the concept of algebra, and their skills in architecture helped them devise the pointed arch that was to grace Europe's lofty cathedrals. Sugar, paper, apricots, and rice were introduced to the West. Constantinople became the headquarters of the Ottoman Empire in 1453, which endured until Arab power diminished in the twentieth century.

What is the key to Islam's current and past successes? The simplicity and directness of the Koran has left no room for compromise. Its history, fables, regulations, and threatening description of hell compel believers into single-minded devotion. Jews are damned by Allah, and Christians are told that faith in Christ as God incarnate is "blasphemy.... whoever joins other gods with God —God will forbid him the Garden, and the Fire will be his abode." (The doctrine of *shirk* forbids associating anyone or anything with God's divinity.)

Islam does accept the virgin birth of Christ and even the scriptural account of his miracles. However, the Muslim's interpretation of how these events occurred is not compatible with biblical theology. The Bible is seen as a corrupt rule of faith inferior to Muhammad's message. Twenty-eight prophets are mentioned in the Koran, but none compares with the last and greatest of all — Muhammad. Though he took ten wives and encouraged military savagery, his tomb draws millions of disciples who pay their respects with solemn admiration. He improved the condition of slaves, and although his ruling that a man could have four wives seems inconsistent with spiritual ideals, it was an improvement over the conditions of his day because he insisted that each spouse had to be treated equally and kindly.

The *surahs* ("chapters") of the Koran are augmented by the *Hadith,* which contains traditions recounting the deeds of Muhammad. As a supplement it serves a role similar to that of the Jewish Talmud. But the Koran is considered to be more than just another Islamic holy book. Muslims believe that every word was literally dictated by God and that its substance is eternal and uncreated. As a result, the Islamic Five Pillars of Faith are binding rules of conduct. These Pillars are:

1. Reciting the *Shahada.* Every day the Muslim must publicly affirm the monotheism of God and the prophetic status of Muhammad.
2. Daily prayer toward Mecca. Morning, noon, late afternoon, sunset, and before bedtime, all Muslims must say their prayers while kneeling with their foreheads touching the ground. Most Muslims go through the procedure in a mechanistic manner, but such constant repetition serves to reinforce the piety of their faith.
3. Almsgiving (*zakat*). Charity was originally a voluntary act to aid the poor and purify one's remaining material possessions. Today, the principle of donating one-fortieth of one's income has become an institutionalized tax in most Muslim countries, averaging 2.5 percent annually.
4. Fasting during the month of Ramadan. Between sunrise and sunset, no eating or drinking is permitted. This occasion is determined by the lunar calendar and commemorates the month Gabriel supposedly delivered the Koran to Muhammad.
5. The *Hajj* (pilgrimage to Mecca). Every Muslim must attempt to make this journey once in a lifetime as a deed of merit facilitating his salvation. Once there, he walks seven times around the *kaaba* (a cubical building housing a black stone). If the jostling crowd permits, he must also kiss the rock (probably a meteorite), which Muslims believe was carried to earth

by Gabriel. The *kaaba* is said to have been originally
built by Ishmael and Abraham on the spot where
Adam uttered his first prayers to God. Other holy sites
in the area are visited, and a ritual sacrifice of goats,
sheep, or camels may be performed. Pilgrims may also
throw stones at the sacred pillar to "stone Satan,"
reenacting the stones Ishmael heaved at the devil
when the Evil One attempted to dissuade Abraham's
son from submitting to his father's plans to offer him as
a sacrifice. (The Koran says it was Ishmael, not Isaac,
whom Abraham laid upon the altar of Mt. Moriah.)
Other beliefs and practices associated with Islam are:
using a ninety-nine bead rosary to recount the
unmentionable names of Allah (the camel is the only
creature said to know the 100th); holding mass-type
services for the dead; forbidding statues and music in
mosques; insisting on circumcision; veiling women's
faces with the *purdah* and draping their bodies in the
ankle-length *chador;* permitting polygamy; abstaining
from drinking alcohol, eating pork, and gambling;
meeting for congregational worship at noon on Fridays;
building *minarets* (towers from which to broadcast the
call to prayer); abolishing a priesthood and having the
Imam serve as spokesman for the faith; believing that
Christ did not die but was taken up to heaven; teaching
that Jesus will return in the last days to convert the entire
world to Islam; and enforcing the "law of apostasy,"
whereby converts to other faiths (especially Christianity)
may be imprisoned or lose their jobs and possibly their
lives! It should be noted that Islam is a complex faith
spanning many cultures and countries; therefore the list
in this paragraph should not be considered categorically.
The beliefs and practices of various Muslim sects are as
diverse as those found in Christian denominations.

The code of ethics known as the *Shari'a* ("the path to
follow") enforces the morals and doctrines of the Koran.
In the face of what the Muslim perceives to be
encroaching decadent Western values, the Shari'a's stern
application of "an eye for an eye" system of penal justice
seems a reasonable deterrant to crime and immorality.
Today, from Bangladesh and Pakistan to Iran and Saudi
Arabia, flogging and stoning is again meted out to thieves
and adulterers. Beheadings and amputations may seem
gruesomely harsh, but to the Muslim the Shari'a

represents 1,400 years of accumulative ethical standards
that impose discipline for the turbulent times. Fortunately,
such brutal punishment is rare since exacting standards
of proof are required. (Even usury is forbidden by the
Shari'a, forcing some Middle-Eastern banks to come up
with novel schemes to charge interest under another
name.)

Not all Muslims regard the Shari'a with equal esteem.
Like all religious movements, Islam is a fragmented faith
with numerous sects. The three most prevalent are listed
below:

1. *Wahhabi.* This group tends to be the most strict and
   "puritanical." Mohammed Ibn Abd al-Wahhab
   founded the sect in the eighteenth century by
   preaching strict adherence to the Koran. Saudi
   Arabia's moralistic, authoritarian rule is an example of
   Wahhabi devotion.
2. *Shiites* (from *shi'ah* meaning "partisans"). They
   believe that only descendants of Muhammad's family
   are the rightful heirs to spiritual leadership. Since
   Muhammad bore no son who survived him, his cousin
   and son-in-law Ali (who married his daughter Fatima),
   are considered to be in the line of the Prophet's
   succession. Found mainly in Iran, Yeman, Algeria, and
   Iraq, Shiites tend to revere the Shari'a (though not as
   fervently as the Wahhabi). About 10 percent of all
   Muslims belong to this branch of Islam. Their leaders,
   Imams, wield dogmatic spiritual authority, as in the
   case of the Ayatollah Khomeini of Iran. Some Shiites
   believe that a twelfth Imam who disappeared in A.D.
   882 will return someday as a Messiah, the *Madhi*
   ("guided one"), to establish a kingdom on earth. In
   Kashmir once a year young Shiahs parade through the
   streets of Srinagar, scourging their bodies with knives
   and chains. This self-mutilation ritual laments the
   martyrdom of Husain, Ali's son and the Prophet's
   grandson, who was massacred in an attempt to restore
   the seat of Islam to Medina. A powerful Islamic leader
   named Muawiya had refused to recognize the
   succession of Ali, taking the title of *caliph* himself and
   moving the headquarters of Islam to Damascus. This
   event lead to perpetual enmity between the Shiites
   and the *Sunnites* (discussed below), who followed
   Muawiya. Subsects such as the *Ismailis* believe that an

Imam of sinless perfection with the power to perform miracles always dwells on earth. During the twelfth century a group of *Ismailis* known as the *hashshashin* (hashish eaters) killed Muslim leaders while in a crazed, drugged state. (From this we get the word "assassin.") They are firmly entrenched today as a merchant class in India and East Africa. The Aga Khan is their Imam.

3. *Sunnites* (from *sunnah,* "the tradition of the Prophet"). Ninety percent of all Muslims consider themselves adherents of this orthodox sect. Since Muhammad left no clear instructions concerning his successor, Sunnites decided their Islamic leader should be nominated by representatives of the community. The *ulama,* Sunnite religious scholars, have less authority than the Imam and are considered to be teachers and wise sages. Sunnites accept the line of succession as passing on through four *caliphs:* Abu Bakr, Omar, Othman, and Ali.

The diversity of Islam is one of its greatest assets. On the steppes of Central Asia, devout Muslims fill mosques every Friday, under the watchful eye of the ruling Soviet Russian authorities. Iran's Imams have assumed dictatorial control to oust the Shah from his Peacock Throne. Across the vast Sahara, black Africans gather beside oases to study the Koran, a book written by an Arab whose descendants loaded their ancestors on slave ships to the New World. And in faraway Indonesia (with the world's largest Muslim population), students memorize the Koran while their elders mix animistic local deities with Islam's fervently monotheistic system.

In America, the estimated 1 – 3 million Muslims maintain a much lower profile. Evangelicals tend to approach them warily, remembering the massacres of Christians (5 million in Turkish Armenia) and persecution of missionaries for which Muslims are infamously known. Of all major religious bodies, the conversion rate of Muslims turning to Christianity is probably the lowest because Islam pervades all areas of a native Muslim's life. For him to turn to Christ is almost the same as committing suicide. Few Islamic countries enjoy freedom of religion, and even where such freedom is sanctioned by the state it is rejected by the culture. When a Muslim decides to place his faith in Christ, for all practical purposes he loses his family, his culture, his history, his economic stability, and his social life. One who leaves Allah for Jesus Christ walks from the life of the Islamic community to the "death" of being a social outcast. Perhaps evangelicals should not be resentful of the seeming arrogance displayed by the present Arabic spiritual descendants of Muhammad. God did promise to make of Ishmael's offspring a great nation (Gen. 16:9-11; 17:20; 21:13,18; 25:12-18). Their ascent to world influence might well be viewed as a fulfillment of biblical prophecy.

Founder: Muhammad the Prophet, born Ubu'l-Kassim in Mecca, A.D. 570. Died in Medina, A.D. 632 in the arms of his favorite wife Aisha.

Text: The Koran, containing prayers, rules of etiquette, and calls to wage "holy wars." It is supplemented by the traditions of the *Hadith*. In addition, Muslims also revere the *Tauret* (Pentateuch) of Moses, the *Zabur* (Psalms) of David, and the *Injil* (Evangel) of Jesus.

Symbols: Crescent moon and star.

Appeal: The simplicity of Islam's message is its chief attraction: one God, a rigidly defined method of worship, and a clearly explained destination of man's soul. Its system of salvation by good deeds and ardent devotion offers solace for those who conform to the outward display of piety without having to experience a spiritual rebirth of their inner nature.

Purpose: All other religions are seen as Satanic expressions of polytheism. Allah alone is to be praised and worshiped. Muhammad originally prayed facing Jerusalem and gave the Jews an opportunity to submit to his spiritual authority. When they refused, he persecuted them severely. Christians must also be opposed, violently if necessary. In the eyes of a Muslim, if Jesus were God, it would have been unjust for God to have punished his own nature. All Muslims have a sacred mission by force or persuasion to bring the entire world under Allah's dominion.

Errors: Though Allah is omniscient, merciful, and compassionate, the Muslim holds him in such transcendent awe that he is virtually unapproachable. The message of John 3:16 that "God so loved the world..." is an alien concept to Islam. God is to be feared and strictly obeyed but his attributes cannot be personally experienced in man's heart. Allah demands a codified system of submission, but he offers no immediate forgiveness of sin in return. The certainty of salvation known by the Christian (John 3:36; 5:24) is but a vague hope to the Muslim who awaits the Day of Judgment when works, not grace, will determine his destination in the next life. Christians cannot accept the authority of the Koran because it seeks to supplant the Bible.

Background Sources: *Great Religions of the World,* 1971, National Geographic Society; *Religions of the World,* 1965, Barnes and Noble, New York, NY; *Cults, World Religions and You,* 1980, Kenneth Boa, Victor Books, Wheaton, IL; *Christianity Today,* 3/21/80, pp. 24-27; *Newsweek,* 2/26/79, pp. 38-41; *Christian Life,* 9/77, pp. 22-67; *Time,* 4/16/79, pp. 40-52.

Address/Location: Since one-sixth of the world's population follows Islam, its disciples are found everywhere. Islamic strongholds are concentrated primarily in the Middle East, Indonesia, and North Africa where more than 90 percent of the population is Muslim.

SUFISM

The most exotic variant of Islam proposes to reach God not through the Five Pillars but by entering trance states induced by dancing. The *Sufis* (their name comes from the wool [*suf*] of their undergarments) are a mystical Islamic branch rooted in the ascetic pietism of Muhammad's followers. Al-Hasan of Basra (643-728) was an early advocate of Sufism as was Melvana Celaleddin Rumi, a Turkish mystic who lived in the thirteenth century.

Sufism's emphasis is on union with God through meditation and ritual rather than Koranic obedience. Combining Islamic doctrines with Christian and Gnostic beliefs, they have developed a pantheistic theology with a spiritual hierarchy of *awliya* ("saints"). Chief of these is

Qutb, the Pole of the World. Sufi leaders known as *shaikhs* are held to be saints, and many of them have practiced celibacy, though it is not a requirement of their office.

While the average Muslim is content in submitting to the will of Allah, the Sufi wants an immediate, ecstatic experience of oneness with God. The means to accomplish this is a once-secret rite of twirling dance maneuvers. It was Rumi who adapted Asian shamanistic practices and formed a ritualistic approach to Islam. His disciples became known as "whirling dervishes" (dervish means "beggar" in Turkish). Until recently, dervishes were illegal in their native Turkey, a ban imposed by Kemal Ataturk who considered their beliefs an impediment to his modernization schemes.

Rumi watched a goldsmith at work one day and as a result was brought into a state of whirling ecstasy. He developed a special dance routine requiring a twirling motion. To master this choreographed movement 1,001 hours of training are required. Dervishes turn for an hour or more at a time without any sign of fatigue, repeating the name of Allah in prayer to the accompaniment of a musical beat. Eventually they enter an unconscious trance-state and fall on the floor, an act which is supposed to represent an "awakening from indifference."

Until recently, this esoteric "metaphysics of ecstasy" was a path available only to initiates. Now, Sufis are performing in public, and their beliefs and practices are being openly explained. The dervish ritual is presented as a way for the teacher to expel from the pupil "gross energy," which would otherwise hinder his spiritual progress. The costume worn is a white skirt which represents a shroud, and a high felt hat symbolizing a tombstone.

Among the eight Sufi precepts are: a concentrated breathing technique, returning to God from the material world, and being aware of the Divine Presence. "When you turn," says a foremost Sufi devotee, "you do not turn for yourself but for God...so the light of God may descend upon the earth."

Though traditional Islam has had little impact on the counterculture of youth in America, Sufism has attracted more than 6,000 adherents. The Sufi goal of higher consciousness through chants and meditative dancing blends well into the mystical landscape of contemporary religious cults.

Founder: Melvana Celaleddin Rumi who established the tradition in Konya, Turkey, in 1273. Pir Vilavat Inavat Khan is the current director and president of the Sufi Order.

Text: Islamic scriptures and Gnostic texts.

Symbol: The *Samazen* (pupil) posing with the circular skirt preparing for circumambulations (walking meditation).

Appeal: Sufism is a way to ecstatically experience oneness with God, if one assumes that the mystical trance-state achieved by dervishes is a form of communion with God. The counterculture fascination with consciousness-expanding modes of religion provides a fertile environment of curiosity among the young, which has led some to experiment with Sufism.

Purpose: Sufi literature declares, "The greatest principle of Sufism is *Isha Allah Ma'bud Allah,* God is love, lover, and beloved." Harmony with all the world's religions and peoples is said to be accomplished by each individual contemplating the immanence of God.

Errors: Sufism virtually ignores the question of sin and redemption. Its lack of fixed doctrinal structure means that belief resides in a subjective, mystical interpretation of truth. The *awliya* could be classified as familiar spirits (demons), with *Qutd* a personification of Lucifer. Dervish trance-states exhibit the characteristics of biblically defined demonic possession.

Background Sources: *The Encyclopedia of American Religions,* 1978, J. Gordon Melton, McGrath Publishing, Wilmington, NC; Sufi advertisements in occult journals; *Time,* 4/16/79, p. 52; *The Denver Post,* 8/29/75, p. 3BB; *Ibid.,* 5/14/76, p. B-9; *Ibid.,* 1/14/77, p. 5BB; *Ibid.,* 2/25/77, p. 5BB.

Address/Location: Sufi Order, c/o Shahnawaz Jamil, 408 Precita Ave., San Francisco, CA 94110.

BLACK MUSLIMS

Mention Black Muslims to the average person and he immediately thinks of incendiary hate rhetoric directed toward the "blue-eyed devil" white man. On second thought, he may recall the day that a spunky boxer named Cassius Clay insisted he henceforth be referred to as Muhammad Ali. The true sports fans would also remember the name of Kareem Abdul-Jabbar, formerly known as the seven-foot-tall basketball wizard Lew Alcindor.

In 1913, a North Carolina black man named Timothy Drew arrived in Newark, New Jersey, under the name Noble Drew Ali. He founded the Moorish-American Science Temples on the doctrine that Negroes were of Moroccan (Moorish) origin, and that Jesus was a black man killed by white Romans. Many of his teachings were taken from *The Aquarian Gospel,* an occult book written by Levi Dowling.

When Ali died, Wallace Ford, a door-to-door salesman from Detroit, suddenly appeared on the scene claiming to be Ali's reincarnation. He asserted that he was born in Mecca and had been sent to America to redeem the black man from the "Caucasian devil." One of Ford's spokesmen, Elijah Muhammad (formerly Robert Poole) helped him to found the Nation of Islam. Muhammad insisted that Ford was an incarnation of Allah. By the time Ford mysteriously disappeared from sight in 1935, Muhammad had assumed leadership of the organization.

While incarcerated as a conscientious objector during World War II, Elijah Muhammad, the Messenger of Allah, effectively recruited black prisoners for his cause. His message to them was simple: Wallace Ford was God — the Messiah predicted by Christians and the *Mahdi* proclaimed by Muslims: the white beast (created by a mad black scientist) has been allowed to reign for 6,000 years, and that period ended in 1914; the time is ripe for the Nation of Islam and the divine black god-men guided by Allah to arise and claim control over the world.

Malcolm X was the mouthpiece of Elijah Muhammad and was an eloquent evangelist until he was murdered by one of Muhammad's rivals on February 21, 1965. Membership blossomed in the turbulent, racially tense sixties. Dozens of temples were opened in ghetto neighborhoods, usually by acquiring the abandoned churches of white congregations who fled to the suburbs. A half-million circulation newspaper, *Muhammad Speaks* (now called *Bilalian News*), was hawked by well-dressed, militantly organized youth.

Black Muslims bought thousands of acres of farmland to promote self-help enterprises. They opened businesses and projected an image of discipline, cleanliness, and morality. Though their racial intolerance separated them from the world community of Islam, they did practice some Muslim precepts. Eating pork, gambling, smoking, and drinking liquor were forbidden. Members prayed five times a day facing Mecca. Women were admonished to respect their husbands and were required to have their heads covered. The Koran was deemed to be the holy scripture of God's prophet, although they also entertained fanciful speculation about the black man having originated on the moon 65 trillion years ago.

Though most critics labeled their theology as "racial hatred," Black Muslims preferred to call their views "social separation." They wanted no part with integration. Why should they? The white man's day of destruction was coming, and blacks should avoid sharing in his judgment. Heaven and hell were considered irrelevant concepts because the black man in America had already gone through the hell of slavery.

Upon the death of Elijah Muhammad in 1965, his son Wallace took over the movement. His initial lackluster leadership left some doubting whether he could adequately fill his father's shoes. His most important accomplishment has been to drop the strident racial invectives that had aroused the fear and dread of whites. This new image has enabled the Black Muslims to gain official recognition as an orthodox Islamic body under the name Community of Islam in the West. Followers are now referred to as *Bilalians* (Bilal was supposedly the first black convert of the Prophet Muhammad). Estimated members of adherents in the Community now range from 50,000 to 150,000. Just how serious they still are about establishing a black separatist nation remains to be seen.

Founder: Timothy Drew, born 1886 in North Carolina. The modern success of Black Muslims is due to leadership of Wallace Ford, Elijah Muhammad, and Malcolm X.

Text: The Koran. The Bible is also considered a source of truth so long as it is reinterpreted without the white man's lies.

Symbols: Crescent and star of Islam.

Appeal: Ghetto black youth who feel exploited by the predominantly white society are promised the vision of a black-ruled nation. The call to nationalistic supremacy promotes self-respect based on a strict moral code that produces individual prosperity.

Purpose: Since God is black, and the black man is a god, recognizing these "facts" will help blacks to shed the "white man's religion." Black Muslims promote a self-sufficient black economy and demand to have seven or eight states ceded to them in order to establish a black nation. Their stern rules and moral conduct aid them in the rehabilitation of societal rejects.

Error: The Black Muslim God is Wallace Ford, believed to be Allah incarnate, the Savior of mankind. This is, of course, incompatible with the unique claim to divinity established by Jesus Christ (Acts 4:12). Peter's vision in Acts 10 leaves no room for any practice of racial superiority. The Bible teaches that all men are sinners (Rom. 3:23; 6:23) and in need of God's saving grace, no matter what the color of one's skin.

Background Sources: *Those Curious New Cults,* 1975, William J. Petersen, Keats Publishing Inc., New Canaan, CT; *The Encyclopedia of American Religions,* 1978, J. Gordon Melton, McGrath Publishing, Wilmington, NC; *Kingdom of the Cults,* 1977, Walter Martin, Bethany Fellowship Inc., Minneapolis, MN; "Black Muslims and the Baptist Witness," Home Mission Board, SBC, Atlanta, GA; *Time,* 3/10/75, p. 83; *Christianity Today,* 5/12/80, p. 29.

Address/Location: Temples found in the urban areas of major U.S. cities.

MAJOR CULTS

15

Survey of Major Cults

Determining the manner in which to categorize today's cults is a subjective decision likely to cause disagreement among both cult members and researchers. The three classifications chosen for this book are admittedly broad, and a particular heading will obviously not apply precisely to all cults listed beneath it. For example, the term "pseudo-Christian" is used with Webster's qualification "deceptive resemblance to." Unquestionably, there are sincere born-again Christians who populate The Local Church and The Church of the Living Word. But because of their aberrational departure from historic orthodoxy and their subservience to authoritarian leadership, these bodies are included in the Pseudo-Christian category. The main criterion determining inclusion in this category was whether or not the cult in question made any attempt (sincere or deliberately deceptive) to follow Christian teachings and traditions.

Some cults are so egocentrically structured that it seems to this author they deserved a special category.

While one sociological mark of a cult is in its centralized control of dogma and practice, some groups seem to be totally structured around the charisma of one man. His teachings are incidental to the force of his personality. It is the subjective commitment to who he is — not what he says — that has formed a following. Not all cult leaders in this category adhere to similar religious systems (for example, William Branham vis-à-vis Sri Chinmoy), nevertheless, most do base their teachings on Hindu theology, since the doctrine of *avatars* naturally lends itself to enforcing the image of a cult leader who practices some form of self-deification. The decision warranting inclusion under Personality Cults was made by observing whether most adherents were initially attracted by the man more than the message.

The Occult/Mystical category includes those cults which base their precepts on non-Christian traditions. No matter how varied their esoteric teachings may be, the essence of their systems is founded on a mystical model. In most cases, the important factor lies in the experience offered by the cult's philosophy, not in its objective perimeters of doctrine. Most of these groups promote an intuitional concept of reality rather than utilizing sensory perception. A complex belief system may emerge as the cult develops, but an altered consciousness is the basis of its appeal. To a greater or lesser extent, most (though not all) cults in this category encourage occult and psychic exploration. As a result, this grouping is more prone to involve spiritually dangerous practices of collusion with supernatural forces.

Please note that the order of listing is alphabetical and does not indicate either size or importance. This method of cult listing also applies to the minor cult section at the end of the book.

The listing of background sources at the end of each cult is not an inclusive reference to all research materials consulted in preparing the cult analyses. These sources only indicate references directly quoted or writers from whom ideas and concepts were borrowed. Also note that the background sources include both cultic and non-cultic writings.

16

Children of God
(Family of Love)

"They went out from us, but they were not of us." The Apostle John's appraisal of first century heretics (1 John 2:19) might well describe how early Jesus Movement pioneers feel about the Children of God. (In 1978 the name Children of God was changed to Family of Love to avoid identification with the bad publicity attached to the COG image.) The far-flung clan of David "Moses" Berg had once spanned seventy-two countries with an estimated membership nearing 10,000. Today, less than 1,000 hard-core followers may remain. Berg's "Royal Family" empire is in shambles, with children, in-laws, and even his legal wife having deserted him. Before closing the final chapter of the COG, we'll look at the opening pages and the sections between.

David Berg was the son of a devout Christian and Missionary Alliance couple. His father, Hjalmer, pastored and taught at a Christian college. Virginia, his mother, was a radio evangelist. David married Jane Berg in 1944 and entered Christian service as an evangelist. Berg gradually soured on organized religion and was associated with fringe religionist O. L. Jaguers and TV evangelist Fred Jordan. During the earlier years of the West Coast Jesus Revolution, Berg joined his mother in directing a Teen Challenge coffeehouse. It was there that his radicalized, antiestablishment gospel took root among religiously zealous hippies.

In 1969 Berg left the coffeehouse and with about fifty followers headed on a trek to Arizona, later described as a time analogous to Israel's wanderings in the wilderness. Maria, a Tucson church secretary, joined the movement and later was elevated to the status of Berg's mistress. (Jane was nicknamed "Mother Eve" and was allowed certain sleeping "rights" with David. In 1980 she ran off with another COG member.) The rag-tag group took organized form with members assuming new biblical names. Twelve groups were formed, named and patterned after Israel's twelve tribes. They couldn't go back to California because Berg had twice "prophesied" the exact date the entire wicked state would slide into the ocean. Their meandering ended when Fred Jordan invited them to locate on his Texas Soul Clinic Missionary Ranch.

When the first wave of controversy hit the COG with charges of kidnapping and brainwashing, Jordan kicked them out. By this time, the COG numbered at least 2,000 and had the strength to go it alone. Communal organizations were divided into colonies, and a subsidiary called THANK COG (consisting of favorably disposed parents of COG members) was activated to counter the charges of FREE COG parents who claimed their offspring were unfairly controlled by Berg. To communicate with his increasingly fragmented followers, Berg hit upon the concept of circulating periodic newsletters that came to be called "MO Letters."

The rambling and grammatically shabby content of Berg's epistles evolved into what were considered divinely commissioned pronouncements. MO letters were said to be God's inspired Word for today, far superior to what was written in the Bible thousands of years ago. Letters were categorized according to the ranks of insiders who had access to them. Considering the pornographic overtones of Berg's sexual preoccupation, it was understandably wise of him to restrict certain MO letters to his immediate intimates.

Though no official systematic theology was promulgated, a philosophical and methodological structure did emerge. A pyramidal system of leadership (with Berg at the apex) placed "babes" (new converts) at the bottom and ensured that Berg's extended "Royal Family" remained in total control. As an autocratic messiah, he claimed to have direct communication with God — the Lord's "Moses" for today. His word was unquestioned, and even "murmuring" against his views was considered a mortal sin. Parents were to be hated and despised along with the corrupt political system of the United States. In fact, he prophesied America's destruction when the comet Kahoutek would collide with Earth. Berg and most of his disciples left behind their doomed native land and set up operations in Europe. His whereabouts remains unknown, though COG international headquarters are in Zurich, and it is rumored that Berg has gone into secluded hiding somewhere in Switzerland.

The practices of COG stir volatile reactions wherever they go. Though Berg once applied for Israeli citizenship, he eventually turned violently anti-Semitic. He courted the favor of Libya's Quaddafi and said about Jews, "devils incarnate . . . if I had a gun I'd shoot them myself!" Commune members languish in often unsanitary quarters, are sometimes refused medical treatment, and are kept on a subsistence diet of food "procured" from local supermarkets. The "Revolutionary Contract" they sign turns over all possessions to the COG, and most contacts with past friends and family are abruptly severed, unless such individuals are considered sources of revenue for the group. Negative comments are forbidden, no member is ever left alone, and daily hours that are not spent pouring over MO letters are dedicated to "litnessing" — evangelizing by literature distribution.

Litnessing is also a primary source of cult income with strict quotas set as a barometer of fervency for the cause. The other basic source of income is through what amounts to religious prostitution, called "FFing" ("flirty fishing") in COG parlance. Female members are encouraged to offer their bodies as an inducement for men to join the organization, though the "fish" are expected to pay for such favors. Husbands are admonished to offer their wives as a symbol of their devotion to the cause. If venereal disease is contracted (Berg admits he himself is afflicted), it is seen as a willingness to suffer for the cause of Christ. In fact, Berg asserts that Jesus practiced sexual intercourse with Mary and Martha and deliberately contracted venereal disease to illustrate his identification with human infirmities.

Sex is a central theme of the salacious MO letters. Nothing is forbidden. Even homosexuality and oral sodomy, which were once considered taboo, have now been legitimized "within the limits of the love of God." Childhood sex is advocated, and children conceived through FFing are called "Jesus Babes." (Unwed mothers are euphemistically referred to as "widows.") Topless bathing is promoted, girls are admonished not to wear undergarments and most go braless. A marriage relationship (approved of first by colony leaders) consists of simply going to bed with the chosen partner — legal civil ceremonies are seen as part of Babylon's corrupt system. Lesbianism and incest are considered particularly desirable.

Berg's system of sexual philosophy also includes the following: wife-swapping — justified by the "all things in common" passage of Acts 2:44; punishing female members by requiring them to masturbate before male observers; fondling children and sleeping with them in the nude; and the belief that God had intercourse with Mary to procreate Jesus! "God is in the business of breaking up families...salvation sets us free from the curse of clothing and the shame of nakedness," Berg writes. "God is a pimp," he blasphemously declares, "...experience a spiritual orgasm by being filled with the Spirit." When questioned about his personal sexual excesses, Berg argues that he is God's King David, and that like his namesake, his own sexual promiscuity has been condoned by the Almighty.

The most startling aspect of Berg's sexual obsessions is his claim to indulge in succubus relationships — sexual intercourse with spirit beings whom he calls "goddesses." In fact, Berg has a long history of flirtation with the occult. He contends that "spiritual counselors" visit him regularly and even enter his body to speak through his mouth. One of them, Abrahim, is supposedly a gypsy king who has been dead for over 1,000 years. Berg has also been involved in palmistry, fortune-telling, and astrology. "Spiritualistic churches are not so bad after all," he concludes.

In Berg's eyes, the COG are the 144,000 of Revelation 7 and 14, the restored Israel. After the United States falls to communism, the anti-Christ will briefly reign until Satan takes over. The majority of professing Christians will take the mark of the beast, but the COG will remain the Lord's faithful. In spite of his unimpressive record of past prophecies, the end, according to Berg, will come in 1993. Non-COG members need not fear, however, since Berg's universalist theology leaves room for a second chance; few will be left to inhabit hell. In fact, those living can even now pray people out of hell.

Berg's course language (MO letters are spiced with four-letter expletives) and immoral philosophy may have finally taken its toll. Defectors abound, including his Barbara Cane ("Queen Rachel") who was Berg's heir apparent. Even the most effectively brainwashed followers of cult leaders cannot permanently overlook their leader's delusions of grandeur and his claims of divine endorsement. As Carole Hausmann and Gretchen Passantino put it in *The New Cults,* "The Holy Spirit is not some love potion. The Father is not some oversexed god. The Son is not a promiscuous bachelor with V.D." That conclusion has also apparently been reached by more than one former COG member.

Founder: David Brandt Berg, born Feburary 18, 1919. The COG coalesced into a viable organization circa 1970.

Text: The Bible, but more prominently the periodic MO letters, rambling discourses by which Berg communicates with his followers. Most letters have strong sexual overtones and artwork and go by titles like "Sex Works!" and "Come on, Ma! Burn Your Bra!" Other letters discuss matters of doctrine and rail against the "Systemites" — anyone not in agreement with COG ideals.

Symbols: None known except the ubiquitous 8½ × 11 folded MO letters that are handed out to passing motorists or pedestrians.

Appeal: COG recruiters concentrate on lonely young people who may be disenchanted with the establishment's economic or religious institutions. Bible verses are quoted out of context along with a positive image of happiness and brotherhood to suggest the COG are truly dedicated Christians. The recruit is bombarded with guilt that he is part of a condemned Satanic system and will never again have a chance to faithfully serve God.

Purpose: "Pull down, destroy, and throw out the old order," Berg implores with revolutionary fervor. Mankind is in the last generation, and the United States is the "great prostitute that sits on many waters" and the "Babylon" of Revelation. Only the COG will remain true to God and escape the world's impending doom. They eventually will rule the Earth as an elitist group through whom God's promises will be fulfilled.

Errors: At times Berg denies the Trinity ("I don't believe in the Trinity.") But on other occasions promotes a Father, Mother, and Son conglomerate. The Holy Spirit, "Holy Queen of Love," is portrayed as a half-naked woman. Christ is declared to be a created being in a misinterpretation of Revelation 3:14. Scriptural injunctions against consulting familiar spirits are ignored (Deut. 18:9–14; Jer. 14:14) by communicating with what he calls "God's Witches." Berg also denies God's promises of blessings to the Jews (Acts 3:18–26; Rom. 9:4, 5) by cursing "May God damn the God-damned Jews." By encouraging fornication, polygamy, incest, and adultery, Berg stands in opposition to the biblical view of sex in marriage as expressed by Paul in Hebrews 13 and Ephesians 5. In his rebellion against the historic church, Berg has, in the words of anticult researcher Jack Sparks, "managed to transform a gigantic personal temper tantrum against authority into a worldwide movement."

Background Sources: *Christianity Today,* 2/28/77, pp. 19-23; *Ibid.,* 2/25/80, pp. 40, 41; Jack Sparks, *The Mindbenders,* 1977, Thomas Nelson, Inc., Nashville, TN;

Ronald Enroth, *Youth Brainwashing, and the Extremist Cults,* 1977, Zondervan Publishing House, Grand Rapids, MI; Walter Martin, *The New Cults,* 1980, Vision House, Santa Ana, CA.

Address/Location: World publication headquarters in Zurich, Switzerland. Colony addresses available for most major United States and European cities.

17

Christian Science

Doug and Rita Swan had watched their sixteen-month-old baby convulse and scream with pain for twelve days. When they finally rushed him to the hospital, it was too late. Little Matthew died six days later. As devout Christian Scientists, Doug and Rita had tried to follow their faith. Their church "practitioner" had told them to stop praying, tell no one, and ignore Matthew's anguished condition. After all, "Mother" Mary Baker Eddy had declared that sin, illness, and disease are all illusions of the mind to be corrected by right thinking.

The tragic story of Matthew Swan is only one of many. Fortunately for Christian Scientists, most states in the U.S. have passed laws that protect them from negligence if they shun medical assistance for a family member. Christian Science rejects chiropractic, vitamins, nutrition, and drugs, as well as immunizations. When pain or sickness strikes, Scientists are admonished to deny "material sense testimony" — what their five senses tell them. Even a mother's protective instinct is derided as a "false, mortal belief." Church members may have broken bones set, but aren't permitted to entertain any medical diagnosis because Mrs. Eddy taught that consulting a physician breaks the first commandment.

How can such an unenlightened belief hold authoritarian sway over an estimated one-half million people? Christian Science has so insulated itself from interaction with other religious groups, that members feel a sense of isolation. They are reluctant to talk with outsiders and are forbidden to read any critical literature. They have reason to be impressed with their church. Mrs. Eddy had declared, "There is one way to heaven... divine science shows us this way. The second appearing of Jesus is unquestionably the spiritual advent of the advancing idea of God, as in Christian Science." Worship is carried on in expensive, beautiful buildings. Reading rooms are well appointed and cheerfully staffed at highly visible locations. The *Christian Science Monitor,* their daily newspaper with a half million subscribers, is a highly respected journalistic organ with several Pulitzer prizes to its credit.

Mary Baker Eddy was certainly not modest in her claims, and most church members admire her as an infallible mother. She proclaimed that her teachings were God's "final revelation." Mrs. Eddy also asserted divine inspiration for her book *Science and Health With Key to the Scriptures.* The very choice of the word Key in its title was based on her belief that she was the woman of Revelation 12. Many of her early followers accorded her a status of equality with Christ, a belief she did nothing to dissuade. Unfortunately for Christian Scientists, the historical record of her life gives one a decidedly different impression.

Mary Ann Morse Baker was the daughter of New Hampshire Congregationalists. Her childhood was characterized by emotional disturbances and frequent illnesses. At the age of twenty-two she married George Glover, who died seven months later. Her second marriage, to a dentist, Dr. Daniel Patterson, ended in divorce. In 1877 she married Asa Eddy, her first disciple and the first Christian Science practitioner. It was while she was married to Dr. Patterson that her life changed abruptly.

Seeking relief from a spinal illness in 1862, she visited a spiritual healer by the name of Phineas Parkhurst Quimby. He practiced a form of mind-over-matter healing that he called Christian Science. Though Christian Scientists disallow the possibility that Quimby had any influence on

Mrs. Eddy, research scholars have proven beyond doubt that she plagiarized heavily from his manuscripts.

In 1866, Mrs. Eddy fell and injured herself. She later claimed that the fall left her with only three days to live (though her physician denied such a diagnosis). On the third day she reported that after reading Matthew 9:2 she experienced a miraculous cure. From then on, she felt her mission was to spread this "new" discovery of Christian Science. In 1875 she published *Science and Health,* offering healing to those afflicted with any number of maladies. The Church of Christ, Scientist, was incorporated in 1879.

Many people are favorably disposed toward Christian Science in spite of its bad publicity regarding cases when medical treatment was withheld. Some have heard glowing testimonials of healing from Church members. Others note the conservative, well-educated, upper socio-economic types who attend Christian Science meetings. They certainly seem well-intentioned, and few would condemn their effective ministry to those plagued with emotional ills and psychosomatic afflictions. But the evaluation of any cult must be based on substance, not image. The source of its authority and power as well as the biblical validity of its views are essential criteria to judge its worth. Such a critical analysis leaves Christian Science lacking in many areas.

Attending a Christian Science service immediately impresses one with its departure from mainstream Christian practices. There is no clergy, only lay readers and designated, full-time practitioners who administer the Church's healing techniques. No ordinances are recognized and the service is ended with a reading of the Lord's Prayer (the verses interspersed with Mrs. Eddy's interpretations). Membership is restricted to only those who sever relationships with any other church or religious organization. *Science and Health* is read alternately with Bible quotations, giving the distinct connotation that the Word of God is useless without Mary Baker's illumination.

The doctrines of Christian Science are not overtly evident to the casual observer. Much of Eddy's terminology sounds good until the surface is scratched to reveal her semantic frame of reference underneath. Influenced by the New Thought fad of her day, she underpins all her doctrines with the Hindu concept of an evil, illusory, material world. In this system, that which is spirit is the only true reality. This notion flavors her concepts of God, sin, and salvation. Here is a sampling of her teachings: man did not fall; death is an illusion; angels are God's thoughts; God is divine Mind; Genesis 2 is a "lie"; the Virgin Birth was a spiritual idea; the Trinity is pagan; evil and sin are imaginary; disease can be removed by right thinking; Jesus was not God; heaven is a state of mind; hell is nonexistent; prayer to forgive sin is pointless; Christ did not die; his resurrection was spiritual and not physical; and the shed blood of Christ is ineffectual for sin.

The core of Christian Science teaching is the doctrine of healing. Nothing else the church propagates draws more potential members. Mrs. Eddy was constantly challenged by the medical leaders of her day to produce evidence of one bona fide healing of a medically diagnosed case of organic disease. She did not and could not. In the end even she turned to physicians and was treated with the painkiller morphine. Still, Christian Science maintains her belief that Jesus revealed to people their illusion of illness and thus cured them. Christian Scientists propose to go and do likewise.

Undeniably there are some cases of Christian Science healing that deserve acknowledgement. Those who believe they have been healed are quick to embrace the entire scope of Church teachings. What really happens? Since medical verification before or after the fact is not allowed, no one knows how many cures were induced by alleviating the psychosomatic root of the problem. Those illnesses which are emotional in nature may have been removed by the psychologically soothing effect of the practitioner's therapy. Some ex-members argue that in Christian Science healing only the symptoms are ignored, a decision which may later result in suffering that could have been alleviated with proper medical treatment. In addition, the encounter of Moses with Pharaoh's magicians in Exodus 7 illustrates Satan's ability to precipitate "miracles." In fact, supernatural healing is a trademark of many demonic cults, including Satanism and Spiritualism. When a healing occurs, it should not necessarily be construed as an indication of Divine approval of what the healer believes.

With rumored declines in membership rocking the
foundation of the Mother Church in Boston, the future of
Christian Science is uncertain. The number of
practitioners has dropped nearly 50 percent in the last
three decades. Mrs. Eddy prophesied that "in fifty years
or less, Christian Science will be the dominant religious
belief of the world." That prediction seems as fruitless as
her contention that, "Man is incapable of sin, sickness,
and death." Auschwitz and Mrs. Eddy's own decayed
body seem sufficient proof to question this optimistic
evaluation as well as her many other claims.

Founder: Mary Baker Eddy, born 1821 as Mary Ann Morse
Baker. *Science and Health* published in 1875 and Church
of Christ, Scientist, incorporated in 1879. She died in 1910.

Text: Matthew 9:2, supposedly an affirmation of Mrs.
Eddy's own healing which led her to formulate Christian
Science beliefs.

Symbols: The seal of a cross ringed by a crown.

Appeal: The healing and health promised by Christian
Science meets man's emotional need to overcome fear of
pain and suffering. Eddy's teachings appeal to those
seeking a philosophical basis for ignoring man's
unregenerate nature and necessity of repentance. The
reality of evil can be excused as an apparition of the
mind.

Purpose: The "myths" of traditional Christian belief must
be eradicated. Man is perfect and should strive for the
same Divine Mind that Jesus attained. Sickness can be
eradicated once a person sees that pure thoughts will
dispel the illusion of disease. As the one true church,
members are encouraged to affirm that God is good and
therefore good is God. In such a system evil cannot exist
since matter (evil) does not exist.

Errors: Few orthodox Christian doctrines are left
unassaulted. Christian Science is biblically not Christian
and it is manifestly not scientific. Its theology is
universalistic. Jesus was said to be hiding in the
sepulcher (he didn't die) so his resurrection holds no
hope for believers, contradicting Paul's exposition of
1 Corinthians 15.

Sources: *Newsweek,* 6/21/76, p. 87; *Christianity Today,* 10/10/75, pp. 6-11; *Christian Scientists and the Baptist Witness,* M. Thomas Starkes, Home Missions Board, SBC; *People,* 3/31/81, pp. 30-32; *Cults, World Religions and You,* 1980, Kenneth Boa, Victor Books.

Address/Location: Mother Church in Boston, MA. Local churches in most U. S. cities of reasonable size.

18

The Church of the Living Word

John Robert Stevens (founder of The Church of the Living Word, commonly called "The Walk") is a classic example of what happens when one is raised in a Christian environment and departs into error. Stevens uses evangelical terminology to justify his private revelations. Consequently, the truth of Scripture is altered slightly enough to be detected, but not sufficient to be overtly obvious. "The Walk" members use colloquial Christian catch-phrases which they have redefined. For example, when Stevens says he is "speaking the Word of the Lord" he is actually referring to a mediumistic revelation of his Christ-attained perfection. Those not familiar with his cult would assume that he is merely talking about preaching. Such a twist in logic and language is consistent with his whole approach to scriptural truth.

Stevens was reared in a Pentecostal preacher's home, though he later departed from Foursquare and Assemblies of God groups after a dramatic vision in 1954. He claims this experience was similar to Paul's encounter on the road to Damascus. After this "revelation," Stevens began the movement which now claims about 100 churches. Headquarters is near his boyhood home in Washington, Iowa, said to be "the most important spot on the face of the earth."

In Steven's scheme of teachings, the Bible is considered to be outdated and thus needs to be supplemented (and eventually replaced) by impromptu, spoken prophecies. During frequent, lengthy, emotion-charged services, members are encouraged to deny reason and yield to extemporaneous utterances that represent "the living word." The one who speaks is more than a mere channel of Christ. He is said literally to become Christ, a self-deification doctrine which is central to the church's beliefs.

Such individualistic revelations are important but they must always be subject to the ones expounded by Stevens, who claims apostolic authority. Members are taught that Scripture will confuse them unless they follow Stevens' interpretation. This authoritarian manner of control also extends to the personal affairs of members. Day-to-day decisions must constantly be subjected to Church supervision, since "The Walk" is assumed to be the only true church capable of guiding one's life.

As the Church has evolved, occult and psychic phenomena have become more evident. Since a central doctrine having to do with perfectionism states that Christians become a part of God in a manner bordering on deification, their divine natures become willing recipients of mystical experiences. This merging of one's nature with God negates the sense of personal identity, further opening up one's spirit to experience transcendent levels of consciousness. At some church services, participants are encouraged to raise the level of their vibrations, a practice bordering on the spiritualistic manner of inducing altered states of mind.

Many "Walk" members are born-again refugees from sterile churches. They have been attracted by a sense of belonging due to the group dynamics and claims of supernatural gifts of tongues, prophecy, and healing. These well-meaning people might overlook the occult nature of references to auras and "transference" of spiritual power. But their sincerity is no excuse for claiming superiority over all other churches and denominations. Such an exclusive attitude is not in harmony with 1 Corinthians 12, which emphasizes the unity of Christ's body in spite of its diversity.

Founder: John Robert Stevens, born August 7, 1919, Washington, Iowa.

Text: Acts 9:3, 4 (Stevens legitimatizes his apostolic authority by equating his visionary experience with Paul's Damascus road encounter); John 16:13 is interpreted to assume that subjective revelation should supplant and augment objective biblical truths.

Symbols: None known.

Appeal: Disaffected Christians from nominal church backgrounds may find in "The Walk" a more spontaneous encounter with spiritual reality. Those familiar with Eastern religions and occult phenomena will easily recognize the similarities between these practices and Stevens' teachings.

Purpose: Members are taught that all other churches belong to a false Babylonian system and that The Church of the Living Word is restoring the active presence of God's truth by the use of supernatural gifts and revelation.

Errors: Stevens' teachings rob Christ of his personhood by claiming that he is now embodied in the Church and that Christians can be a deified extension of Christ. "Be robed with deity itself — God's very nature being reproduced in you," Stevens implores. A conclusion of this belief is that The Church of the Living Word essentially represents the Second Coming of Christ, replacing the literal return of the person of Christ in the clouds (Acts 1:11). 1 John 2:2 admonishes that Christians can and do sin. They are to repent and ask forgiveness (1 John 1:8, 9), not strive for a sanctified state of self-deification.

Background Sources: "John Robert Stevens and The Church of the Living Word," Spiritual Counterfeits Project Newsletter, 9/76, vol. 2, no. 7; *The New Cults,* 1980, Walter

Martin, pp. 269-296; miscellaneous writings by John Robert Stevens, including *To Every Man That Asketh,* etc.

Address/Location: Cult headquarters is in Washington, Iowa. The greatest concentration of churches is in California.

19
Holy Order of MANS

Publicly distributed literature describes the Holy Order of MANS as a "discipleship movement," not a religion. "Seekers" who inquire are told that the Order's purpose is to teach the Universal Law of Creation revealed by ancient Christian mysteries. A list of Twelve Rules of Living guide the search, including admonitions to tithe ($5.00 per month for beginners) and render absolute obedience to the Class Master to whom the inquirer is assigned.

Entry into the Order (it's coeducational) starts when the initiate fills out an application form. He must also pledge his willingness to receive the teachings of Master Jesus. This nominal reference to Christ is consistent with the Order's position that Jesus was a great teacher, but only one of several great *avatars.* The Holy Order of MANS purports to have a Christian belief system. There are frequent references encouraging the seeker to maintain "high Christian morals." However, the Order's true mystical nature is revealed by its allusions to concepts such as "Self-Realization," the "Aquarian Age," the "Christ Light Within," the "Esoteric Council," and "Attainment of the Illumination."

The so-called Basic Course takes about two years to complete. Then, the entrant (who is now a Lay Brother or Sister) may proceed on to the Advanced Course or may even pursue to the highest level of Discipleship Instructor. From that point onward each member is expected to exhibit qualities of self-control, charity, and detachment from material and physical desires. Dark-colored clothing with a clerical collar is standard attire, a dress style designed to spiritually distinguish members from "the common folk." Such garb also emphasizes the Catholic-type overtones of the Order.

Rigid moral codes are not assigned. Instead, the Order seems to assume that a subjectively acquired Christ-consciousness will dictate positive conduct. Members are told that they do not need to forsake their existing church or religious faith affiliations because the precepts of the Order are "not doctrines." (For those who make a total commitment to MANS teachings, there are cloister and monastic orders.) By denying that Christ is the only Savior/Creator and relegating him to an infusion of "radiant energy," the Holy Order of MANS places itself in opposition to orthodox biblical belief.

More serious spiritual dangers may be encountered by meditation techniques designed to "reach the higher beings and your own inner being." Such a solicitation may result in spiritistic practices, though there is no reason to suggest that any active attempt at spiritualism or necromancy is intended. They do, however, promote involvement in tarot cards, astrology, psychic power, Kabbalah, and parapsychology.

The main thrust of the Order is an appeal to achieve a higher consciousness. This exalted state is to be achieved by attaining the same "Christ consciousness" as Jesus, who was merely a god-realized man. Members will then be prepared to enter the New Age of man's spiritual understanding. Their slogan, "And by their work ye shall know them," is paraphrased from Matthew 7:20. The substitution of the word "work" for "fruit" may or may not have been deliberate, but it does reveal the essential difference between the Order and biblical Christianity. The ethical aims of the Order are commendable, but ultimately unattainable. The true Christian is to be known by the Spirit's fruit (Gal. 5:22, 23) which comes from the indwelling Person (not consciousness) of Christ.

Founder: Earl Blighton, an ex-engineer who claims "divine revelation" prompted him to start the Order.

Text: The Bible (preferably the New Testament) with mystical emphasis on the Pauline epistles; seminars and correspondence study.

Symbol: Golden Cross overlaid with a flaming sword. MANS is an acronym denoting *mysterion* (mystery), *agape* (divine love), *nous* (knowledge), and *sophia* (wisdom).

Appeal: Moral asceticism and ethical honesty are strongly emphasized to attract those who have been victimized by society's moral vacuum. The image of the Order is noncontroversial and so little is known about it that prospective members have no predispositions about its secret teachings.

Purpose: The Holy Order of MANS promises to reveal hidden, ancient Christian Mysteries. These "truths" will elevate one's spiritual consciousness and prepare him for the New Age which will soon dawn upon humanity. Members are promised entry into "the Greater Brotherhood," a company of "Christed" individuals who will someday reign with "the Cosmic Christ."

Errors: Christ is not Eternal God but merely a great teacher. God the Father is "the highest initiate among the humanity of the Saturn Period," Jesus is "the highest initiate of the Sun Period," and the Holy Spirit is "the highest initiate of the Moon Period." Mystical wisdom is considered to be a valid source of truth and equal in authority to biblical revelation.

Background Sources: Holy Order of MANS solicitation correspondence; introductory brochure, "Steps Along the Way"; *S.C.P. Newsletter,* 2/76, vol. 2, no. 2.

Address/Location: Holy Order of MANS, 2101 Seymour Ave., Box 308, Cheyenne, WY 82001 (Discipleship Headquarters).

Holy Order of MANS, 20 Steiner St., San Francisco, CA 94117 (International Headquarters).

20

International Community of Christ/The Jamilians

Would you be willing to believe that Christ has come again in the form of Jamil Sean Savoy, the child of Eugene Douglas Savoy, born in the United States (1959) and passed away in the Peruvian Andes in 1962? And would you also be willing to accept the fact that the miracles of Christ were performed by solar energy? If not, then this "secret community" based on "the System" as revealed by Gene Savoy is not for you. If these beliefs do seem plausible, you are welcomed to enroll in The Academy and Sacred College (with a minimum pledge of $734.40 annually) to discover the esoteric, true teachings of Jesus as revealed in *The Decoded New Testament.* To begin, just fill out the "Spiritual Awareness Aptitude Test" advertised in major occult journals.

Gene Savoy, a writer and explorer of some renown, was the grandson of a Baptist minister. At the age of six he witnessed the first of several visions and psychic experiences which led him into a study of world religions. At age twenty-eight, he came upon the teachings of the Essenes and other Middle-Eastern mystic orders. Savoy became convinced that Jesus was a mere "inspired man of God" whose most important teachings were not included in the New Testament. He concluded that Christ orally communicated a secret closed system to his followers that is only cryptically revealed in the Gospels. The time has now come to restore to the Church this message which has been lost for centuries.

As a result of explorations in the Peruvian mountains, Savoy became convinced that ancient sun worship was based on the premise that all humans are actually "light-beings." By a technique of gazing at the sun, initiates of the cult are taught to absorb solar energy so they can experience a "new birth" and increase their life span by "fifteen to twenty percent." By "feeding upon the invisible light that is being shed through the sun," each person can become more aware of his "true nature" as a "light body." Savoy contends that "the creative energy of the universe begins in the sun." His ultimate goal is "intercommunication with some greater intelligence via the sun."

The rationale for his "cosolary" teachings lies in the assertion that his only child, Jamil, was actually a divine being who came to Earth as Christ. Taking his cue from Christ's references to receiving the Kingdom of God as a child (Matt. 18:3) and Isaiah's prophecy that "a little child shall lead them" (Isa. 11:6), Savoy claims Jamil is the fulfillment of these Scriptures. Jamil's purpose was to amend Christianity through his prophecies and restore its original form. Though any adept student of occult and Eastern philosophy will find nothing new in Jamil's discourses, Savoy is convinced that the child's words were divinely inspired. When Jamil died in 1962 ("returned to the World of Light," is Savoy's way of putting it), Savoy came back to the United States. In 1972 he established the Community near Reno, Nevada. The ministry went public in 1975.

In Savoy's scheme of theology, "Christ is a universal force to be experienced [instead of worshiped as a deity]" and "man, too, is a Son of God." His writings denigrate the blood atonement and promise to "open the Book of Life." When Christ returns, he will not be a "man-savior. . . to redeem mankind," but a "new spiritual Sun, unlike any sun that ever shone." Among the practices used to develop Savoy's concept of solar energy are pyramidology, dream analysis, altered states of consciousness, vision analysis, biorhythms, auras, the study of light and color bodies, and other indulgences from the world of spiritualism. The promotion of occult phenomena along with persistent references to "light-beings," are uncomfortable reminders of the Apostle Paul's warning of 2 Corinthians 11:14 — "For Satan himself is transformed into an angel of light."

Founder: Eugene Douglas Savoy, born May 11, 1927, in Bellingham, Washington.

Text: *The Essae Document, The Decoded New Testament, The Lost Gospel of Jesus,* and *The Jamilians.*

Symbols: A four-pointed cross with radiants of equal length.

Appeal: Those with a nominal Christian background and metaphysical inclinations may be fascinated by the idea that Savoy has discovered the true, hidden teachings of Jesus.

Purpose: The Community reveals the secret teachings of Christ orally communicated to his disciples, and now interpreted through the writings of Savoy. These doctrines are substantiated by the "prophecies" of Savoy's late, three-year-old child, Jamil.

Errors: Savoy refuses to accept the Bible as inerrant and assumes that the supernatural power of Jesus was from solar energy. Christ is a mere prophet of no greater significance than others. Jesus was a messenger, not a Redeemer.

Background Sources: Miscellaneous Community documents, advertisements, and published texts: *The Emerging New Christianity, A Confidential Prospectus,* 1975; *The Child Christ,* 1973, Gene Savoy; "Dawning of a New Creation," *East/West Journal,* 12/76, pp. 19-21; *Ibid.,* 4/81, p.7; membership solicitation letter, 5/19/76 (signed by Gene Savoy); *East/West Journal,* 3/80, pp. 40-49; *Project X: The Search for the Secrets of Immortality,* 1977, Gene Savoy.

Address/Location: International Community of Christ, Chancellory Building, 643 Ralston, Reno, NV 89505.

21

Jehovah's Witnesses

She died on her sixth birthday. She could have lived. A blood transfusion would have saved the life of Ricarda Bradford, who was critically injured in a car accident. But her father, a chiropractor and devout Jehovah's Witness, refused the life-giving procedure. He quoted Genesis 9:3, 4 and Leviticus 17:10-15, explaining that Witnesses consider taking blood in the veins to be the same as eating it.

Refusing to accept blood transfusions is just one of several distinctive beliefs associated with Jehovah's Witnesses. They do not donate vital organs nor receive transplants. Until 1952, they were forbidden smallpox vaccinations. They also refuse to vote, salute the flag, sing "The Star Spangled Banner" (or any nationalistic anthem), and will not serve in the Armed Forces. Witnesses who depart from such injunctions are disfellowshiped. From then on, Kingdom Hall worshipers (even family members) consider them as dead. The excommunicated "apostate" is told he will not rise from the grave on Judgment Day.

In 1879 a Bible study leader named Charles Taze Russell was looking for a way to expound his somewhat peculiar teachings. He had departed from orthodoxy by denying the existence of hell, the Trinity, and the deity of Christ, and felt compelled to reach a larger audience. He co-published *The Herald of the Morning* magazine with its founder, N. H. Barbour, and it is here that we find the first records of Russell's movement. By 1884 Russell controlled the publication, renamed it *The Watch Tower Announcing Jehovah's Kingdom,* and founded Zion's Watch Tower Tract Society (now known as the Watch Tower Bible and Tract Society). The first edition of *The Watch Tower* magazine was only 6,000 copies each month. Today the Witnesses' publishing complex in Brooklyn, New York, churns out 100,000 books and 800,000 copies of its two magazines — daily!

Russell's theology established the foundation for the Witnesses' militant opposition to all other church organizations. Until his death in 1916 aboard a train in Texas, Russell insisted that the Bible could be understood only according to his interpretation. At the heart of his system was a prophetical chronology that predicted the Gentile era would end in 1914. (Russell had already concluded that Christ had returned in 1874, but as a "presence in the upper air," not a visible manifestation.) The end of the sealing of the 144,000 saints who would be "Kings and priests in heaven" was also designated to occur in 1914. Those saved after that would belong to a servant class, "the great company," who would rule on earth under the tutelage of the 144,000.

After the death of Russell, a Missouri lawyer named Joseph Franklin Rutherford took over the presidency of the Watch Tower Society. At a Columbus, Ohio, convention in 1931, he cited Isaiah 43:10 as the pretext for changing the name of the organization to "Jehovah's Witnesses." Thus, the stigma of Russell's questionable scholarship (he had only a seventh-grade education) and morals was resolved. Rutherford assumed total charge of the organization, and from then on his prolific writings were the source of divine mandate. This consolidation of power enabled him to discard some of Russell's less desirable teachings about the gathering of the Jews and the great pyramid theory.

After Rutherford's death, Nathan Knorr took over. In the same way that Rutherford had sought to supplant Russell's influence, Knorr ignored the works of

Rutherford. Today, the Society is led by Frederick William Franz, a widower in his eighties, who wields papal power over the lives of 4.1 million Witnesses all over the world.

The pronouncements that issue forth from the Brooklyn headquarters (known to members as "Bethel") are binding, and no deviation is tolerated. Strict theological control insures a consistency of doctrine. Witnesses avoid contact with outsiders, and the rare chance to meet one usually occurs when they knock on the door. Never identifying who they are, these friendly but persistent zealots deserve high marks for perseverance. Society statistics indicate that 740 house calls are required to recruit *each* of the nearly 200,000 new members who join every year.

The first thing to notice once they're inside the front door is that they do bring a Bible, *The New World Translation* — their especially prepared version. Its translators are anonymous, so neither credentials nor their manuscript sources can be checked. But astute students of the Word will readily notice that the Society's theological stance is enhanced by significant changes from the Authorized Version.

Debating with a Witness requires skill and a thorough knowledge of Bible doctrines. They have been taught that all other beliefs are Satanic and have been programmed with stock answers for questions that are often raised. Even if they don't know an answer, they're confident that their leaders back at the Kingdom Hall will provide the correct response. Evangelical Christians need to be aware of Witness beliefs so that a clever choice of words doesn't disguise their extremely unorthodox doctrine. The following paragraph points out some of their more controversial views.

To begin with, the Trinity is seen as a demonic doctrine. The Holy Spirit is robbed of his personality, and Jesus is stripped of his deity. Their *Translation* renders John 1:1, "the Word was *a* god," introducing the Witness belief that Christ, the Archangel Michael, was created by Jehovah. The appearance of Jesus on earth was not an incarnation but an example of human perfection in response to Jehovah's moral law. Witnesses do not consider Christ to be Eternal God, the Creator of the universe, and our Great High Priest as declared in Hebrews 4:15 and Colossians 2:9, 10.

Other Jehovah Witness doctrines that may be encountered are soul-sleep and the annihilation of the wicked (along with Satan and his demons). They deny the existence of a soul which can exist apart from the body. To Witnesses, the soul is just the life-animating force which gives life to a material body. When a human being dies, his soul ceases to exist and his body ultimately deteriorates. There is no hell since there is no conscious existence after death. Hell, for the Watch Tower, is the grave. Faithful Witnesses hope one day to be recreated (resurrected) from Jehovah's memory. Those destined for resurrection will inhabit either paradise, earth (the large earthly class), or heaven (the elite spiritual class, the 144,000 of Revelation 7 and 14). The earthly class will live as they have here with a body and life-animating force (soul). The heavenly class will "give up" any right to a resurrected body and will live as spirits, as they believe Jesus did after his "recreation" or spirit resurrection.

Witnesses make much of their devotion to Jehovah and eschew any reference to God by another name. Ironically, respected Greek and Hebrew scholars tell us that the word Jehovah is nonexistent in the Bible, no matter how many times it appears in *The New World Translation*. There is no pretext to assume that the Hebrew consonants referring to God (YHWH — Yahweh) could not be Jehovah. But neither is there sufficient proof to assume that any designation other than Jehovah is a deliberate distortion of God's name. The greatest challenge to Watch Tower Society doctrine is the fact that the Bible presents Jesus as Jehovah-God, a fatal blow to their entire belief system.

But one need not be a Hebrew scholar to be aware of the most glaring inconsistency in the teachings of Jehovah's Witnesses. A brief study of the Society's history shows a confused view of the end times as indicated by their record of erroneous dates for Christ's return. The world's end has been prophesied for 1914, 1918, 1920, 1925, 1941, and more recently, 1975. Since Adam's creation was presumed to occur in 4026 B.C., Witnesses taught that 6,000 years of human history would end in A.D. 1975. When the date passed, thousands left the sect. But President Franz had an explanation all ready. The 6,000-year chronology was set forward to begin with Eve's creation, and how long that occurred after Adam's advent is an interval not yet revealed by Witness leaders. Still, members believe the end can't be far off. They have been told that the war of Armageddon will be waged, and the Millennium must dawn before all of the 144,000 "anointed class" from 1914 have died. Less than 10,000 of the "anointed" are left.

Founder: Charles Taze Russell, born 1852 in Pittsburgh, Pennsylvania. Died 1916.

Text: Isaiah 43:10 —"Ye are my witnesses...."

Symbols: The ubiquitous castle-shaped "watch tower" that appears on almost all their literature.

Appeal: Those with an apocalyptic mentality may be enticed by the zealous desire of Witnesses who want to evangelize all the world before the end. Some not well-versed in Scripture may be attracted by what seem to be logical and reasonable explanations for hard-to-explain doctrines, such as the Trinity and the eternal punishment of the wicked.

Purposes: To usher in the Kingdom age of the Millennium and join Jehovah's forces who will triumph at Armageddon. Only faithful Witnesses will survive the battle. Since the 144,000 already sealed will remain in heaven with Christ, most current-day Witnesses look forward to living eternally on a perfected Earth.

Errors: Faulty biblical scholarship and out-of-context interpretations allow Witnesses to discard most orthodox doctrines. The 144,000 cited in John's Revelation obviously refers to 12,000 Jews out of each tribe of Israel, not a sealed company of heavenly "spirit brothers" as Witnesses contend. The death of Christ is not seen as a ransom for sin but rather as the procurement of a second chance to be offered in the Millennium.

Background Sources: *Cults, World Religions and You,* 1977, Kenneth Boa, Victor Books; *Kingdom of the Cults,* 1977, Walter Martin, Bethany Fellowship; *The Truth That Leads to Eternal Life,* Watch Tower Society; *The Denver*

Post, 6/10/77; *Christianity Today,* 12/12/80, pp. 60-71; *Time,* 7/11/77, pp. 64, 65.

Address/Location: Watch Tower Society, 117 Adams Street, Brooklyn, NY 11201.

22

The Local Church

Most people think of religious leaders as somewhat attractive individuals with forceful personalities and gifted leadership abilities. To see Witness Lee is to shatter all illusions. This bespectacled man in his seventies hardly looks like the type to wield persuasive influence over thousands of lives. And if you can't trust a man who constantly exhorts you to say, "Oh, Lord Jesus," then who is credible? No one could have predicted that this one-time, China-born disciple of Watchman Nee would take the former's "Little Flock" philosophy and turn it into an exclusive organization. Witness Lee claims that only one gathering of believers in each city truly represents Christ — *The* Local Church.

Unlike other authoritarian groups, The Local Church is not comprised of burned-out rejects of society. Many members are genuinely born-again, but their personal testimony can often be less important than the corporate identity they have found in The Local Church. Consequently, they have unwittingly accepted a variety of unorthodox doctrines. Lee's approach causes his disciples to seal themselves off from the checks and balances of interaction with other Christians by insisting that their congregation is the only authentic representative of Christ's Church. As Lee explains it, "Catholicism is demonic, Judaism is satanic, and Protestantism is without Christ."

It is ironic that many of Lee's followers are genuinely converted believers since he significantly departs from several historic Christian doctrines. His most prominent differences with orthodoxy are found in his teachings regarding God, whom critics claim he sees in a modalistic concept. Ex-Local Church members charge that Lee teaches the Father, Son, and Holy Spirit are really one person in three different modes of manifestation. Lee's concept of sin and redemption also contradicts the historic Christian viewpoint. As stated in his writings, the fall of man permitted sin and Satan to literally take up residence in man's flesh. As a result, the devil is no longer seen as the personal, fallen angel of 1 Peter 5:8. Because of this, it was necessary for God to place himself in man's flesh by the incarnation of Christ. When Christ died on the Cross, Satan also died. When Christ rose from the dead, the devil was left behind in the grave, completing Christ's victory. Thus, since Satan dwells in the flesh of all men, God must incarnate himself in man's flesh if this sin/Satan nature is to be overcome. "Regeneration," Lee states, "is the mingling of God, Himself, with our spirit."

This unusual view of sin, evil, and salvation, results in an approach to conversion which is quite different from that experienced by most evangelicals. "We have seen that to reach unbelievers, no preaching is necessary," Lee writes. "If we can get them to say, 'Oh, Lord,' three times, they will be saved. It is not a matter of teaching; it is a matter of touching the seven Spirits of God." Belief and faith (Heb. 11:6 and Acts 16:31) are not seen to be absolute prerequisites to salvation. The mere repetition of Lee's prescribed words appears to be sufficient.

In fact, such an emphasis on literally spoken words is a primary tenet of The Local Church. Adherents are told that the Bible is "a book of life, not a book of knowledge." Therefore, "It is better for us to close our minds." This leads to what Lee calls "pray-reading." Followers are sometimes instructed to open the Bible to any page (even at random) and recite passages, interspersed with phrases such as, "Oh, Lord Jesus," "Amen," "Hallelujah," and "Praise the Lord." This practice can encourage a mechanistic approach to Scripture that is much like the "meaningless repetition" Christ condemned in Matthew 6:7.

Questioning of Lee's methodology and doctrines is seldom permitted. He tells his flock to be "drunkards" for the church, intoxicated with a constant hubbub of activity centered around The Local Church. Consequently, there is little time left for outside activities, and almost no opportunity to think reflectively on what Lee is teaching. This is why some members develop an outlook which sees all other religious groups as part of the harlot Babylon. They do admit that other churches contain some committed Christians. But in the final analysis, Lee's followers are ultimately the only true local church faithfully representing the body of Christ.

Members are very reluctant to question Local Church beliefs. Lee has told them, "Do not think this is my teaching; it is the Lord's revelation." Unfortunately, some Christians who are confused about their faith find their way into Lee's groups. These highly susceptible believers are impressed by the zeal and lively fellowship found in The Local Church. When they are told that leaving may result in Divine Judgment, many find it easier to stay and accept Lee's doctrines, no matter how much they seem to conflict with those of other Christian churches. Adherents of The Local Church need to be loved and received with caring concern when they become disenchanted with Lee's teachings.

Founder: Witness Lee, a disciple of Watchman Nee who later split with his mentor and brought The Local Church to America in 1962.

Text: "Oh, Lord Jesus," a frequently quoted expression.

Symbols: None known.

Appeal: Christians who are nominal in their commitment, and new believers are prone to be impressed by the zealous dedication and enthusiastic song and "pray-reading" services.

Purpose: The Local Church is God in the flesh and purports to represent God on earth as his literal manifestation. Each Local Church body is the only

properly unified functioning church in that city.
Gatherings are called to "feast" on Christ to "eat and
drink" him, to mingle with his nature so that The Local
Church member and Christ form an "intrinsic union."

Errors: In the first century, the Apostle Paul sanctioned
the existence of more than one church per city (e.g., Rom.
16:3-5). Lee's doctrine of Satan residing in man's flesh
confuses the personality of Satan with the attitudinal act of
disobedience to God (sin). His concept of regeneration
suggests that the human nature of man mingles with the
divine nature of God. In effect, one can conclude this
doctrine to mean that Christ becomes literally incarnated
in the flesh of converts. This teaching borders on the idea
of self-deification found in many Eastern mystical cults.

Background Sources: *The Denver Post,* 10/13/78, p. 2BB;
"Witness Lee and The Local Church," Christian Research
Institute; "The Teachings of Witness Lee and The Local
Church," *Ibid.*; *The Mind Benders,* 1977, Jack Sparks,
Thomas Nelson, Inc., pp. 219-255; *The New Cults,* 1980,
Walter Martin, Vision House, pp. 379-407; miscellaneous
writings of Witness Lee, including *The Economy of God,
Stream,* "A Time With the Lord," *Christ vs. Religion,* et al.

Address/Location: The Church in Anaheim, CA, is
considered the world headquarters (large followings also
in Taiwan and the Philippines).

23

Mormonism

They're easy to spot. First of all, they always come in
two's. Then, there's that closely cropped hair and regalia
of dark suits, white shirts, subdued ties, polished shoes,
and plastic name cards with the impressive title "Elder."
Their sincerity is beyond question. And they represent
the most basic of human values — patriotism, sobriety,
familial responsibilities, and hard work.

While they spend two years of their lives propagating
the gospel of Mormonism, these young missionaries are
subsidized by their parents, friends, and relatives. Each of
them must file a weekly report accounting for every hour
of the day. Their task isn't easy. Only nine of every 1,000
doors they knock on is opened to them. But it's worth it. In
one and one-half centuries, the Church of Jesus Christ of
Latter-day Saints has grown from six adherents to nearly
5 million members.

Why such zeal? Founder Joseph Smith declared that he
had a vision of God the Father and Jesus Christ. They
revealed to him that all churches and creeds were an
"abomination" unto the Lord. He, Smith, was to be a
prophet proclaiming a "restored" message of the true
gospel. Today, 30,000 Mormon missionaries garner
200,000 converts each year, while the church pulls in an

estimated $1.3 billion annually. The twenty-eight story headquarters in Salt Lake City, Utah, might well bear the inscription "success" emblazoned from its top.

Mention "Moonies" or "Hare Krishna" to the average person and he'll respond with disdain. But the word "Mormon" generally evokes an immediate nod of approval. The Donny-and-Marie-Osmond image is no sham. Mormons are known to eschew tobacco, cigarettes, caffeine, and premarital sex while revering family life and free enterprise. They have a low cancer rate and score higher than the general populace when it comes to physical fitness. Who wouldn't admire a religious group that promotes the Boy Scouts and receives "fast offerings" to care for widows as well as the poor and indigent? The suspicious history and strange beliefs of Mormonism are often overlooked on the assumption that sound morals make a good religion.

Most people know little of Mormonism's doctrines and beginnings. They may be familiar with the names Joseph Smith or Brigham Young. Ezra Taft Benson and George Romney have been visible Mormons on the political scene. And the Tabernacle choir's concerts have earned the respect of music critics. Only a few have heard about the odd practices of proxy baptisms and celestial marriages. To truly understand Mormonism, one must sift through all the arcane doctrines and public relations ploys of Latter-day Saints and go back to the small town of Palmyra, New York, in the year 1820.

Joseph Smith, Jr., is revered by millions of Mormons as a seer and prophet. The contemporaries who knew him and his parents were less gracious. Neighbors viewed the Smith family as "illiterate, whiskey-drinking, shiftless, and irreligious." Joe (as he was known) was said to be indolent with a penchant for exaggeration and untruthfulness. His mother, Lucy Mack, practiced magic and had visions. His father, Joe, Sr., was known as a persistent treasure-seeker, always trying to dig up the fabled booty of Captain Kidd. The founder of Mormonism often accompanied his father on these expeditions and was himself fond of the occult, especially divining and fortune telling by "peep stones."

Then one day in 1820, while praying in the woods, Joseph Smith, Jr., received his fabled vision of God and

Jesus. In 1823 another personage, an angel named
Moroni, appeared at his bedside. The visitor claimed to
be the son of Mormon, the departed leader of an
American race known as Nephites. Moroni told him about
a book of golden plates that contained "the fullness of the
everlasting Gospel." Four years later, in the hill named
Cumorah (near Palmyra, New York), Smith unearthed the
plates. Buried with them were a pair of large,
supernatural spectacles known as the "Urim and
Thummim." They were to be used in translating the
hieroglyphics on the plates, a language called "reformed
Egyptian." (Archaeologists and Egyptologists deny there
is any historical evidence to validate the existence of
such a form of communication.)

Joseph immediately began his work of translating the
plates. He claimed later that during this time John the
Baptist (sent by Peter, James, and John) appeared to him
and administered a divine ordination. When the
translation work was completed (with the help of Oliver
Cowdrey, an itinerant school teacher, and Emma Hale, his
first and only legal wife) he returned the plates to Moroni.
The *Book of Mormon* was published in 1830. On April 6 of
that same year, Cowdrey, Smith, and his brothers Hyrum
and Samuel officially formed the Church of Jesus Christ,
now known as the Church of Jesus Christ of Latter-day
Saints.

The *Book of Mormon* is the cornerstone of Mormon
faith. It (along with the other Smith volumes, *Doctrines
and Covenants* and *The Pearl of Great Price*) is
considered to be a divine revelation superior to the Bible.
In actual practice, whenever the *Book of Mormon*
contradicts the Bible, the former is considered to be the
final authority. Just what exactly does the *Book of Mormon*
contain?

It purports to tell the story of two Middle-Eastern
peoples who migrated to the Americas. The tale unwinds
in a series of books written between 600 B.C. to A.D. 400.
An ancient civilization called Jaredites came from the
Tower of Babel to Central America. A wicked group, they
perished as a result of their own immorality. (This author
has visited a number of ancient Mayan ruins in Central
America where Mormon archaeologists search for clues
to verify Mormonism's historical claims. At Tikal in
Guatemala and Copan in Honduras I have viewed

carvings resembling a star of David which Mormons say prove their assertions.)

A later group of Jews led by a righteous man named Nephi fled Jerusalem to avoid the Babylonian captivity and ended up in South America. They divided into warring factions, the Nephites and Lamanites. The latter annihilated the Nephites in a fierce struggle near Palmyra, New York in A.D. 428. The victory earned them a curse — dark skins. They continued populating the continent and became the American Indian race. Before his demise, Mormon, the Nephite leader, compiled a record of his civilization and of the appearance Christ is supposed to have made to them after his resurrection. He described how the Lord met them in South America and commissioned them to institute the ordinances of communion, baptism, and the priesthood. The entire account was recorded on the golden plates which Mormon buried and were found by Joseph Smith 1,400 years later.

Before continuing with the historical saga of Smith and his successor (according to the Utah branch), Brigham Young, the *Book of Mormon* deserves some scrutiny, for it claims equality with the Bible. It purports to be the sealed book mentioned in Isaiah 29, and a record of the "other sheep" Jesus spoke of in John 10:16. But its proofs are questionable and its inconsistencies glaring.

While it aspires to be an additional revelation to the Bible, it contains verbatim references in King James English, though it was supposedly written many centuries before the A.D. 1611 Authorized Version. These analogous passages even include some seventeenth-century translators' errors, a strange coincidence for a book supposedly predating the KJV scholars' efforts. In addition, the *Book of Mormon* credits these New World immigrants with metal-producing capabilities, a claim not confirmed by archeological research. Mormon even described elephants roaming the Western hemispheres, though no skeletons have ever been found.

The Smithsonian Institute flatly denies any correlation between American archeological discoveries and the information contained in the *Book of Mormon*. A Mormon publication, "Joseph Smith's Testimony," concludes its glowing appraisal of the *Book of Mormon* by citing a total of eleven witnesses. What the pamphlet's author failed to note is that three of them (Oliver Cowdery, David Whitmer, and Martin Hanes) were later denounced by Smith. The other eight include five who were related to David Whitmer. Of the final three witnesses, one was Smith's father and the other two his brothers, hardly an objective company of jurists.

Who wrote the book of Mormon? God, Satan, Smith, or another mortal are the only possible sources. Some who doubt its divine inspiration suggest that Smith may have been a fanciful thinker who borrowed King James' English and nineteenth-century historical speculation to produce a fictitious novel. Others contend that one of his converts, Sidney Rigdon, stole a manuscript entitled *Manuscript Story* by Solomon Spaulding, a minister-writer who died in 1816. A few insist Smith's writings bear strong similarity to that of Rev. Ethan Smith who authored *View of the Hebrews.* Most evangelical critics espouse the Spalding-plagiarism explanation, noting that Smith always dictated his writing from behind a curtain.

No matter who really wrote the book, its revelations and its followers caused quite a stir wherever they went. Mormons were a combative lot, challenging all other sects, and flaunting their polygamous ways. (Smith, it was said, had twenty-seven wives.) Persecution drove them from New York to Ohio and then Missouri where the governor asked them to leave. Smith's clan ended up in Nauvoo, Illinois, where, with hard work and dedication, they built the largest city in the state. He told his followers that Nauvoo meant "beautiful plantation" in Hebrew, and obtained a charter that made it a city-state with its own military. But Joseph and his brother Hyrum ran afoul of the law and ended up in jail in 1844. An outraged mob beset their cell and murdered both. This tragic, lawless act of intolerance insured instant martyrdom for Smith.

A split immediately followed the shooting. One group led by his widow felt that the mantle of leadership should fall on Joseph's son. They left for Independence, Missouri, to settle on the site where the prophet had declared Christ would return. That body, now known as the Reorganized Church of Jesus Christ of Latter-day Saints, parted ways with some major Mormon doctrines. Though they claim a common origin and reverence for the *Book of Mormon,* the Reorganized Church repudiates several vital beliefs of the Utah group — i.e. secret rites, a plurality of gods, and sealed marriages. Above all, they claim to be the only legitimate Latter-day Saint body, saying that Joseph Smith appointed his son to succeed in the Church Presidency. A recently discovered document in Smith's handwriting, dated January 17, 1844, seems to confirm their contention.

But such historical verification matters little now. The fact is that after Smith's assassination, Brigham Young persuaded a majority to follow him on the arduous trek to Utah. In July 1847 Young and his band looked on the Salt Lake Valley and declared, "This is the place." Brigham encouraged polygamy, took twenty-five wives, and by the time of his death in 1877 had collected 140,000 followers. He strongly adhered to the little-talked-about Mormon doctrine of blood atonement. Christ's blood, he believed, could not atone for certain sins. Such deeds required a man's own blood. Another could kill him as a righteous act he described as, "loving our neighbor as ourselves... if he wants salvation and it is necessary to spill his blood...spill it." Modern Mormons have suppressed (but not officially repudiated) the doctrine. But they still have stinging memories of the day their second "prophet" ordered his fellow Mormons to attack and slaughter 120 men, women, and children of the Fancher party who crossed Mormon land on their way to California.

Brigham Young also espoused two other doctrines which Mormons would like to forget. He taught that Adam was actually God who took on a body and came to Eden (in Missouri) with one of his heavenly wives, Eve. This Adam-God (the Archangel, Michael) begat Jesus by sexually cohabiting with the Virgin Mary in a physical, flesh relationship. "He [Christ] was not begotten by the Holy Ghost," Brigham declared emphatically. It was Young's espousal of polygamy that gained Mormons the most bad publicity. He instructed his followers, "The only men who become gods are those who enter into polygamy."

Even today, Utah is pocketed with fundamentalist Mormons (an estimated 30,000) who engage in plural marriages. They are devout in their belief that they will be barred from heaven unless they follow the covenant of polygamy set forth by Joseph Smith in 1843. In the late 1800s, the U.S. Congress became so concerned with the conduct of Mormons that it passed the Edmunds-Tucker Act, threatening to confiscate Mormon property and jail its leaders. The Church recanted in 1890, and today most mainline Mormons maintain an image of monogamous bliss.

But polygamy and the Adam-God theory are not the only unorthodox doctrines of Mormonism. They subscribe to the idea of an anthropomorphic God with physical, material dimensions. He is a procreating father (all humans were preexistent spirits he begat) with a divine mother-wife. It is this conviction that undergirds the Mormon emphasis on marriage and parenthood in this life and the next. Some Mormons believe that Jesus was married to both Mary and Martha, and that he bore children on Earth. Good Mormons enter their secret temples and don white garments to indulge in esoteric, Masonic-like rituals that seal their marriages for eternity.

The most famous of all Mormon aphorisms declares, "As man now is, God once was; as God now is, man may become." God himself was once procreated in another world, and now humans may aspire to the status of procreator that he has obtained. Adam did right by eating of the forbidden fruit because it made him capable of fathering the human race. In other words, "Adam fell that men might be." The right to godhead is not earned by the grace of Jesus, but by being a good Mormon. Followers of Joseph Smith prove their faithfulness by being baptized and married in the temple, being a member of the priesthood and tracing genealogies. As potential father and mother gods, Mormons will ultimately have their own planets to populate.

All those born prior to Mormonism's founding in 1830 cannot enter the celestial state without a little help from present-day adherents. The Church has blasted a tunnel out of Utah granite (capable of withstanding a nuclear explosion) to house the ancestral records of devout Mormons. Once departed kin have been identified, posthumous, proxy baptisms are performed. Mormons spend $10 million a year to maintain the facilities, but for them it is well worth it. Some go through the three-hour ceremony on behalf of a nonrelative they have never known. Mormons are universalists and believe that everyone will eventually have immortality with only baptized Mormons attaining godhead. (Article of Faith number two states, "...all mankind will be saved.")

The priesthood concept, a belief in a restored
priesthood of Aaron and Melchizedek, represents one of
Mormonism's most distinctive departures from Christian
tradition. All Mormon males over fourteen years of age
are eligible for the Aaronic priesthood. At twenty years of
age they may enter the higher office of Melchizedek and
be designated an elder. They can then perform all the
ordinances of the church. Until 1978, those with black
skins were forbidden this status. Mormonism's seventeen
temples were off limits to blacks because Joseph Smith
taught that they were the descendants of Cain and
therefore cursed. The church rejects the doctrine of
original sin and believes that sinners are punished on
Earth for failures in their past spirit lives. Blacks were thus
guilty of the preexistent sin of rebelling with Lucifer and
barred from the priesthood until Mormonism's leader,
First President Spencer Kimball, received a "revelation"
abrogating this injunction.

Most aspects of church structure are seldom known to
outsiders. The First President is considered to be a
prophetic successor to Smith and thus is a prophet and
revelator who speaks in God's name. From there,
authority descends in a nondemocratic fashion to the
President's advisors (two other high priests), the twelve
apostles, the presiding quorum of seventy, and the
presiding bishopric. Individual members are organized
into wards of 500 to 1,000. Wards are consolidated into
stakes. Space does not permit a detailed discussion of
other unique Mormon practices. Some of them are as
follows: de-emphasis of Easter and the Cross, speaking in
tongues and spiritual healing, the ability of individuals to
receive private revelations from God, emphasis on
Monday as family night, storing of food supplies for times
of famine, insistence that the U. S. Constitution is divinely
inspired, believing that the state of women is inferior to
that of men, opposition to the use of birth control,
opposition to interracial marriages, binding temple oaths
(breaking them can jeopardize one's hope of eternal life),
and belief in the brotherhood of Jesus and Lucifer.
Mormons also believe in a three-tiered heaven with
separate sections for heathens, non-Mormon Christians,
and those with sealed marriages whose earthly
matrimonial unions will endure forever.

Some may wonder how such exotic ideas could be
compatible with the seeming love and care exhibited by

most Mormons. The evangelical Christian questions how such unorthodox theology could produce such pleasant people who knock on doors and warmly present their case. This irony is not so hard to understand when one comprehends why an individual may have joined the Mormon Church. For one thing, the new Mormon finds an instant social community of God-conscious values. The positive emphasis on Christian virtues and the intense involvement on a layman's level causes most new members to simply overlook the blemished history of the LDS's origins. Family pressure prevents many disillusioned Mormons from forsaking the Church, particularly if they are second or third generation adherents. People today often have a pragmatic approach to religion that tends to see theology as a cumbersome commodity. They want something that works, something that will bring them emotional security and shared goals. Mormonism delivers, and for millions, that is good enough.

Founder: Joseph Smith, born in Sharon, Vermont, December 23, 1805. Killed June 27, 1844, Nauvoo, Illinois. The *Book of Mormon* was published in 1830 and the Church of Jesus Christ of Latter-day Saints was founded April 6, 1830. (It was originally named the "Church of Jesus Christ." The official name was adopted in 1837.)

Text: John 10:16, "Other sheep I have, which are not of this fold," supposedly refers to a Middle Eastern civilization that migrated to the Americas. Christ preached to them (the Nephites) after his resurrection. The Bible is the Word of God only "as far as it has been translated correctly." A Mormon article of faith states that "we also believe the *Book of Mormon* to be the Word of God."

Symbols: The angel Moroni, usually perched atop temple spires, with trumpet in hand.

Appeal: Outside observers who do not scrutinize Mormon doctrine may be attracted by their avoidance of unclean physical habits and the seriousness with which they take their faith. Members believe in the continuing function of divine revelation which gives a vitality and authority to their faith.

Purpose: Since Mormonism is the only restored, true church, its concept of salvation must be strictly followed. The highest heaven is open only to faithful Mormons who will become gods and join in procreative partnership with God who was once as humans are now. Life on Earth is a discipline where one develops one's potential to rule a celestial kingdom with a spouse and children. Marriage and large families on Earth are encouraged as part of this evolving process toward equality with Christ who is the Mormon "elder brother." After death, Mormons in the heavenly realms seek to convert non-Mormons who dwell in the lower realm so these "gentiles" can also accept the revelations of Joseph Smith.

Errors: Mormons find themselves in the conundrum of having to modify or deny some of their more embarrassing past doctrines (e.g. blood atonement, Adam-God concept, polygamy, anti-Negroid beliefs) while according prophetic status to the men who taught such beliefs (i.e. Joseph Smith, Brigham Young, et al.) The priesthood concept is repudiated by Hebrews 7 and 1 Peter 2:9, 10. The Aaronic and Melchizedek orders were consummated in Christ and now all believers are part of a "royal priesthood." The Mormon Jesus is not eternal God-Jehovah (Elohim), able to "save them to the uttermost" (Heb. 7:25). He is therefore "another Jesus," and Moroni is the false angel of the "accursed" gospel of which Paul speaks in Galatians 1:8, 9.

Background Sources: "Joseph Smith's Testimony," Desert News Press, LDS publication; *Book of Mormon, Doctrine and Covenants, The Pearl of Great Price,* books by Joseph Smith; *Moody Monthly,* 6/80, p. 32; *Newsweek,* 3/1/76, p. 71; *Ibid.,* 11/21/71, pp. 113-119; *Ibid.,* 9/1/80, pp. 68-71; *Ibid.,* 4/27/81, pp. 87, 88; *The Kingdom of the Cults,* 1977, Walter Martin, Bethany Fellowship, Minneapolis, MN; *Time,* 7/11/77, p. 69; *Ibid.,* 6/19/78, p. 55, *Ibid.,* 8/7/78, pp. 54, 55; *Ibid.,* 12/4/78, p. 30; *Ibid.,* 10/21/77, pp. 38, 39; *Ibid.,* 5/23/80, pp. 42, 43; *Ibid.,* 4/24/81, p. 42; *The Vancouver Sun,* 4/19/80, p. 5B; *The Denver Post,* 10/1/76, p. 4BB; *Ibid.,* 7/1/77, p. 4BB; "Journal of Discourses," LDS publication.

Address/Location: The Church of Jesus Christ of Latter-day Saints, 47 East Temple Street, Salt Lake City, UT.

24

Neo-Gnosticism

As the infant Church sought to formalize its beliefs into a doctrinal structure, the heresy of Gnosticism prompted Paul to write an epistle to the Colossians. Taking their name from the Greek word for "knowledge" (*gnosis*), the Gnostics taught that Jesus was either a magician, an ascetic, or a sexual deviate who initiated his followers by means of secret ceremonies. The Apostle found it necessary to defend the uniqueness of the *person* and redemptive *work* of Christ in the face of suggestions that Jesus was only one of many angelic intermediaries between God and man. He also emphasized that salvation was completed in Christ, countering the legalistic asceticism of Gnosticism (Col. 2:20-30).

A major conflict erupted between the orthodoxy of codified beliefs as expressed in the Bible and mystical philosophical concepts held by those who claimed they were the true followers of Christ's esoteric teaching. Orthodoxy eventually triumphed. Today, however, this early A.D. heresy is alive and well and debated in prestigious seminaries. Neo-Gnosticism forms the theological foundation for many modern cults and has even formalized a belief structure of its own. Though it has no official organizational apparatus, the tenets of

Neo-Gnosticism are held by an increasing number of the educated elite.

Gnostic belief, as expressed in the fourth-century Nag Hammadi Codices (and more recently published volumes such as *The Secret Gospel, The Gospel of Thomas,* and *The Forbidden Gospel),* may be summarized as follows: God is actually an abstract figure in an invisible realm. The Judeo-Christian Creator is replaced by another deity named Yaldabaoth. The serpent in Eden heroicly reveals to Adam and Eve secret knowledge which Yaldabaoth had hidden from them. The Gnostics guarded this knowledge carefully throughout history. The Flood and the destruction of Sodom and Gomorrah were Yaldabaoth's way of getting revenge upon the Gnostics. However, that divine light of *gnosis* has continued in some enlightened souls even to our present age.

Jesus, according to Gnostic belief, was one of those who possessed a higher consciousness. How he attained this knowledge and what he did with it is a point of conjecture among current Gnostics. Some believe he clandestinely traveled to India to learn the way of the Buddha and the wisdom of the Brahmans. Others suggest that Christ was actually raised by the hermetic Essenes who schooled him in mysterious rituals. All Gnostics agree that Christ did not die for man's sin, even suggesting that the Savior tricked Simon of Cyrene into enduring the fate intended for him.

Gnosticism finds fertile ground in two camps. The atheist and agnostic find comfort in believing that Christ was a mere man whose charisma was due to hypnotic techniques or sexual baptismal ceremonies. The mystically inclined student of Eastern philosophy discovers a presumed harmony between the Gnostic Jesus and the avataristic concept of spiritual leadership as expressed in Hindu texts. Though Neo-Gnosticism expounds theories too abstract to interest the average person, it does appeal to those whose education has placed them in the upper socio-economic strata. As an elitist cult, Neo-Gnosticism is a serious intellectual challenge to Christianity. Those interested in its teachings will acquire an elaborate rationale for rejecting the deity and sacrificial atonement of Christ.

Founder: First century heretics (or earlier mystical religions).

Texts: Nag Hammadi scriptures; miscellaneous Gnostic manuscripts; modern books with conjectures based on ancient texts; the Bible.

Symbols: None known.

Appeal: Secret knowledge not available to the uninitiated is the main lure of Neo-Gnosticism.

Purpose: Orthodox Christian doctrine is refuted and replaced with an alternate explanation for Creation, the Fall, and Redemption.

Errors: The inspired Scriptures are denied in favor of the "true" teachings of Christ. These esoteric doctrines are available to the adepts of Neo-Gnosticism who achieve the same level of consciousness as Jesus.

Background Sources: *Time,* 6/4/73, p. 73; *Ibid.,* 6/9/75, pp. 46, 47; *Newsweek,* 3/3/75, p. 65; *The Denver Post,* 12/2/77, p. 6BB; *East West Journal, 1/78,* pp. 76-87.

Address/Location: Primarily Western countries, especially the United States and Europe.

25

Penitentes

High in the remote mountain areas of southern Colorado and northern New Mexico live a people caught in a time warp, playing out centuries-old rituals of penance. Each year at Easter, members of the Brothers of Our Father Jesus, or the Penitentes, as they are commonly known, reenact Christ's crucifixion. Their devotion includes painful self-flagellation and stark suffering. According to some witnesses, actual crucifixions take place every year during Holy Week. Spokesmen for the Brothers deny this claim, but several outsiders who have observed the ritual insist that the ceremony concludes with a man being raised on the cross. There are also tales of literal nails being used and of the participants actually dying, though such versions of this religious drama are hard to verify.

The history of Penitentes can be traced to a fifth-century movement within the Roman Catholic Church. Spanish followers of the discipline emigrated to the New World and subsequently retreated to the rugged mountain regions of the Southwest where they were cut off from civilization. Two centuries later, public knowledge of their activities began to emerge. Though the Catholic Church officially denounced their gory activities, the bizarre and clandestine nature of their devotion continued to attract followers.

Unlike their bloodier better-known counterparts in Brazil and the Philippines, the American Penitentes rigorously guard their secrecy. Eyewitness accounts of present-day cross-bearing, self-whipping, and other torturous acts of penances are hard to verify. Some who claim contact with this strange sect believe that it is currently experiencing a resurgence of interest from those wishing to join its ranks. It has even been suggested that chapters exist in some urban centers of the West. Whether the present fascination with the darker side of occult practices has contributed to such a revival of these ancient masochistic techniques is open to question.

In an age of apathy and contentment, it is only logical that the sufferings of Jesus would incite fascination in the human spirit. To those who fail to see these agonies as the finished work of atonement, there may still lie the haunting appeal of personally reliving such pain to seek favor with God. Known Penitentes in America are confined to the active involvement of several thousand Hispanics. But the ritual has an uncanny attraction for new, curious members who seek to share the Lord's passion. They remind us that the Church may have lost a valuable incentive for spiritual fervor by emphasizing the glory of Christ and forgetting that "learned he obedience by the things which he suffered" (Heb. 5:8).

Founders: Spanish Catholic immigrants, circa 1700.

Text: Bible, folklore.

Symbols: Revered religious statues and icons.

Appeal: Adherents share companionship with Christ's passion.

Purpose: To obtain favor with God by self-inflicted penance.

Errors: Penitentes believe atonement comes by personal bloodshed rather than Christ's death and suffering.

Background Sources: *National Courier,* 4/16/76, p. 5; "Guarded Secrets of the Penitentes," *Denver Monthly,* 5/80, pp. 24-33; *Dallas Times Herald,* 4/12/81, pp. 20-27.

Address/Location: Ceremonies are practiced in the Philippines, Brazil, and the southwestern United States.

26

Unity School of Christianity

"This has been a message from Unity," the announcer intones. It certainly sounds good. Who wouldn't want such a pleasant approach to life? Just think of it. No more guilt, disease, or financial worries. Every problem solved. Why not write the Missouri address and find out what it's all about?

This scenario is an example of the way thousands of people every year fall prey to Unity's slick advertising campaign. The Unity Village headquarters in Lee's Summit (near Kansas City), Missouri, enhance their radio and TV promotions with a slick, well-financed printing operation. Periodicals like *Wee Wisdom* appeal to Sunday school children, and Ernest Wilson's book, *Have We Lived Before?* hones in on adults ripe for reincarnation teachings. Such media exposure has paid off. Unity's mail-order approach has resulted in 4.2 million "readers and followers" worldwide (1.2 million in the U.S.) with centers in nine countries. Active membership is closer to 1.2 million.

To the casual observer, Unity's beliefs may seem like nothing more than power-of-positive-thinking homilies.

But those acquainted with the fertile ground of late nineteenth-century pantheistic philosophy will readily see Unity's similarity with Christian Science and New Thought. That is to be expected. A Belfast, Maine, clock maker, Phineas Parkhurst Quimby, fathered all three cults. His theories of animal magnetism and mental healing were plagiarized by Mary Baker Eddy (Christian Science founder), and Julius and Annetta Dresser along with Warren Felt Evans (New Thought creators). Charles and Myrtle Fillmore adopted their brand of Quimby's teachings to launch Unity in 1889. (The actual name Unity was designated in 1895.)

Myrtle claimed she was tubercular until she learned, "I am a child of God; therefore, I do not inherit sickness." Charles, a cripple with tuberculosis of the hip, had explored Spiritualism and Hinduism. Both later testified that living by Christian Science and New Thought principles cured their ills. Eventually they split with the two groups on minor points of theology. The Fillmores dropped the Christian Science belief that matter is not real. They added a reverence for Jesus and the doctrine of reincarnation to New Thought philosophy. In fact, Charles Fillmore believed he was a reincarnation of the Apostle Paul.

Reincarnation is one of Unity's least publicized but most distinctive doctrines. Charles and Myrtle borrowed heavily from the Hinduistic teachings of Swami Vivekananda from India. But sensing that the idea of soul transmigration back to an animal form might not set well with Westerners, they insisted that reincarnation could only occur in human bodies. Several Bible references are used to justify this teaching, such as the instance where Christ is called the Son of David. (To Unity this is an indication that Jesus had been previously incarnated in King David.) Confronting such scriptural perversion with proper biblical exegesis would be pointless. Charles Fillmore declared that the Bible is only one of many sacred books to be revered. He went so far as to suggest that the Word of God is an inferior form of revelation for those "who are not themselves in direct communication with God."

It should, therefore, come as no surprise that the belief system of Unity severely departs from orthodox Christian doctrine. As in Christian Science, God is said to be a principle of love, and his Son is only an example of how we too can come to our own Christ-consciousness. Since, according to Fillmore, there are other "spiritually illuminated persons" who can "help one get started on the right path for finding God," Christ does not have an indispensable role in Unity's perception of "salvation." Unity believes that "atonement means reconciliation between God and man through Christ." Such an evangelical-sounding statement is clarified by the qualification that "reconciliation means a reuniting of our consciousness with the God-consciousness." The traditional Christian position is that reconciliation should be based on forgiveness of sin and removing the barrier of rebellion between man and God. In Unity, redemption isn't necessary because evil and sin do not exist. Since God is in everything (including plants and inanimate objects), this premise of pantheism does away with both the devil and man's fallen unregenerate nature.

The average person who explores Unity probably never delves that deeply into its theology. Like many such cults, participants experience the benefits of its principles without necessarily adhering to its more refined doctrines. Initiates are discouraged from leaving their own churches, though they later encounter pressure to more closely align themselves with Unity Centers (some of which are called churches). Most inquirers are attracted by the core of the cult, Silent Unity. This group handles prayer requests and expresses apparently genuine concern for the problems brought to them. Letters from Silent Unity recommend "affirmations" or "meditations" to get the inquirer's thinking back into the right mode to solve his problems. By thus adjusting their mind to the "divine mind," physical ills and difficulties will vanish.

Will they? For some the answer is decidedly, "Yes." Those with physiological or emotional symptoms resulting from mental stress are bound to experience some relief by adopting a positive outlook on life. Even organic disorders may have the healing process accelerated by the right frame of mind. But such a commonly accepted fact of medical science is a long way from Fillmore's belief that "thoughts of disease will produce microbes of destruction." Still, there is no doubt that many are impressed with the religious warmth by

which Unity's emotional guidance is dispensed.
Psychological aid is a worthy merit, but it should never
take the place of adherence to spiritual truth rooted in
objective revelation. The question is not whether Unity
works, but how it works without having any biblical basis
for its benefits.

Founders: Founded in 1889 by Charles and Myrtle
Fillmore of Kansas City, Missouri. Myrtle died in 1931.
Charles died in 1948. His son, Lowell, is now the leader of
Unity.

Text: The Bible, though passages are spiritualized and
alllegorized to fit Unity teachings. All sacred writings of
world religions are accepted. Charles Fillmore wrote:
"Unity believes there is good in every religion on earth
and that we should keep our minds open."

Symbols: A number of them: a circle with wings on both
sides and the word "Unity" across the front; the
several-storied tower that rises above the Unity Village
complex; a light shining at night from a lone window
symbolizing "The Light that Shines for You," a reference
to Silent Unity's constant prayer vigil.

Appeal: Christian terminology is used to promote
syncretistic metaphysical beliefs. Some with a poor
mental perspective on life may be uplifted by Unity's
emphasis on love and positive emotions. Their restoration
to psychological health would undoubtedly accrue
certain physical benefits. In addition, Unity's optimistic
attitude toward material prosperity may have compelled
some toward greater financial gain.

Purpose: Charles Fillmore viewed physical ills and failure
as an outgrowth of mental disequilibrium. One must
overcome this by affirming that God is the source of all
desirable values, and that God and man are inseparable.
The divine mind of God is in all men and perfection (as
attained by Jesus) is possible by acknowledging this
inner divinity and removing the illusion of sin.

Errors: Unity's goal of harmony with the mind of God
ignores the scriptural truth that union with God requires a
penalty for sin and the shedding of blood. In the words of

Charles Fillmore, "The number and seriousness of our past mistakes do not matter to God. He holds no grudges and has no account book." A mere affirmation denying the existence of evil does not eradicate its effect on man's soul. Fallen humanity bears guilt for transgression and good thoughts and beneficent feelings will not suffice to remove the consequences of Divine judgment.

Background Sources: *The Denver Post,* 11/28/ 75, p. 5BB; writings of Charles Fillmore including *Talks on Truth, Jesus Christ Heals, Prosperity* et al.; *Kingdom of the Cults,* 1965, Walter Martin, Bethany Fellowship, *Cults, World Religions, and You,* 1977, Kenneth Boa, Victor Books; "The Adventure called Unity," Charles R. Fillmore; "Daily Word," Unity devotional publication (various issues); *Unity — A Way of Life,* Unity periodical (various issues).

Address/Location: Unity Village, Lee's Summit, MO 64065.

27

The Way International

What happened when four clean-cut young people (two male, two female) descended upon a small, midwestern town and took up residence, calling themselves "dedicated servants of God"? Plenty. Local citizens were alarmed when they found out that the new visitors were luring young people into The Way. The faithful four held a public meeting and acknowledged that the $200 "voluntary" fee required for their Power for Abundant Living course was, in fact, mandatory. No one is admitted without prepayment of the "donation."

The majority of people in this sedate community felt their provincial charm had excluded them from the cult incursion found in big cities. But this invasion of The Way Corp. sent local citizens scampering for information as to whether or not The Way is really *the* way of Jesus Christ. Here's what they found out.

In 1957 a United Church of Christ minister, Victor Paul Wierwille, resigned his Van Wert, Ohio, pulpit to set up his own independent ministry. Wierwille began informing his followers that in 1942 God had spoken to him audibly. The message was simple: "God told me he would teach me the Word as it has not been known since the first century, if I would teach it to others." Sometimes the message is carried by rock bands like Takit and the Take a Stand Caravan which presents both music and drama. No one can question Wierwille's success. Membership in The Way is estimated between 40,000 to 100,000 in sixty-two countries.

New believers are enticed and inducted by Wierwille's Power for Abundant Living (PFAL) Sessions. Over a period of thirty-six hours, the initiates listen to tape or video recordings of Wierwille's teachings. No notes are allowed and only ten minute breaks are permitted every three hours. Questions are not permitted during the three-week course, which is strong on indoctrination but weak on objective inquiry.

PFAL sessions center on Wierwille's teaching that "About 85 percent of what is believed as being Christian is not Christian if the Bible is right." Wierwille's system of theology blends elements of Armstrongism and Jehovah's Witnesses' beliefs with a mixture of orthodox doctrines. His book, *Jesus Christ Is Not God,* explains his position that "Jesus Christ is not God but the Son of God....If Jesus Christ is God, we have not yet been redeemed.... Jesus Christ was not literally with God in the beginning; neither does he have all the assets of God."

The Way not only denies the Trinity and Christ's divinity and incarnation, but also teaches that Christ was resurrected on Saturday, and that four (not two) were crucified next to Jesus. Only believers after Pentecost will be saved, and they must remain dead until the final resurrection. Water baptism is discouraged in favor of holy spirit (lower-cased "h" and "s") baptism with accompanying speaking in tongues, a technique which, unlike its spontaneous charismatic counterpart, is "taught." Members are encouraged to cultivate this glossolalia thirty minutes every morning because it is an indispensable part of salvation.

Opponents and some ex-members claim that far worse heretical goings-on take place. They argue that Wierwille's extreme Calvinism has led to sexual indulgences based on the theory that once you're saved, sinful practices are no longer forbidden. Some have even charged that extreme licentiousness is found among the advanced groups in the Way International. Such conduct is said to be based on Wierwille's teaching that once one is saved he can no longer sin "in his spirit," although he can still sin in his body. This is construed by certain of his followers to be permission for smoking, drinking, drug taking, and even fornication. Other eyebrows were raised when a quadriplegic sued Wierwille for $300,000, claiming that he had given The Way $210,000 with the promise he'd be healed in a year's time. (The Way teaches a 15 percent tithe called "abundant sharing.") Some skeptics also point with alarm to the armed, private police force that watches over the 147-acre world headquarters of the cult near New Knoxville, Ohio. Rumors persist that some members hold marksmanship classes at the organization's Bible College in Emporia, Kansas, and on their 105-acre ranch near Gunnison, Colorado. Way officials say the courses are for hunting safety. Former members charge that it's all part of a plan "to take to the streets and defend the Word."

Such charges contrast with The Way terminology which includes evangelical phrases such as "born again," "Jesus Christ our Savior," and "the Word of God is the Will of God." The Way, like many cults, deceives many young Christians by using semantic deceptions which allow it to define words according to its own perception. When young "WOW Ambassadors" ("Word Over the World") are confronted with these semantic inconsistencies, they conveniently respond, "You'll have to write or call our headquarters about that."

Wierwille claims his organization is not a church but rather a "biblical research teaching and fellowship ministry." Such fellowships are called twigs (each individual member is called a leaf). Twigs are grouped into branches, and several branches make a limb. Limbs are then organized into trunks, with all trunks leading to the root at New Knoxville, Ohio. These structures have holdings estimated at $20 million with an annual income in the range of $1 million.

Youthful followers of The Way are exuberant and even arrogant at times when ridiculing orthodox beliefs. They mock the "martyr, self-sacrifice" attitude of traditional Christians. "God dying on a cross is a standard by which man can achieve his own righteousness. It is an image that binds man into continuous slavery and self-idolatry," wrote one student in the official newspaper of The Way College of Emporia. Such language, along with their strange nomenclature of "Bless Patrol," "First Family

Corps," and "Limb Leader," leaves the average evangelical a little bewildered. Though many of Wierwille's followers are sincere, their belligerence may stem from a disillusioned background in orthodox but sterile churches. The evangelical's best response is not one of strident counterattacks, but a compassioned example of Christian faith which will cause the disciples of Wierwille to question if The Way really is *the* Way of John 14:6.

Founder: Victor Paul Wierwille, born 1917.

Text: John 14:6, though Wierwille denies the substitutionary atonement of Christ and the propitiatory blood sacrifice of the cross.

Symbols: Slogans such as "One God," and "The Word means what it says and says what it means."

Appeal: The Way attracts those turned off by the institutional church and offers them an interpretation of Scripture supposedly ignored by other Christians who have followed the biblical scholarship of established denominations.

Purpose: The "abundant living" philosophy must be brought to those who have been deceived by pagan doctrines which have infiltrated the Church.

Errors: Wierwille's interpretation of the Bible is considered to be *the* Word. No attempt is made to remain faithful to the objectively tested text of the Bible. He rejects the doctrine of the Holy Trinity, seeing God as one Person (the Father) who is holy and spirit and therefore can be called "the Holy Spirit." This Holy Spirit is to be distinguished from "holy spirit" which is God's gift of spirit-life to those who turn to him in repentance. Wierwille denies the absolute deity of the Lord Jesus Christ, using sophisticated Unitarian arguments to say that Jesus Christ is not eternal and was created by God the Father.

Background Sources: "The Way Seemed Right," *Eternity,* 11/77, pp. 23-35; *The National Courier,* 2/4/77, p. 3; *Ibid.,* 4/1/77, p. 4; *Ibid.,* 8/5/77, p. 27; *Christianity Today,* 9/26/75, pp. 40-42; *Columbus Citizen Journal,* 2/1/79,

p. 1; *The McCook Gazette,* 9/5/80; *Ibid.,* 9/8/80; *Newspaper of Students of The Way College,* Vol. 2, No. 6, p. 4; *Toronto Star,* 2/28/81, p. H6; *Omaha World-Herald,* 2/11/81.

Address/Location: Box 328, New Knoxville, OH 45871.

28

Worldwide Church of God
(Armstrongism)

The orchestra swells, the music crescendos, and a deep-throated voice intones, "The World Tomorrow, with Garner Ted Armstrong." Or at least that's what used to be said before Garner Ted's philandering with money and women (a reported 200 consorts) resulted in a four-month exile in 1972 and final expulsion in 1978. Octogenarian Herbert W. Armstrong has gone back on the tube himself and has reclaimed total autocratic control over the 68,000 members of the Worldwide Church of God (WCG).

His domain includes Ambassador College campuses in Pasadena (California), Big Sandy (Texas), and St. Albans (England). (The Big Sandy, Texas, Institution was recently closed.) H. W. is known for his frequent association with distinguished officials and world governmental leaders. He travels aboard a private jet, a symbol of the opulent lifestyle for which he has been criticized. Armstrong fancies himself as an international statesman and has gained access to high offices (Egypt's Sadat, Israel's Begin, India's Gandhi) by bestowing philanthropic gifts. Critics charge him with having $30,000 worth of carpet in his office, and lavishing $500,000 on the Vienna Symphony which performed at the opening of his extravagant ($11 million) Ambassador Auditorium.

Armstrong, self-styled prophet of the "one true church," started out as an advertising salesman in Des Moines, Iowa. After being influenced by the teachings of an Adventist offshoot, his wife convinced him that salvation was only possible by keeping all of God's commandments. These injunctions were later to become an integral part of WCG doctrine: Sabbath-keeping, Old Testament kosher laws, and observance of Jewish feasts. Other precepts adopted by Armstrong are: rejection of the Trinity, noninvolvement in governmental affairs, denial of hell, annihilation of the wicked, and Anglo-Israelism (a belief that caused him to split with the Church of God Seventh Day).

His background in promotion alerted him to the possibilities of media exposure. From an initial broadcast on a 100-watt station in 1934, the Armstrong empire has grown to include scores of radio and TV outlets (500 in Garner Ted's heyday). In addition, *The Plain Truth,* a slick four-color monthly magazine (two-million circulation in five languages) entices future Church recruits. Its patriotic, morally concerned, editorial slant caters to middle-Americans. To those frustrated with crime, pornography, and political uncertainty, it promises a brighter "world tomorrow" without saying exactly how it is to be achieved and who is to lead the way. (*Quest* magazine, an expensive, glossy bimonthly, serves as a public relations vehicle dedicated to "the pursuit of excellence," and is published by Ambassador International Cultural Foundation, a WCG front-organization. As of the writing of this book, *Quest* was rumored to be for sale.)

Almost never mentioned are the WCG beliefs that make this home-grown sect an enigma. Some of these strange doctrines have recently been modified to accommodate a more open, public image. Others remain intact. These teachings (which may or may not have been rescinded by the time this book reaches the reader) include: triple-tithing on one's gross income, racial superiority for whites, prohibitions against doctors and surgery, requirements that members dissolve post-divorce marriages, and condemnation of recognizing birthdays as well as Easter and Christmas. Until recently, knowledge of any WCG teachings was scarce to come by. Church meetings were held in public buildings, services were unannounced, and uninvited visitors were politely ushered out.

It is Armstrong's belief in Anglo-Israelism that draws the most theological attention. Though Herbert denies it, his doctrine meshes perfectly with the founder of this theory, Canadian Richard Brothers, a psychic visionary who lived in London in the eighteenth century. (His ideas were later popularized in 1840 by Scotsman John Wilson.) Ignoring sound rules of linguistics and hermeneutics, the theory suggests that England (Ephraim) and the United States (Manasseh) are what is left of the so-called ten lost tribes of Israel. Ancient Judah and Israel are believed to be two separate entities (the former are Jews as they are known today). After the Assyrian captivity, Israel migrated northward to eventually become the Anglo-Saxons of British heritage.

Armstrong teaches that the promises of God due to his chosen people have been transferred to America and the United Kingdom. He also declares that Queen Elizabeth sits on the throne to which Christ will return. Although sound Bible scholarship questions whether or not Israel and Judah should be separated and debunks the idea that any tribes were ever lost, the WCG maintains that the British Coronation Stone of Scone was actually brought to the Emerald Isle by the prophet Jeremiah. Armstrong believes the war of Armageddon is near and that Germany (modern Assyria) will lead a ten-nation confederation into this battle.

Worldwide Church of God members need not fear the coming conflagration. God's "true church" (i.e., WCG) will be raptured to Petra (the ancient rock-city south of the Dead Sea in Jordan). When will all of this take place? Armstrong has variously set the dates for 1936, 1943, 1972, and 1975. When the last date passed without prophetic fulfillment, H. W. imposed a permanent silence on the issue. He had already goofed in 1965 by declaring that Jerusalem would remain in Gentile hands until the return of Christ. Then came the Six Day War in 1967.

If a predisposed view of Jewish history and a predilection for expensive tastes were his only shortcomings, Herbert W. Armstrong might be dismissed

as easily as any other religious zealot. However, his
ubiquitous broadcasts and publications reach (by his
estimates) 150 million people weekly. Therefore, closer
scrutiny is in order to determine if his doctrines are
merely fanciful or heretical. Those who are easily
impressed by his railings against society's ills ought to
explore the solutions offered by his system of theology.
Identification with his moral viewpoint may cause one to
accept uncritically a belief structure that doesn't mean
what it appears to say.

Speaking of his "conversion," the elder Armstrong
declares, "God called me . . . for the most important
commission in 1900 years." That message, as he explains,
teaches the born-again experience is a process, not an
instantly imputed act. "We are not yet born of God — only
heirs — only begotten," he emphasizes. H. W. insists one
cannot be truly "saved" in this life since redemption will
not be completed until the resurrection. In the meantime,
WCG followers live in fear of offending God and losing
their salvation, careful not to miss a Church feast or fall
short of their financial obligations to the WCG.

Perhaps the most dangerous Armstrong doctrine is the
contention that deity is an attainable goal of man. A recent
WCG publication insists, "We are to be changed from
physical to spiritual [a denial of the bodily resurrection]
. . . into the spirit of God. We must be God. Blasphemy?
No. Believe it or not, you are a potential omnipotent
power. You were born to become God!" Note, the writer
doesn't say *a* god. He says *God.* This view, of course, robs
Christ of his unique position as eternal God. Man, who
was created by Christ, is thus elevated from his finite
position to a status equal with Infinity. (Armstrong also
believes that man will someday join God in recreating the
entire universe.)

Right now, Armstrong's focus on the future has been
overshadowed by the legal and financial battles he faces
today. Garner Ted's sexual misconduct has driven away
many members to splinter groups. Since the younger
Armstrong's face is no longer seen on television
promoting the WCG, an economic vacuum restricts the
elder's plans for expansion. Top Church leaders have
resigned, and the government temporarily placed
Herbert's purse strings in receivership. All this has left a
pall over the Church's fortunes. In addition, his closest

associate and heir-apparent, Stanley Rader, left his position as treasurer and board member. (In 1980, Rader reportedly drew a salary of $350,000 to serve as the Church's executive manager.) With H. W.'s son, Garner Ted, living in Tyler, Texas (where his own church led by ex-WCG officials is rapidly growing), the "apostle" of Anglo-Israelism faces a bleak "world tomorrow."

Founder: Herbert W. Armstrong, born 1892, Des Moines, Iowa; cult founded in Eugene, Oregon, 1934.

Text: Emphasis on Old Testament Scriptures regarding feasts, festivals, and dietary laws.

Symbols: Visual — none known; verbal — "The World Tomorrow," a theme of media broadcasts.

Appeal: Conservatively inclined people concerned about moral decay may be attracted by Armstrong's denunciation of social evils and calls for biblical allegiance. WCG broadcasts and publications contain a measure of truth that draws disaffected traditional church members. The absence of overt fund solicitation and the sobering style of their news commentaries give a respectability that belies the true nature of Church activities and doctrines.

Purpose: Herbert W. Armstrong believes that the true Church and its pure message has been underground for 1900 years. Now, just prior to the return of Christ, he has been called of God to bring a message that will dispel the confusion of all other false denominations who consider themselves Christians. The Worldwide Church of God is the only legitimate representative of the Gospel of Christ.

Errors: Mr. Armstrong has Galatianized the gospel by adding laws and commandments to the message of grace, a violation of the principles set forth in Colossians 2 and Romans 14. Ephesians refutes the ethnic and nationalistic superiority inherent in the unbiblical theory of Anglo-Israelism.

Background Sources: *The Good News,* 7/76, p. 28; various issues of *The Plain Truth,* including 4/77, p. 3, and 5/77, p. 39; *Christianity Today,* 12/17/71, pp. 6-9; *Ibid.,* 4/1/77, pp. 20-24; *Ibid.,* 2/20/81, p. 41; *Time,* 5/15/72,

p. 87; *Ibid.,* 3/4/74, p. 50; *Ibid.,* 6/15/78, p. 54; *Ibid.,* 2/23/81, p. 54; *Eternity,* 5/81, p. 15.

Address/Location: Worldwide Church of God, Box 111, Pasadena, CA 91123; foreign offices in England, Australia, Canada, and South Africa.

PERSONALITY CULTS

29

Baba Ram Dass
(Hanuman Foundation)

What Harvard student in the sixties would have
suspected that his bespectacled psychiatry professor,
Dr. Richard Alpert, would someday become a Hindu guru
whose main focus of attention is a monkey-god?

The year was 1961 and a fellow professor named
Timothy Leary had started dropping LSD. Alpert literally
joined the trip. After six years of getting high, only to
come back down to the same problems, Alpert decided
to visit India. There he met a twenty-three-year-old man
named Bhagwan Dass. Alpert was so profoundly
impressed with Dass that he took up fasting, yoga, and
meditation. Eventually, Alpert was taken to Dass's guru,
Maharaji, who lived in the foothills of the Himalayas.
Dr. Alpert changed his name to Baba Ram Dass, returned
to America, and wrote a book entitled *Be Here Now.* It
emphasized his philosophy of "living each moment
meaningfully."

Ram Dass believes that everyone is on the same
spiritual journey to recognize the oneness of all religions
and the "truth" that God's spirit resides in each person. A
guru is needed to reveal this "truth." A spiritual teacher
will suggest the seeker's most expedient way to

experience being "here now." Some might be recommended to indulge in yoga or sex while others are encouraged to meditate or chant mantras. Certain disciples are even given the same psychedelic drugs that failed to satisfy Alpert. Ram doesn't exactly eschew drugs. He credits their role in his own spiritual enlightenment by providing hallucinogenic experiences that paralleled spiritistic descriptions in *The Tibetan Book of the Dead.*

As Baba Ram Dass, Richard Alpert has forsaken his Jewish upbringing in Boston. In 1974, he formed the Hanuman Foundation, named after the monkey-god of Hindu scriptures. Ram Dass sees this animal-god as an example of the devoted service he wishes to evoke from his own followers. The Foundation program includes counseling the terminally ill, involvement in prison work, and maintaining the Hanuman Temple.

Ram Dass has left Dr. Alpert far behind, as if his former vocation took place in another incarnation. He often travels the lecture circuit exuding an apparent happiness he never had during his Mercedes Benz/private airplane/materialistic days at Harvard. As a father-figure from the turbulent days of flower-power, Ram Dass brings a message that meshes well into the Eastern/mystical mainstream of contemporary thought.

Founder: Dr. Richard Alpert, whose following developed in the early seventies with the publication of *Be Here Now.*

Text: Hindu scriptures.

Symbols: None known.

Appeal: Those who look to drugs as a means of transcending reality see Ram Dass as a psychedelic pioneer who has "been there" and knows what he is talking about. His views on religion, even though they are warmed-over *Raja Yoga* beliefs, are perceived as authoritative because of Dass's past.

Purpose: Baba Ram Dass teaches that fulfillment comes from avoiding introspection about the past and future. Instead, his disciples are encouraged to acknowledge their inner divinity and oneness with the universal deity.

He claims the result is a nonhedonistic compulsion to explore momentary satisfaction.

Errors: The Hinduistic roots of his teachings are incompatible with a Christian world-view. Moral restrictions are ignored in favor of a pleasure principal which assumes that reveling in "now" is a desirable way to work out one's karma. The biblical concept of future accountability for sin is replaced by the assumption that inner peace today is more important than preparing for judgment tomorrow.

Background Sources: *Be Here Now,* 1971, Baba Ram Dass, Lama Foundation, San Cristobal, NM; *Circus,* 7/71, p. 40; *The Denver Post,* 5/15/81, p. 35.

Address: None available.

30

Bhagwan Shree Rajneesh

To most mystical gurus, sex, drugs, and hedonism are impediments on the path to enlightenment. Not to Bhagwan Shree Rajneesh. "I don't profess anything," he declares, and his disciples act accordingly. For students of Eastern religions who consider asceticism too confining, this is it. Until recently, all one had to do was grab the next plane to Poona, India (a route taken by notables such as Diana Ross, Ruth Carter Stapleton, and 50,000 others).

Once there, all clothes were shed for the orange robes one sees everywhere. Candidates for Rajneesh's brand of spirituality must prostrate themselves the moment Rajneesh enters the room. The seeker then receives a new Hindi name and a beaded necklace with Rajneesh's face in a locket. One important warning: devotees must wash thoroughly — especially their hair. Though he lays claim to being a "living God beyond time in a state of continuous bliss," Rajneesh has diabetes and a horrible case of asthma. Guards stand ready to sniff the hair of each entrant whose every lock must be clean and free from oil before being allowed into his divine presence.

Bhagwan's teachings abound in eighty books and more than 500 tapes. The message is simple — anything goes. He preaches indiscriminate premarital sex, open marriages, and the abolition of the family, which he says is "the biggest threat to human progress." In his perception of religion, Christianity is a "cult," and even the Pope and Mother Teresa receive his castigation. Traditional *sanyasis* (holy men who meditate and renounce the world) may pursue the path to God for years. The Poona guru offers the state of *sanyas,* with all of its bliss, immediately. *"Neosanyas,"* he calls it. "Westerners want things quickly, so we give it to them right away." He promises nothing less than "freedom from everything!" Weekly one-third-page ads in *Time* magazine proclaim messages such as, "Repression should not be a word in the vocabulary of a *sannyasin* [seeker]."

For years, the balded and bearded Rajneesh was referred to as India's sex-guru. At his resort in Rajasthan State he dispensed *tantric* (sex) yoga and meditation. Western pilgrims at his Poona *ashram* received more of the same. Adhering to his admonition that "the path to desirelessness is through desire," they would smoke pot, disrobe, dance, jump up and down, and pursue sex however and with whomever they wished. The sterilization of female members avoids having to cope with one possible consequence of such libertine ways. Such antics have attracted 200,000 followers in 500 centers worldwide (100 of them in the U. S.). The estimated income totals between $5 million to $7 million a year, with Rajneesh being chauffeured about in a Rolls Royce Silver Shadow.

Born nearly a half century ago as Rajneesh Chandra Mohan, Bhagwan Shree Rajneesh ("The Blessed One Who Has Recognized Himself As God") was raised as a Jain in a small village in Madhya Pradesh province. After receiving a master's degree in philosophy, he served for a while as a professor. In 1966 he left the teaching profession to fulfill what he saw as God's plan for his life — spiritually transforming humanity. Various techniques are suggested as to how one may achieve this goal on an individual level.

Meditation at Bhagwan's *ashram* goes through five stages, from hyperventilative breathing to Sufi dancing. Participants are often required to wear blindfolds, and many discard their clothing. Since Rajneesh sees the logical mind as a barrier to spiritual progress, it is stilled by such exercises as staring at his picture without blinking for an hour. Even his endless list of irrelevant rules is designed to rid one's thinking of questioning processes. He also encourages "rebirthing," a state of returning mentally and emotionally to mother's womb before the traumas of birth. Eventually, disciples may believe they are actually rebirthing to previous incarnations; the idea is to rid the subconscious of any neuroses. Ultimate illumination comes when Bhagwan presses his thumb into the center of the initiate's forehead to awaken the mystical third eye.

The Poona *ashram* usually had approximately 5,000 to 7,000 in residence at any given time. As Rajneesh attempted to create a communal theocratic state, area citizens were offended by the way his followers displayed uninhibited sexual affections in public. Circulated stories about erotic licentiousness and physical violence inside the *ashram* walls eventually provoked harassment from the townspeople. To escape the criticism (and avoid a crackdown from Indian tax officials), Rajneesh packed up his collector's 150,000-volume library and headed for New York, along with twelve tons of luggage.

For years, he had been seeking "a new site, isolated from the outside world." As the dismantling of the Poona *ashram* was taking place, word surfaced that officials of the Chidvilas Rajneesh Meditation Center had already purchased (with $1.5 million in cash) more than 100 square miles of ranch land near Antelope, Oregon (120 miles southeast of Portland). Disciples attending his meditation sessions would observe the sex-guru sitting motionless for long periods of time as he entered a self-proclaimed period of "speaking through silence." It is now apparent that Rajneesh was formulating plans to establish the world's largest spiritual community on these shores — much to the chagrin of many solid Oregonians!

Founder: Bhagwan Shree Rajneesh, born 1931 (also known as Acharya Rajneesh).

Text: Hindu scriptures and Rajneesh's books including *Beyond and Beyond* and *Above All, Don't Wobble.*

Symbols: None.

Appeal: Graduates of consciousness-raising cults in the so-called "human potential movement" are often looking for a new discipline or experience beyond what they have already encountered. Rajneesh gives them a spiritual rationale for uninhibited self-gratification, especially of the sexual variety. To one unfamiliar with biblical guidelines regarding meditation and self-expression, his therapeutic approach of negating all hang-ups may sound like good advice.

Purpose: The goal of God-realization is accomplished when thinking and knowledge have been circumvented. One can then live in a constant meditative state, an existence of innate responses to Bhagwan's programmed precepts. Each *sannyasin* (follower) is encouraged to live a sexually vigorous life with spiritual sanction.

Errors: Bhagwan Shree Rajneesh departs from traditional Hindu morality as well as biblical standards of sexuality. Man is the center of determining what conduct is permissible. Christianity enhances self-identity in contrast to Rajneesh's attempt to destroy one's emotionally protective barriers of self-worth. Meditation should be a concentrative act of the will, not a chaotic, mindless, drug-like state of emptying out the consciousness.

Background Sources: *Time,* 1/16/78, p. 59; *Ibid.,* 3/23/81, p. 78; *People,* 2/16/81, pp. 36-38; *Radix;* "A Journey Towards Faith," date unknown.

Address/Location: Main Rajneesh Meditation Center formerly in Poona, India. Primary U. S. Centers: Chidvilas, 154 Valley Road, Montclair, NJ 07042; Geetam Rajneesh Sannyas Ashram, Box 576 E, Lucerne, CA 92356; Antelope, OR.

31

Branhamism

When a drunken driver killed William Branham in 1965, most people assumed that the fame of this itinerant "Jesus only" (nontrinitarian) preacher would fade into obscurity. But Branham was not just another evangelist. He claimed to be *the* prophet for this dispensation (presumed to be the Laodicean Age), the voice of Revelation's seventh messenger.

Today, Branhamites can still be found from the backwoods of Appalachia to the prairies of Saskatchewan. They gather in small groups to study the few books he wrote and listen to primitively recorded tapes of his sermons. To such zealots, there is one born among men greater than John the Baptist, and that man is William Branham.

Branham was born in 1909 in the hills of Kentucky, the son of a bootlegger. At seven years of age, he experienced the first of several visions that were destined to guide his life. On May 7, 1946, he spent a night in a cave where an angel supposedly appeared unto him and explained his past and future. The angel also revealed how God would enable him to heal people. Many of his contemporaries were concerned about the spiritualistic overtones exhibited by Branham's gift of healing. The presence of a disease would set off vibrations causing his hand to swell. Sometimes he would see a fiery ball dance about the room and then hover over those upon whom he would pronounce healing. (This author was present during a 1965 Branham meeting when the ball of fire supposedly appeared. No visible phenomenon was evident to the audience, but many of those present accepted Branham's explanation without question.) But despite persistent warnings from fellow ministers that his visions might be demonic, Branham was undeterred.

Branham traveled widely overseas and achieved a wide measure of acceptance among some mainline Pentecostal groups. But his small congregation in Jeffersonville, Indiana, provided the primary channel for his teachings. Branham told his parishioners that God spoke to him out of a pillar of fire and revealed the mysteries of Revelation 5—8. This led him to predict future events, including Hitler's rise to power (correct), and the destruction of America by an explosion in 1977 (incorrect). In fact, the book which contains this later prophecy (*The Seven Church Ages*) also designated 1977 as the first year of the Millennium.

During the forties, Branham held large healing campaigns during which thousands experienced miraculous cures. Those who knew Branham intimately claimed he was a humble, self-effacing, withdrawn man who, in spite of an unlearned background, had a remarkable sense of spiritual understanding. Was he a person who started out sincerely, but later succumbed to doctrinal error because he lacked adequate theological training? Were his visions and angelic visitations of Godly origin, or was he cleverly deceived by Satan?

Retrospective analysis cannot conclusively answer these questions. But it is possible to decipher Branham's theology and weigh its inconsistencies against orthodox Christian doctrine. Even Branham's most devout followers would have to admit that his unscriptural views generate some measure of skepticism regarding his claim to be a prophet for the end times.

Branham was nontrinitarian, claiming that Jesus was created and not the eternal Son of God. He also believed that Cain and Abel were born from separate impregnations, the former by the serpent's seduction and the latter by Adam. Though he accepted the existence of a literal lake of fire, he contended that it would be destroyed eventually. Some of his prophetic statements were fulfilled while others contain glaring errors.

Analyzing the credibility of living cult leaders is relatively easy. But those vanguards who have passed away can only be judged by the memories of persons who knew them and by the written documents they left. Without question, Branham sincerely believed he was a servant of God whose revelations were from the Lord. To question his theology is not to suggest his conversion was false or that all he did was in error. Even if God did confer spiritual gifts upon the life of William Branham, his current followers seem to have forgotten Paul's warning of 1 Corinthians 3. Christians are not carnally to adulate men, no matter how dynamic or charismatic they may be. It is God who gives the increase and he, alone, deserves total devotion.

Founder: William M. Branham, born 1909, died 1965.

Text: Malachi 4:5 (Branham claimed to be the fulfillment of this prophecy, the "Elijah" of the so-called Laodicean Age).

Symbols: None.

Appeal: To those who feel the organized church world is apostate and in need of divine revelation by a prophet from God.

Purpose: To perpetuate Branham's teachings by tract distribution and listening to his tape-recorded messages in small groups.

Errors: Branham denied the Trinity and eternal punishment; inaccurate foretelling of future events; wrong interpretation of Eve's fall; possible satanic deception by supernatural occurrences.

Background Sources: Western Tract Mission, Saskatoon, Saskatchewan, Canada; "Is It Later Than You Think?" tract by O. A. Jorgensen; "William Branham," Cal Beisner, Christian Research Institute; "God's Word Came to the Prophet William Marion Branham," tract by Spoken Word

Publications; *William Branham, A Man Sent from God,* Gordon Lindsay, published and copyrighted 1950 by William Branham; ''The Laodicean Church Age,'' William Branham; *An Exposition on the Seven Church Ages,* William Branham.

Address/Location: None known.

32

Bubba Free John

What kind of God would sit by the bedside of a sick person and mockingly tease him about his illness? Or accept a $250,000 gift from a disciple and then forbid him to live in the spiritual resort purchased with the money? Hindus have a term to describe such contradictory conduct on behalf of a God-man: *lilas,* the humorous, irrational disregard of convention. Followers of Bubba Free John call his *lilas,* "Bubba theater."

Franklin Jones (his real name) is not exactly modest about his person and purpose. He claims to be nothing less than an incarnation of God, a guru to be worshiped. "Surrender to me all your seeking, the very sense of your separate self, all thoughts, all desires, every circumstance, even your body." Those who do are promised "freedom" and the joy of constant laughter. All this supposedly comes from being in the presence of one (Bubba) who is "perfect love," a siddha guru "descended directly from God."

Jones started out life rather normally as a college student at Columbia and Stanford. He experimented with LSD and studied at a Lutheran Seminary. In the late sixties, he made several pilgrimages to India where the Hindu Swami Muktananda Nityananda influenced him so strongly that he experienced visions of the teacher. He also saw apparitions of the Virgin Mary whom he considered to be Mother Shakti, the Hindu goddess. By 1970 he felt he had attained enlightenment and hence formed the Dawn Horse Fellowship, now called the Free Primitive Church of Divine Communion. Other organizational entities under his leadership include the Free Community Order and the Laughing Man Institute.

Bubba's claim of divinity isn't unique in today's marketplace of mystical gurus and cult leaders. But he is the only American-born domestic product available. Thus when he claims to fulfill the traditions of Moses, Krishna, Jesus, and Buddha, he does so as one who (according to him) only assumed the identity of Franklin Jones to provide a lesson for his disciples. The late Zen authority and Eastern religious gadfly, author Alan Watts, studied Bubba on videotape. Watts wept and declared, "It looks like we have an *avatar* here. I've been waiting for such a one all my life."

The teachings of Bubba Free John are dispensed by videotape, film, cassettes, pamphlets, and his four published works: *The Knee of Listening, The Method of the Siddhas, Garbage and the Goddess,* and *No Remedy.* His doctrine is simple. Objective truth and reality do not exist. Life is an unexplainable mystery. One's only choice is to be subjectively absorbed by the impersonal Divine. This is done by sacrificing ego and consciousness and abiding in the presence of a guru. All negative *karma* will thus be dissolved spontaneously. To embark on such a journey and join one of Bubba's Communities, the seeker has to hold down a steady job (and tithe 10 percent to Bubba's work), adapt to a lactovegetarian diet, confine sex to marriage, and contemplate Free John's teachings every day.

Following Bubba is not just a matter of intellectual acknowledgment. His avataristic claims are substantiated by what seem to be amazing supernatural phenomena. Disciples are privileged to see him heal and perform miracles. They credit him with causing violent thunderstorms and creating coronas around the sun. Some students claim to have experienced dynamic *kundalini* phenomena such as *kriyas* (automatic purifying movements), *mudras* (spontaneous yogic postures), visions, revelations, and states of indescribable bliss (*samadhi*). The close comparison of such experiences with similar occurrences in demonism and classical spiritualism should not be a comforting thought to followers of Bubba.

Founder: Bubba Free John, born Franklin Jones, November 3, 1939.

Text: Hindu scriptures.

Symbols: None known.

Appeal: Bubba's claim to be an *atman,* a self-realized soul and avatar, is stamped "made-in-America." His pompous claims of enlightenment are rare for a Westerner and thus intriguing to students of Eastern mysticism. Some followers are drawn by hearing stories about his disciples experiencing a spontaneous kind of hilarity in his presence. Others are attracted by tales of devotees receiving powerful psychic experiences by the mere touch of his hand.

Purpose: By abandonment of independent thought and moral judgment, the disciple becomes absorbed by his guru (Bubba) and thus merges his consciousness with God (since the guru *is* God). "You do not even know what a single thing is. Then rest-abide in that Ignorance," Bubba teaches. Presuming to know and think and be is the cause of all unhappiness. Seeking for solutions to problems is pointless. All dilemmas can be solved by one's abiding in a relationship to a God-realized guru.

Errors: Second Thessalonians 2 describes the nature of the Antichrist, which is to exalt himself above God to the point of actually claiming to be God. Bubba Free John certainly possesses the same motivating spirit of self-deification. He makes of himself the supreme source of truth and spiritual knowledge and claims equality with Christ as an incarnation of God.

Background Sources: *The Knee of Listening,* 1972, Franklin Jones, The Dawn Horse Press, Los Angeles, CA; *No Remedy,* 1976, Bubba Free John, The Dawn Horse Press, Lower Lake, CA; *East West Journal,* 5/76, pp. 60, 67; *Ibid.,* 7/76, pp. 20-25.

Address/Location: Dawn Horse Press, P. O. Box 3680, Clearlake Highlands, CA 95422.

33

Gurdjieff/Subud/ Renaissance

George Ivanovitch Gurdjieff didn't have the kind of household name that ensures popularity as a cult leader. His personality traits weren't any more endearing. Gurdjieff was an erratic despot with a habit of unpredictability. He was known often to drive down the wrong side of the road at high speeds, accelerating until he ran out of gas. Even his death in 1949 didn't bring an end to his uncanny influence over men's lives. Today, an estimated 5,000 disciples follow his teachings. They are organized into secret societies located all across the United States, from California to Washington, D. C. The life of Gurdjieff was an enigma, but his teachings endure as the number of his followers continues to grow.

The birth and background of Gurdjieff are shrouded in the same mystery that characterized his life. It is likely that he was of Armenian origin. His father first interested him in the occult, and this fascination with the supernatural continued throughout his life. *Meetings with Remarkable Men,* his most widely read book, was recently made into a major motion picture. The volume recounts his travels throughout Central Asia, from Tibet to

Russia, and on to France where he settled in 1922. It was there that his investigations into secret Sufi brotherhoods and Asian mystery schools prompted him to form the Institute for the Development of Man.

The actual teachings of Gurdjieff, which came to be called "esoteric Christianity," are hard to decipher. G-O groups ("G" for Gurdjieff and "O" for Peter Demianovich Ouspensky, his foremost contemporary disciple) don't advertise their gatherings. Disciples meet for the purpose of discussing Gurdjieff's books and indulging in whirling dervish-type dances, known as "spiritual gymnastics." Their intent is to embark upon "the great adventure of the search for self."

Gurdjieff sought to open up man's consciousness to higher planes of awareness. He believed that most people are "asleep," but they can be "awakened" by having a greater sense of self-awareness. Then they will be able to see their various egos and proceed to seek out which part of them is the real "I." This "Fourth Way," as it is called, is the path to self-transformation. Seekers are encouraged to begin each morning concentrating on putting their real "self" into each part of their bodies, beginning with the toes and so on. Eventually such "self-consciousness" enables one constantly to observe his body and become aware of unconscious mannerisms.

The purpose of such exercises is to shatter the illusion that reactions and intentions are a choice of free will. The next goal is attaining "objective consciousness," by which a person finally discovers his true self. Human effort thus enables one to "save" his own soul.

There is definite value in recognizing that man's heart and his spiritual aims are in a state of disequilibrium. But looking to human merit as a source of right thinking overlooks the fallen nature of man which clouds any attempt to achieve a truly objective state of mind.

Gurdjieff's teachings are found in books such as, *All Is Everything* (sometimes known as *Beelzebub's Tales to His Grandson*), *Meetings with Remarkable Men, The Fourth Way,* and *Life Is Only Real When I Am.* In the first of these he speaks of a future prophet of consciousness. Many believe that Muhammed Subuh, a Javanese government official, fulfilled that role. In 1925 a ball of light descended on Subuh and overwhelmed him, an event he called a *latihan* (God's power purifying the soul).

Subuh combined three Sanskrit words to come up with the name of his movement — Subud.

Subuh went to England in 1956 and gained a following among former disciples of the late Gurdjieff. He developed a process for surrendering to God's power *(latihan)*. Prospective recipients enter a darkened room and await contact with someone who has already experienced *latihan*. When the power enters, participants exhibit body contortions and vocal utterances. Healings may occur (along with moans and screams) as the goal of an altered consciousness is achieved.

One of the most visible and controversial offshoots of Gurdjieff's philosophy is the Fellowship of Friends. This monastic, well-educated group (more generally called Renaissance) is led by a forty-two-year-old former grade-school teacher named Robert Burton. Burton, who intimates he may be the embodiment of the Second Coming of Christ, lives with a portion of his followers (about 1400 worldwide) in affluent splendor on a Northern California ranch.

Gurdjieff's ideals of self-improvement receive a special application from Burton. He contends that the quality of life is enhanced by a worship of beauty and materialism. Higher consciousness is possible by filling one's environment with beauty and comfort. As a result, his disciples provide Burton with a new Mercedes-Benz and a lavish mansion filled with priceless works of art. Followers (virtual servants) attend his bidding and provide free labor for the ongoing construction of cult facilities. Most of Burton's time is consumed in world travel, a task he undertakes to scout for new paintings and porcelains to be added to Renaissance's growing collection of artifacts. He explains to critics that it is his duty to elevate the culture and tastes of those who surround him.

Burton also prophesies a worldwide economic collapse and nuclear holocaust. His hideaway in the Sierra foothills will escape this disaster. The priceless art objects he has purchased will allow him and his group to be surviving apostles of an advanced culture and civilization.

Such refined ideals seem hollow when compared with Burton's moral flaws. When his mother was dying in the hospital he was practicing a period of self-imposed silence. In spite of her suffering, he refused to speak, an act that he sees as exemplifying virtuous self-denial.

Founder: George Ivanovitch Gurdjieff, born 1872, died 1949. Teachings established in Fontainbleau, France, 1922.

Text: Books of Gurdjieff and P. D. Ouspensky.

Symbols: None.

Appeal: Gurdjieff's teachings represent a thinking man's cult. Philosophical speculation and the potential for self-discovery attract some. Others are intrigued by the clandestine nature of Gurdjieff groups which give the illusion of being an elitist corps possessing superior knowledge about the mysteries of life.

Purpose: It is obvious that true happiness consists of that which is beyond immediate conscious perception (Gurdjieff called it the "something else"). Gurdjieff followed in the tradition of the ancient admonition to "first know thyself." The Work, as it is now called, believes that humans can evolve to spiritual understanding once they become aware of their own imperfections.

Errors: Gurdjieff taught that the highest goal is to have self-knowledge. Proverbs 1:7 states, "The fear of the Lord is the beginning of knowledge." The quest for higher consciousness always portends the danger of invasion by an alien spiritual intelligence. That "something else" Gurdjieff sought with his blend of Gnostic and occult philosophy is found in Christ who transforms and regenerates the "I" to be a recipient of "abundant life."

Background Sources: "S.C.P. Newsletter," vol. 5, no. 4, 6/79; *The Denver Post,* 12/9/77, p. 8BB; *Those Curious New Cults,* 1975; William J. Petersen, Keats Publishing Inc., New Canaan, CT; *San Francisco Chronicle,* 4/20/81.

Address/Location: Headquarters in New York City. Affiliated groups in major U. S. cities. Published locations and addresses not available. Prospective members often learn of the groups through advertising bookmarks which have been inserted in the pages of works by Ouspensky. The bookmarks have phone numbers of local centers.

34

Guru Maharaj Ji
(Divine Light Mission)

"God has retired and now resides in comfortable affluence amid the placid splendor of a Malibu, California, mansion." That might well be the epitaph on the tombstone of Divine Light Mission. In the early seventies, Guru Maharaj Ji commanded one of the largest and fastest-growing followings of all imported cult leaders.

At one time he confidently declared, "The key to the whole life, the key to the existence of this entire universe rests in the hands of Guru Maharaj Ji." Then, it all fell apart. Reorganizational efforts failed to salvage the momentum of the days when he was worshiped as one "greater than god, because he showed men to god." But don't count him out yet. A hard core of an estimated several hundred to several thousand disciples still believe he is *the* incarnation of God, the Perfect Master for our age.

Guru Maharaj Ji owes the founding of Divine Light Mission (DLM) to his wealthy, revered father, Brahma Samaj Shri Hans Ji Maharaj, who headed the Prem Nagar *Ashram*. Shri Hans was considered to be a *Satguru*

(Perfect Master) by many of his countrymen. When
Maharaj Ji was born December 10, 1957, in Hardwar,
India, no one paid much attention. The family already had
three older sons and one of them was presumed to be
next in line as Satguru. But Maharaj Ji was remarkably
precocious. By age two he was meditating and giving
satsang ("holy discourses").

When Maharaj Ji was eight years old, his father died.
The boy addressed the grieving devotees by declaring,
"Why are you weeping? Haven't you learned the lesson
that your Master taught you? The Perfect Master never
dies. Maharaj Ji is here amongst you now." As his father's
disciples bowed at Maharah Ji's feet, his mother
Rajeshwari Devi (usually known as Mata Ji) confirmed the
passing of the spiritual mantle to him. He was invested
with the crown of Krishna and thirteen days later, while
praying to his father's cremated ashes, an inner voice
spoke. The message was simple: Guru Maharaj Ji was
destined to become the savior of humanity.

On November 8, 1970, Maharaj Ji led an entourage of
thousands of followers through the streets of Delhi.
Arriving at the India Gate he declared, "I will establish
peace in this world." Strange words, indeed, for a
ninth-grade dropout from a Catholic mission school.
Several million Indian disciples believed his claim, but
only a handful of *premies* (devotees — literally "lovers")
greeted his arrival in the West as he touched down at Los
Angeles International in 1971. Yet, there was something
fascinating about this pudgy teenager whose tastes ran to
Baskin Robbins and horror movies.

The turning point came the following year in Montrose,
Colorado. Two thousand converts were solicited from an
audience of 5,000, and suddenly Maharaj Ji was on his
way. By the time another year rolled around there were
480 DLM centers and 35,000 members in the United
States. The organization opened up a variety of
businesses and communes along with a record company,
a film production house, and a printing establishment.
Then came "Millennium 1973," an extravaganza held in
the Houston Astrodome.

This author witnessed the events of that festival which
was supposed to draw a potential attendance of 144,000.
Though only approximately 20,000 showed up, the

worship accorded to Maharaj Ji testified to his uncanny
power. Dopers-turned-devotees, fornicators-turned-
celibates, hippies, and straights all united in their
shouting praise: "Bholie Shri Satguru Dev Maharaj Ki Jai,"
a Hindi "hip, hip, hooray" to the Lord of the Universe. To
this author's amazement, the entire audience of
thousands prostrated themselves before Maharaj Ji's
throne, which was elevated nearly forty feet above the
Astroturf.

Controversy soon followed glory. A reporter who threw
a cream pie in Maharaj Ji's face was mercilessly beaten by
the Guru's disciples. Maharaj Ji was accused by Indian
customs officials of trying to smuggle $80,000 worth of
jewels into his native land. The Astrodome gathering rang
up huge debts, and questions were raised about the
Guru's true age and materialistic preoccupations. Still,
dedicated followers declared they would die or kill for
the corpulent kid whom Rennie Davis, the ex-leftist
radical, called "the power of creation itself."

The biggest upheaval occurred in 1974 when he
married a former United Airlines stewardess who was
eight years his senior. He pronounced her the incarnation
of the ten-armed, tiger-riding goddess Durga. When the
new bride refused her mother-in-law access to their
$554,000 Malibu estate, that was the last straw. Mother
Mata Ji denounced her son as a drinking, dancing,
nightclub-haunting meat-eater. She changed the name of
the U. S. organization to The Spiritual Life Society and
installed Maharaj Ji's eldest brother Shri Satyapal Ji (Bal
Bhagwan Ji) as the new Perfect Master. Even the birth of
two grandchildren (Premlata and Hans Paul) didn't mollify
her anger. However, Maharaj Ji was unperturbed,
wondering aloud how anyone could claim to tell God he
was no longer qualified to hold office.

For a while things picked up. Income averaged over
$400,000 a month, mostly due to a mandatory tithe.
Maharaj Ji's passion for automobiles extended to a
Jensen, Mercedes-Benz, Maserati, Lotus, and a mobile
van. The *Divine Times,* a slick four-color publication,
reported on the Guru's activities to communities in
sixty-six countries. He still continued holding large
festivals and *lilas* (god-games where audiences of
disciples were doused with water and red paint from

huge pressurized nozzles). But as Goomerajee (as he is affectionately known by close associates) grew more obese, his following conversely diminished.

Plans for his divine city were shelved. Almost 100 DLM-owned vehicles were sold. All but one of thirty-four food cooperatives were shut down. The staff of 250 at the Denver international headquarters was reduced to a mere forty. Maharaj Ji's scores of hand-picked evangelists, called *mahatmas,* were reduced to twenty and renamed "initiators." Income plunged to less than $100,000 per month. Estimates of followers worldwide still remained slightly above a million, but in the U. S. that total went from a heyday high of 50,000 to about 10,000. Some critics suggested the figure might be closer to 3,000. Worst of all, his former head, Bob Meshler, left the DLM amid a series of accusations.

But before any final obituaries on Guru Maharaj Ji are pronounced, it would be wise to ponder the teachings and practices that precipitated his sudden rise to power. In the seeds of his fame may be the genesis of other cult leaders having an Eastern inclination. Understanding what the DLM taught and represented may give a clue forewarning society of other personality cult figures.

Followers of Maharaj Ji are encouraged to live by his Five Commandments: (1) Do not put off until tomorrow what you can do today; (2) Constantly meditate and remember the Holy Name; (3) Leave no room for doubt in your mind; (4) Never delay attending *satsang* (one of Maharaj Ji's discourses of rambling stories and illustrations); (5) Always have faith in God (which is translated as complete devotion to Maharaj Ji).

The theology of DLM may be summed up by understanding its view of God, guru, mind, and Knowledge. To begin with, God is a form of energy, a cosmic vibration. As such, "the Word" extends itself to everything, making even man's soul part of God. This author once heard Guru Maharaj Ji exclaim in a speech that he did not desire a relationship with God. To do so would imply that deity is separate to man, undercutting the doctrine of oneness which is central to Hinduism. Hence DLM has as its ultimate goal the merging of man's soul with the Infinite Absolute — the soul's energy being reabsorbed into the universal energy of God.

Guru Maharaj Ji's variant of Hinduism emphasizes the *Siddha Yoga* school of thought. In this tradition, god-realization can only be accomplished with the aid of a guru who leads one forward on the path of enlightenment. All the better if this guru is a Perfect Master greater than God himself. The Perfect Master is sinless, since his subjective consciousness is the only standard by which he is judged (God is inside him). No external principles of absolute values guide him because he responds spontaneously to his own divinity. This living Master deserves and has the right to demand total submission from his followers. In Maharaj Ji's case, such subservience is reinforced by his ubiquitous visage adorning every trinket and magazine produced by DLM.

But there is an impediment to following the Perfect Master on the path toward knowledge of God — the mind. Guru Maharaj Ji insists that the rationalistic West has given too much prominence to reasoning faculties. The mind, in his estimation, is delusive, unreliable, and imperfect. It is the spirit which contains the capacity for love and peace. Therefore, the Knowledge of God is unattainable by objective information. It can only be received by experience. Maharaj Ji describes the mind as a snake to be killed so the direct revelation of divine Knowledge can be transmitted. "Give it [your mind] to me," he implores. "I am ready to receive it. Because your mind troubles you, give it to me."

The devotee who surrenders his mental capacities is ready to receive the Guru's Knowledge. It is this experience which transforms the lives of his disciples and makes them into robots to do his bidding. When pressed to explain this phenomenon, *premies* give glowing testimonials of its benefits but never divulge its process. Only diligent research has uncovered the four-fold procedure which consists of a blinding light (seeing with the so-called third eye), hearing celestial music (supposedly referred to in Revelation 22), tasting a sweet substance called nectar (which presumably has curative powers), and sensing a primordial vibration (representing the internalized Word of God).

A devotee is considered ready to receive Knowledge once his unfettered submission to Maharaj Ji has been proven. This may be evidenced by signing away one's possessions to DLM or listening to extended hours of *satsang.* At the appointed time, the candidate enters a darkened room. He may sit there, draped in a sheet, for several hours. All the while a *mahatma* lectures him on the importance of the Knowledge he is about to receive.

Finally the initiator places his thumb and middle finger on the devotee's temples and presses inward with the index finger at a spot near the center of the forehead (claimed to be the location of the spiritual "third eye," the pineal gland). The optic nerve is pinched and a neurological light results from pressure upon the retina. *Premies* learn how to duplicate this experience at will by merely closing their eyelids and letting their eyeballs roll back in their sockets.

Divine music is heard with the "third ear." The *mahatma* places his fingers in the initiate's ears long enough for the recipient to be conscious of the sounds of his own internal organs and systems. One *premie* described the sound as "loud rock and roll" while another insisted she was hearing the same vibrations she experienced in her mother's womb.

Tasting divine nectar isn't as easy. The substance is said to be a fluid flowing from the brain, the very elixir which sustained Christ forty days in the wilderness. With the devotee's mouth open, the *mahatma* places his fingers in the *premie's* throat and forces his tongue backward until it rests against the uvula. The resulting mucous of post-nasal drip is interpreted as being "sweeter than honey."

Finally, John 1:14 is quoted to justify the theory that God's Word is in man's flesh. The candidate is told that a repetitive pattern of rhythmic breathing actually constitutes a mantra. In reality, this experience of the "primordial vibration of the divine word" is a hyperventilative technique which leaves the *premie* in an altered state of consciousness much like a drug-induced high. This concluding experience conveys a sense of omnipotence producing a feeling of oneness with the universe. Followers of the Guru refer to this ultimate high as being "blissed out."

The dynamics of the four states of Guru Maharaj Ji's Knowledge can be explained on a naturalistic basis. After the *mahatma* has predefined each experience, the candidate can easily be manipulated by autosuggestive hypnosis. At each stage, he is prone to interpret the phenomenon according to the expectations his spiritual leader has previously explained. Undoubtedly, the passively receptive state of the willing devotee also allows demonic forces to enhance the dimensions of each aspect of the Guru's ritual of receiving Knowledge.

Now that the image of the organization has been revamped, the procedure of transmitting Knowledge has become refined and dignified. Guru Maharaj Ji no longer sits on a throne, and devotees do not have to practice the Indian custom of *darshan,* literally kissing his feet. *Mahatmas* have exchanged their robes for business suits, and even Maharaj Ji's divinity is being downplayed. It remains to be seen whether Maharaj Ji's duodenal ulcer will be placated by the less frantic pace of his activities. Perhaps he was only a confused adolescent being exploited by a "holy" family lusting for power. If he really is an antichrist convinced of his own divinity, he'll soon need to fulfill his lofty predictions before another Perfect Master comes along.

Founder: Balyogeshwar Param Hans Satgurudev Shri Sant Ji Maharaj (Guru Maharaj Ji), born December 10, 1957, Hardwar, India.

Text: Hindu scriptures.

Symbols: Pictures of Maharaj Ji seated on a throne wearing the Crown of Krishna.

Appeal: During the early seventies, the rebellion of youth against established institutions made them susceptible to a strong disciplinary structure. The age of Maharaj Ji was an ironic contrast appealing to their loss of adult authority. Today's disciples tend to be older and better educated, responding to the DLM's current goals of peace through meditation and selfless service.

Purpose: The only pathway to God is by submission to an *avatar,* a fully god-realized guru. This Perfect Master helps one to remove the resistance of the logical mind which is the only block between man and his divine inner soul. Maharaj Ji's Knowledge is equated with the Holy Spirit, an experience which conveys a heightened sense of well-being and union with the Infinite.

Errors: All the requirements of the DLM are based on pleasing God by the works of submission and service, a contradiction of Ephesians 2:8, 9. Since the experience of Knowledge communicates a euphoric feeling, it is wrongly assumed to substantiate the teachings of Maharaj Ji. Proverbs 1:7 states that true knowledge is "the fear of the Lord," not a hypnotic series of psycho-neurological manipulations. Clearly, according to 1 John 2:18-23, Maharaj Ji fulfills the role of an antichrist as prophesied in Matthew 24.

Background Sources: *Who Is Guru Maharaj Ji?,* 1978, Bantam Books, New York, NY; various issues of DLM publication *Divine Times;* miscellaneous DLM pamphlets and materials published for release to the press; *The Guru,* 1974, Bob Larson, Bob Larson Ministries, Denver, CO; *Cults, World Religions and You,* 1980, Kenneth Boa, Victor Books, Wheaton, IL; *Empire Magazine,* 4/28/74, pp. 52-61; *The Denver Post,* 4/2/76; *Ibid.,* 8/13/76; *Ibid.,* 2/18/77, p. 3BB; *Ibid.,* 12/15/78, p. 3BB; *Time,* 4/28/75, p. 75; *Ibid.,* 3/13/78, p. 39.

Address/Location: Divine Light Mission, Box 532, Denver, CO 80201.

35

Meher Baba
(Sufism Reoriented, Inc.)

Ever been kissed on the forehead? Probably lots of times, especially as a child. Most likely your reaction was to respond with affection or embarrassment. Meher Baba was kissed on the forehead, and he became God — or at least *he* thought so.

The fame of Jesus spread after his death because of the Resurrection. When Meher Baba "dropped his body" (Baba's term for death) on January 31, 1969, it remained in the grave. Ironically, his fame too has grown, but not because of any miracles he performed. In fact, Baba was prone to catch colds. He rationalized the seeming contradiction of being God yet not being disease-resistant by saying, "...the physical body of even a God-realized Perfect Master is subject to ordinary contagion."

There certainly is no dearth of Baba-lovers (as they are called) more than a decade after his passing. They range from sophisticated socialites to college students on the latest Eastern-consciousness trip. Peter Townshend, leader of the British rock group The Who, has been an unabashed Baba-lover since his doper days of the sixties. "Baba is Christ," Townshend declares, because being a

Christian is "just like being a Baba-lover." He dedicated a
solo album to Baba which featured songs extolling
reincarnation, and a final tune adopted from Baba's Hindu
prayer, "Parvardigar."

Townshend's devotion exemplifies the status of deity
accorded Baba by his followers. "A mere twitch of his
nose could split the planet," Townshend says, "and a
twiddle of his finger could save your life. Luckily his
infinite power is used with compassion." If he were God,
then why was there not more evidence of his
omnipotence? Townshend explains: "Baba rarely
interferes. He said, 'Why alter events that occur in a
system that is self-perpetrating, self-correcting, and
self-destructive when it goes too far?' "

Who is Baba and how did he come to be worshiped as
an incarnation of Jesus Christ? Meher Baba was born in
1894 in Poona, India, near Bombay. His parents were
Zoroastrians and named him Merwan Sheriar Irani. While
attending college he developed an affection for an old
Muhammadan woman believed to be a Sufi saint, one of
the five Perfect Masters of the Age. One day she kissed
him on the forehead, an event which Baba claimed
triggered an instantaneous God-realization. From that
moment on, Baba was never the same.

He proceeded to spend seven years studying with the
Perfect Masters of his time. One of them, Upasni Maharaj,
threw a stone at Baba, hitting him in the exact spot where
the old woman had planted her kiss. Presto! The event
triggered Baba's instantaneous God-realization and he
became aware of his new destiny as *the* Perfect Master.
From then on he became known to his followers as Meher
Baba (the "Compassionate Father"), the *avatar*
(incarnation of God) for this age, in the lineage of
Zoroaster, Krishna, Rama, Buddha, Jesus, and
Muhammad. But more than that he claimed to be the final
incarnation of the godhead.

In 1921 he gathered a group of disciples and
established a colony including a hospital and school. The
unique distinction that set him apart from other *sadhus*
and holy men of the East was the self-imposed silence he
declared on July 10, 1925. "You have had enough of my
words, now is the time to live by them," he declared. By
"my words" he meant the precepts of all the religious

leaders of his previous incarnations. As Jesus et al. he had said enough. Now was the time to act.

His communications continued by means of an alphabet board and hand gestures. Baba promised this self-imposed silence would someday be broken before he dropped his body. He predicted the words he would speak would bring a surge of spirituality throughout humanity. Needless to say, Baba-lovers waited breathlessly at every public appearance, thinking each occasion might be the time for Baba's anticipated utterance. The Compassionate Father had indicated over and over, "I love you more than you can ever love me or yourself." This intensity of devotion to his disciples made them eagerly await his final words as if they were tantamount to the Second Coming of Christ.

In the meantime, Baba crystallized his teachings by issuing the five-volume *Discourses.* He also published a document entitled "Chartered Guidance from Meher Baba for the Reorientation of Sufism as the Highway to the Ultimate Universalized." His theology was rooted in the Hindu tradition of *Bhakti Yoga* which teaches that the pathway to God is facilitated by devotion to an earthly yogi. All the better if this yogi claims to be *the* ultimate avatar. And Baba was not shy about demanding followers to yield totally to him. He pompously declared, "I am neither a mahatma, nor a Saint, neither a sadhu or a yogi. I am the Ancient One. The Highest of the High."

What truths then did "God" expound? Basically, Baba introduced Western minds to a warmed-over, syncretistic combination of Hinduism, Buddhism, Zoroastrianism, and Islam. Souls come to earth, he taught, from two sister planets. These souls begin their evolutionary journey upward by incarnating first in stones, then to metals, then onward through vegetables, insects, reptiles, spiders, fish, birds, kangaroos, monkeys, and humans. The human form may dwell on one of seven planes of existence, decided by man's degree of adherence to what Baba called the "seven realities." The final plane is nirvana where one's consciousness merges with God. But Baba-lovers must be careful. One false step of failed devotion to Baba, and it's right back down to the lowly rocks to start all over again.

But was Baba's silence ever broken? What were those

divine words he promised would transform mankind? No one knows, and it seems that Baba died before being able to utter the truths for which his "lovers" had longed. The reader may reach his own conclusions about this man who claimed divinity and yet was smitten by death before being able to fulfill his most-heralded prophecy.

Founder: Meher Baba, born Merwan Sheriar Irani, in 1894, Poona, India. Died January 31, 1969.

Text: Hindu Scriptures; *Discourses, God Speaks,* and *Listen Humanity* (books by Baba).

Appeal: Baba's claim of divinity must be accepted or ignored. He either was the Christ, an incarnation of God, or a deluded sham. For certain people who have an authority vacuum in their lives, Baba provides both a father-figure as well as a deified object which to worship. Devotees can thus immerse themselves in Baba, tossing reason aside, and heed his call, "Come unto me."

Purpose: "All religions are basically dear to me," Baba taught. "It is not so much what you believe that counts, but what you are." In other words, happiness in this life and preferential reincarnations in the next life are not dependent upon doctrine, but rather on devotion — to Baba. Baba claimed to be God, and his religious philosophy is rooted in the impersonal concepts of divinity explicit in Hinduism; therefore, the goal of his disciples is to become at one with their avatar.

Errors: Baba was a created being, and thus his desire to be worshiped as God falls under the judgment of Romans 1. Jesus warned of false Christs and declared, "Go ye not therefore after them" (Luke 21:8). Romans 12:1 implores men to present themselves as a "living sacrifice" to God, not to a mustachioed Indian whose most important prophecy (breaking silence) was unfulfilled.

Background Sources: *Rolling Stone,* 11/26/70, pp. 25-27; *Those Curious New Cults,* 1975, William J. Petersen, Keats Publishing Inc., New Canaan, CT; *God Speaks, Discourses,* vol. I-V, by Meher Baba.

Address/Location: Former U. S. headquarters, Myrtle Beach, SC; Sufism Reoriented, Inc., 1300 Boulevard Way, Walnut Creek, CA 94595.

36

Muktananda Paramahansa
(Shree Gurudev Siddha Yoga Ashram)

Joe Don Looney was a terror off the field as well as on during his pro football days of the sixties. Now he's a docile, disciplined truck driver. John Denver sang of being "Rocky Mountain High" with literal reflection on the drug-induced altitude in his own life. Now he sings of nothing higher than transcendental bliss. Both Joe and John credit their transformation to the pressure of two fingers placed against their closed eyelids. The fingers belong to seventy-one-year-old Swami Muktananda Paramahansa.

Baba ("father") Muktananda, surrounded recently by 2,500 blissed-out showbiz folk who came to do him honor, has come a long way from his home in Mangalore, India. At age fifteen he left his parents to spend more than twenty years seeking spiritual truth. In 1947 he met Guru Bhagwan Sri Nityananda. Nityananda claimed to be a *siddha* yogi, a person whom Hindus believe is a Perfect Master being capable of awakening the latent spiritual power of *Shakti*. (Shakti is the Hindu Supreme Mother goddess lying at the base of the spine.) He told

Muktananda that man has forgotten his divine nature and that awakening Shakti brings forth God-realization. Unlike most gurus who may take years to arouse a student's Shakti power, Nityananda transmitted the experience to Muktananda immediately. He was instantly overwhelmed by rays of light and a hot, burning fever.

This system of enlightenment known as *shaktipat* was passed on to Muktananda. When Nityananda died in 1961, the Shree Gurudev Siddha Yoga *Ashram* was founded. Muktananda came to America on his 1970 world tour and was accompanied by Baba Ram Dass. Today, Muktananda claims over 100,000 U. S. followers who have experienced *shaktipat* at his hands. Three hundred meditation centers carry on the work in the United States (est founder Werner Erhard sponsored one of his American tours). Followers say they have seen visions, heard ethereal sounds, and even, among women, undergone orgasms. All this for only a $100-per-day "intensive meditation" fee. "God is within you," Muktananda declares. "Honor and worship your inner being." The audience is relatively mature, containing a high proportion of professionals. To Westerners geared to instant-everything, his version of God-realization is particularly appealing.

Founder: Swami Muktananda Paramahansa, born 1908, Mangalore, India.

Text: Hindu scriptures.

Symbols: None.

Appeal: Muktananda is less secretive and not as ostentatious as most Eastern gurus. This makes him appear to be more credible. Followers testify of spontaneous, emotionally and physically charged experiences resulting from his initiation ceremonies. They feel this encounter gives meaning to their lives without having to believe or renounce any religious dogmas.

Purpose: With a brush of his peacock feather fan, or the thrust of his fingers into a disciple's eyes (an old Hindu ploy of creating neurological pressure on the retina), Muktananda claims to awaken the elemental energy force of Shakti. Followers are then admonished to direct their devotion and meditation toward Muktananda with unconditional zeal. In exchange, they receive God-realization.

Errors: The entire system of Siddha Yoga is based on the false premise that a human being can be a channel to God-realization. First Timothy 2:5 states, "There is one God, and one mediator between God and men...Christ Jesus." The so-called awakening of the *Kundalini* power of Shakti may be the result of an anticipatory, psychological response. This experience may also be induced by demon activity.

Background Sources: *People,* 5/24/76, p. 83; *Ibid.,* 12/3/79; *Ibid.,* 3/9/81, p. 89; *Time,* 7/26/76, p. 78, 79.

Address/Location: In India, Muktananda's Center is known as the Shree Gurudev Siddha Yoga Ashram. U. S. Centers are known as the Siddha Yoga Dham of America with headquarters in Oakland, CA. His meditation community, formerly in New York's Catskill Mountains, has been moved to a Miami Beach hotel, address not available.

37

Rev. Ike

"The lack of money is the root of all evil." So says black preacher Rev. Frederick Eikerenkoetter, better known as Rev. Ike. This distorted paraphrase of 1 Timothy 6:10 is representative of Ike's Science of Living philosophy, a mixture of black pentecostalism and Christian Scientism, laced with evangelical terminology. "Forget about the pie in the sky," this monetary messiah proclaims, "get yours here and now. You can't lose with the 'stuff' I use."

What is Ike's "stuff?" While some cult leaders obscure their true doctrines with a veneer of orthodox Christian theology, Ike's aberrant beliefs are openly expressed. He sees the Bible as "a book of psychology rather than a book of theology." Satan is "the negative thoughts of lack and limitation" and Deity is "the Presence of God in you." Ike says the purpose of his preaching is to "teach the individual to be master of his own affairs by manipulating his own self-image." Heaven is replaced by "the eternal now" since there are no literal, spiritual realities. Sounding like Mary Baker Eddy, Ike declares, "Everything is a condition of the mind."

The cornerstone of Ike's appeal is rooted in an admittedly materialistic view of success and happiness. He makes no apologies for insisting that those who give generously to finance his own extravagant lifestyle will, in turn, receive similar benefits from the god-who-is-in-them. Ike's audiences at his Joy of Living meetings empty their pocketbooks in the hope of getting rich quick. Ghetto blacks who see little chance of upward economic mobility are easy prey for Ike's promises. As a result, the biblical concept of receiving from God by giving to God is set aside in favor of unadulterated greed. "The Bible says that Jesus rode on a borrowed ass," Ike explains. "But I would rather ride in a Rolls Royce than to ride somebody's ass!"

The fallacy of such unbiblical motives may be easily recognized by the evangelical Christian. But for those who are biblically illiterate Ike has cleverly filled a vacuum that may have been unwittingly left by the Church. Some segments of Christianity have experienced a dearth of strong biblical preaching coupled with an emphasis on the so-called "prosperity-gospel." Consequently, some nominal church members feel justified in seeking financial gain in the name of religion. Marginal Christians infected with this "disease" may be concerned very little that Ike's doctrines are nothing more than a rehashed Science of Mind approach. It might be argued that the appeal of the Rev. Eikerenkoetter would be greatly diminished if Christians sincerely reflected God's concern for the poor and lived like they truly believe that "a man's life consisteth not in the abundance of the things which he possesseth" (Luke 12:15).

Founder: Rev. Frederick Eikerenkoetter, born 1935.

Text: "The lack of money is the root of all evil," a misstatement of 1 Timothy 6:10. Rev. Ike also restates John 3:16 to read, "God so loved all of mankind that he gave every man Divine Sonship. And whoever believes in his Divine Sonship, whoever believes in his relationship to God, shall not perish but shall have everlasting life."

Symbol: None.

Appeal: Ike's goal is self-improvement and financial advancement by visualizing one's self in a positive frame of mind. Since all reality is a mental state, those who may not have natural or educational abilities to improve their socio-economic standing are told that by a developed pattern of giving (to Rev. Ike) they release some inner potential for wealth.

Purpose: Ostensibly, Ike proposes to abolish negative thoughts which induce poverty and replace them with positive mind power which produces unearned wealth. In reality, it is Ike's financial status that is most directly enhanced, as evidenced by his unabashed and ostentatious display of diamonds and sixteen Rolls Royces.

Errors: Orthodox Christian beliefs in self-sacrifice, denial, a personal devil, a transcendent God, the hereafter, and the importance of spiritual values more than material concerns are all negated. These doctrines are replaced by a mind-science approach that emphasizes immediate financial gain over future moral considerations. Ike says, "There is no God outside of you to do a d— thing for you. Your only Savior is your own realization that you are the Christ, the Son of the Living God." His entire system is in contrast to the command of Christ in Matthew 6:33: "Seek ye first the kingdom of God."

Background Sources: Miscellaneous issues of *Action* magazine published by United Christian Evangelistic Association; *People,* 11/1/76, pp. 101-103.

Address: United Christian Evangelistic Association, 910 Commonwealth Ave., Boston, MA 02215.

38

Rev. Sun Myung Moon

(Unification Church)

"The Cross is the symbol of the defeat of Christianity."
This author was stunned at that statement and wondered
if the speaker really meant what he said. Rev. Sun Myung
Moon had harangued the audience through his Korean
interpreter for over two hours. His message was filled
with many theological absurdities, but this last statement
topped them all. "The Cross is the symbol of the defeat of
Christianity," he repeated.

Full page newspaper ads had stirred this writer's
curiosity. "Christianity in Crisis — New Hope for
America," the headlines declared. The year was 1973 and
few people had yet heard of this militant messiah. The
word "Moonie" had not yet entered the average person's
vocabulary. Today, Rev. Moon, "Lord of the Second
Advent" to his disciples, has stirred international
controversy.

Did he actually intend to ridicule the cross of Christ as
representing the hallmark of Christianity's failures? Moon
went on to explain the theology which hatched this

conclusion. Before Adam had a conjugal relationship with Eve, she was sexually seduced by the serpent, none other than the Archangel Lucifer. The evil offspring of this union (Cain) became the seed from which communism sprang. Abel, Adam's child, started the lineage resulting in the spiritual democracies of South Korea and the United States. With the blood line of humanity tainted by Eve's sexual sin, God's original purpose in creating Adam and Eve was thwarted. He had wanted them to procreate a perfect human family; therefore, Christ came to Earth as a man to correct Adam's failure.

Moon says that Jesus of Nazareth was the bastard offspring of Zechariah and Mary. ("Jesus is not God himself," he states.) Since God intended for Christ spiritually and physically to redeem mankind, he needed to marry, father children, and begin rearing the perfect family. But before he could find the Eve he searched for, the Jews killed him. As a result, his death on the cross fulfilled only half of God's plan, the spiritual redemption of man. Since then, God has searched for 2,000 years to find someone who would redeem the human race by becoming the True Parent — the Third Adam, who must have a sinless life and be completely dedicated to God's will. If he qualifies, he will succeed where the First Adam (in Eden) and the Second Adam (Christ) have failed.

Such theological assertions are only a small part of the highly unorthodox world-view held by Rev. Moon. He could easily be ignored as another Oriental fanatic were it not for the fact that over 2 million people worldwide (30,000 or more in the United States) take his doctrinal fantasies as their supreme spiritual authority. As a result, this millionaire industrialist from South Korea has enslaved the minds of thousands of young people, stripped them of their personal belongings, and pressed them into virtual servitude. In doing so, he has amassed a fortune for himself and his church.

Moon's bold denouncement of Christ's crucifixion is only one of his many notable and outlandish statements. He has also been quoted as follows:

"I will conquer and subjugate the world. I am your brain."

"He [God] is living in me. I am the incarnation of himself."

"I want to have members under me who are willing to

obey me even though they may have to disobey their own parents."

"In restoring a man from evil sovereignty, we must cheat."

"Master [Moon] here is more than any of those people (saints and prophets) and greater than Jesus himself."

How did the Rev. Moon develop the egomania which led to such pretentions of self-deification? He was born in 1920 as Yong Myung Moon and was reared in a Presbyterian family. His childhood clairvoyant inclinations climaxed at the age of sixteen when Moon claims he had a vision of Jesus. He claimed that Christ commissioned him to fulfill his interrupted task of physically saving humanity. Moon married his first wife in 1944 and began gathering a following. After meeting Park Moon Kim, a self-proclaimed messiah, Moon changed his name from Yong Myung Moon (Dragon Shining Moon) to Sun Myung Moon (Sun Shining Moon).

The next few years were spent in prison. Moon says he was persecuted for opposing communism, though his contemporary critics claimed that accusations of ritual sex practices were the real reason behind his incarceration. In 1954 his wife divorced him. Shortly after this he officially organized the Unification Church. Three years later he published his spiritual manifesto, *Divine Principle.* Meanwhile he searched for the perfect woman. His marriage to a fourth wife Hak Ja Han (some say he never divorced number two before going on to number three) was proclaimed as the "marriage of the Lamb" prophesied in Revelation 19. Such eccentricities brought charges of moral improprieties and excommunication from the Presbyterian church.

This rebuke certainly didn't affect his business success. His Korean conglomerates of munitions, tea, and titanium accumulated an estimated worth of $20 million. His next target for money and Moonies was the United States, where he headed in 1972. The stage had already been set in 1959 when Young Oon Kim, an associate, brought Moon's message via an English translation of *Divine Principle.* Spiritualistic medium Arthur Ford extolled Moon as the New Age voice of religious thought.

Once he arrived in America, Moon wasted no time in getting on with his job in high style. He purchased a million-dollar headquarters complex and a $625,000 residence in upstate New York. The New Yorker Hotel and Tiffany Building were also added to his real estate portfolio, with rumors of overtures to buy the Empire State Building. A large circulation newspaper called *News World* was launched and nationwide tours heralded his message. Moon defended the beleaguered Richard Nixon and was photographed with Hubert Humphrey and Ted Kennedy. His political aspirations were as exaggerated as his spiritual goals. He wanted nothing less than to organize a religious party and institute a worldwide, theocratic rule.

As Moon and his followers gained the attention of a skeptical press, a national controversy erupted. Parents charged him with brainwashing and hired deprogrammers to rescue their children from his clutches. Questions were raised regarding the legality of immigrant status for his Korean followers. Moonies swarmed Capitol Hill to cajole members of Congress. Meanwhile, other followers invaded shopping centers and airports hawking flowers and candles to the tune of millions of dollars every year.

Not so long ago, all this would have seemed like the plot line from a novel. In this case, fact is indeed stranger than fiction, providing an interesting commentary on the religious climate of America. It can't be denied that Moon's teachings obviously strike a responsive chord with many. Young people disillusioned with the institutional church and yearning for security within an authoritarian structure have been the fuel for his spiritual fuselage. Invited to a weekend retreat of flattery, smiles, and "love bombing," initiates hear nothing of Moon or his claims. It is later that the cult tactics of sensory deprivation, physical exhaustion, and intense indoctrination are used to introduce neophytes to their "True Father and Mother" — Mr. and Mrs. Moon.

Moon's theological scheme is based on a scope of history divided into an Old Testament Age, a New Testament Age, and the present Completed Testament Age. The latter requires a new revelation of truth to supplant the Bible, and Moon's 536-page *Divine Principle* fills the bill. It was dictated, he explains, by God to him through the process of automatic handwriting. Its "truths" were compiled only after Moon had conferred in the spirit world with Buddha, Jesus, and other notable religious figures. All bowed in acquiescence to Moon, imploring him to bring humanity the unuttered revelations supposedly mentioned by Jesus in John 16:13. Moon also reserves the option of continuing to add supernatural revelation or adjusting his "divine principle" at a future date.

Central to his belief system is the concept of a Third Adam, the Messiah and Lord of the Second Advent. Moon declares that this world Savior will "appear in the East," that he will unify all religions, and that his birth date (determined by numerological calculation) was sometime about 1920. More specifically, this messiah must come from an Oriental land populated by Christians. He will be persecuted by the masses who reject him. Like John the Baptist who came as Elijah, this "Lord" will appear in a physical body.

Though Unification Church leaders are careful publicly to avoid naming Moon as this messiah, the deductive conclusions are inescapable. The suffering, torture, and bloodshed he claims to have endured in communist prisons is supposed to be further proof of his redemptive mission. Moon neither confirms nor denies that he is the Promised One but does purport to have personally conquered Satan. The present battle line between good and evil, God and the devil, is the 38th parallel between North and South Korea. Since the Almighty has chosen the United States as the bulwark against Satanic communism, it is Moon's duty to reverse America's moral and spiritual decline.

Moon promises more than a message. It is his duty to take up where Christ left off. The union with his present wife is presumed to result in a new humanity, not polluted by Lucifer's bloodline. Do the failed marriages of Moon disqualify him to be a messiah? "No!" Moonies respond, emphatically. His mission to save humanity is so crucial that more than one perfect woman could have been the "True Mother." God prepared several "Eves" and the first three failed. Hak Ja Han is *the* Mother of mankind who has finally been chosen of God. Sin, in Moon's estimation, is a matter of genetics, not moral choice. And salvation is a matter of being born of his physical bond or entering a marriage union chosen and blessed by him.

Knowledgeable critics charge that when the cult was

small, the doctrine of "blood cleansing" (removing Lucifer's genetic interference) was accomplished by having female Unification members engage in sexual intercourse with Rev. Moon. The dramatic growth of the cult necessitated that this premise be expanded to include purification for any male who has had relations with a woman "cleansed" by Moon. Now, those who totally submit to his authority may consider their devotion to be a spiritual kind of purification not requiring sexual cohabitation.

The absolution Moon offers may require members to turn over all their financial assets to the Unification Church. Any children may be removed from personal parental guidance and placed under the Church's corporate care. Prior marriages have to be ended and resolemnized by Moon. Those who are single must wait until after seven years of service to Moon before he chooses a mate for them. Some do not meet their future marriage partner until the day of the wedding, and are not allowed to consummate the union until forty days thereafter. To conserve Moon's time and energy, mass wedding ceremonies are held where as many as 1,800 are joined in matrimony at one time.

There are many other strange beliefs held by Moon. In some cases, members are encouraged to isolate themselves from all contacts with parents and past associates. Mother and Father Moon are the True Parents (the term "Heavenly Father" is reserved for God) and the only ones worthy of devotion. In exchange for this submission, all the necessities of life are provided. Food, clothing, and accommodations, everything from toothpaste to trousers, are served up communal-style for those members who forsake all to pound the streets selling wares to augment Church income. A minimum quota is suggested (such as $100 or more a day) though some ex-members claim to have brought in as much as $1,600 in one outing. Estimated totals indicate this approach brings in about $1 million every five days. Deliberate misrepresentation ("heavenly deceit") is used when a customer inquires regarding the destination of the proceeds. People are far more inclined to give to a "drug rehabilitation program" or to "feed starving children" than to fill the coffers of a self-anointed

messiah. Members have also been known to solicit from
wheelchairs in order to enhance the sympathy motives of
potential contributors.

Moon's theology is a mixture of Christian concepts and
spiritistic practices. He teaches that heaven is a realm of
the spirit world. Hell is inconsequential because it will
"pass away as heaven expands." One's destination after
death depends on his spirit's "quality of life on earth; by
the degree of goodness we build into them through our
actions." Unlike the Christian promise of immortal
perfection, Moon insists that in the afterlife his followers
will experience the same "desires, dislikes, and
aspirations as before death." Any spot sprinkled with soil
from Korea is considered to be Holy Ground. Evil spirits
may be expelled by a sprinkling of Holy Salt. An
application may be surreptitiously applied from behind
whenever someone considered evil enters one of their
centers.

Sunday mornings are set aside to pay homage to the
True Parents. Rising at 5:00 A.M., the Church Family bows
three times before a picture of Rev. and Mrs. Moon. A
pledge follows in which members vow to do whatever
necessary to bring about Moon's will on earth. At times,
prayer sessions (with petitions directed to Moon himself)
become loud, frenzied affairs. Observers report seeing
some devotees sob and wail, pounding their fists on the
floor in explosive outpourings of grief and exclamations
of victory. Moonies were described by one reporter as
jerking spasmodically "in spiritual transport like
participants in a voodoo ceremony." Such traumas of
self-evaluation are better than receiving a humiliating
tirade from Moon. To those who fail his goals, the True
Father is merciless. He scathingly attacks slothful
members, accusing them of not helping to build the
kingdom of heaven on earth.

From the beginning, occult practices have overshadowed Moon's approach. He admits communicating with familiar spirits by means of seances.
Though the Christian ordinances of baptism and
communion are avoided, the Unification Church accepts
clairvoyance, automatic handwriting, and mediumistic
trances. Moon confidently predicts, "As history
approaches its end point, more and more people will

have spiritual and psychic experiences." He promises followers that those who are completely surrendered to his precepts will witness spirit materialization of their Father (Moon). Certain members claim to have observed this phenomenon while others credit Moon with the ability to read their minds. Some initiates have been lured by dreams in which Moon and his wife have appeared to call them to service in the Church. Ironically, those who consider forsaking Moon's teachings are warned that such actions may result in Satanic possession.

Moon has now fallen out of grace with Seoul's new governmental leaders and favorable mention of him in the press is barred in his homeland. Most Koreans seem genuinely embarrassed by Moon's image. In the United States, public consciousness of his unsavory activities is better known than the tactics of most cults. This has created a plethora of problems. Some of his church-owned buildings in New York have been declared taxable. And the U. S. Immigration and Naturalization Service has recommended Moon's deportation based on the falsified credentials of his wife's application for permanent resident alien status. A federal grand jury in New York handed down a twelve-point indictment charging Moon and an aide with tax evasion. A court found him guilty of conspiracy to avoid taxes on $162,000 in personal income. This unfavorable publicity forces Moon to keep his recruiting tactics at a feverish pace to balance the estimated 50 percent attrition rate of disillusioned followers. But so long as America remains a society of rootless youth, Moon's vision of hope for the future will continue to attract a sizeable following. In fact, Moon's disciples are so confident of the days ahead that Church President Mose Durst now openly declares Moon to be the "second Messiah" succeeding Jesus.

Founder: Rev. Sun Myung Moon, born January 6, 1920, in Kwangju Sangsa Ru, Korea. That portion of Korea is now controlled by communistic North Korea.

Text: *Divine Principle,* by Rev. Moon. Moon's revelations are said to be the "things to come" referred to in John 16:13.

Symbol: A square surrounded by a circle. Four spokes radiate from the outer circle to the center where they meet a smaller darkened sphere inside the square. This inner circle radiates spokes to the edge of the square.

Appeal: Many Moonies are former evangelicals or frequent churchgoers. Their frustrations with hypocrisy and lack of dynamic leadership led them to Moon. In the Unification Church they discover authority, a nonjudgmental, accepting kind of love, and a vision for world unity and peace.

Purpose: Cult literature states, "In the work of restoration [mankind's salvation], God worked to find one individual who could overcome his evil nature, and on the foundation of that person's faith to find a family around him, a society, a nation, and finally to restore the whole world." Christianity holds no hope since God has discarded it as a corrupt and outdated religion. God is pictured as a sad creature, surrounded by evil and estranged from his creation. Moon is the man who will cheer God's heart by accomplishing what Christ failed to do: redeem man physically from the curse of the serpent's sexual seduction of Eve.

Errors: The God depicted in *Divine Principle* is neither omnipotent nor sovereign in earth's affairs. Assigning a female nature to the Holy Spirit and ridiculing Christ's resurrection is blasphemy of the highest order. Moon's doctrine of sinless perfection by "indemnity" (forgiveness of sin by works on Moon's behalf), which can apply even to deceased ancestors, is a denial of the salvation by grace offered through Christ (Gal. 1; Eph. 2: 8, 9). The warning in Matthew 24 regarding false prophets is clearly fulfilled in Moon's doctrines and claims to spiritual authority.

Background Sources: *Divine Principle,* 1973, Sun Myung Moon, The Holy Spirit Association for the Unification of World Christianity, New York; *New Hope,* 1973, Sun Myung Moon, The Holy Spirit Association for the Unification of World Christianity, Washington, DC; "The Unification Church — Who We Are," introductory pamphlet; *Psychology Today,* vol. 2, no. 8, 8/76, pp. 16-21; *Circus,* 4/13/76, pp. 50-53; *Time,* 11/10/75, p. 44; *Ibid.,* 6/14/76, p. 49; *Ibid.,* 7/6/81, p. 37; *Christianity Today,*

3/1/74, p. 101; *Ibid.,* 2/28/75, p. 42; *Ibid.,* 12/19/75, pp. 13-16; *Ibid.,* 3/12/76, p. 45; *Ibid.,* 10/8/76, pp. 59-62; *Ibid.,* 7/20/79, pp. 38-40; *People,* 10/20/75, pp. 7-9; *The Lure of Cults,* 1979, Ronald Enroth, Christian Herald Books, Chappaqua, NY; *Heavenly Deception,* 1980, Chris Elkins, Tyndale House Publishers, Inc., Wheaton, IL; *The Denver Post,* 2/1/74, p. 6FF; *Ibid.,* 12/5/75, p. 5BB; *Ibid.,* 2/18/77, p. 8BB; *Ibid.,* 3/3/78, pp. 4, 5BB; *Ibid.,* 5/8/81, p. 5BB; *Newsweek,* 3/26/75, p. 63; *Ibid.,* 6/14/76, pp. 60-66; *Ibid.,* 5/19/80, p. 27.

Address/Location: The Holy Spirit Association for the Unification of World Christianity.
U. S. Headquarters
1365 Connecticut Ave., N. W.
Washington, DC 20036
International Training Center
723 South Broadway
Tarrytown, NY 10591

39
Sathya Sai Baba

We've all seen the magician who gestures with his hands and out pops a bird. But he generally has on a coat and you wonder just what he had up his sleeve. What would you think of a man with no sleeves who waves his hand and produces a U. S. gold coin (the feat took place in India) minted in the year of your birth? That's just one officially recorded "miracle" of Sathya Sai Baba, perhaps the most phenomenal guru of this century. Since his own sympathetic biographers provide the major source of information regarding Sai Baba, much of this chapter is based on their account. Consequently, what is known about his background is undocumented, leaving some of his claims open to the possibility they are based more on legend than fact.

The forerunner of Sathya Sai Baba, Sai Baba of Shirdi, was born in the middle 1880s in Hyderbad State, India. Before his death in 1918, he had convinced area devotees and skeptics alike that he was an incarnation of God, an *avatar.* Legends declare that he cured leprosy, cast out spirits, appeared in animal as well as human forms, and was especially fond of holy ash, which he produced out of thin air by a gesture of his hand. The ash, called *udhi,*

was used for curing ailments and miraculous purposes.
When he died, mourners wondered whose body would
be the recipient of his next incarnation. Though countless
Indian gurus lay claim to the office of an avatar, Hindu
theology clearly states that only one incarnation of God
may exist at one time.

Entering on the stage of potential avatars, Sathya Sai
Baba was born in 1926 in Prasanti Nilayam, India. Even
before his birth as Satyanarayana Raju (his given name),
strange things happened in his home. Musical
instruments would twang unaided in the night and
unseen hands would pound rhythms on a *maddala*
(drum). On a certain occasion after his birth, he was laid
on top of some bedclothes on the floor. His parents
noticed movement in the cloth and looked to see a cobra
entwined about the baby's body. Incredibly, no harm
came to the child. (Later, devotees took this to mean that
his incarnation also included the role of Sheshiara, Lord of
Serpents.)

As a youngster, Satyanarayana would produce candy
and fruit for his friends — out of an empty bag. When
asked how these and other paranormal feats were
performed, he explained that an invisible helper named
Grama Sakti obeyed his will to give him whatever he
wanted. At age thirteen he suffered a scorpion bite
(though no one could find the culprit) and lapsed into a
coma. Shortly after this he exhibited different
personalities and various voices spoke from his body.
Some of these entities quoted lengthy portions of Hindu
scriptures the boy had never learned. His parents
consulted a witch doctor who failed in an attempt to
exorcise any evil spirits from the lad. Two months and
fifteen days after the bite he suddenly started producing
objects out of the air with a mere flick of his hands. "I am
Sai Baba," he declared. No one knew who he was talking
about.

Eventually, people in the village of Prasanti Nilayam
learned of Sai Baba of Shirdi and became convinced that
Satyanarayana Ruja was an incarnation of the late Hindu
saint. From then on, Satyanarayana became known as
Sathya Sai Baba. (*Sa* means "Divine," *ai* means "mother"
and *Baba* means "father" — "the Divine Mother/Father.")
Tales of Sai Baba's miracles began to abound. To convince
men of his reincarnation as Sai Baba of Shirdi, he related

conversations that were known only to the departed guru's disciples. He also supernaturally produced articles of devotion that had been placed at the shrine of the Shirdi tomb many miles away.

Whether or not any or all of the supposed miracles attributed to Sai Baba are true is open to question. Such claims either represent exaggerated legends or phenomenal psychic feats. Consider these examples of Sai Baba's powers: Flower petals thrown on the floor fall in the pattern of his name. Pendants, chains, rings, necklaces, and photographs can be plucked from the air by his bare hands and are then dispensed as gifts to devotees. Disciples may name a fruit and it instantly appears on a tree. Food supply is multiplied. A blinding jet of light streams from his forehead. Cancer is cured. *Devas* (Hindi for "angels") hand him a carved glass bowl that materializes out of nothing. Idol statuettes suddenly appear. Psychic surgery is performed. Rocks turn into candy. A flower bud is transformed into a diamond. Demons are driven out. And a man is raised from the "dead," in a fashion that bears striking similarity to Christ's miracle in Luke 8.

His favorite "miracle" is to produce sacred ash from his waving hand. The ash (vibhuti, he calls it) is said to represent the regenerative aspect of the Hindu god Shiva. When given to devotees it becomes a curative powder for all sorts of ailments. At Shiva's annual festival, Baba always performs two miracles. One is the creation of a mound of ash from a small urn. The other is more repulsive to the Western mind.

Hindus sometimes worship Shiva in the form of a *lingam.* Though intellectual Hindus have elaborate explanations about the philosophy of *lingams,* these objects actually represent fertility symbols. The most common form is that of an elongated oval, effecting the shape of a male phallus. During the annual Shiva observance, Sai Baba may speak for an hour or more, and then writhes and twists in apparent pain. His temperature rises to 104 degrees. Suddenly, he ejects an object from his mouth — a five-inch by three-inch solid *lingam!* He has been known to spit out as many as nine *lingams* on one occasion.

What is the purpose of such paranormal phenomena? A chronicler of Sai Baba's life put it this way: "The miracles of Christ must be taken on faith; those of Sai Baba you can see for yourself." In other words, Sai Baba's miracles are the pudding-proof of the "truths" he teaches. As one writer explained, "They [Baba's miracles] build our faith...toward the production of a divine edition of ourselves."

Sai Baba's theology is classical Hinduism. Man is essentially *atma* (soul/spirit), an entity which is formless. It is manifested in five sheaths (spiritual essences) of man, who is divine but has forgotten his god-nature. "Man is not born in sin," Baba declares. Eternal bliss is only possible by conquering earthly desires to reveal the spark of divinity. "If you realize the atma-principle, you become God himself," according to Baba. There are three ways to attain this: karma (action), *jnana* (knowledge) and *bhakti* (devotion to a guru). The latter is Sai Baba's preference. In his perception, The *Sadguru* (God-realized guru) *is* God to the disciple. Only by putting himself completely in the hands of Baba may the devotee be guided to the knowledge of God-love. But who guides the hands of Sai Baba?

As he stands before his disciples, red silk robe flowing and afro crinkled like a circular mop, he evokes tears and sighs of awe. The contrast between Jesus and Sai Baba is apparent. Though the latter lays claim to being Christ, the avatar for our age, the proofs of divinity both offer are distinctly dichotomous. Sai Baba's feats may not need an element of faith. But a man who claims to be God and then regurgitates replicas of sex organs brings into question the motive of his miracles. Charlatan or psychic, Sai Baba will need more than holy ash to cure what ails him.

Founder: Sathya Sai Baba, born 1926 as Satyanarayana Raju in Pratsanti Nilayam, India.

Text: Hindu scriptures.

Symbols: None known.

Appeal: Unlike most Indian gurus who claim to have achieved God-realization, Sai Baba produces apparent miracles as a proof of his avataristic claims. His powers are seemingly greater than those of other *siddhis* and he performs his feats more frequently. Those who do not believe in the devil or are unaware of the extent to which his powers may be manifested, will be impressed by Sai Baba. They must decide if the source of his phenomena is Satanic, psychic, divine, or merely trickery.

Purpose: Baba's miracles are intended to validate his claims of divinity and cause devotees to submit to his wishes and teachings. By thus concentrating on their guru (Baba) who is the form of God, disciples are said to become more placid and thus realize their own oneness with the Supreme. Baba teaches that scriptures are partially effective spiritual guide books, but devotion to the *Sadguru* is the easiest and quickest way to the knowledge of God.

Errors: Sai Baba's miracles, though impressive, are limited in scope and degree. When confronted with this inconsistency of his presumed omnipotent nature, he argues that man has accumulated too much *karmic* sin to heal all those who seek relief. When Christ's resurrection and power over death is compared to his own eventual demise, Baba insists he has conquered death, too. By this he means that he has the power to choose his time and manner of death as well as his next incarnation. The fallacy of these rationales is self-evident.

Background Sources: Miscellaneous materials published by Sai Baba Center and Book Store, including "Who Is Sai Baba?", "Sathya Sai Baba Speaks"; *Baba,* 1975, Arnold Schulman, Pocket Books; *Sai Baba, Man of Miracles,* 1971, MacMillan Company of India.

Address/Location: India: Prasanti Nilayam (Home of the Supreme), Anantapur District, Andhra Pradesh; "Brindavan," Kadugodi, Near Whitefield, Bangalore, Karnataka State. U.S.: Tacete, CA, and Sathya Sai Baba Center and Book Store, 7911 Willoughby Ave., Los Angeles, CA 90046.

40

Sri Chinmoy

He now prefers to be called *Devadip,* a Hindu word
meaning "the lamp of the light of the Supreme." Rock
fans know him better as Carlos Santana, lead guitarist and
guiding force of the rock group Santana. The name
Devadip was given to him by his guru, Sri Chinmoy, the
son of a West Bengal, India, railroad inspector.

Carlos is joined in his devotion by another famed guitar
player, John McLaughlin. McLaughlin calls Chinmoy
"Perfection. . . a Divine Being." McLaughlin begins his
concerts with meditation and proceeds to sing
metaphysical lyrics that sometimes praise Chinmoy with
unabashed devotion. Though Chinmoy's actual following
consists of less than a thousand fully committed disciples,
his influence is far-ranging. He has talked with the Pope
and lectured at Yale. In a stroke of "enlightened" genius,
Chinmoy has established a headquarters at the United
Nations where he supervises the bimonthly U. N.
meditation program.

The Hindu doctrine of yoga is at the heart of Chinmoy's
system of salvation. Students go through a process which
may include *Hatha Yoga,* vegetarianism, and meditation.
Chinmoy's way to God is by devotion and surrender to
one's guru. Though such a mentor may not be absolutely

essential, Chinmoy tells followers that having such a private tutor is certainly the quickest way to achieve the enlightenment he has known since age twelve.

It is crucial that a guru take his disciple through *Siksha,* the yielding of one's life to this teacher. Chinmoy's ritual of *Siksha* begins with a trance state during which his eyes roll back into their sockets leaving only the whites visible. This state of meditative bliss (known in Hinduism as *samadhi*) has a powerful effect on the disciple who kneels before Chinmoy. Finally, the devotee receives a portion of Chinmoy's soul, in exchange for unswerving service from that day forth. Those who have undergone Siksha claim the experience is so overwhelming they never again doubt Chinmoy's authenticity as a spiritual leader.

Unlike some Indian gurus whose personal charisma outshines their intellectual capacity, Chinmoy apparently has prolific creative talents. He claims to have completed over 16,000 paintings in a single day, though such a pace would mean an incredible two per second! A more believable output was his record of 843 poems during a twenty-four hour period. He has published dozens of books and pamphlets as well as two periodicals, *Chinmoy Family* and *Aum.*

Unlike so many other gurus, Chinmoy does not promise instantaneous enlightenment. Potential followers are warned that they may spend a dozen or more years before they experience their oneness with the Supreme (Chinmoy's designation of God). His mission to America since 1964 is the result of a deliberate attempt to blend the East and West. "There are two aspects of God," he declares. "One is realization and the other is manifestation." To him, Eastern disciplines bring the realization of God while the Supreme's manifestation is seen in Western approaches to spirituality.

Founder: Sri Chinmoy, born 1931, East Bengal, India. Came to the United States in 1964.

Symbols: None known.

Text: Hindu Scriptures.

Appeal: Since Chinmoy's personal lifestyle is less extravagant than the demeanor of most imported gurus, his following (though small) is more fervent. This laid-back image gives him the appearance of being more genuine.

Purpose: The guru-student relationship is central to his teachings. Total submission to one's guru facilitates the process of God-realization. His spiritual path is more in line with traditional Hinduism than some other yoga masters, lending emphasis to his selective approach of quality over quantity of disciples.

Errors: Jesus plainly stated that he was the only way to God (John 14:6), and this access is through his redemptive death. Chinmoy seeks to replace the mediatory status of Christ by putting a human channel (himself) between God and man. Chinmoy's doctrine of submission to a guru is the same lie of self-deification the serpent in Eden expounded.

Background Sources: *The Denver Post,* 5/6/77, p. 3BB; *People,* 12/12/76, p. 50; *The Encyclopedia of American Religions Vol. 2,* 1978, J. Gordon Melton, McGrath Publishing, New York, p. 376.

Address/Location: Centers in the U. S., Canada, Europe, and Australia.

OCCULT/MYSTICAL CULTS

41

Association for Research and Enlightenment
(Edgar Cayce)

"All healing comes from God," declared the prim, pleasant-looking lady, lecturing to a group of curious tourists. The statement seemed suspect in view of her earlier complimentary remarks about American psychic Edgar Cayce. She had already pointed out that in Cayce's theology "sin is separation from that which is correct, such as wrong diet or negative thoughts." For an example, she explained that Cayce once declared constipation to be a "sin" since it disrupted the body's normal functions. With that in mind, this author wasn't going to let her comment on healing go unchallenged. After all, this was the headquarters building of the Edgar Cayce organization, and she was their official representative to address visitors. If anyone was authorized to speak on behalf of Cayce's beliefs, she certainly ought to be the one.

"Who is God?" was the question it seemed logical to pose.

"God is whatever you perceive him to be," was the
reply. "The One Source, the Creator, the First Cause, That
from which all emanates. . . . "

Such ambiguity certainly contrasted with the personal
deity revealed in the Holy Scriptures. Perhaps that should
have come as no surprise. Cayce, the "sleeping
prophet," who as a child aspired to be a missionary and
claimed to have read the Bible completely through for
each year of his life, eventually departed from orthodoxy.
His theology mixed metaphysics with mysticism, flavored
by strong doses of reincarnation.

Cayce's life was replete with strange phenomena. As a
baby, he cried for the entire first month until an old black
woman suggested pricking the nipples of his breasts with
a pin. When it was done, milk came out. From that point
on, young Edgar rarely ever cried. Later in life he
recalled that during childhood he was constantly
surrounded by what he called "play folk." They
disappeared when others were around, although his
mother saw them occasionally. As Edgar grew older and
increased in size, these "play folk" also seemed to
increase in stature. One day they simply failed to show
up, and that was the end of their communication with
Cayce.

A turning point in his life occurred at age thirteen. The
presence of a woman appeared and offered to grant him
any request. Edgar responded that he wanted to help
others when they were sick. No sooner had his petition
been stated, than the apparition vanished.

He was not the first in his family to exhibit psychic
tendencies. His father had a strange power over snakes,
and his grandfather had a widespread reputation as a
water witcher. The elder Cayce could also make tables
move and brooms dance. But Edgar's supernatural
powers were even more strange. For one thing, he
discovered at an early age that he could sleep with a
book under his pillow and awake the next morning with
its entire contents indelibly fixed in his mind.

When D. L. Moody was passing through town, Edgar
shared with the famous evangelist his story of visions and
voices. Moody warned him that possession by an evil
spirit could create such things. According to Cayce's
official biography, *There Is a River,* the evangelist also left

open the possibility that Edgar might be a prophet as described in Numbers 12:6.

Edgar Cayce's psychic meanderings came to a crossroads at the age of twenty-four when he lost his voice. Doctors failed to offer a cure, so hypnotists were consulted. After being subjected to a deep trance state, Cayce's voice returned, and his throat was instantly healed.

Shortly after this, Cayce's technique of hypnotic self-cure was expanded to diagnose the ills of others. A. C. Layne, the hypnotist who had facilitated Cayce's voice restoration, suggested that Edgar self-induce a sleep/trance condition and attempt to see what was wrong in another person's body. Cayce did just that and described in detail Layne's physical condition. Physiological, biological, and pharmacalogical terms were uttered from Cayce's mouth although he had only a grammar school education. Even Cayce admitted the voice was not his own.

Layne enlisted Cayce as an assistant to his lucrative practice of suggestive therapeutics and osteopathy. It was Layne who told Cayce he had a clairvoyant gift and called his diagnoses "readings." Cayce started out with altruistic motives and refused to accept any money for his cures. As his fame spread he became convinced that all this success was the fulfillment of the request granted him by the woman who had appeared to him many years before.

Cayce continued teaching Sunday school and rationalizing his psychic experimentation by claiming it was a God-given calling. He remained reasonably orthodox in his doctrines until 1923. That's when he met Arthur Lammers, a student of Theosophy and occultism. Lammers encouraged Cayce to go beyond his physical readings of ills to cultivate the practice of life readings. These revelations contained analyses of spiritual and philosophical matters. From then on, Cayce departed sharply from biblical truth.

During his lifetime, Edgar Cayce gave in excess of 16,000 readings. Of that total, 14,246 were stenograph-ically recorded and are indexed and filed in the locked, fireproof vaults of the headquarters building of the Association for Research & Enlightenment (A.R.E.). The A.R.E. was founded in 1932 to research and preserve his readings. Virginia Beach, Virginia, was chosen as a location because Cayce had prophesied it would be a haven safe from future cataclysms (earthquakes, floods, etc.) that would befall America. The A.R.E. is now under the leadership of Cayce's son, Hugh Lynn Cayce.

The physical readings of Cayce were the main source of his attraction. Over a period of forty-three years, he gave 8,985 readings proposing cures for the body and mind. In his state of altered consciousness, he expounded on diet, eating habits, and diagnoses for patients who sometimes were miles away. His home-spun remedies often had remarkable curative effects. Some of his prescriptive suggestions were a little farfetched. He told cancer victims they need never worry if they ate three almonds a day. (A.R.E. literature points out that almonds contain laetrile, the discredited cancer-cure.) Patients who smoked moderately (six to eight cigarettes a day) were informed that their habit was harmless, a position not supported by modern research. He also counseled that moderate use of liquor was no hindrance to spiritual growth.

Some of Cayce's physical readings were undoubtedly beneficial for their practical, medicinal effect. Natural remedies for natural maladies should not be seen as being indicative of miraculous cures. And the success of such therapy should not be a validation for the source of its information. The authenticity of the elocutions from Cayce's vocal chords rests on whether their comments on scriptural matters are biblically sound. It's faulty logic to suggest that religious pronouncements can be trusted if the same voice uttering them is also correct when analyzing ills. Psychic success is not a sufficient gauge for spiritual validity.

To trust Edgar Cayce because he was a sincere, devout man who read the Word and taught Sunday school is dangerous reasoning. His charitable platitudes can't be used to judge the veracity of his readings, even when some of them seem to square with the Bible. Ardent altruism is no substitute for total harmony with the revelational truth of Scripture. It is by this calibration that Cayce's lofty sentiments fall far short of biblical standards.

Much of what Cayce taught is extrabiblical. When questioned as to why he placed so much emphasis on the

Essenes (a monastic sect not mentioned in Scripture), he replied, "We have received it [this information] psychically." Psychic revelation was also the source of information for his contention that Jesus was initiated into secret societies in India and Egypt. Cayce also rambled on about souls descending from apes and expounded theories concerning advanced civilizations in the lost lands of Atlantis and Lemuria. He encouraged nearly every form of occultism from astrology to auras, from astral-projection to ancient Egyptian mysteries.

But reincarnation is the cornerstone of his belief system. Cayce admitted that reincarnation is not taught in the Bible but blamed the omission on third-century translators whom he claimed deliberately excised it from canon. Reincarnation is even used to justify sexual perversion. In the official A.R.E. publications, *Many Mansions,* a homosexual's conduct is excused as resulting from a psychological imprint from a former incarnation.

According to Cayce, God created all souls in the beginning, and they enter the material, earthly plane by choice to work out their faults and thus achieve atonement with God. Jesus Christ of Nazareth was appearing in his thirtieth incarnation, having been on earth before as Adam, Enoch, and Melchizedek among others. In Cayce's view, Christ has now worked out his karmic debt and become a Christ-soul. Cayce referred to Jesus as the "Master," and "our Elder Brother." The latter term probably came from the influence of a Mormon lady who lived in the Cayce home during Edgar's childhood. She claimed to have been a wife of Brigham Young.

A.R.E. literature calls Cayce's readings the "most impressive record of psychic perceptions ever to emanate from a single individual." That may be true, but even his proponents admit his prophecies have proved to be only 90 percent accurate. Critics place his rate of accuracy even lower. He failed by underestimating Hitler's inclination for evil, and struck out again by declaring that New York would be dumped into the sea in the seventies. People are still looking for the elusive Atlantis he prophesied would arise in the twentieth century.

How much of Cayce's readings came from his

subconscious mind which was influenced by outside sources cannot be determined. Those familiar with demonic phenomena find in Cayce's readings a curious consistency with the kind of utterances associated with spiritism. One thing is certain. Though the extrabiblical aspect of Cayce's interests cannot objectively be evaluated, his claim to be a prophet is clearly without a scriptural base. One hundred percent accuracy (Deut. 18:20–22) is the requirement for those who speak on behalf of God, whether awake or asleep.

Founder: Edgar Cayce, born March 18, 1877, on a farm near Hopkinsville, Kentucky. Died January 3, 1945, in Virginia Beach, Virginia.

Text: Numbers 12:6 — "If there be a prophet among you, I the Lord will make myself known unto him in a vision, and will speak unto him in a dream."

Symbol: Dove and cross or letters A.R.E.

Appeal: Those suffering painful and incurable illnesses may turn to Cayce's physical readings when medical science cannot help. If their suffering is alleviated, they consider his life readings a source of truth explaining the nature of their cure.

Purpose: The A.R.E. exists to index and catalog Cayce's readings for those seeking help for physical maladies. Inquirers may be referred to one of 400 physicians who are A.R.E. members and utilize Cayce's approach to health. Publications and lectures disseminate further information regarding Cayce's life readings on religion. The headquarters building houses a large occult/metaphysical library for research.

Errors: Cayce's undocumented revelations of historical events, erroneous prophecies of geologic alterations, and unsubstantiated tales of lost empires, should cause serious students of history and the Bible to question his credibility. If Jesus was once incarnated as Adam, then he is not a sinless Redeemer. Cayce's solution for sin is not forgiveness in this life but the promise of many future lives to make ourselves acceptable to God.

Background Sources: Various A.R.E.-approved publications, including *Many Mansions, There Is a River, The Edgar Cayce Reader, The Sleeping Prophet,* A.R.E. membership solicitation letter.

Address/Location: Association for Research and Enlightenment Inc., Box 595, Atlantic Ave. at 68th St., Virginia Beach, VA 23451.

42

Astara

"It is possible that I may have erred in receiving them [messages from the teachers of the spirit world]. Therefore if errors are brought forth in the lessons, it is I who am to blame. I alone must be held fully responsible," says Earlyne Chaney, as quoted in "Astara's Book of Life," First Degree Lesson 1.

Mrs. Chaney's admission of fallibility is rare among spiritualists. But lest anyone should think she approaches the teachings of Astara with ambivalence, she confidently declares (in the same booklet from which the above quote was taken): "It [Astara] guides the disciple toward the inner mysteries of life, death, God, man — and the ultimate initiation: immortality." Critics of Astara may wonder if the journey into such knowledge is really advisable. After all, it is hardly credible to claim supernatural spiritual inspiration while at the same time acknowledging that such inspiration may contain error.

Astara means "a place of light" and is taken from the name of the Greek goddess of divine justice, Astraea. The teachings form an eclectic cult that encompasses spiritualism, Theosophy, yoga, Christianity, mystery schools, Rosicrucianism, and various occult orders and disciplines. For those who ask, "Why then follow Astara?" Mrs. Chaney answers, "Astara has come forth as

a Light Bearer in the latter part of this century."
(Evangelical Bible students will find that comment
noteworthy since "light bearer" is the meaning of the
name Lucifer, the devil.)

Astara certainly promises a lot. Among its claims are
soul progression, the solving of life's enigmas, the
developing of "inner faculties," the healing of illnesses,
spiritual brotherhood, expansion of consciousness,
self-unfoldment, and God-realization. Membership in
Astara is said to be like a "Cosmic Bank Account where
you earn interest in peace of mind and enlightenment."
Members are told that when death comes they will "fade
from consciousness and go to the Valley of Rewards"
where they will "find again all they have deposited in the
Cosmic Bank."

When she was twenty-eight years of age, Earlyne
Chaney's world was shattered by the death of her fiancé.
The event had been prophesied by a spirit-being named
Kut-Hu-Mi, with whom she had communicated
clairvoyantly since she was a child. (Kut-Hu-Mi had taught
her to develop psychic powers, including a methodology
called *The Great Work of the Penetralia* which contains a
secret yoga system called *Lhama Yoga.*) Two years after
this tragedy she met and married Robert Chaney, a
spiritualist who had his own spirit guide named Ram.
Earlyne then left the acting profession, and in 1951 she
and Robert moved to California where they formed the
Astara Foundation.

Though regular services are held at the organization's
headquarters in Upland, California, most of the teaching
is carried on through correspondence courses. Astarians
are led through four degrees containing at least twenty
lessons each. The first few instructions explore
elementary occult/mystical practices. As the studies
progress, the initiate is gradually introduced to Secret
Documents revealing the Astarian sign, word, and hand
grip. It is then that the techniques of Lhama Yoga are
taught. Almost every kind of psychic phenomena is
pursued, with the exception of Ouija boards and
automatic handwriting. Chaney acknowledges the
demonic nature of such practices by warning members
against the "disastrous consequences of those who
indulge in them."

Healing plays a central role in Astarian philosophy. The *Voice of Astara,* the Foundation's monthly publication, abounds with testimonies from those who have experienced supposedly miraculous cures. Members are encouraged to send their healing petitions to the headquarter's shrine where a group of four Astarians, known as the Circle of the Secret Seven, will intercede on their behalf. Neophyte Astarians are told that these individuals are "dedicated ones who touch and influence the cosmic powers of etheric realms for cosmic assistance."

The Chaneys draw from Masonic, Rosicrucian, and Theosophic beliefs. But their central doctrines are rooted in the teachings of Hermes Trismegistus, the ancient Egyptian magician who is believed to be the organizer of the original Mystery School from which all others have derived. Another Egyptian named *Zoser* is the Chaneys' current spirit guide. His god-name is *Neterkeht,* which literally means "God in flesh," and Astarians are told to call on his name if in need of healing. Members have been known to see materializations of Zoser, whom it is said gives of his efforts exclusively to Astara.

Despite these pagan overtones, Astara still endeavors to hide itself behind a veneer of Christian beliefs. While accepting the tradition of *avatars,* including Buddha, Astarians insist that God was most completely revealed in Christ, whom the Chaneys profess to revere as "the Light of the World." This "Cosmic Christ" is said to be "the Lord of our planet, begotten before the beginning of our time and age." The Astarian denial of Christ as Creator/God, eternal and the Only Begotten of the Father, is consistent with the minor role he actually plays in Astara. Issues of the *Voice* abound with messages from Kut-Hu-Mi, but few biblical references are cited. The lessons do quote certain scriptural passages, but only out of context to support occult principles.

The whole system of Astara is highly complex and includes phenomena such as Arcane Biorhythms, *prana* breath techniques, ethereal bodies, astral projection, polarity, and laws of vibrations and correspondence. The secret word, sign, and hand grip are apparently taught during trance states. Members are told that the "Divine Hierarchy of Great Beings who once brought wisdom and knowledge to man" have come again from the "Universal Brotherhood" to reveal life's mysteries through Astara. Considering the possibility that these Great Beings may be familiar spirits, there is little comfort in Earlyne Chaney's admonition that "the presence of Astarian Masters overshadows your life."

Founders: Robert and Earlyne Chaney.

Text: Genesis 1:1-3 is paraphrased without any indication that the Chaneys' version is extrabiblical: "And God said, 'Let there be Light in the minds of men.' And God created channels through which the Light might come. And one of them was Astara. And God looked upon Astara and He saw that it was good."

Symbol: Seven-pointed "star of the West," merging inside with the "Lotus of the East."

Appeal: Those with an interest in occult and psychic phenomena find what appears to be an historical basis for discovering hidden truths. Its secret ceremonies and promises of miraculous healing are also an attraction.

Purpose: To blend Eastern religious philosophy and ancient mystery schools (especially Egyptian) with Christianity.

Errors: Astarians decree verbally, "I am perfect," denying man's sinful nature. Without historical evidence, Astara claims Christ traveled to Egypt, Tibet, and India and there was initiated by mystery schools. The Bible is said to have hidden truth which requires special interpretation to be "rightly understood." The exclusive nature of Christ's salvation is denied by Astara's teaching that there are many paths to the Infinite Being. The founders of Christianity are said to have "brought forth the doctrine of the resurrection of the physical body at Judgment Day. A blind, believing humanity accepted the doctrine, and some still do." The Bible warning against familiar spirits (Isa. 8:19, 20) is ignored, and spirit guides (demons) are revered and elevated above Christ.

Backgound Sources: Miscellaneous Astara literature: "Astara's Book of Life," "You and Astara," *Voice of Astara* (various issues); *The Encyclopedia of American Religions,* 1978, J. Gordon Melton, pp. 183, 184.

Address/Location: 261 So. Mariposa Ave., Los Angeles, CA 90004.

43

Astrology

It's there in your newspaper every day. You don't really believe in it, but the horoscope is fun to read. Most of the time it's just good for a laugh. You don't take it seriously like some people. What harm is there in just casually checking to see what's in store for your sign of the zodiac? Sure it's an occult practice, but you don't look at it that way. On the other hand, there was that one day the prediction for your sign did come true. You wonder if....

Astrology, along with palmistry, witchcraft, numerology, and other forms of occultism, has always interested a few, but today a fad has turned into a phenomenon. George Gallup says that 32 million (one in five adult Americans) believe in astrology, and that eight of ten can name the sign under which they were born. Right now there are three times as many astrologers as there are clergymen in the Roman Catholic church. Nearly 2,000 newspapers carry a daily horoscope.

Recently, 186 distinguished scientists issued a no-nonsense statement savagely attacking astrology. Their declaration pointed out, "The time has come to challenge directly and forcefully the pretentious claims of astrological charlatans. It's simply a mistake to imagine that the forces exerted by stars and planets at the moment of birth can in any way shape our future." In spite of such a scathing condemnation, belief in the effect celestial bodies can exert over human affairs continues unabated.

Does astrology work? Is it a harmless pastime? Is there anything wrong with casually consulting one's daily horoscope? What does the Bible say about astrology?

Fifty centuries ago the Chaldeans of the Babylonian empire observed the influence of the sun upon the Earth and the moon upon the seas. They concluded that the planets were gods and, therefore, certain conjunctions of their movements would have an effect upon wars, governments, and the destinies of men. There were other methods of fortune-telling, such as surveying the entrails of animals, but these often proved unpredictable. The positions of the stars were dependable.

The ancients, as well as current astrologers, computed their predictions with a geocentric view of the universe. Imagine a spoked wheel. The center where the spokes meet indicates the location of the Earth and the outer rim signifies the path the sun takes through the heavens each day as it revolves about the Earth. According to the astrologers, the area indicated by the outer rim is about sixteen degrees wide and represents the zones of the zodiac. What concerns zodiac consultants are the star constellations that appear within the pathway of the sun as it travels through the heavens. This band is divided into twelve equal sections representing the twelve divisions, or "houses," of the astrological zodiac.

During the course of a year, the twelve constellations, or signs of the zodiac, move through each of the twelve houses. In addition, each of the nine planets as well as the moon and sun move through each house every twenty-four hours. There are many other constellations besides these twelve, and just why the ancients did not take them into account isn't certain. It may be that they reasoned the sun's rays would have to shine through the constellations to affect the people on the Earth below, keeping in mind that the Earth is at the center of the model of the universe we're referring to.

To determine one's horoscope, the exact geographical spot of birth is coordinated with the date and hour of delivery. The conjunctions and relative positions of all heavenly bodies are considered by the angles they form with relationship to each other. From this information the horoscope is eventually computed.

As reasonable as this simplified illustration sounds, it is based on a faulty premise. Astrology originated in the pre-Copernican age when the Earth was thought to be the center of the universe. Now, scientists assure us that the sun does not circle the Earth but vice versa. Because astrology is based upon an erroneous, geocentric concept (the sun circling the Earth), its suppositions and conclusions have no scientific basis.

Astrology also has other factual discrepancies. The Earth has an uneven wobble as it spins on its axis. As a result, there has been a shift in the zodiac. Today, the sun's rays actually enter each of the constellations about one month earlier than they did centuries ago when the present astrological charts were finalized. This means that current horoscope readings are inaccurate by a factor of thirty days. Even if the predictions of astrology were true, the characteristics of each sign would not apply to the months they have been assigned.

A new book by an astrologer entitled *Astrology Fourteen* asserts that there are actually fourteen constellations in the zodiac. If the predictions of astrology were to be scientifically correct, these two extra constellations would have to be included when casting a horoscope. And what about the billions of other celestial bodies outside our own galaxy? Why aren't their influences considered? The answer is that the heavens were not fully explored when the practice of astrology was developed.

Some people are born without a horoscope. What about those who live north of the Arctic Circle? No planet assigned to the zodiac is visible there for several weeks out of the year. Does this mean that Eskimos and some Norwegians have no celestial influences upon their lives and no astral destinies to guide their behavior?

Astrology is a universal practice in pagan religions. But no two false religions agree on the same attributes for each sign. If you were to have your horoscope computed by a Hindu in India, it would read much differently from that of a Buddhist in Bangkok. The arbitrary character-istics assigned to constellations seem inconsistent. One horoscope may say Aquarians are practical and patient while another designates them as restless and skillful. The only constancy appears to be a suitable ambiguity designed to apply to almost any personality.

The predictions of horoscopes are not only capricious, but these prophecies are also prone to have a high degree of error. If most astrologers had their forecasts periodically reviewed for accuracy, their reputations would fade quickly. Carroll Righter, whose syndicated column is read by millions, once predicted that Spain's Franco would remain healthy (he died) and that J. Edgar Hoover would have an improved physical condition (he, too, expired less than five months later). Jeanne Dixon, who credits the Almighty with her foreknowledge, once declared that Jackie Kennedy would not remarry. Apparently her zodiac charts never bothered to consult a Greek ship owner by the name of Aristotle Onassis. Those who say their astrological talent is a "gift from God" need to be reminded that the Lord's qualifications for a prophet leave no room for error (Deut. 18:22).

Astrologers depend heavily upon the accuracy of determining the exact moment of birth in relationship to the position of heavenly bodies. But who determines when a child is born? Mother Nature? More often the doctor decides the hour of birth for the convenience of his schedule as well as the mother's welfare. Would it then be possible for a physician to thwart one's astrological destiny by using drugs to manipulate the moment when the baby emerges? Also, since life begins at conception, wouldn't that moment more accurately reflect the choice of one's astrological sign?

Astronomers, those who engage in the true science of stargazing, completely reject astrology, relegating it to the ranks of superstition. Yet there are millions of people who waste multiplied hours and countless dollars studying the signs of the zodiac. In the end, they usually learn nothing about themselves except what they read into their horoscopes (which generally is of a complimentary nature).

The first Bible reference to astrology is in Genesis 11. Here we find the story of the building of the tower of Babel. Archaeologists have now discovered that this structure and similar towers were actually *ziggurats* which the early Chaldeans erected to survey the heavens. Some ziggurats have been unearthed to give evidence of zodiac signs actually inscribed on the circumference at the top. The Bible says the purpose of the tower of Babel was to "reach unto heaven." This

biblical metaphor could more accurately be paraphrased, "a tower whose top may be used to reach out
unto the heavens." The Chaldeans were not simple and
ignorant but a highly advanced civilization. They had
sense enough to know it was not literally possible to build
a tower which would actually extend that far into the
atmosphere. There is little doubt its real purpose was to
survey the stars for astrological purposes. Because these
men sought to discover their destiny in the stars rather
than communicate with God, judgment was brought upon
them.

The Bible explicitly denounces astrology in many other
passages. In Jeremiah 10:2 we read, "Learn not the way of
the heathen, and be not dismayed at the signs of heaven;
for the heathen are dismayed at them." The prophet goes
on to equate astrology with idolatry and describes the
vain way in which the heathen seek to please and follow
their astrological gods.

The clearest command against astrology is found in
Deuteronomy 18, beginning with verse nine. As the
children of Israel were about to enter the Promised Land,
God issued severe warnings against the practices of the
heathen in that territory. One such warning is against any
Israelite becoming an "observer of times," which is an
astrologer. This practice, God declares, is "an
abomination unto the Lord." The penalty for its practice
was death by stoning. Consulting one's horoscope,
whether seriously or casually, is an act defying one of the
most solemn warnings of Scripture.

The futility of trying to use astrology to interpret
correctly God's dealings with man is portrayed in Daniel
2:27, 28 and 4:4–17. In the former instance, Nebuchadnezzar's dream confounded the wisest of the court
astrologers. Even though they were pagans, these seers
were quick to recognize that true perception of the
unknown is an attribute of "a God in heaven that
revealeth secrets." Many years later, Belshazzar was
reminded of the dilemma his father Nebuchadnezzar
faced when he, too, was confronted by a mystery that his
most trusted soothsayers could not unfold. Once again it
was the Lord's servant, Daniel, who was called upon
because his "wisdom" excelled that of Satan's
prognosticators.

Those who consult astrology are displaying an anxious and fretful attitude. Jesus said in Matthew 6:25 that we should "take no thought" for what might happen in the future. He declared that the necessities of life would be provided by our Heavenly Father if we would seek him first. Man does not need to know what lies ahead if he faces tomorrow with the help of God. The Christian may not know the future, but he does know the One who holds the future in his hands.

Psalm 19:1 says: "The heavens declare the glory of God; and the firmament showeth his handiwork." The emphasis of astrology is upon nature rather than the God of nature. This Psalm points out that the purpose of the heavens is to declare the glory of God, not the affairs of men.

The underlying philosophy of astrology declares that one's destinies can be found in the stars. In contrast, Christianity teaches that the events of life are determined by a combination of God's sovereign will and man's personal moral choices. Astrology, on the other hand, attempts to destroy man's accountability to God. Horoscope devotees may think they can fall back on blaming the stars for their actions. But the Bible teaches that someday all mankind will stand before God to be judged (Rom. 14:12). Man is responsible for his conduct and the Lord will not take into consideration the lame excuse that certain stars and planets were in the wrong conjunction.

Christians are to trust the Holy Spirit to guide their lives, knowing that "the steps of a good man are ordered by the Lord" (Psa. 37:23). The guesswork predictions of astrology should hold no interest for believers who follow "a more sure word of prophecy" (2 Pet. 1:19). God, in his mercy, has veiled the future from man's eyes (except for those events detailed in eschatological biblical references). If it were possible to know the events of tomorrow in detail, most people would not place their confidence in God's wisdom to look lovingly after our future. Satan, who, according to Isaiah 14:14, wanted equality with the Lord, still desires to be man's substitute god. Astrology is a tool of the devil to entice men to replace trust in God with a faithless dependence upon the whimsical uncertainties of the horoscope.

Founders: Chaldeans of the ancient Babylonian empire.

Text: Various occult volumes and oral traditions. Some Bible scriptures are taken from context to condone astrology.

Symbols: Twelve zodiac signs.

Appeal: In an age of uncertainty, people look for something which brings structure to their lives. Political, economic, and social turmoil creates fear and uncertainty which some feel could be assuaged by knowing the future. Astrology becomes a faith system, with the horoscope its liturgy. Those who have abandoned the Church find solace in its tenets.

Purpose: Astrology postulates that human lives are influenced (and in some cases predetermined) by the fixed position of certain heavenly bodies at the moment of birth. Earthly events are also affected by the relative positions of the planets and stars. Important decisions and momentous occasions should be considered with respect to their relationship regarding the horoscope.

Errors: The scientific discrepancies are well documented and acknowledged by the majority of scientists and astronomers. Numerous Scriptures (several already cited) denounce astrology for its erroneous prophecies and its false worship of the creation rather than the Creator (Rom. 1). The eternal destiny of each soul is determined by man's volitional choice, not a fatalistic conjunction of heavenly bodies.

Background Sources: *The Toronto Star,* 4/16/77, p. A3; *Hell on Earth,* 1974, Bob Larson, Creation House, Carol Stream, IL.

Address/Location: None applicable.

44

Bahaism

"We may never pass this way again." This melody has wafted over the airwaves of a thousand radio stations, along with songs like "Year of Sunday." The lyrics of the latter implore, "People, return to the tree of oneness." Both tunes were the composing and performing product of Jimmy Seals and Dash Croft, two of modern music's more successful minstrels. Both songs contain an explicit endorsement of the religious faith Seals and Croft have in common — Bahaism.

Bahaism promotes noble and altruistic goals. Above all, it desires to unify mankind into one religious kingdom. This attempt to be a watershed for all faiths in the oneness of God is laudable but impossible to be achieved. The doctrines taught by the religions of this proposed union are in many instances quite contradictory. Thus, any effort to accomplish a global, religious synthesis is a futile task. Still, Bahaism continues to pursue its goal of reconciling religious opposites. Such idealism has attracted 4 million followers in almost every country, including 70,000 in America.

The Bahai concept of religious unity, international government, and planetary interdependence began in Persia over a century ago. A businessman known as Mirza Ali Muhammed (1819-1850) announced in 1844 that he was the Bab ("the Gate") who would be the forerunner of the "Promised One" who would be a manifestation of God. Six years later he was killed. One of his followers, Mirza Husayn Ali, known today as Baha'u'llah, ("the glory of God"), came to believe he was the one prophesied by Mirza Ali Muhammed. Baha'u'llah spent most of his life in prison for plotting against the Shah. In 1863, in Bagdad, he declared that he was the promised *Madhi* (Messiah) a progressive revelation of God onward from Abraham, Moses, Krishna, Buddha, Zoroaster, Jesus, and Muhammad.

As the Comforter of John 14:16, the "second coming of Christ," Baha'u'llah had a big task to fulfill. His divine claims were cut short in 1892 when he died at the age of seventy-five. His son, Abdul Baha, brought the message of Bahaism to the United States in 1912. He spent eight months spreading the faith to Americans and laid the cornerstone at the $2.5 million Bahai temple in Wilmette, Illinois. Upon Abdul Baha's death, the mantle of Bahai leadership was passed to his grandson, Shoghi Effendi, who expired in 1953. Since then, the rulership of Bahaism has been in the hands of a National Spiritual Assembly.

Bahai belief has been summed up in the dictim, "The earth is but one country and mankind its citizens." Underlying this statement of faith are thirteen principles: the independent search after truth, the oneness of the human race, the unity of all religions, the elimination of all prejudice, the harmony of science and religion, the equality of men and women, universal education, a universal language, abolition of extreme wealth and poverty, world court, work as worship, and justice with universal peace. As Bahais see it, mankind is currently headed toward a socio-economic cataclysm. Out of this tragedy a "golden age" will dawn, and Bahais will be the only ones prepared to rule in this new world order. "War shall cease," said Baha'u'llah, "and all men shall live as brothers." Unlike more passive cults, Bahais evangelize vigorously to help fulfill their founder's prophecy.

The religious practices of Bahaism are similar to Islam (with a modified Western twist), though the two faiths are entirely separate religious systems. Nine members constitute an assembly. There are weekly gatherings, an annual fast, and a special calendar with New Year's Day occurring on March 21. There is no professional clergy, and leaders are forbidden to reveal exact membership figures to the public. The estimate of more than 17,000 localities is based on the assumption that even one member living in an area constitutes a locality. In a manner similar to Moslems, Bahais are expected to pray at certain times during the day; they are also encouraged to make at least one pilgrimage to their Mecca — the temple in the city of Acre (near Haifa, Israel) where Baha'u'llah died, and where Mirza Ali Muhammed was buried (on nearby Mount Carmel).

As with most religious systems which emphasize their inclusiveness, the inherent result of Bahai teachings is exclusiveness. Bahaism claims to be the ultimate fulfillment of Judaism, Buddhism, Islam, Zoroastrianism, Hinduism, and Christianity. While proclaiming the merits of all world religions, Bahaism also insists that these faiths must now concede to the supremacy of God's fulfilled revelation in Baha'u'llah. Disagreements between the disciples of Krishna, Muhammad, and Buddha are sufficient to preclude any hope of their uniting. The suggestion that they could also mute their differences with Bahaism is equally unlikely.

It is impossible for biblical Christianity to amalgamate with Bahaism. Those who believe that "all the fulness of the Godhead bodily" dwells in Christ (Col. 2:9) would be unwilling to demote their Savior, accepting him as only one of nine manifestations of God. Acceptance of Bahaism means that one must deny the substitutionary atonement of Jesus Christ and ignore the distinctions of other world religions. Bahais teach that all major religions hold to essentially the same truths. If this is the case, why are the tenets of Bahaism and Christianity mutually exclusive? The conclusion of this question cannot be ignored no matter how loving, kind, and considerate the followers of Baha'u'llah may be.

Founder: Baha'u'llah proclaimed in 1863 that he was the manifestation of God for this current age.

Text: The writings of Shoghi Effendi and Baha'u'llah (especially his *Tablets* which are considered as authoritative as the Bible). Their teachings may be summed up in the saying, "Oneness of humanity, oneness of religion, oneness of God."

Symbols: The number nine, a sacred designation dictating the structure of their temples (nine sides) and the size of local organizations (a minimum of nine members).

Appeal: Those who long for world peace and elimination of religious divisions over peripheral differences see Bahaism as a gracious faith with high ideals.

Purpose: Since all religions are presumed to have some merit and essential agreement, Bahais hope to unite all faiths to prepare man for spiritual advancement in this life as well as in the next.

Errors: Christ is robbed of his incarnate deity by placing him on the same level as other religious teachers. He is also accorded a position inferior to that granted to Baha'u'llah. Bahais do not believe in the bodily resurrection of Christ, the inerrancy of the Bible, eternal punishment, a literal hell, or the blood atonement of the cross. In the place of these doctrines is a syncretistic religious system with Baha'u'llah as the central figure and fountain of all truth. The paradox of differences in the nature of God as he is viewed by various world religions is ignored in favor of the oneness theme of Bahaism.

Background Sources: *Newsweek,* 3/24/80, p. 61; *East/West Journal,* 12/77, pp. 80-83; *The Denver Post,* 6/20/75, p. 2BB; *Ibid.,* 10/18/74, p. 7BB; *The Kingdom of Cults,* 1965, Walter Martin, pp. 252-258; "The World Centre of the Bahai Faith," informational brochure handed to visitors of the Shrine of the Bab in Haifa, Israel.

Address/Location: World headquarters in Haifa, Israel. Main U.S. temple in Wilmette, IL. Centers and teaching groups in most major world cities.

45

Church Universal and Triumphant

"I am that I am," says Elizabeth Clare Prophet as she conveys her blessing on the audience who has just heard her discourse. "Guru Ma," as she is known to her followers, has not only plagiarized God's reply to Moses (Exod. 3:14), but she also makes some other phenomenal claims. She purports to be a reincarnation of the biblical Martha, stating that in a former life Jesus spoke directly to her one day while she was kneading bread with her sister, Mary. Christ commanded her to keep incarnating until God's Spirit would be poured out at the dawning of the Aquarian Age. Elizabeth Clare Prophet believes that hour has now come, and she is the only present-day medium of truth endorsed by the Ascended Masters (beings who have passed on to an elevated spirit plane). Those who follow her teachings, as received from the Great White Brotherhood (a community of Ascended Masters said to be sages of hidden wisdom and knowledge), will have their souls purified by the Violet Consuming Flame so that they may achieve Christ-consciousness.

To the uninitiated such ideas may seem a little confusing. But to indoctrinated followers of the Church

Universal and Triumphant, it's all part of an effort to transcend the laws of karma and acknowledge one's inner divinity. Some cult groups can be explained in fairly simple terms. But the Church Universal has concepts and nomenclature which need defining before any analysis of Church belief is possible.

During the early twentieth century, occultists and Theosophists, such as Guy and Edna Ballard, developed a system of religious philosophy around the concept of "Ascended Masters." The theory is similar to a gnostic belief that God, who is impersonal and unknowable, must be approached by deified, human intermediaries. These "Masters" are the messengers whom God uses to reveal his truth. They have passed beyond the cycles of reincarnation to merge their consciousnesses with God. Now, these "elder brothers and sisters who have gone before" divulge the hidden mysteries of truth by discourses transmitted through selected human messengers, of whom Elizabeth Clare Prophet is their sole channel of communication for this hour. Foremost among these "Ascended Masters" is Saint Germain, a French eighteenth-century occultist. His associates in this spirit realm include Jesus the Christ, Mary, his mother, Master Kuthumi, Master Godfre, and El Morya (the main source for Prophet's messages). This fraternity is known as "The Great White Brotherhood."

Building on the spiritualistic concepts of the Ballards and other Theosophists/occultists, Mark L. Prophet founded the Church Universal and Triumphant (known then as Summit Lighthouse) in 1958. While serving as a medium, Mark met Elizabeth Wolf at a meeting in 1961, and two years later they were married. The union was a logical one since Elizabeth claims her first spiritistic encounter occurred at age three when she was surrounded by "angelic hosts." While she attended college, voices directed her to books about St. Germain. Through the years, a variety of spirit beings communicated with Elizabeth. But it was not until she met Mark that she felt her calling in life was fulfilled. Mark Prophet, twenty years her senior, died of a stroke in 1973. (He is now deemed to be among the other Ascended Masters communicating with the spirit name, "Lanello.") The mantle of serving as a messenger for the Ascended Masters fell upon her, and today 30,000 followers (15,000 in the United States) believe she is the absolute authority on all spiritual matters.

The "gospel," as preached by the Ascended Masters and mediumistically dictated through Elizabeth to her *chelas* (disciples), is a mixture of Christian terminology and Eastern/mystical concepts. Each person is believed to be on a spiritual pilgrimage (through a myriad of reincarnations) from his lower self to his higher self. Prophet ignores the warning of 1 John 2:22 that the spirit of antichrist denies Jesus is *the* Christ. She contends that the historical Jesus was a mere human who became *a* Christ. Thus, he is not God who is "able to save to the uttermost" (Heb. 7:25), but merely an example of how we, too, can ascend spiritually by acknowledging our inner Christ-presence.

Chelas are assisted in their pilgrimage by a variety of occult/mystical practices. Foremost among these is the use of "decrees," the mantra-like chanting of incantations. A favorite is, "I am that I am," an affirmation of self-deity which ensures ascension. Devotees also seek to cleanse their *karma* by being surrounded by the "Violet Consuming Flame," a sacred fire said to be made available by the spiritual merit of St. Germain. As a substitute for the blood of Christ, it provides a source of salvation from any negative influences. The spiritual smorgasbord in Prophet's theology also includes *chakra* purification, reflexology, healing, fasting, diet, auras, and cosmic astrology.

As a point of interest, this author has received letters of support and appreciation from followers and officials of the *Church Universal and Triumphant.* This correspondence has been in regard to the author's books on the occult and the immoral aspects of rock music. In fact, these books are promoted and sold at the public appearances of Mrs. Prophet. In light of the presumption that the Ascended Masters might well be masquerading familiar spirits and that Prophet's messages from them are demonic utterances, how could these same powers then promote the cause of one who represents orthodox, historic Christian theology?

The answer may be that Prophet and her followers are sincere in their religious devotion. In spite of their violation of scriptural commands against attempted communication with the dead (necromancy — Deut.

18:11), they genuinely believe they are defenders of moral purity and opponents of witchcraft. Prophet and her followers should be approached with loving concern that they may discover a personal faith in Jesus *the* Christ, who is above all principalities and powers, including the Ascended Masters (Eph. 1:20, 22).

Founder: Mark L. Prophet (1918-1973); Elizabeth Clare Prophet, current leader.

Text: "I am that I am" (Ex. 3:14). In Scripture, this statement affirms the eternal, omnipotent, omniscient nature of God. I AM cults say this phrase can be spoken to testify of the God-presence in each person.

Symbols: Cross with dove emerging from center of the quadrants; flame representing the sacred fire; chart of "divine self" illustrating man's transition from lower self; pictures of miscellaneous Ascended Masters.

Appeal: Those interested in spiritualism and Eastern religions find a Christian frame of reference for pursuing these beliefs in a syncretistic manner. Some are attracted by the awe of receiving directly from Prophet's lips supernatural messages of departed spiritual masters.

Purpose: Stated — "To publish the teachings of the Ascended Masters and to shed light on the lost and distorted teachings of Christ"; Inherent — From a biblical perspective, devotees become entwined in a web of occult practices and psychic experiences which portend a grave risk of spiritual bondage.

Errors: The biblical injunction against necromancy and consultation with familiar spirits (Ascended Masters) is ignored (Deut. 18:9–14). In this context (Lev. 19:31), Elizabeth Clare Prophet fulfills the Bible's description of a witchcraft medium. In Church Universal theology, Christ is not God in flesh worthy of worship (Phil. 2:9, 10), but rather "the mediator between God and man, the Christ-self, or the Christ-consciousness." Man's need is not forgiveness by God's grace but rather a purging of his karma to ascend spiritually in future reincarnations, or to directly join the other Ascended Masters.

Background Sources: Church Universal and Triumphant literature and miscellaneous mailings. Among these are "Pearls of Wisdom" (weekly organ), "The Teachings on the Path of Enlightenment," "Only Love," "Sing a New Song," *Climb the Highest Mountain, The Coming Revolution,* Winter 1981; *The New Cults,* 1980, Walter Martin, pp. 203-236.

Address/Location: Box A, Colorado Springs, CO 80901; Box A, Malibu, CA 96265.

46

ECKANKAR

Of all the new religions to enter the spiritual marketplace in this century, few are more confusing than ECKANKAR. The individual who picks up one of their promotional pamphlets in the local grocery store may be intrigued by so-called "ancient science of soul-travel." Followers of ECKANKAR are often intelligent, well-meaning people who constitute an estimated membership of 50,000. (ECKANKAR's leaders claim three million followers worldwide.)

Paul Twitchell, a journalist and frequent dabbler in occult and mystical practices (including having served as a staff member in the Church of Scientology), formed the first public ECKANKAR group in 1965. His theology, a restatement of Hinduistic precepts, teaches that ECKANKAR ("co-worker with God") came into being as a result of his contact with the two ECK Masters, Sudar Singh in India and Rebazar Tarzs in the Himalayas. No documented proof has been presented that Twitchell ever visited either place or that either man actually existed. The terminology of ECKANKAR is said to come from the Amdo dialect of the Tibetan language. Twitchell offered no explanation for claiming such expansive knowledge regarding this tongue, which is unverified by linguists. (One cult expert claims that ECKANKAR is a semantic perversion of "Ek Onkar," the name of the supreme deity in *Shabda Yoga.)*

Sudar Singh and Rebazar Tarzs designated Paul Twitchell to be the 971st living ECK Master, a *mahanta* (living manifestation of God). Twitchell says such a person is "above the laws of man...omnipotent and omniscient...." The ECK Master's purpose in life is to lead the souls of men to "that realm of spirit which is known as the Kingdom of Heaven where God (known as SUGMAD) dwells." Life flows from SUGMAD in the form of a cosmic sound current called ECK. (ECK is also often used as an abbreviation for ECKANKAR.) Twitchell taught a variety of occult exercises by which the ECK student could tune into this ethereal sound of God. Foremost among these phenomena is an out-of-the-body experience Twitchell originally called "bilocation," and later changed to "soul-travel," which he declared is "the secret path to God." (Occultists generally refer to this phenomenon as "astral projection.") Twitchell claims that Jesus, Buddha, and St. Paul indulged in the practice of bilocation.

The *Shariyat-Ki-Sugmad* are sacred ECKANKAR scriptures which Twitchell declared to be located in a monastery in the Tibetan mountains. *Anami Lok* is the name given to the true heaven where SUGMAD dwells. *Atma Sarup* is the soul body which travels astrally from the *Nuri Sarup,* the physical ("light") body. Such language (along with hundreds of other ECKANKAR-invented words) would be of little interest to the average person were it not for Twitchell's contention that by soul-travel one can achieve "omniscience...through the release of the soul from the bondage of flesh." In fact, ECKANKAR claims to provide "a key to heaven." Even the inventions of Alexander Graham Bell and the Wright brothers are said to be the result of astral journeys they made to a great museum in the capital of the spirit-world, *Sahasra-dal-Kanwal.*

The outward image of ECKANKAR is friendly and tolerant. An advertisement circulated in major newspapers stated that ECKANKAR "...does not condemn any person or teaching. If a person is involved in any world religion, he is encouraged to stay there." However, other statements found in ECKANKAR literature do not necessarily support this declaration.

In his book, *ECKANKAR — The Key to Secret Worlds,* Twitchell described God as being "unconcerned about any living thing in this universe. He is detached and unconcerned about man" (pg. 42). Christ taught that love is the greatest commandment, but Twitchell asserted that Rebazar Tarzs has instructed man to "love only those whom you must!" *Kal* (an ECK word denoting the devil) is identified in Twitchell's theology as the Father of the Christian faith, and Jesus is "a son of Kal, King of the lower worlds." The inclusive, conciliatory language used in ECKANKAR ads is contrasted by its published claims to be "the path of Total Awareness," "the everlasting gospel," and the one true source of all religions, "the most ancient religious philosophy known to man." In Twitchell's booklet, "ECK and Music," he states, "The ECK, therefore, is the Way.... Without this heavenly music, or the WORD, no one can reach God again." Other religions may not be openly condemned, but the teachings of ECKANKAR certainly relegate them to an inferior position.

To replace the Christian doctrines of sin and redemption, Twitchell proposes a Hinduistic concept of *karma* and reincarnation. Those who wish to avoid the countless cycles of rebirth must learn to ascend through a series of eleven astral planes by OBE's (out-of-the-body experiences). Success on this journey depends on the guidance of a Living ECK Master, who is assisted by other spirit guides. This Master will facilitate astral travels by helping the student discard the karmic debt he has accumulated in past lives.

The ECK Master is no mere way-shower. He is believed to be god-in-the-flesh, an incarnation of SUGMAD. The Master teaches the student that by sensory deprivation, altered states of consciousness, mantra-chanting, trancing, and contact with spirit guides, he can advance to higher planes of enlightenment. Twitchell claimed to have witnessed frequent appearances of entities who asserted they were "translated" (ECKANKAR for "dead") Masters. Students are encouraged to think upon the current living Master until he, too, manifests himself to them as a glowing, light-entity.

On September 17, 1971, in a Cincinnati, Ohio, hotel room, Paul Twitchell suddenly died of a heart attack. ECK

Master number 972 is Sri (an honorific Hindi title) Darwin Gross. Gross claims to be God's guru for our age, "the most splendid specimen of manhood, the noblest of the noble," "the most gifted spiritual leader alive today," and "a healer who has rescued many from physical ills and mental anguish." As the "Divine One," he received Twitchell's "Rod of Power," an event said to have taken place in the spirit world since Twitchell died too suddenly for an orderly transfer of leadership. Now Gross must continue "the longest unbroken line of spiritual teachers on this planet."

The teachings of ECKANKAR according to Gross continue Twitchell's tradition. Of love he says, "Many are teaching the masses to love everyone, to love their neighbors, and that's fine, if it's with a detached love. You have to be very careful who you give love to." Morality is described as ". . . an individual thing established by our own inner authority." He supports abortion by declaring that the soul does not enter the body until ". . . after the child has been brought into the outer world, and sometimes later than that." According to Gross, animals have a soul and their own heaven; Christianity adopted the idea of the virgin birth from Hinduism; and the current spiritual awakening is ". . . not due to evangelists like Billy Graham. It is due to ECK Masters."

Evangelical Christians are troubled by the spiritistic overtones of ECKANKAR. Others are skeptical about its deified, authoritarian leadership. In "ECK and Music," Twitchell addressed such apprehensions by saying, "If the individual is under the Living ECK Master, then he has no worry, for the Master is taking care of him." ("I am with you always," Twitchell's Master Rebazar Tarzs once told him, an adaptation of Christ's promise in Matthew 28:20.) If ECK advocates believe that Twitchell's Master appeared to him, the stage has been set for Master number 971 (Twitchell) to appear to his followers. A masquerading familiar spirit could easily assume the role of Twitchell (necromancy) to guide students of ECK onward to SUGMAD.

Founder: John Paul Twitchell, born sometime between 1908 and 1912 in Paducah, Kentucky (Twitchell's biography claims a birthdate of 1922).

Symbols: A funnel-shaped series of ascending ovals representing the eleven astral planes or "God Worlds of ECK"; a series of five stick-shaped human figures ascending horizontally (the fifth figure encircled), representing spiritual progress on the path of ECKANKAR.

Appeal: ECKANKAR offers dramatic psychic, out-of-the-body experiences and purports to give the student direct access to departed Spiritual Masters who appear as light-being entities. These astral projection abilities supposedly offer the opportunity to predict one's future, acquire healing, and eventually obtain omniscience. One practitioner claimed he would leave his body while driving to work so he could check traffic flows and avoid any bottled-up intersections which might be ahead.

Purpose: Stated — "Soul travel is the means we use as the vehicle of return to our true home." Actual — To "invent" a new religion based on a variety of occult phenomena.

Errors: Every cardinal Christian doctrine is denied, including original sin, intercessory prayer (called "an occult form of black magic"), the virgin birth, Christ as Creator and sole Incarnation of the Father, and the absolute goodness of God (Satan, "Kal," is a partial manifestation of God's character). Participants of astral travel may make themselves vulnerable to demon possession.

Background Sources: *ECKANKAR — The Key to Secret Worlds,* 1969, Paul Twitchell; "ECKANKAR — Ancient Science of Soul Travel," pamphlet by Paul Twitchell; "ECK and Music," 1971, Paul Twitchell; *Spiritual Counterfeits Journal,* 9/79, vol. 3, no. 1; "Open Letter to All Christians," advertisement placed in various newspapers and paid for by ECKANKAR; *Your Right to Know,* Sri Darwin Gross, 1979, IWP Publishing, Menlo Park, CA.

Address/Location: Box 3100, Menlo Park, CA 94024.

47

est

"Obviously, the truth is what's so. Not so obviously, it's also so what." If that sounds like a conundrum, don't be fooled by the apparently harmless confusion of the statement. Behind these words of Werner Erhard lies a system of religious philosophy rooted in Mind Dynamics, yoga, Silva Mind Control, gestalt psychology, Dale Carnegie, Subud, and most importantly, Zen Buddhism and Scientology. Those who indulge in Erhard's est training are told they are "perfect...gods who have created their own world." This teaching has led Erhard to conclude, "How do I know I'm not the reincarnation of Jesus Christ?"

Born Jack Rosenberg in 1935, Erhard left a wife and four kids in his early twenties. While traveling on a plane, he met a woman named Ellen who would become his second wife. He happened to be reading an article entitled "The Men Who Made the New Germany." His long enchantment with the German nihilistic philosopher Nietzche (who believed in a super-race, the foundation of Hitler's political approach), compelled Erhard to choose a new identity with a German name. Werner came from Werner Heisenberg (not Werner von Braun as est literature claims) and Erhard from Ludwig Erhard.

In the company of friend Bill Thaw, he explored an interest in a succession of Eastern religions and mind-science cults. Finally (according to Thaw), Erhard read a book entitled *est: The Steersman Handbook.* The author, L. Clark Stevens, used the abbreviation est to denote "electronic social transformation." Erhard borrowed the term and redubbed it Erhard Seminars Training — est (lower-cased "e") for short. While driving his wife's Mustang one day, he experienced a Damascus-road-type enlightenment. Erhard says he "got it," and est became the vehicle for propagating "it."

In the Zen Buddhist tradition of subjective, relative, intuitive enlightenment, no one in est (including Erhard) really knows what "it" is. But the goal of getting "it" is to conclude that there is nothing to get. In est, there is no objective reality, only experience. "Being" is said to be more important than "doing." Thinking is forbidden, and terminology is twisted. "Wrong is actually a version of right. If you're always wrong, you're right," est declares. Singer-composer John Denver, an est advocate, extolls Erhard's view of life in his song "Looking for Space." ("If there's an answer, it's just that it's just that way.") "Seek and ye shall find," Jesus said. In contrast, Erhard declares, "What isn't, isn't. You can't put it together. . . what you have to do is experience it being together."

Such doublespeak and intellectual dishonesty is more than a clever way to dispose of the definitions used in normal language. It is also an elaborate fund-raising vehicle ($16 million per year) and a public extension of Erhard's ego-oriented goal to remake the world. It all begins when interested parties plunk down $250 to join 249 other people for two weekends of group-therapy encounter sessions, totaling sixty hours. The inductee is initially greeted with smiles and hugs. But all that changes quickly once the hotel room doors are closed to begin the first fifteen to eighteen-hour period. Pen, paper, watches, tape recorders, and cigarettes must be left outside. Until recently, participants needed to be certain they had not eaten or drunk too much before entering. They were only allowed one bathroom break from start till finish (unless they had a doctor's signed statement indicating physical necessity). Numerous trips to the restroom are now permitted.

An est seminar is a calculated process of breaking

down the inductee's personality and then rebuilding it by harassment and intimidation. A trainer begins immediately to abuse the audience verbally with repeated obscenities. All ego defenses are ridiculed by means of demeaning epithets hurled at anyone who resists the tactics of the trainer. Eyewitnesses report that scores of people urinate, defecate, convulse, sob, scream, and vomit (in specially provided, silver-colored est bags). The only relief comes in the form of "meditation practices" (to acquire an altered state of consciousness), and exercises of lying on the floor to "find one's space." The latter practice has its relaxing effect quickly ended by the trainer who proceeds to create feelings of fear and danger, causing some to respond hysterically.

After three days of such psycho-manipulative and hemorrhoid-causing activity, participants are expected to "get it" on the fourth day. What they get is not an improved self-image, but a totally transformed perception of reality which is consistent with a Buddhist/occult view of the universe. "You are part of every atom in the world and every atom is part of you," estians are encouraged to affirm. This all-is-one, merging-of-consciousness doctrine of Eastern thought is what leads most est graduates to reject all other belief systems. After all, to know est is to know *you* are god.

The elementary student of psychology can easily recognize est's potential for creating psychosis. By the confrontational stripping away of coping mechanisms, some emotionally unstable individuals can be left in a dangerous, vulnerable condition. Even more serious to consider is the possibility that evil powers may take advantage of such a psychologically defenseless state to precipitate a demonic invasion. At the very least, the destruction of one's concept of self-worth may result in the violent release of suppressed traumas. Without an understanding of God's love, healing, and forgiveness to fill this void, the est participant can only deal with such feeling by retreating from reality and adopting a mystical view of life as an illusion.

In est, Christ's commands to "love your enemies" (Luke 6:27) and "Love thy neighbor as thyself" (Luke 10:27) are replaced with a self-centered approach to life. Since there is no God but one's own ego, moral conduct is judged according to self-serving satisfaction. The cult est doesn't tell you what not to do. It is understood that those who experience their "space" are practicing perfection, no matter what their moral beliefs may be. What an estian decides is good for himself is good. With no gods to worship, some est graduates adulate Erhard to a point of near perfection. His word is *the* word. What they do with guilt is another matter. No reinterpretation of reality can completely assuage one's conscience. That takes much more than four days locked in a hotel room, for it requires the shed blood of Jesus Christ (Heb. 9:22).

Founder: John Paul Rosenberg, born September 5, 1935, Philadelphia, PA. Renamed Werner Erhard. The cult was officially launched in 1971.

Text: "What is, is." — Werner Erhard

Symbol: None.

Appeal: Those with a poor self-image learn to assert themselves by ignoring reality. For some it is another "trip" to experience along with involvement in other consciousness-raising groups. People whose lives are meaningless or have experienced rejection and depression may view est as a quick, "cheap" form of psychotherapy.

Purpose: Compels people to get "it" though no one, including Erhard, can define what "it" is. The est manual reads: "The purpose of est training is to transform your ability to experience living so that the situations you have been trying to change . . . just clear up in the process of life itself." Life is not to be understood (understanding is irrelevant), but rather experienced.

Errors: Love, concern, compassion, sorrow, and other Christian and human values are considered an illusion. For example, the Hunger Project started by est proposes to eliminate world famine by 1997. This laudable goal is not to be achieved by feeding the hungry, but by simply declaring that "the end of hunger is an idea whose time has come." Man is his own god, the center of the universe. Sin does not exist and all personal conduct is justified by one's own perfection. As in Zen, reality is a matter of perception, not objectivity.

Background Sources: *Newsweek,* 8/28/78, p. 50; *Ibid.,* 5/9/77, p. 95; *Ibid.,* 6/15/81, pp. 18-21; *Time,* 6/7/76, p. 53; *Circus,* 2/76, p. 45; "Spiritual Counterfeits Project Newsletter," 3/76, vol. 2, no. 3; *The New Cults,* 1980, Walter Martin, pp. 105-141; "The Fuhrer over est," *New Times,* pp. 36-52 (issue date unknown).

Address/Location: The cult's centers are located in more than a dozen U.S. cities. Seminars are held in various locations using hotel and auditorium facilities.

48

Foundation Faith of the Millennium

(Foundation Faith of God)

Its name is difficult to define, and its evolving doctrines are even harder to pin down. In the beginning (1963) it was known as the Process Church of the Final Judgment (The Process). In 1974, as a result of a break with its founder, Robert de Grimston, its name was changed to The Foundation Church of the Millennium (with the word "Church" changed to "Faith" in 1977). For practical purposes, today it is usually referred to as "The Foundation."

Grimston's original group followed his psychic teachings with rapt enthusiasm. But his theology of dualism (supposing the universe is dominated by two opposing spiritual forces, neither being omnipotently supreme) eventually received bad press. Even non-Christians didn't like being stopped on street corners by robed zealots wearing silver crosses entwined with a red serpent. What Processians taught was even more offensive. "Christ said, 'Love your enemies,'" they declared. "Christ's enemy was Satan. Through love, Christ and Satan have destroyed their enmity and come together for the end, Christ to judge, Satan to execute judgment." Growing out of this doctrine was the belief that "process" by spiritual knowledge would allow members of the Church to provide moral leadership in a New Age led by a God-sent Messiah. All this would take place after a Bible-like apocalyptic period when Christ and Satan would finally be reconciled.

But the black garb, somber theology, and Satanic symbolism was too hard to accept, even for Processians. Grimston was ousted, though he continues to lead smaller groups of leftovers under the original name. The Foundation clothing was changed to blue, and the serpent-cross was replaced by the star of David with two *F's,* one inverted. Occult practices such as Tarot cards, psychic healings, and astrology persist, but elements of Judaism, including Sabbath ceremonies, have been added to upgrade the cult's image. The past and its spooky overtones are de-emphasized, though the belief in a soon-to-appear savior still undergirds Foundation philosophy.

Father Lucius (Christopher de Peyer) and Father Malachi (Peter McCormick), the current leaders, claim an estimated 500,000 are affiliated with their efforts, including 20,000 hardcore members. Foundation advocates certainly seem more palatable since they no longer publicly promote the Christ/Satan reconciliation theory. But they have not abandoned their basic belief in a coming Messiah. Bible students are left to wonder whether such a person might well be the Antichrist, the representative of the once-revered serpent that Foundation Faith advocates now seldom discuss.

One of the more successful off-shoots of the original Process Church is the Foundation Faith of God, with a devoted clergy committed to a vow of perpetual celibacy as a testimony to "the existence of the Kingdom." This group claims twenty ordained ministers with a growing number of followers in Canada.

Christ has a prominent role in the Foundation's teachings, with special emphasis on spiritual healing. However, its most distinctive doctrine maintains that everyone has a personal guardian angel who can be invoked for guidance in daily living. The clergy will conduct "angel listenings" (for a suggested donation of ten dollars), claiming they can actually hear the angel voice and write down his instructions. Most angelic messages are generalized and concern removal of barriers preventing one's spiritual growth, but additional questions may be asked of these angels for a tax-deductible fee of three dollars per inquiry.

Two other prominent tenets of the Foundation Faith include reincarnation, and the importance of controlling one's own life by personal choices.

Founder: Robert de Grimston, 1963, London, England.

Text: "Love your enemies — including Satan."

Symbols: Formerly, a cross with a snake entwined upon it; today, a star of David with two opposing (one inverted) *F's.*

Appeal: In the early days of the cult, initiates were intrigued by the exotic doctrines that combined elements of Satanism and Christianity. Current appeal centers more in the area of occult phenomena.

Purpose: Originally, Grimston endeavored to explain how a good God had created the devil and evil. (Answer — The devil is not truly evil and, therefore, he will eventually be a cohort of God.) Today, the emphasis is more on understanding the nature of the coming Apocalypse and the role Foundation members will play in the social order that follows.

Errors: The absolute nature of God's goodness and Satan's depravity is denied. Christ is only one of a succession of prophets including Moses, Buddha, etc.

Background Sources: *The Processians* (cult magazine), 3/74; *The Denver Post,* 7/27/73; *Ibid.,* 5/31/74, p. 5HH; *The Encyclopedia of American Religions, Vol. 2,* 1978, J. Gordon Melton, p. 229; *Toronto Star,* 1/24/81, p. H6.

Address/Location: Headquarters in New York, Chicago, New Orleans, Toronto, Miami, and Cambridge, MA. (Some of these offices may no longer be open.)

49

International Society of Krishna Consciousness

(Hare Krishna)

"Get out of here. You're a demon — a fornicating meat-eater." That kind of rebuke would be harsh anywhere, let alone in a crowded airport concourse. The epithet was directed toward this author for butting in on what, to that point, had been a successful attempt to con an unsuspecting tourist out of his money. He was an Israeli citizen visiting America. If I hadn't stepped in, he might never have known he was the victim of what Hare Krishna devotees call "transcendental trickery." The victim had been told he was giving his $100 traveler's check "donation" in exchange for a book about the Jewish religion.

Of all the imported cults to land on American shores in recent times, none is more ubiquitous and scorned than Hare Krishna. (The official organizational name is the International Society of Krishna Consciousness. For sake of brevity, the rest of this analysis will use the acronym ISKCON.) Even though the saffron robes and shaven heads publicly have given way to wigs and conventional clothing, the public image of ISKCON remains a negative one. Members are seen as deceptive, pushy beggars who frequent public places to prey on the naive. But beneath the *dhotis* and *saris* they wear is more than a collection of societal dropouts with brainwashed minds.

Thirty percent of the devotees have spent at least a year in college, and 70 percent formerly attended church with regularity. What they found in Hare Krishna is not just an exotic system of authoritarian asceticism. The 50 percent who remain permanently with the cult claim a deeply personal relationship to their Lord similiar to the devotion expressed by evangelical Christians to Christ. Hare Krishna members are dedicated to a set of sacred scriptures and seek to surrender their lives to a supreme power. They acknowledge man's inherent desire to worship a deity beyond himself and have plunged into their belief system with total commitment.

This is not to suggest that Christianity and Krishna Consciousness are in any way compatible. Far from it. An exploration of the history and nature of ISKCON readily establishes the pagan and mythological roots of this fervent faith. The worship of Lord Krishna began in the sixteenth century in Bengal, India. It was then and there that Caitanya Mahaprabu, inspired by the *Bhagavad-Gita* (one of Hinduism's sacred books), sought to revitalize a religion that had become heavy on philosophy and weak on participative devotion. Hinduism had split into two schools: those who worshiped Shiva as the greatest of the godhead (Brahma, Vishnu, Shiva), and those who considered Vishnu to be supreme. Caitanya insisted that Vishnu was actually an incarnation of Krishna (narrator of the *Gita*), and that Lord Krishna was the ultimate god. Even more revolutionary was his idea that Krishna would intimately commune with his devotees on a personal level, a foreign concept to the traditional Hindu perception of God's impersonality. This communion could be possible by the practice of exuberant chanting and dancing, known as *sankirtana*.

This concept of worshiping Krishna was revived in the early 1900s by the Indian sages Bhaktivinode Thakur and Sri Srimad Bhaktisiddhanta Saroswati Gosvami Maharaj.

One of the latter's disciples was a University of Calcutta
philosophy and economics major named Abhay Charan
De. In 1922 Gosvami initiated Charan De into the
discipline of *Bhakti Yoga* and instructed him to take the
message of Krishna Consciousness to the Western world.
Abhay Charan De became known as Bhaktivedanta
Prabhupada ("at whose feet masters sit"). At age
fifty-eight he left his wife and five children and a
prospering pharmaceutical business to pursue the life of
a *swami.* In 1965 he boarded a steamer for the United
States and on September 18 sailed past the Statue of
Liberty with eight dollars in his pocket. At the time of his
death, His Divine Grace A.C. Bhaktivedanta Swami
Prabhupada was chauffeured in black limousines and
could claim to his credit forty Krishna temples and an
estimated 5,000 to 10,000 followers in the United States
alone.

At any other time, this seventy-year-old man sitting in a
Greenwich Village park and chanting strange words
would have been an oddity. In the burgeoning
counterculture milieu of the sixties, he was considered
hip. Beat poet Allen Ginsberg, along with an array of
hippie-types, gravitated to Prabhupada's message.
Ex-Beatle George Harrison wrote a song extolling
Krishna's virtues ("My Sweet Lord") and dedicated an
entire album ("Living in the Material World") to ISKCON
belief. With the proceeds from these and other
recordings, Harrison bankrolled Prabhupada's efforts to
evangelize. In those days Bhaktivedanta had confidently
declared, "This is a prediction that in all the villages and
towns of the entire world, the Krsna [his preferred
spelling] Consciousness movement will be known." For a
while, it looked like he might be right.

What was the message he brought? Many people have
heard of the repetitive Hare Krishna chant and have
witnessed devotees ecstatically dancing on urban street
corners. But few understand the aim of such activity and
even less have any knowledge about their object of
devotion, Lord Krishna. Dismissing ISKCON antics as
weird and offensive is an understandable response of
Westerners. What may not be apparent to the occidental
mind is the complicated system of religious philosophy
behind the conduct of Krishnaites.

The religious philosophy of ISKCON is found in the

Bhagavad-Gita, an eighteen-chapter Hindu poem written (according to most credible scholars) sometime in the first century A.D. (not 5,000 years ago as Krishna devotees claim). The *Gita* is a virtual Bible to Krishnaites, so long as it is consulted in the form of Prabhupada's commentary, *Bhagavad-Gita As It Is.* The Gita is an allegorical story (in Krishna's words) of a certain war. The dialogue between Krishna and Arjuna, his warrior charioteer, is purported to represent a conversation between deity and humanity. This exchange is said to embody the ultimate wisdom of the ages.

Arjuna bravely enters the battle until he learns that his relatives are among the opposing forces. He hesitates to fight and is understandably overwhelmed with concern for the coming death of his kinsmen. Krishna stirs him on, advising him to avoid feelings of attachment to his loved ones. This approach of detachment from earthly desires and emotions is central to Krishna's message and ISKCON's theology. *Gita As It Is* contains a picture of devotees calmly walking past the poor and suffering. The caption explains such indifference by quoting Krishna's command, "Those who are wise lament neither for the living nor the dead." Prabhupada agreed. He wrote, "Philanthropists who build hospitals and churches are wasting their time."

Such a callous rationale is nothing compared with the twist in logic necessary to justify Krishna's character. The *Gita* and other legends portray ISKCON's deity as a blue-skinned, flute-playing prankster. He hid the clothes of girls bathing in a river and enticed the wives of other men to frolic with him in the moonlight. They became so overwhelmed by his romancing that each felt as if she were the only one having intercourse with him. Though Krishna did have a favorite mistress named Radha, he also consorted with 16,108 *gopis* (women cowherds). Over a period of 125 years he fathered ten children with each of them.

Such orgiastic abandon is a far cry from the behavior demanded of present-day Krishna devotees. Their lives are carefully regimented in a fashion that eradicates the need for personal choices or decisions. Everyone rises at 3 A.M. for a cold shower before "awakening" the temple idols. These "deities" are then dressed and "fed." Devotees chant, count their japa beads, and head for the

streets to solicit funds and fill the surrounding landscape
with Krishna's praises. Evenings are spent with more
chanting and idol worship before an early retirement. Six
hours of sleep on a hard floor is all that is between most of
Krishna's disciples and another day.

Life is austere in many other ways. There is no alcohol,
drugs, coffee, meat, fish, gambling, or conversation
unrelated to Krishna devotion. Reading of magazines or
newspapers is strongly discouraged. Contact with the
outside world, including family and friends, is infrequent
and sometimes nonexistent. Personal possessions are
disposed of, leaving the devotee solely dependent on the
temple for food and shelter. Children born of
temple-sanctioned unions are taken from the parents to
be placed in special ISKCON schools.

In fact, the marriage relationship is viewed as an inferior
state for those unable to answer the higher calling to
celibacy. Couples live in separate quarters and sexual
intercourse is allowable only by permission of the temple
priest. At the most, conjugal relationships are restricted
to one per month, at the wife's optimum time of fertility,
preferably at the time of a full moon, and only then for the
purposes of childbearing, not pleasure. In addition,
consummation is possible only after each partner has
completed chanting fifty rounds of the Krishna mantra, a
feat requiring about five hours. Finally, avoiding
hand-holding and kissing, the act is performed to the
accompaniment of a cassette recording of Prabhupada's
voice. It should come as no surprise that one former
member claims 90 percent of ISKCON marriages fail.

Obviously, the mind and body of a Krishna devotee is
not his own. To signify this fact, every day each member
places thirteen clay markings *(tilaka)* on his body. The
clay is flown in all the way from India and these marks
signify one's total servitude to Krishna. Those who stay in
the cult more than six months are given a new sanskrit
name and a secret mantra. Men must shave their heads
leaving only a hand of hair (a *sikha*) by which Krishna can
pull them up to heaven if he so desires.

The shaven heads also remove what Prabhupada
declares is the symbol of man's vanity. Balded pates are to
be indicative of denying any means of sexual attraction.
Women, who are said to have inferior brains and be
worthy only of serving men, must adorn themselves in

plain, Indian *saris.* This long, loose-fitting garment is
prescribed as a deterrent to arousing male passion. Such
practices are central to the Krishna doctrine that all
desires must be suppressed. The body is the enemy of
the spirit, and only by denying it comfort and attention
can one reach the high goal of intimacy with Krishna.

Prabhupada expounded a strict, fundamentalist form of
Hindu philosophy. In essence his main goal was to help
disciples liberate their pure souls from the spiritually
inferior nature of their bodies. "I am not this body,"
devotees are fond of saying. What they mean is that all
matter is *maya* (illusory and transient) and only the spirit is
worthy of eternal attention. Man's primary dilemma in life
is his ignorance of the Krishna god-nature of his spirit.
This unfortunate state has been caused by the bondage
resulting from the spirit's encasement in flesh. The only
merit of having a human body at all is the alternative of
having been incarnated in a lower animal form. At least
having a human body means one's previous incarnation
must have exuded good *karma.*

How does one escape the confines of the sensory
temptations of flesh and blood? ISKCON teaches that the
way of salvation can be shown only by a guru whose
spiritual succession is legitimate. Prabhupada lays claim
to such a lineage, insisting he is the spiritual heir of
Caitanya (mentioned earlier) who was Krishna's
incarnation for this present age. (Some devotees believe
that Prabhupada was himself an incarnation of Krishna,
and thus greater than Christ.) Prabhupada taught that
liberation of the soul in this age called *kali-yuga* ("the dark
age") is possible only by *kirtana:* reciting the Hare
Krishna chant. The devotee who does this is freed from
samsara (endless cycles of reincarnation) and begins his
pilgrimage "back to the Godhead."

One must admire the zealous success of Krishna
devotees. Their relatively few numbers have managed to
familiarize the public consciousness with their
sixteen-word chant: Hare Krishna, Hare Krishna/Krishna,
Krishna, Hare, Hare/Hare Rama, Hare Rama/Rama, Rama,
Hare, Hare. Even though it is brief, amazing powers are
claimed for the mere utterances of this *maha* ("great")
mantra. Accompanied by the "transcendental sound
vibrations" of drums and finger symbols, these words are
said to embody Krishna himself. (Rama is an alternate

name for Krishna and Hare expresses his creative energy.)

Devotees often do the chant in correspondence with each of the 108 japa beads on the "rosary" kept in a bag hanging around their necks. And they may repeat the entire cycle as many as sixteen times a day. It is of no concern to the chanters that the curious observers who watch them during public displays may mock or listen with disinterest. Prabhupada has told them that "there is no need to understand the language of the mantra." Anyone who hears it will be automatically affected by Krishna's name. For a similiar reason, ISKCON's own "spiritual sky" incense is often burned during chanting to provide an aroma in which Krishna may dwell. Devotees believe that those who smell it will literally inhale Krishna.

And there's more to chanting than that silly, blissful smile on the face of devotees. They are promised by His Divine Grace that eventually they may experience hair standing up on their bodies, dislocation of the voice, crying in ecstasy, and going into trance states. The result of this form of suggestive hypnotism is that the participant may enter a condition which would facilitate control by demonic possession. At the very least, such an enforced method of divorcing the mind from reality can turn devotees into robots who will act blindly in response to whatever they perceive to be Krishna's will. The potential misuse of such exaggerated devotion should cause alarm to those initiates who are just beginning the pathway of temple service.

The Hare Krishna chant is essentially an invocation to the pantheon of Hindu deities. Such paganism is also evident in a variety of temple duties and rites. Krishna is believed to be resident in the metal and wood idols maintained in ISKCON facilities. These statues are offered food (six times a day) which is later eaten by devotees (an act called *prasada*) as a way of actually ingesting Krishna. (This ritual is a kind of Hare Krishna "eucharist.") When water is used to bathe the deities, it is collected for the disciples to drink. A sample of the Indian *Tulasi Devi* plant is kept in each temple as an object of worship to eradicate sin and disease.

In spite of all this, Prabhupada declares his religious system is not idolatrous. To him, idolatry is the "worship of a material *form* of God." He insists that in Hare Krishna the devotee is not worshiping a *form* of God. "The form *is* God," Prabhupada declares. In Krishna's case, "There is no difference between the form of the Lord and the Lord himself." Whatever the excuse, such practices are inconsistent with Exodus 20:4. 5.

But accusations of idolatry are mild aberrations to defend compared with more recent charges leveled at ISKCON. Since the passing of Bhaktivedanta the organization has faced accusations of drug-smuggling, firearms-hoarding, suicides, murder, and outright thievery. The solicitation methods directed toward nonbelievers *(karmi)* have fostered court investigation of tactics including short-changing donors, participating in false pretense, and even using experienced thieves to train devotees on how to lift wallets. Critics suggest that such sources of income enabled the cult to erect the elaborate onyx, teakwood, ebony, marble, and gold-adorned temple in the West Virginia hills.

With Prabhupada gone, leadership has passed on to eleven gurus, each with his own geographical jurisdiction. This new breed still defends its fund-raising policies by insisting that even deceptive tactics serve a useful purpose. The *karmi* who is unwittingly separated from his money partakes in his own salvation by giving to Krishna. Thus, the solicitor has actually favored the donor by enticing him to give back to Krishna what really belonged to him in the first place.

On the other hand, some of the practices offensive to non-Krishnaites are being modified. In the future, members will not necessarily need to forsake everything and move into the temple, so long as they maintain a vegetarian diet and construct an altar in their home. Health food stores and society-owned farms will channel energies that may result in less public chanting exercises. And other religious viewpoints may be viewed a little more tolerably. Krishna is reported to have said, "There is no truth superior to me." What he will think of such liberalization is anyone's guess. What is certain is that after 100 million books distributed (plus 500,000 copies per month of the periodical "Back to the Godhead"), the "innocence" of those flower-power days is gone. Hare Krishna faces a more skeptical world where promises of ecstasy by chanting may no longer keep either the coffers or membership rolls filled.

Founder: His Divine Grace, A.C. Bhaktivedanta Swami Prabhupada, born Calcutta, India, September 1, 1896, as Abhay Charan De. Died of heart failure, November 14, 1977.

Text: The Hindu sacred texts, especially *The Bhagavad-Gita* according to Prabhupada's interpretation.

Symbols: Traditional Indian-style devotional paintings of gods and demi-gods, especially Lord Krishna as the Supreme Personality of the Godhead driving the chariot of Arjuna.

Appeal: Youth in the sixties were ripe for exotic, simplistic answers to questions unfulfilled by technological advances. Even today, those frustrated by the vanity of materialism may resort to a system which totally rejects all pleasure from sensory gratification. The authoritarian structure of temple life may fill a need for the disciplinary lifestyle being sought by some victims of this permissive age.

Purpose: ISKCON offers a highly religious life with dedication and the fellowship of like-minded adherents. All rituals and devotions are designed to free man from the ignorance of having forgotten his true personal relationship with Lord Krishna. This can be accomplished only by freeing the spiritual body from the physical body. Chanting Hare Krishna bypasses the intellect to cleanse the mind and heart of their false concept of concern for the material world.

Errors: The entire religious system of ISKCON is built upon mythological scriptures of legendary events and people (including Krishna). There is no sin to be saved from, there is only the illusion of evil to be eradicated. Jesus warned in Matthew 6:7 that "vain repetition" was a fruitless form of prayer. According to 1 Corinthians 8:6 there is but one Lord, Christ, and not Krishna. Jesus died of his own choice and rose from the dead. Krishna expired from an arrow in his foot and failed to conquer death.

Background Sources: *Bhagavad-Gita As It Is,* 1975, Bhaktivedanta Prabhupada, The Bhaktivedanta Book Trust; *The Nectar of Devotion,* 1970, Bhaktivedanta Prabhupada, The Bhaktivedanta Book Trust; *The King of*

Knowledge, 1973, Bhaktivedanta Prabhupada, The Bhaktivedanta Book Trust; "On Chanting Hare Krishna," ISKCON pamphlet; various issues of ISKCON periodical *Back to the Godhead,* especially vol. 10, no. 7; *Newsweek,* 12/27/76, p. 26; *Ibid.,* 1/30/78, p. 57; *Ibid.,* 9/29/80, p. 83; *Time,* 9/15/80, p. 71; *Life,* 4/80, p. 44-51; *The Denver Post,* 7/11/75, p. 3BB; *Ibid.,* 4/15/77, p. 4BB; *Ibid.,* 8/26/77, p. 2BB; *Ibid.,* 3/17/78, p. 1BB; *Ibid.,* 3/6/81, p. 5BB; *Ibid.,* 5/29/81, p. 1BB; *Circus,* 2/28/77, p. 48; *The Mystical Maze,* 1976, Pat Means, Campus Crusade for Christ; *The Mind Benders,* 1977, Jack Sparks, Thomas Nelson, Inc.; *Cults, World Religions and You,* 1980, Kenneth Boa, Victor Books, Wheaton, IL; *Hare Krishna, Hare Krishna,* 1978, J. Isamu Yamamoto, Inter-Varsity Press; *Forward,* vol. 4, no. 1.

Address/Location: International Society for Krishna Consciousness, 3764 Watseka Avenue, Los Angeles, CA 90034.

50

Martial Arts

He stands motionless, draped in his flowing white uniform called a *ghi*. Silence fills the room. With eyes closed in mute contemplation, one thought possesses his mind. Finally, he is ready.

Bowing slightly to his *sensei* (honorable teacher), he steps near the object of his concentration. In the center of the main room of the *dojo* (training center), someone has stacked six, one-inch-thick pine boards on top of each other. Each end of the pile rests on two cement blocks which suspend the center of the boards about twelve inches off the floor.

For several moments he glares at those inanimate boards as if attempting to stare down a dangerous opponent intent on his harm. Suddenly, he draws several deep, quick, rhythmic breaths and lunges toward the stack. His arm is raised in the air as though it were a chopping axe, and he lets forth with a piercing yell (*kiyai*). Almost simultaneously, faster than the eye can follow, his hand strikes the center of the stacked boards with one violent thrust.

Crack! Six, one-inch pine boards splinter and fall to the floor, victim to the force of nothing more substantive than human flesh.

An audible sigh of relief is heard from those watching.

Some nod in approval while others shake their heads in disbelief. Few, if any, realize that what they have just seen is an ancient spiritual discipline designed to harmonize the body with the energy forces of the universe in order to achieve religious enlightenment.

Tales abound (some spurious, some true) relating the paranormal feats of adept *senseis.* Such claims are truly astounding. Bullets can be caught between one's teeth. Punches can be pulled (i.e., stopped short of striking the body) and yet their effects can still be felt. Psychokinetic phenomena (the movement of material objects by immaterial, "mental" power) may be displayed.

These accomplishments have a name: *noi cun.* The source of power for such feats is said to be *ki* (sometimes written as ch'i). *Ki* is widely known in the occult arts as the "life-energy-creative force of the universe." Advanced practitioners of the martial arts credit *ki* with enabling them to knock a man down by barely touching him or by merely pointing a finger at him. Some have cultivated *ki* to such an extent that they can floor a man by their breath or a look from their eyes. One martial arts practitioner interviewed by this author said his *sensei* could place his knuckles on the man's chest and send a burning, electric shock through his body, driving him up against a wall.

Most people are interested in the martial arts for less exotic reasons. Concerned with warding off muggers or attaining physical prowess, they spend evenings at a store-front *dojo* learning kicks and punches. They are more concerned with downing an opponent than with attaining spiritual insight. Those of small stature may be seeking an effective means of self-protection that will enchance a macho image to friends and lovers. But the inherent principles of paganism underlying the martial arts, promises the novice he may get more than he bargained for.

Interestingly enough, the centuries-old practices of martial arts are relatively new to the Western world. The boom started when returning World War II servicemen brought back such arts from the Pacific. Later, the Hong Kong movie industry churned out films such as "Five Fingers of Death" and "Duel of the Iron Fist." But it took American movie star Bruce Lee to popularize the arts for the masses. His 1972 movie "Kung Fu" was turned into a successful TV series which spun off magazines and

T-shirts with an appeal far beyond board-breaking. Lee, to whom kung fu was more than a physical practice, explored its spiritual depths until he met an untimely, mysterious death. David Carradine, who took kung fu to TV, told his fans, "When Bruce Lee died, his spirit went into me. I'm possessed."

There are many conflicting historical theories regarding the origin of martial arts. The account stated here is a widely accepted survey which traces the general history of the martial arts and goes back to the dawn of civilization in India. Three millennia ago in China the arts were developed even more extensively. By the establishment of the Feudal States in 770 B.C., kung fu was widely practiced. Only during the Boxer Rebellion of 1900 were the martial arts partially eliminated from the mainland. In 1928 they were renamed War Arts and were accorded national recognition.

Over the centuries various aspects of the arts were modified and eventually evolved into more or less violent types. Northern and Southern schools, and hard and soft forms also developed. Kung fu was the original, all-inclusive term describing the martial arts. Later, specific names were applied to its variations: karate, tai chi, judo, jujitsu, and aikido. In Korea, the arts were known as Tae Kwon Do, and they were honed into their highest forms of proficiency in Okinawa. Though one often thinks of the arts as "made in Japan," they have many roots and cultural variations.

The original religious philosophy of kung fu dates back as far as 2696 B.C. where it was rooted in the occult forms of divination known as the I-Ching and the "Book of Changes." Lao-Tse, the Chinese sage born in 604 B.C., added further embellishments. His teachings were set forth in a 5,280-word manuscript called *Tao Teh Ching,* often called simply "the tao," or "the way." He taught that salvation could not be found in prayer but rather by the observance of nature, the natural way. As the trees bend with the wind and the rivers follow the path of least resistance, so must man adapt to the rhythm of coexistence with evil and wrong.

The next development in the history of kung fu took place when a monk named Bodhidharma brought Buddhism to China in the sixth century A.D. When he discovered the monks sleeping during his lectures, he introduced exercises to assist them in meditation. Known as *I-chin Sutura,* his system combined kung fu with the philosophical principles of Zen to develop a highly sophisticated form of weaponless fighting. The monks at his Shaolin Temple became famous for their savage abilities of defense which they employed whenever they were attacked in the course of pilgrimages. Eventually two schools of martial arts evolved: *Ch'uan Fe* (kung fu) based on the hard (external) school of Buddhism and other arts founded on the soft (internal) school of Taoism. As the martial arts spread beyond the monastery to the fields of war, some of the religious flavor was lost. But the essential belief system behind these disciplines has never been completely lost, even today.

After centuries of countless adaptations, the martial arts have evolved into six basic forms by which they are known in the Western world. Other variations exist, but for the sake of brevity, categorizing these six headings will be sufficient.

KUNG FU

Originally used as a colloquialism referring to any martial art, kung fu is considered to be the mother of all such physical disciplines. The alchemists who developed it were said to be literally "possessed" with kung fu. In *The History and Philosophy of Kung Fu,* Earl C. Mederiros states, "Kung fu represents the development of man as a complete person. It combines the theological with the philosophical and blends these with the physical, thus evolving those attitudes which are in keeping with the natural laws. . . a perfect harmony of the physical and metaphysical."

Kung fu is known best for its "hard" school which emphasizes kicking, striking, and punching with strength and speed. The power is said to be derived from *ki* and may also be directed toward improvement of one's health as well as for self-defense. But its appeal to the average person lies more in its offensive character which emphasizes force to break force. It also may include the striking of vital points, delayed action "death touches," and the use of psychic powers.

T'AI CHI CH'UAN

Some historical evidence indicates that this art evolved from the "soft" school of kung fu. It was founded by Chang San-feng who meditated on the occult I-Ching for three weeks while watching a snake and crane fight. Like Lao-Tse, he was interested in the balanced interplay of opposites known as *yin* and *yang.* In Ta'i Chi Ch'uan, these negative *(yin)* and positive *(yang)* principles are supposed to reach a harmonious duality when mind, breath, and sexual energy come together. In this state, *ki* will produce quietness and cure impotency and depression.

All this is achieved by practicing "shadow-boxing" while concentrating on the body's psychic center located below the navel. Participants often arise early to practice the fluid, rhythmic motions of T'ai Chi. Some claim it produces natural health (a famous participant was said to have lived for 250 years). One of the West's foremost T'ai Chi teachers, T. T. Liang, states, "The ultimate goal of learning and practicing T'ai Chi is to become an immortal." This is accomplished by placing the body in harmony with the laws of nature. Some proponents claim supernatural strength and warn of its devastating power as a combative form.

KARATE

For Westerners, this is the best known and the most practiced of all the martial arts. Today it is used basically as a form of self-defense and sport-fighting, using bare hands, arms, and wrists. American occupation forces brought karate back from Japan where it had been imported from Okinawa and China. It developed in these countries because the Japanese rulers had forbidden their people the use of weapons. Gichin Funakoshi, who developed it as Shotokan Ryu, emphasized that the student must empty his mind of wickedness in order to react cognitively, and from this philosophy we get the term *karate,* meaning "kara" (empty) "te" (hand). In Okinawa, karate became imbedded with its Zen philosophy.

The undercurrent of Buddhism found in some martial arts is illustrated by the emphasis on bowing, breathing exercises, seated meditation, intense concentration, and heightened awareness. Reflective thinking is discouraged — another influence of Buddhism. Since karate is a practice of the spirit, its stated purpose is to unite mind, body, and spirit to achieve the unity envisioned by Zen.

The most distinctive practice in karate is called *kata,* a choreographed combination of kicks, punches, and breathing techniques. It is like a graceful, yet powerful dance performed alone because the blows are deadly enough to kill. Fortunately, sport karate does not cultivate the intent of taking another life or painfully disabling an opponent. And most instructors do not pursue the spiritual purpose of cultivating *ki* to achieve union with an internalized god. But it is questionable whether any devotee may be totally free of the distinctly pagan frame of reference associated with karate.

AIKIDO

This martial art is the most overtly religious. Literally, it means "the road" *(do)* "to a union" *(ai)* with the "universal spirit" *(ki).* It was founded by Morihei Uyeshiba who became concerned that he couldn't control his strength without controlling his mind. Ultimately, after entering many temples he arrived at "enlightenment" and viewed himself, in the Buddhist theological concept, as "at one with the universe." At that moment, he declared, "The fundamental principle of the martial arts is God's love and universal love. The true martial arts," he said, "regulate *ki* of the universe."

All of the body movements of aikido are said to agree with the universal laws of nature and bring to the follower the power of *ki,* which is inhaled into the lower abdomen and exhaled through the hands. When the innate psychic powers of all men are united with the spirit and body, aikidoists predict the world will be composed of one family.

A tenth-degree black belt aikido instructor from Japan states of his art, "We create a universal harmony which ties together all of the worlds, the phenomenal world we see around us, the world of the kind of spirits we cannot see, and the pure world of energy. This building of harmony, and harmonizing the universe with ourselves so we may become one, is the essence and ultimate purpose of aikido."

Morihei Uyeshiba (O'senei as he is known by devotees) once described a strange psychic/occult visionary experience of seeing rays come down from the sky. "I felt my body growing larger and filling the entire cosmos. While I was exalted by this vision, I acknowledged suddenly I should not want to win: a martial art should be a form of life."

JUDO AND JUJITSU

Jujitsu is a blending of kung fu and Japanese martial arts. By the twentieth century, it was the Japanese national sport. A basic factor is knowing the vulnerable portions of an antagonist's anatomy and how to attack those areas.

Judo is basically jujitsu minus the killing aspects. It was founded in 1882 by Jogoro Kano, a student of jujitsu. Unlike karate, which may be compared with boxing, the "gentler" art of judo is similar to wrestling. It employs the use of balance and leverage to throw an enemy. Devotees are warned in some judo manuals that the art should not be learned without the inclusion of meditation exercises. Its founder agrees, calling it a "method of arriving at self-realization."

While it may be true that the various disciplines of martial arts have different forms, they all have similar religious backgrounds and goals. Because of their roots in Taoism and Buddhism, they view the entire universe as an interplay of harmonizing opposites, the *yin* and *yang*. These principles are expressed by the relaxed state of equilibrium produced with meditation and body movements. "The way" of Tao is accomplished by yielding and never resisting, and by responding sympathetically to each action of one's opponent. As illustrated in kung fu, each movement is uninterrupted and flowing. The end of one action is the beginning of the next, thus balancing the *yin* and *yang*. When the Zen goal of stilled senses is also achieved, this balanced harmony is supposed to help one merge with the Universal Consciousness.

To the Christian, salvation comes by the finished work of the cross where Christ was sacrificed for man's sin.

And it is by his resurrection that man has hope of eternal life. Salvation in Zen is achieved by comprehending the divine essence of man, who is a manifestation of the Universal Soul. Followers of Zen believe that such enlightenment may be shared by sending forth *ki* to illuminate the spiritual darkness of the world. Whether the form of martial art one practices is based on the doctrine of naturalism found in Taoism or the doctrine of illusion found in Buddhism, the philosophical basis of both explicitly deny the blood atonement of Christ. The Christian practitioner of the martial arts must ask himself whether or not any involvement in such physical disciplines implies an inherent approval of the religious principles behind them.

Founder: Most historians credit the Buddhist monk Bodhidharma in the sixth century A.D.

Text: Zen Buddhist doctrines; *Tao te ching.*

Symbols: So-called "spiral configuration" from the I-Ching representing the belief in reincarnation and cyclical evolution; double fish shown as a curved line in the shape of an *s* bisecting a circle. One side of the *s* is dark and the other is light. This represents the harmonizing opposites of yin and yang.

Appeal: Self-defense as a crime deterrent; physical conditioning; sport; fascination with martial arts movie and TV idols; desire to achieve physical and spiritual composure; as a way of life to arrive at immortality.

Purpose: The intent depends on the form of discipline and the instructor. Traditional Eastern *senseis* will possibly present the arts as a religion with meditation techniques and idolatrous trappings. Western instructors will more likely emphasize the initial sport stages and appeal to a more casual fascination with the arts as a fad.

Errors: The religious and philosophical roots of most martial art forms presuppose a pantheistic perception of the cosmos. Even the curious student runs the risk of being conditioned by the techniques which pursue a goal of impersonal oneness with the universe. The Taoistic and Buddhist overtones represent more than an historical root. These principals are an integral part of fulfilling the ultimate spiritual aims of most art forms.

Background Sources: *Aikido in Daily Life,* 1966, Koichi Tohei, Rikugei Publishing House, Tokyo; *Handbook of the Martial Arts and Self Defense,* 1975, William Logan and Herman Petras, Funk and Wagnalls, New York; *The History and Philosophy of Kung Fu,* 1974, Earl Mederiros, Charles E. Tuttle Co., Rutland, VT; "Women Liberating Themselves with Karate," *East West Journal,* 9/76, pp. 14-16; *Ibid.,* 11/78, p. 72; *Sports Illustrated,* 8/18/75; *Newsweek,* 1/2/78, p. 40.

Address/Location: Martial arts training centers *(dojos)* in most major cities.

51
Nichiren Shoshu/ Soka Gakkai

Most Eastern cults offer psychic experiences, authoritarian father-figures, or ascetic rules which are in contrast to hedonistic Western lifestyles. How could anyone be attracted by the thought of chanting strange syllables while kneeling before a black-lacquered box containing a small, sacred scroll? Until a recent scandal (involving charges of misappropriation of funds and sexual misconduct by its leader) jolted the Nichiren Shoshu organization, 200,000 Americans and 10 million foreigners were performing this ceremony each day. (Current membership is still estimated to be more than 3.5 million.) If that seems hard to believe, then consider the testimonials of practitioners who claim that Nichiren Shoshu has brought them love, health, wealth, and whatever else their hearts desire.

In his search to discover the essence of diverse Buddhist teachings, a thirteenth century Japanese monk named Nichiren Daishonen claimed to have found the "true Buddhism." It was embodied, he said, in the *Lotus Sutra,* a writing attributed to Buddha but actually written much later. Nichiren wrote scores of books, but the real

growth of his teachings awaited the formation of the Soka
Gakkai (Value Creation Society) in 1930. (Soka Gakkai is
the politically active, evangelistic branch of the
organization. It operates a 4.5-million-circulation daily
newspaper and has constructed a huge Temple near
Mount Fuji.)

After World War II, the movement grew rapidly under
the leadership of Daisaku Ikeda. He made Soka Gakkai a
significant force in Japanese politics by establishing its
own political party under the name Komei ("Clean
Government") Party. In contrast to Christ's teaching that
the chief should be servant of all (Matt. 20:27), Ikeda
declared, "You have to have power to do anything at all
meaningful."

This power originates in a series of pagan rituals and
beliefs. Members are acquired by a conversion
technique known as *Shakubuku* ("brow-beating"), a
controversial kind of forced persuasion that borders on
brainwashing. An NSA (Nichiren Shoshu of America)
document calls it "a merciful method of introducing True
Buddhism to nonbelievers." Once they join, many
members become convinced that NSA holds the keys to
world unity and peace. Such laudable goals are to be
obtained by chanting *nam-myoho-renge-kyo* ("glory to
the lotus sutra of the mystical law") before an altar upon
which sits the *butsodon* (a black box) containing the
Gohonzon (sacred scroll). All the while, the devotee
fingers the 108 beads of a rosary.

The goal of such devotion is to merge one's self with the
essence of Buddha. Repeated chanting of the *Diamoku*
(worship formula) is said to place one in tune with the
rhythm of the universe. As a substitute for psychotherapy,
chanting *nam-myoho-renge-kyo* is much easier and
cheaper. Perhaps more important, its spiritual goals of
working out one's karma take second place to the more
immediate purpose of satisfying selfish desires. "Happy
individuals can build a happy world," is NSA's creed, a
hedonistic motto that is well received in affluent, Western
cultures. If he were alive, Buddha (who taught principles
of denial and withdrawal from material pursuits) might
look askance on such egocentric goals.

While most of NSA's emphasis is on acquiring wealth,
power, and personal happiness, the pagan religious
overtones cannot be overlooked by evangelical

Christians. Chanting to the *Gohonzon* constitutes an idolatrous act, and the belief in its supernatural properties could be a dangerous opening for demonic subjection. The *Gohonzon* takes the place of God, while implying at the same time a pantheistic version of deity. NSA's espousal of karmic philosophy and reincarnation place it yet another step away from biblical Christianity. The Buddhist goal of fusing one's nature with the universe negates any individual accountability for sin or salvation. While certain material benefits may be incurred by NSA's chanting, conformity with God's moral laws and forgiveness of sin are something that meaningless repetition can never achieve.

Founder: Nichiren Daishonen (A.D. 1222-1282); modern founder, Tsunesaburo Makiguchi (1930). The cult's main growth occurred under the leadership of Daisaka Ikeda, who was ousted in 1979 due to charges of sexual misconduct and misappropriation of funds.

Text: The *Lotus Sutra* (writings erroneously attributed to Buddha), and *Gosho* (collected volumes of Nichiren Daishonen).

Symbols: Prayer beads; *gongyo,* a booklet with the words of the *Lotus Sutra; butsodon,* black box containing the *Gohonzon* (sacred scroll).

Appeal: Some members are attracted by the admirable goals of world peace, nuclear disarmament, and abolition of war. Others join in the pursuit of personal desires without moral regard for Christian beliefs or the wishes of others.

Purpose: New members are proselytized with the eventual goal of world domination through political power.

Errors: Nichiren Shoshu promotes a Christless belief with a Buddhist view of reality, while denying Buddha's basic teachings. Salvation is by enlightenment and the attainment of Buddhahood. Occult and spiritistic practices of idol worship, shrines, talismans, false scriptures, and repetitious chants are included.

Background Sources: *Newsweek,* 6/5/73, p. 68; *Ibid.,* 8/27/73, p. 60; *Time,* 1/13/75, p. 12; *The New Cults,* 1978, Walter Martin, pp. 321-350; *The Mystical Maze,* 1976, Pat Means, pp. 169-180; *Christianity Today,* 1/23/81, p. 57.

Address/Location: Headquarters and main temple in Japan. Cult branches throughout the Western world, especially the United States.

52
Rosicrucianism

Who they are, where they came from, and what they really believe is a matter of controversy with most secret organizations. With Rosicrucians, these uncertainties are amplified by the volumes of undocumented literature they distribute. They insist that their belief is not a religion, not an occult organization, has no relationship with Freemasonry, and has nothing to do with spiritism. Though there is ample evidence to refute these assertions, Rosicrucians still claim they are nothing more than a "fraternal order" with the intent of awakening "the dormant, latent facilities of the individual whereby he may utilize to a better advantage his natural talents and lead a happier and more useful life."

This statement of purpose seems laudable, but it obscures the somewhat tainted history and esoteric practices which dominate Rosicrucian beliefs. If, in Webster's view, religion is a system of "faith and worship," then the Rosicrucians surely qualify. Those who begin a study of its teachings soon discover that self-advancement is no mere psychological goal. It is dependent upon a complex system of doctrines, rituals, and ceremonies laced with Judaic and Christian concepts, based on pagan mythology and occult practices.

In the seventeenth century, a pamphlet entitled *Fama Fraternitis* appeared in Germany under the authorship of Johann Valentin Andrea (1586-1654). The book described the religious discoveries of Christian Rosencreutz who claimed to have traveled to Egypt and uncovered the mystery of the "rose cross." Though historical dates for his existence are available (1378-1484), Rosicrucians claim the name Christian Rosencreutz was symbolic, enabling them to assert a much earlier origin for their Order. Wherever their prior historical roots may lie, Rosicrucian Societies flourished in seventeenth- and eighteenth-century Europe. Some evidence indicates they exchanged ideas with Freemasonry. Current-day Rosicrucians deny this philosophical cross-pollination. Freemasonry does include a Rosicrucian degree, and there appears to be a strong historical link between these two closed societies.

Rosicrucians claim that their Order first came to the United States in 1694 under the leadership of Grand Master Kelpius who was connected with a European lodge. After a time of flourishing activity (Benjamin Franklin and Thomas Jefferson are said to have been Rosicrucians), the Order went into a self-proclaimed period of "outer silence" lasting 108 years. Secret work continued, but overt knowledge of the organization awaited a twentieth-century resurrection. In 1909, Order literature states that Dr. H. Spencer Lewis met with officials of the French Rosicrucian Order. Dr. Lewis was initiated, and returned to spark a revival of the Order in America. His efforts continued until his "transition" (Rosicrucian for death) in 1939 when his son, Ralph, took over.

What Rosicrucian literature fails to mention is Lewis's contact with the occult group Order Templi Orientis (O.T.O.) and the infamous British spiritualist Aleister Crowley. (Crowley was a homosexual, murderer, and practitioner of black sex-magic. He sought to violate every moral law possible, and actually renamed himself "Beast 666.") Lewis founded the Ancient and Mystical Order of Rosae Crucis (AMORC for short) in 1915. Apparently he was not at all embarrassed to receive the endorsement of the O.T.O., in spite of its unsavory practices. Religious researcher J. Gordon Melton claims that various emblems of the AMORC, including the Rose

Cross symbol, were actually borrowed from Crowley's periodicals. Such information makes even more suspect AMORC's statement that it does not endorse any occult or superstitious beliefs. (Several other Rosicrucian Orders exist: for example, the Rosicrucian Fellowship founded by Max Heindel, and the Societas Rosicruciana, an American variant, which requires its members to be Masons. Since AMORC is the largest and most visible representative, further discussion will be limited to it.)

To validate its authenticity (and perhaps obscure its more recent checkered history), the AMORC insists its roots extend back to ancient Egypt. In 1500 B.C., Thutmose III is said to have established certain "mystery schools" of the Great White Lodge. His successor, Amenhotep IV, is claimed to be the "most enlightened man of his time" and the object of much AMORC reverence. No substantial evidence exists to connect these ancient rituals with a continuing observance leading to modern Rosicrucian practices. AMORC justifies this link by declaring that during certain periods of inactive cycles of "outer silence," Rosicrucian ceremonies and rituals were kept alive by secret practices. Therefore, with or without historical evidence, one cannot test the belief system. Its validity is asserted regardless of reason or proof.

Modern AMORC beliefs are a mixture of Egyptian religious tenets, paranormal and psychic interests, and pseudo-scientific pursuits based on alchemy. Members attempt soul travel, development of inner "intuition," healing, and also conduct chemical experiments. The absorbing nature of this approach permits Rosicrucians to encompass almost every form of mystical/transcendent experience, from waterwitching to mind control. Training for members takes place primarily by correspondence through a series of mail-order *Mandamus,* which are secret, sealed instructions. Neophytes are warned to never reveal the content of such literature nor to explain to outsiders their clandestine ceremonies. "Simply tell them you study one night a week," new members are instructed. "Always emphasize that AMORC is *not* a religion."

The facts indicate otherwise. Members are encouraged to construct what is essentially an altar (they call it a *telesterion*) in their homes. Emblems may include incense, an ankh, candles, and idols of Egyptian deities and rulers. They may hang on their walls a document entitled "Confession to Maat." *(Maat* is supposed to be Egyptian for "truth.") The affirmation begins, "Homage to thee, Great God, Thou Master of all Truth, I am pure." Neophytes are told they are petitioning the "forty-two principal gods...expressions of the principal god, the Sun-God, AMEN-RA."

Each lesson gradually introduces more AMORC theology. Since the neophyte affirms he is pure, there is no need for sins to be forgiven. Only "psychological obstacles" are acknowledged, and these are "confessed" to one's self. Prayers are made to "the God of your heart." The penalty for bad *karma* one has accumulated can be expiated by the law of *AMRA.* (A check donated to AMORC is suggested.) God is defined as the "Supreme Intelligence," a form of "pure energy," "The First Cause of All." This Brahmanistic-type deity is totally impersonal and is also said to be a "number endowed with motion."

The Bible takes a special drubbing from AMORC. Genesis is dismissed as "a beautiful poem." The New Testament is said to be devoid of the most important, private teachings of Jesus. Several books are recommended in the stead of Holy Scripture, such as *The Secret Doctrines of Jesus, The Book of Jasher,* and other volumes supporting reincarnation. Bible beliefs are replaced with a concoction of teachings about the lost continent of Atlantis and a race of Negroes called Lemurans. Jesus is said to be the highest initiate of the sun period, and the Holy Spirit is the foremost initiate of the moon period.

Though the AMORC officially denigrates spiritism, the sealed instructions encourage members to contact departed spirit-Masters. These are called "psychic contacts with soul personalities" who are now part of "the Universal Soul." These "personalities" are said to be in need of an "identity" to find expression, therefore, the neophyte becomes that "physical medium." Christian theology would view this phenomenon as an example of demonic control when the "personality" (evil spirit) enters (possesses) the "physical medium" (body) of the unsuspecting initiate. In this perspective it is perhaps appropriate AMORC denies that its "Rosy Cross" represents the Christian crucifix, since the cross of Christ symbolizes the defeat of Satan's kingdom.

Founder: According to historical scholarship, Johann Valentin Andrea (1586-1654), a Lutheran pastor who may have been writing about Christian Rosencreutz (1374-1484); the AMORC claims its origins are found in ancient Egyptian "mystery schools"; modern American Rosicrucianism dates from its founding in 1915 by Dr. H. Spencer Lewis.

Text: Various geometric and hieroglyphic symbols along with the hidden, esoteric knowledge of the Kher-Hebs who are said to be the Masters of ancient, Egyptian mystery schools.

Symbols: Foremost among their symbols is the "Rosy Cross" (a Christian cross with a rose in the center). Rosicrucians claim that Christians chose the cross as an "arbitrary symbol." To the AMORC, the cross represents "the body of man" with the rose symbolizing "man's soul unfolding and evolving."

Appeal: Extensive use of advertising entices the prospect to "develop your psychic power of attraction." Ads proclaim that Isaac Newton, Francis Bacon, and Descartes were Rosicrucians and suggest "they were inspired and moved by the teachings and knowledge of Rosicrucianism."

Purpose: The exoteric aim is to help people achieve "an understanding of natural, cosmic laws" as the "only means of mastership of life."

Error: The esoteric ceremonies of Rosicrucianism lead its followers into ancient Egyptian secret rites which may result in demonic phenomena, including possession and spirit conjuration. (Initiation rituals are verbally affirmed with the words, "So mote it be," a standard oral oath of witchcraft cults.)

Background Sources: Miscellaneous AMORC literature including "Master of Life," "Who and What are the Rosicrucians?" "Rosicrucian Digest" (3/75), "History of the AMORC," "Rosicrucian Initiation — Neophyte

Guide," "Recognition," various issues of "Master Monograph," "The Celestial Sanctum"; *The Kingdom of Cults,* 1965, Walter Martin, pp. 428-432; *The Encyclopedia of American Religions,* 1978, J. Gordon Melton, pp. 177-184.

Address/Location: Rosicrucian Park, San Jose, CA 95191.

53

Scientology

Make it past the Hare Krishna chanters on the streets of any large city, and you're likely to run into a more conventionally dressed, clean-cut young man or woman offering you a "free personality analysis." Who would suspect that the 200 questions to be posed are part of the recruiting program for the Church of Scientology? Why be skeptical of "an applied religious philosophy" which offers "a clear, bright insight to help you blaze toward your mind's full potential?" After all, Dianetics (meaning "through the soul") promises to reveal "the single source of all man's insanities, psychosomatic illnesses, and neuroses."

Scientology attempts to give the appearance that it is both a science and a religion. Whatever it is, it isn't cheap. Fifty hours of Scientology counseling can cost $2,350. Some former members say they invested up to $30,000, which may explain some claims that the organization's take is over $1 million per week. With guru-like control, its founder and mentor, L. Ron Hubbard, oversees all Scientology activities from a floating fleet of ships.

Lafayette Ronald Hubbard published his book, *Dianetics — The Modern Science of Mental Health,* in

1950. It was originally intended to be his psychother-
apeutic answer to the techniques of modern psychiatry.
The medical community responded with alarm, forcing
Hubbard to formalize his theories into a religion and thus
seek tax-exempt status and freedom from governmental
interference for some of his organizations. Since then, it
has blossomed to command the attention of an estimated
600,000 followers and 4 million sympathizers. Hubbard's
reputation as an explorer, science fiction writer, and
parabotanist (he was one of the first to expound the idea
of communicating with plants) has now enlarged to make
him the worldwide spokesman for this fast-growing cult.

It's difficult to understand Hubbard's teachings without
a crash course in Scientology nomenclature. The Church
has found it necessary to publish a dictionary with 7,000
definitions for the use of over 3,000 Dianetic words.
Hubbard teaches that mankind is descended from a race
of uncreated, omnipotent gods called *thetans,* who gave
up their powers to enter the Material-Energy-Space-Time
(MEST) world of Earth. Gradually, they evolved upward
by reincarnation to become humans who could not
remember their deified state. Scientologists are
encouraged to awaken their dormant thetan potential by
removing all mental blocks called *engrams.* By doing so
they can realize their true personhood, achieving total
power and control over MEST.

Engrams are said to be traumatic experiences in past
lives. The "analytical mind" reasons, but the "reactive
mind" simply records engrams which impede spiritual
progress. Dianetics teaches the techniques for removing
(clearing) all engrams. The one who joins Scientology, a
preclear (PC), is said to be in need of *auditing* to discover
his engrams. This is done by using a galvanometer called
an E-Meter which measures the resistance to electric
current by recording galvanic skin responses. As with a
polygraph (lie detector), the instructor (auditor) asks a
series of questions while the student holds the two tin
cans of the E-Meter in his hands. (More elaborate models
are available for a "donation" of $215.) Scientologists
insist the auditing procedure is like a church
confessional. Those who have removed the psychic
hindrances of their engrams are said to be *clear.* The
clear one is a thetan who has audited out his reactive
mind responses.

While *Today's Health* contends that Scientology attracts the "weak, confused, lonely, and emotionally ill," there are others who genuinely look to Dianetics for altruistic reasons. Scientologists have tried to keep a clean image, publicly eschewing drugs, adultery, and premarital sex. Members are usually well-scrubbed, respectable, middle-class types. Church ministers wear the conventional black priest-suit and white collar, and even sport crosses, though they point out it isn't representative of Christ's crucifix. Scientologists talk at length about their antidrug abuse program called Narcanon, and their efforts with prisoners and the mentally retarded.

When their teachings and tactics are questioned, Scientologists are not prone to turn the other cheek. "Ron [Hubbard] says you only get hurt when you duck," explains Jeff Dubron, a Church leader. Reports have continually surfaced regarding the Church's alleged tactics of harassment, intimidation, and defamation of critics. An FBI raid on Church quarters revealed a hit list of enemies. Included were the Mayor of Clearwater, Florida, who exposed their clandestine activities regarding a hotel purchase, and Paulette Cooper, who wrote *The Scandal of Scientology.* The government finally charged Church officials with spearheading break-ins at several government offices. The purpose was to acquire documents which might embarrass and silence certain opponents. Seven Scientologists, including Mary Sue Hubbard, L. Ron's wife, were found guilty of conspiring to obstruct justice.

But ethics and legality of conduct are not the foremost criteria for evaluating any system of belief. Christians are concerned with Scientology's relationship to the Bible. A major creed of L. Ron Hubbard states that "man is good." This tenet is consistent with the Dianetic belief that man is descended from the gods and may someday evolve to reclaim his thetan potential. Other doctrines and practices include astral travel, regression to past lives, and the "urge toward existence as spirits" (Scientology Dynamic number seven).

Hubbard sails the seas with his Sea Org (organization) claiming that his teachings are "the road to spiritual freedom." Those who question the compatability of Scientology and Christianity need to be reminded that Hubbard declares Dianetics to be "the spiritual heir of Buddhism in the Western world." The regal thirty-room mansion and fifty-seven acre estate the church occupies in England symbolize Scientology's success on Earth. But Christians who are preparing for life after death feel a sense of compassionate concern for those who fruitlessly search for meaning in nonexistent past lives.

Founder: L. Ron Hubbard; Church of Scientology founded in Washington, DC, 1955.

Symbols: A cross, believed to have ancient religious connotations with the bar denoting matter and the vertical symbolizing spirit.

Appeal: Among those drawn to Scientology are disaffected youth looking for a simple, structured view of life; emotionally distraught individuals who shun traditional psychiatric techniques because they are too complex; and seekers of truth who are impressed with the dramatic claims of physical well-being and positive mental development promised by Dianetics.

Purpose: Scientology purports to explain all of life's difficulties and contradictions in terms of occurrences in past lives. These mental blocks are removed so the individual can return to the deified state from which he came many incarnations ago.

Errors: Occult practices of age regression and astral travel are based on theories of reincarnation. Extrabiblical information regarding man's origin (as a god called thetan) and mystical beliefs regarding the relationship of spirit and matter are essential to Dianetics. Man is good, Christ was merely a "cleared" individual, and the existence of an eternal heaven and hell is denied.

Background Sources: *The Denver Post,* 9/7/76, p. 2BB; *The Kansas City Times,* 7/14/77, p. 2B; "Scientology," a cassette recording by Walter Martin (no "P" date given); *Newsweek,* 9/23/74, p. 84; "Dianetics," Scientology introductory pamphlet; *Dianetics — The Modern Science of Mental Health,* 1950, L. Ron Hubbard; *People,* 8/17/78, pp. 20-24; *Christianity Today,* 12/7/79, pp. 54,55; *Celebrity,* no. 19, Scientology publication.

Address/Location: Various world locations, including Washington, DC, and Sussex, England; 2723 West Temple St., Los Angeles, CA 90026.

54
Spiritualism/Spiritism

"But it is Elvis!" she declared emphatically. "I was his fan for years. I know his voice and mannerisms. I'm telling you it is Elvis Presley who comes to see me at night."

The lady speaking to this author claimed to be an evangelical Christian. Before his death in 1977, she had idolized Elvis Presley. When he died, it was as though a loved one had passed away. Now, she felt comforted thinking that his spirit was reappearing to console her grief.

"I don't believe it's a masquerading demon," she insisted. "Elvis always tells me to worship God. He just talks to me, touches me, and assures me that he's gone to be with Jesus."

It was no small task to convince her that whatever had appeared to her had nothing to do with the person or spirit of Elvis Presley. Though her situation was unique, this author has counseled scores of individuals who feel they are communicating with the actual presence of a departed friend or relative. Not only do such occurrences "confirm" an eventual reunion with loved ones, they also provide information about life beyond the grave. In a time of sorrow, many are tempted to look past death's veil for some seemingly objective "proof" that those for whom they grieve continue their existence in some other realm.

After a period of demise due to the onslaught of scientific rationalism, Spiritualism is once again on the rise. Our post-Christian age has produced a biblically illiterate populace unaware of the Scripture's stern denunciations of any who attempt to seek knowledge or comfort by contacting the spirit world. Such conduct in Old Testament times was punishable by death (Lev. 20:6, 27). Today, these laws are seen only as the unenlightened injunctions of a theocratic state.

In recent times, the late Arthur Ford, a Disciples of Christ minister, served as a medium to perform seances on live television. Episcopal Bishop James A. Pike endorsed Ford's blasphemy by seeking to contact his son who had committed suicide while on LSD. A best-selling book, *The Other Side,* explored Pike's burgeoning fascination with paranormal realities. Pike's ecclesiastical superiors neither censored nor defrocked the Bishop for daring to attempt what cost King Saul his kingdom and his life! (1 Sam. 28).

Spiritualism/Spiritism is mankind's oldest religion. From the shamans of primitive cultures and the seers of ancient paganism to the psychics who frequent today's TV talk shows, Spiritualism has an unbroken history in almost every culture. In the strictest sense of the term, Spiritism is the overt worship of spirit beings, exemplified by voodoo practitioners in Haiti, macumba devotees in Brazil, and black magic advocates in Africa. However, since any form of contact with spirit beings results in a deeply felt sense of devotion, obeisance, and honor for these entities, there is little real difference between Spiritism and Spiritualism. For practical purposes, any technical semantic distinctions will be ignored in this chapter. The term Spiritualism will be understood to also encompass the activities of most Spiritists with our major focus being directed toward organized Spiritualism as it exists in Western culture.

Psychic activity in the eighteenth century centered on the life and work of Emanuel Swedenborg (discussed in the Minor Cults section of this book), as well as the experiments of Franz Anton Mesmer. Mesmer's investigations into hypnotism and magnetic healing sparked the interest of a shoemaker named Andrew Jackson Davis. In 1843 Davis was hypnotized, and while in a trance he displayed clairvoyant abilities and experienced visions. He philosophized about a system containing six spheres of existence in the afterlife by which man spiritually progresses upward. Davis' theories were explained in the volumes *Principles of Nature: A Divine Revelation* and *The Voice of Mankind,* books still revered by Spiritualists.

A more precise birthday of modern Spiritualism took place March 31, 1848, in the Hydesville, New York, residence of John Fox. Mrs. Fox became aware of some strange rapping sounds emanating from her upstairs and cellar. Margaretta, fifteen-years-old, and Katie, twelve, her two daughters, claimed they were communicating with a disincarnate entity they called Mr. Splitfoot. Splitfoot informed them he was actually Charles B. Roena, a peddler who had been murdered in the house some years previously. The sisters worked out a code (one tap —no; three tapes — yes) with Splitfoot.

Newspaperman Horace Greeley endorsed the "Rochester rappings," and hundreds of curiosity seekers descended on the Fox home. All across the country, other mediums began making similiar claims and Spiritualism entered its golden age. Advocates included James Fenimore Cooper, Sir Arthur Conan Doyle, Elizabeth Barrett Browning, Daniel Webster, and William Cullen Bryant. It was even rumored that Abraham Lincoln's wife was holding seances right in the White House.

In 1888 the Fox sisters confessed that the rappings were accomplished by a method of cracking their toes. (Margaretta, who had become an alcoholic convert to Roman Catholicism, later retracted her confession and was readmitted into Spiritualism's good graces.) Despite this damaging admission, the Fox home in modern Lilydale, New York, is still considered a mecca of Spiritualism and bears a shrine marker declaring, "There is no death."

Spiritualism was introduced to England and Germany in the 1850s, and in the United States, mediums flourished during the years 1880-1920. According to the National Spiritualistic Association, its ranks have increased to 160 member churches in America today.

The essence of Spiritualism is talking with or receiving information from beings who have departed this life. Communication with the beyond takes place at a seance.

Interested parties gather in a darkened setting, since the entities are said to be less likely to appear in the full gaze of either too much light or too many people, especially if some are nonbelievers. Ectoplasm, the foul-smelling, milky-white murky substance that exudes as an "umbilical cord" from the medium's mouth, is said to be an energy-form that will not function properly without darkness. Since ectoplasm may be the essence out of which the apparition and/or voice trumpet (the video and audio of the spirit world) emanates, seances are always held in dimly lit surroundings.

What goes on at a seance is unpredictable, though certain occurrences are standard fare. As the participants sit quietly in a circle, lights may appear, ghosts may materialize, a trumpet may convey the message of disembodied speech, objects may levitate, and the medium may be taken over by a spirit *control* who answers the inquiries of those who have gathered. The spirit guide, who generally is already known *(familiar)* to the medium, may control his subject's mind or subject the medium to a trance state. The voice and personality of the medium then changes as the spirit imposes his will and character upon his vehicle of communication.

Mediums usually specialize in a particular type of spiritistic phenomenon. While a trance state is the type most commonly effected, others may use automatic handwriting, table-tipping, or actual materializations. In the latter case, the spirit is often recognizable (either facial or fully human dimensions appear) to someone present at the seance. This presumed visitation by a loved one seems incontrovertible proof of life after death, especially if the spirit relates information known only to the grieving participant.

What is the source of such eerie goings-on? Some are unquestionably fraudulent. The contrived activities of magicians and hucksters have long been the nemesis of "respectable" Spiritualists. Swindlers have often preyed upon the grief of those who are bereaved and have staged seances for handsome fees. Henry Sedgwick, founder of the Psychical Research Society which investigates the claims of supernaturalism, remained a skeptic until his death. However, the history of Spiritualism presents too many bona fide claims to dismiss such evidence outright. Only the nonbiblicist who ignores the sorcery of Pharaoh's magicians (Exod. 7:11) and the "signs and wonders" of the anti-Christ (Rev. 13) would conclude that the feats described by the Spiritualists are beyond the realm of possibility.

Some researchers and certain Christian writers (this author excepted) feel that some paranormal happenings at seances may be attributed to the extraordinary psychic abilities of the medium. It has been speculated that a universal subconscious mind exists and that certain highly skilled experts can plug into the information it contains, much like getting information out of a computer. Such nonsupernatural ESP and telepathy may enable some mediums to draw knowledge out of the seeker's subconscious. However, certain documented cases of seances exist where the information interchanged was beyond the realm of any conscious or unconscious ideation of those present. While it may be arguable that the spirit of man possesses latent, untapped powers, two things seem certain. First of all, God never condones nor promotes the exploration of these powers, especially when telepathic phenomena violate the moral sovereignty of another person's mind. Second, most phenomena of Spiritualism seem to exist in a realm that defies naturalistic explanation and confound the investigations made by scientists and parapsychologists. Most evangelical observers would acknowledge that some Spiritualists genuinely communicate with spirit beings. The serious student of the Bible believes such entities are fallen angels, the demonic emissaries of Satan's kingdom of darkness.

It should be noted that Spiritualists claim there are biblical pretexts for their activities. The Transfiguration in Matthew 17 is viewed as an example of spirit materialization. Pentecost is said to have been the "greatest seance in history." In fact, Spiritualists believe that Jesus was the master medium of all time. They hold that the stone was levitated from his tomb, and that his own disincarnate entity materialized before the gaze of the disciples. One Spiritualist writer suggests that "by a slight change of name, 'medium' for 'prophet,' 'clairvoyant' for 'discernment of spirits,' 'psychic phenomena' for 'miracles,' 'spirit lights' for 'tongues of fire,' the close affinity of the two systems [Spiritualism and biblical Christianity] becomes apparent to all sincere investigators and students."

Gordon Lewis, Christian apologist and cult expert, has contrastingly observed that this word-game "makes the Bible endorse what its writers emphatically opposed! The prophets received their messages, not from the spirits of the dead, but from God. Spirits were discerned (1 Cor. 12:10), not by clairvoyant apprehension, but by their teaching of Jesus Christ (1 John 4:1-3). Biblical miracles, unlike Spiritualistic phenomena, took place in nature and in broad daylight. They served not to entertain nor comfort individuals, but to establish God's redemptive program."

Having discarded objective biblical truth on the basis of subjective, speculative spirit communication, Spiritualism has developed its own belief structure. Though many Spiritualists prefer to consider themselves Christians, The National Spiritualistic Association of Churches officially affirms that Spiritualists are not Christians. (They also disavow any endorsement of belief in reincarnation). That is to be expected since one of their spokesmen has declared, "Advanced spirits do not teach the atonement of Christ...."

Seeking to mimic Christian forms of worship, Spiritualistic churches conduct services that resemble the church gatherings of most denominations. There are, however, some significant differences. Though furnishings may include a pulpit, pews, crucifix, and organ to accompany singing, members receive "spirit greetings" in place of the pastoral blessing. The presiding minister's sermon may be delivered while in a trance. Psychic readings replace prayer, and familiar hymns such as "Just As I Am" and "Holy, Holy, Holy," have subtle lyric changes to avoid affirming Christian doctrine.

Spiritualism is a system of theories based on whatever information has been supplied by spirit-beings who range from the profane and blasphemous to the refined and intellectual. Over the years, organized Spiritualistic churches have codified their beliefs into "Seven Principles" and "Nine Articles." These "doctrines" are listed below, allowing Spiritualists to speak for themselves as to their view of God and spiritual realities.

SEVEN PRINCIPLES

1. The Fatherhood of God
2. The Brotherhood of Man

3. Continuous Existence
4. Communion of Spirits and Ministry of Angels
5. Personal Responsibility
6. Compensation and Retribution Hereafter for Good or Evil Done on Earth
7. A Path of Endless Progression.

NINE ARTICLES

1. We believe in Infinite Intelligence.
2. We believe that the phenomena of Nature, both physical and spiritual, are the expression of Infinite Intelligence.
3. We affirm that a correct understanding of such expression and living in accordance therewith, constitute true religion.
4. We affirm that the existence and personal identity of the individual continues after the change called death.
5. We affirm that communication with the so-called dead is a fact scientifically proven by the phenomena of Spiritualism.
6. We believe that the highest morality is contained in the Golden Rule: "Whatever ye would that others should do unto you, do ye unto them."
7. We affirm the moral responsibility of the individual, and that he makes his own happiness or unhappiness as he obeys or disobeys Nature's physical and spiritual laws.
8. We affirm that the doorway to reformation is never closed against any human soul here or hereafter.
9. We affirm that the precept of Prophecy contained in the Bible is a divine attribute proven through Mediumship.

What the Articles and Principles do not tell about Spiritualist beliefs may be summarized in the following statements: Every human is a divine child of God, no less a part of the Infinite Intelligence that was Christ. There is no lake of fire and no ultimate judgment of man's life. The crucifixion of Jesus was no more than "an illustration of the martyr spirit." Original sin, miracles, and the virgin birth have no place in Spiritualism.

What may be concluded about mediums whose receptivity to vibrations from the spirit world welcome poltergeists (ghosts), apports (movements of objects by psychokinetic means), and clairvoyant powers to see beyond the five senses? Their search for secretive knowledge violates God's prohibitions on such behavior ("The secret things belong unto the Lord" — Deut. 29:29). Luke 16 clearly illustrates that an impassable gulf separates the dead from the living. And if they could return, Jesus declared that anything the dead might say would have no ultimate moral consequences on the living (Luke 16:31). Jesus himself came back from the dead, and yet the undeniable proof of his resurrection is not accepted by many.

There is nothing the "initiates of a higher order" have to offer by way of comfort that has not already been offered by the Holy Spirit, the Comforter. The capricious messages of ghostly apparitions at mysterious seances can hardly promise more than the certainty of life after death assured to Christians by the One who conquered the grave. Spiritualists are generally not devious individuals, though many are enticed into the darker realms of black magic. They are often kindly people, who make warm friends and avow to promote morality for the common good. But their good intentions cannot remove the sting of death. Death is the result of sin, and only by facing that fact squarely through repentance can the resurrection promise of Christ offer hope.

Founder: Spiritualism is the outgrowth of Spiritism, a universal pagan practice of fallen man outside the Judeo-Christian tradition. The National Spiritualistic Association of Churches, the oldest and largest of Spiritualistic bodies, was formed in 1893. Also prominent among the nearly twenty Spiritualist denominations are the International General Assembly of Spiritualists and the National Spiritual Alliance of the U.S.A. Hardcore membership of Spiritualist churches probably numbers less than 10,000, though church officials estimate there are more than one-half million adherents.

Text: Books by Andrew Jackson Davis, as well as *Oahspe* by John Newbrough, and the *Aquarian Gospel of the Jesus Christ* by Levi Dowling.

Symbol: The Spiritualist creed, affirming "the belief in personal survival of death, which can be demonstrated by mediumship."

Appeal: Spiritualism capitalizes on the distraught emotions of those who have suffered the loss of loved ones and desire to communicate with them after death. The spirits which are contacted may offer to reveal the past, prophesy the future, and divulge spiritual "truths." The bereaved, the curious, and those fascinated by the paranormal may be enticed to experience the apparent "proof" of an afterlife.

Purpose: Spiritualism is defined by the National Spiritualistic Association of Churches as ". . . the Science, Philosophy, and Religion of a continuous life, based upon the demonstrable fact of communication by means of a mediumship, with those who live in the Spirit World." Contact with the dead is presumed to bring consolation to the living. The information obtained from departed spirits is said to produce spiritual growth and moral advancement. In this way sin and wrong conduct will be overcome by personal effort.

Errors: The key test of any spirit's validity has nothing to do with the accurateness of its information but rather its views regarding Jesus Christ. Prayer is the only spirit-world contact sanctioned by God, and the Holy Spirit is to be the only guiding source of spiritual information. Scripture abounds with prohibitions regarding the practices of Spiritualism (Lev. 19:31; Deut. 18:10, 11; 1 Chron. 10:13; 2 Chron. 33:6; Isa. 8:19; Gal. 5:19-21; 1 Tim. 4:1). The Bible warns of "lying spirits," and the Spiritualist has no gauge to objectively determine the credibility of his sources, since the biblical standards for discerning spirits have been discarded. The hope of reformation in the hereafter removes the urgency of correct moral choice in this life. Messages from subjectively identified spirits takes precedence over the revelation of Christ's gospel. Spiritualism's main tenet is but the paraphrase of Eden's serpent, "Ye shall not surely die," a spokesman whom Christ identified as a "liar" and a "murderer" (John 8:44). The Apostle Paul clearly condemned the mediumship of Barjesus (Acts 13), declaring that one who participates in such sorceries is a "child of the devil."

Background Sources: *Cults and the Occult,* 1980, Edmond Gruss, Baker Book House, Grand Rapids, MI; *Confronting the Cults,* 1966, Gordon Lewis, The Presbyterian and Reformed Publishing Co.; *Kingdom of the Cults,* 1977, Walter Martin, Bethany Fellowship, Inc., Minneapolis, MN; *The Encyclopedia of American Religions, Vol. 2,* 1978, J. Gordon Melton, McGrath Publishing Co., Wilmington, NC; *Those Curious New Cults,* 1975, William Petersen, Keats Publishing Co., New Canaan, CT.

Address/Location: The National Spiritualist Association offices are in Washington, D.C. Those wishing ordination as a Spiritualist minister may attend the Morris Pratt Spiritualist Institute in Whitewater, WI. Spiritualism is more prevalent in Europe than in the United States, especially in France and the United Kingdom. It also has a stronghold in South America, particularly in Brazil, which probably has more practitioners of Spiritualism than any nation in the world (see the author's book *Babylon Reborn*).

55

Theosophy

Robert Kennedy lay dead on the floor of a Los Angeles ballroom. Another Kennedy had been assassinated! What was the motive this time? There was no doubt who did it. The gun had been wielded by a young Middle Eastern fanatic named Sirhan Sirhan. Why did he pull the trigger? Investigators might have found the answer if they had bothered to thumb through the pages of the first book Sirhan requested after he was jailed — *The Secret Doctrine* by Helena Petrovna Blavatsky. The principles of Blavatsky's Theosophical doctrines may well have guided the murderous thoughts of Sirhan Sirhan. Sirhan's expedient philosophy of superior spiritual knowledge (which was inspired by Blavatsky's Theosophical teachings) may have made Sirhan feel he had the right to take matters into his own hands.

Helena Petrovna Blavatsky was born in 1831 of an aristocratic Russian family. She exhibited psychic tendencies at an early age, a portent of things to come later. Her marriage at the age of seventeen to a much older Czarist general lasted only three months. Her perfidious marriage vows were symptomatic of her basic lack of moral character. Biographers report that she swore fluently in several languages, went through two marriages and many lovers, and gave birth to an illegitimate child. Mrs. Blavatsky exhibited a violent temper and was addicted to hashish. Of her ability to sway masses to accept her teachings, she once declared that people "in every part of the world have turned into asses at my whistle, and have obediently wagged their long ears as I piped the tune."

Blavatsky's corrupt character hardly qualified her to inaugurate a global religious movement with the motto: "There is no religion higher than truth." Yet, the Theosophical Society owes its conception to her guiding hand.

Through the years, her mix of Hinduism and Spiritualism has attracted the likes of George Bernard Shaw, Thomas Edison, William Butler Yeats, and Jawaharlal Nehru. Such access to influential people has given Theosophists power beyond their numbers, an estimated 25,000 in sixty countries including 6,000 in the United States. Recent interest in the occult has swelled the ranks of this organization which was once dwindling in size partly due to strife from internal dissention.

After her divorce from the elder Mr. Blavatsky, Helena Petrovna proceeded to travel widely. While visiting the United States, she became intensely involved in Spiritualism. She claimed that during her journeys to Tibet she had made contact with disembodied higher spiritual beings whom she called *mahatmas.* HPB told how these masters of the spirit-world had guided her entire life through letters and messages, with even her home containing an altar to the *mahatmas.* In New York she met Col. Henry Steel Olcott, who shared her occult interests. Along with another of her admirers, William Quan Judge, the three formed the Theosophical Society in 1875. Her first book, *Isis Unveiled,* became the Society's central document, and a year later *The Secret Doctrine* was added to Theosophical "canon."

To outsiders, Theosophy presents a benign image of religious liberals intent only on fulfilling three major tenets: (1) forming a universal brotherhood of mankind; (2) investigating the unexplained laws of nature and the latent powers of man; and (3) encouraging a comparative study of religion, science, and philosophy. A closer look at Theosophical thought reveals a complicated system of cosmological theories based on Hinduistic doctrine.

Blavatsky's universe contains a pantheistic plethora of gods, lesser deities, and *devas* ("angels" in Hindusim) arranged in a hierarchical pattern based on numerological symmetry.

Both man and Earth are destined to evolve through seven stages. Earth is in its fourth cycle and man is in his Fifth Root Race, from which point he will evolve upward spiritually. The human body is composed of seven qualities: divine, monadic, spiritual, intuitional, mental, astral, and physical. To evolve spiritually, man must raise his consciousness beyond Earth's material plane with the aid of occult phenomena and the *mahatmas.* Though Blavatsky owed a debt of gratitude to Spiritualism for sparking her early endeavors, she eventually became an ardent foe. According to her, Spiritualists were erroneously engaged in contacting the lower levels of psychic entities. Helena Petrovna was more concerned with directives from the ruling masters of the spirit world.

Foremost among these deities is a being known as the Lord of the World. Under his authority are a Trinity of Buddhas and a variety of "rays" and emanating spirits, including Master Morya and Master Koot Hoomi. Master Jesus is considered to be a reincarnation of Lord Krishna, the Hindu deity. The cosmological status now held by Christ had once been filled by the Greek god Apollonius. The desired destination of man's soul is *devachan,* "heaven" to Theosophists. "Hell" is known as *kamaloka,* a purgatory type of existence where souls await another chance in a new reincarnation. Even the most evil offender need not fear a permanent, final divine judgment. "Man is a god in the making," wrote one leading Theosophist.

Blavatsky traveled to India in 1879 and declared that the Theosophists' headquarters would be in Adyar, a suburb of Madras. It was there that the vocal and written communications from the *mahatmas* became more frequent. However, during a return visit to England in 1884, Blavatsky's spiritualistic messages came under closer scrutiny. She was accused of being a magician, hypnotist, and charlatan. The prestigious Society of Psychical Research investigated her claims and found them to be considerably lacking in credibility. This blow to Blavatsky's veracity nearly destroyed Theosophy.

One major accomplishment of her stay in London was

meeting Annie Besant, a radical activist. Upon joining the Society, Besant's oratorical skills brought about a resurgence in Theosophy's growth. She eventually became head of the Society after Blavatsky's death in 1891. Though Helena Petrovna had once been toasted as a "world traveler, multilinguist, psychic, knowledgeable occultist, and altruist," she died as a lonely, obese, and miserably sick woman who was considered a fake and deserted by most of her followers.

With Blavatsky gone, Henry Olcott and William Quan Judge struggled for control of the U. S. Society. They eventually split into two factions, with Olcott, who was more interested in Eastern occultism, directing the European group. Before his death in 1907, Olcott claimed to receive messages from the *mahatmas* indicating Besant was next in line to lead the flock. In the United States, Judge tried to synthesize Western philosophy with occult theories and openly split with the London/Adyar division in 1895. Shortly after Judge died in 1896, Katherine Augusta Westcott Tingley (she had been thrice married), a Spiritualist with amazing occult powers, took over the American branch of Theosophy.

Most of today's Theosophists belong to the Olcott/ Besant wing, though a smaller group faithful to Judge and Tingley continues with headquarters in Altadena, California. The Theosophical Society of America, with headquarters in Wheaton, Illinois, keeps close ties with the British Theosophical Society. Current president is John B. Coates. Remaining true to the vision of Blavatsky, he has encouraged modern Theosophists to dabble in contemporary occult phenomena such as Kirlian photography, and in paranormal practices like psychokinesis. Coates cautions those who look to Theosophy as a spiritual lodestone by saying, "We have more questions than we have answers."

Though Theosophy seeks to encompass all religions, the Christian message understandably comes in for considerable drubbing. Theosophists have no need for the cross since *karma* and reincarnation guide their search for "redemption." The atonement of Christ is dismissed as a "pernicious doctrine" perpetuating the deplorable idea that "wrongdoing by one can be set right by the sacrifice of another." After all, the incarnation of Christ had no unique significance since, according to

Theosophy, ". . . christs and saviours of the age have been appearing at propitious times since humanity began existence."

Its foremost leaders have led undistinguished lives, its leadership has historically been rocked by scandal and internal dissent, and its teachings have been tinged by the dark, spiritistic arts. Yet, Theosophy survives, and indeed, thrives in the fertile soil of today's disenchantments with materialism. A leading Theosophist once declared, "Theosophy evokes a philosophy so profound and recondite, trying to explain it to someone is impossible. It takes years — lifetimes." And, it might be added, it also takes rosy-tinted glasses to overlook the foibles and fables of its founders.

Founder: Madame Helena Petrovna Blavatsky was born in Russia, 1831, the daughter of Peter Hahn, descendant of a noble German family. She died in 1891 while living in exile in Germany. The Occult Theosophical Society was founded in New York in 1875 by Blavatsky and Henry Olcott, aided by William Quan Judge.

Text: Writings of H. P. Blavatsky, including *The Secret Doctrine, Isis Unveiled, Cosmosgenesis,* and *Anthropogenesis.* Though Blavatsky's books are considered divinely inspired, other books and authors are also revered: Besant — *Ancient Wisdom;* Judge — *Ocean of Theosophy;* Leadbeater — *At the Feet of the Master;* L. W. Rogers — *Elementary Theosophy.* The religious philosophy of Theosophy is rooted in Hindu religious texts *(Vedas, Upanishad, Bhagavad-Gita)* and other occult sources.

Symbol: A combination of religious designations including the Egyptian ankh fertility symbol, a backward swastika portraying energy, the Sanskrit word *om* meaning "oneness," and the Jewish Star of David.

Appeal: It's lack of official public dogma makes Theosophy attractive to religionists who take a universalist view. Many find its inclusion of mystical practices (vegetarianism, yoga, *mahatmas)* a way to incorporate Eastern ideas into a Western tradition without turning to more extreme cults such as Hare Krishna.

Those enamored by psychic phenomena may be intrigued by stories regarding the supposed occult powers possessed by Blavatsky. (Theosophists proudly displayed at their centennial meeting a pair of sugar tongs she allegedly "called into existence through an effort of her will.")

Purpose: "We are seekers of truth," current leader Coates declares. Though the esoteric teachings of Theosophy constitute a complex system of doctrines based on Hinduism and various mystery cults, members insist their Society represents a philosophy and not a religion. Theosophy espouses goals of world peace, brotherhood without distinction of sex or creed, and investigation of occult and paranormal phenomena that presumes to reveal unexplained laws of the universe. Though Blavatsky officially denigrated Spiritualism in her later years, the realm of psychic powers is of special interest to Theosophists.

Error: Theosophy comes from the Greek word *theosophia,* meaning "divine wisdom." In reality, theosophical thought is merely a modernized version of the pantheistic Gnostic teaching so sternly condemned by the Apostle Paul in his letter to the Colossian church. The supremacy of Christ as extolled in Colossians 2:10 ("the head of all principality and power") is reduced in Theosophy to a "christ principle" apart from Jesus. This cosmic christ-consciousness is claimed to be attainable by all men, since in Besant's words, ". . . all men become christs." By asserting that humanity is but "a spark of the divine fire," Theosophy deifies the created and denigrates the Creator. Instead of walking "in the light" to know "the blood of Jesus Christ his Son cleanseth us from all sin" (1 John 1:7), Theosophists flounder in the "darkness" of reincarnation beliefs, which they call "the religion of self-respect."

Background Sources: *Newsweek,* 11/24/75, p. 110; *The Herald Weekend Magazine,* 12/7/80, pp. 16-20; *Madame Blavatsky, The Woman Behind the Myth,* 1980, Marian Meade, Putnam; *The Kingdom of the Cults,* 1977, Walter Martin, Bethany Fellowship Inc., Minneapolis, MN; *Encyclopedia of American Religions, Vol. 2,* 1978, J. Gordon Melton, McGrath Publishing Company, Wilmington, NC.

Address/Location: International Headquarters are in
Adyar (Madras), India. U. S. headquarters: The Theo-
sophical Publishing House, P. O. Box 270, Wheaton, IL.
The address of the Blavatsky Foundation (dedicated to
promoting her "life and works") is: P. O. Box 1543, Fresno,
CA 93716.

56

Transcendental Meditation

He can't trademark the name. The words "transcendental" and "meditation" are not exclusively definitive. And even the Maharishi Mahesh Yogi acknowledges in his writings that some Hindus believe this ancient spiritual discipline was conveyed to man centuries ago by one of their gods, Lord Krishna.

Worse yet for the Maharishi (devout disciples insist "the" must be dropped when referring to him), the pretense that TM (as it is popularly known) "isn't a religion" is no longer defensible. On October 19, 1977, U. S. District Judge H. Curtis Meanor issued an extensive eighty-two page opinion upholding the plaintiff's claim regarding the religious nature of Transcendental Meditation. In Judge Meanor's words, "No inference was possible except that the teachings of SCI/TM and the *puja* are religious in nature. No other inference is 'permissable' or reasonable, especially because the court is dealing with the meaning of the constitutional term and not with a factual dispute . . . . " Seventeen months later, the United States Court of Appeals for the Third Circuit, sitting in Philadelphia, affirmed this ruling.

The legal opinion regarding TM is of value to those

Christians concerned about its incursions into public schools, prisons, the military, and other government-funded institutions. Government grants (seventeen in all at one time, including $21,540 from the Department of Health, Education and Welfare destined to show 150 high school faculty members how to teach TM) may grind to a halt. But with an estimated one million adherents in the United States alone, TM isn't going to fade away quickly. Senators, sports stars, movie idols, businessmen and even doctors continue to tout its benefits. And Americans who are generally ignorant of religious traditions outside of the Judeo-Christian model may dismiss references to Hindu gods as so much gobbledygook. The old Yankee maxim, "If it works..." could yet give impetus to the Maharishi's plans for the future.

To a generation raised on quick-relief commercials, expediency is all important. Thus, when an M. D. advises, "...no technique of meditation is as effective as TM in producing deep rest and consequent psychophysiological integration," who really cares about the intrinsic pagan nature of such a practice? After all, the publicized benefits of TM include relief from insomnia, normalization of weight, beneficial effects on asthma, faster time reaction, broader comprehension, and improved ability to focus attention.

Maharishi Mahesh Yogi was born Mahesh Brasad Warma, 1911, in Jabalpur, Madhya Pradesh, India. At thirty-one years of age he graduated from Allahabad University with a degree in physics. He worked for a while in a factory until crossing paths with Swami Brahmananda Saraswati, Jagadguru, Bhagwan Shankaracharya of Jyotir Math (commonly known as Guru Dev — "Divine Teacher"). Guru Dev had left his home at age nine to seek enlightenment. Under the teachings of Swami Krishanand Saraswati he achieved his god-realization and became known as an *avatar,* a manifestation of the divine.

Guru Dev had revived a technique of meditation which originated from the Hindu monastic tradition of Shankara, a philosopher who established the practice in the ninth century A.D. For twelve years, Maharishi ("Great Sage" — a name he adopted in 1956) was the favorite student of Guru Dev. When his spiritual mentor died in 1953, Maharishi retreated to a Himalayan cave for two years. In

1958 he ended up in Madras where during a lecture he spontaneously announced a plan to spread TM all over the world. He formed the International Meditation Society and headed for the West. In Los Angeles, he chartered the Spiritual Regeneration Movement in 1959. He finally settled in a London apartment where nothing much happened until 1967.

Flower-power was in bloom, but the sex and drug-crazed ways of the Beatles had brought the Fab Four disillusionment and frustration. George Harrison met the Maharishi and persuaded Ringo, Paul, and John to join him on a pilgrimage to India. There the Beatles, with Mia Farrow in tow, sat at the Maharishi's feet to be schooled in the ancient Vedic practice of transcendental meditation. The Rolling Stones and the Beach Boys joined the bandwagon. Of the latter group, Mike Love and Al Jardine became TM teachers. Brian Wilson augmented the faith of his comrades by lyrically declaring, "Transcendental Meditation, it works real good/More, much more than I thought it would." With such heady endorsements, the Maharishi confidently boasted, "I shall bring fulfillment to the hippie movement."

The Maharishi pocketed a week's pay from his followers (a substantial sum for a Beatle) and blitzed the United States with a lecture tour. The disarming smile of this giggly guru ubiquitously dominated magazine covers and TV talk shows. With flowers in hand he repeated the basic theme that the mind has a natural tendency to seek happiness. But peace and serenity are only possible if one passes beyond the normally experienced states of consciousness: sleep, dreaming, and wakefulness. Man must learn to "meditate" so he can "transcend" to the fourth state of "bliss consciousness," a condition of "pure awareness" where one is tuned-in to "creative intelligence."

The promises were euphoric. Maharishi confidently predicted that just one percent of the population practicing TM in any locality would reduce crime and empty the hospitals. Many victims of stress and hypertension gave glowing testimonials. Some argued that such relief was merely due to an anticipatory attitude aided by the forty minutes of restful posture which TM required each day. But supporters seemed to far outnumber detractors until the bubble of optimism burst.

"We were wrong," the Beatles concluded, with John accusing the Maharishi of being a "lecherous womanizer." His following was nearly defunct and crowds no longer seemed charmed by his Hinduistic platitudes. Though he had once hobnobbed with celebrity luminaries, the Maharishi headed home with the pronouncement, "I know that I have failed. My mission is over." His stay in his Rishikesh, India, *ashram* was cut short by a government-launched financial inquiry, so he set up shop in Fiuggi Fonte, an Italian resort community. There he decided to revamp his entire approach and vocabulary. His resplendent beard and hypnotically dark eyes disappeared from American TV screens. But not for long.

Religious terminology was dropped in favor of psychological and scientific language. The Spiritual Regeneration Movement became the Science of Creative Intelligence, and the Maharishi presented an image of a friendly psychotherapist rather than a Hindu monk. His inner circle may have heard him call the *Bhagavad-Gita* "an anchor for the ship of life sailing on the turbulent waves of time." But outsiders only heard the oft-repeated litany, "It's not a religion."

The ruse worked. By the mid-seventies, more than one million Americans had tried TM. Seven thousand teachers were propogating the Maharishi's gospel in more than 100 U. S. centers. Income jumped to over $20 million a year as 30,000–40,000 followers a month joined the movement to meditation. For an introductory fee of fifty-five dollars for college students and $125 for adults (now up to eighty-five dollars and $165), anyone was guaranteed inner peace. Best of all, there was no renunciation of materialism nor desire in the Buddhist tradition, and no repentance of sin nor reformation of character in the Christian tradition. All around the world, in prison cells and military barracks, TM'ers gathered twice a day to chant their *mantras.* Everyone, that is, except for the Maharishi. He was virtually deified as a yogi who had achieved "a perpetual fourth state of consciousness" with an "awesome" clarity of mind.

Though TM has popularized the terms "meditation" and "mantra," most people are still a little vague about their precise definitions. They mean more than "deep thinking" and "a funny sounding word." To understand their usage in TM, it is necessary to decipher the religious framework of the Maharishi's entire system.

The religious philosophy of the Maharishi is rooted in Vedantic Hinduism. God is a pantheistic, pervasive Absolute Being (*Brahman*). Even man's inner self is part of this divine Being. In Christianity, man's dilemma is separation by sin from a transcendent deity. The Maharishi sees man's foremost problem as alienation from his true Being. Salvation is derived by contacting this inner state of pure-consciousness. Meditation is the key to transcending ("going beyond") the three levels of normal consciousness (discussed earlier) to the fourth state where one is cognizant of his soul's true nature.

Three additional levels exist: cosmic consciousness, complete God consciousness, and Unity consciousness. Beginners in TM hear only about the first four, but the Maharishi's ultimate goal is to eventually lead all humanity to Unity consciousness. At that point, the meditator is liberated from the karmic cycles of reincarnation by achieving sinlessness.

For the present, the Maharishi is content with introducing adherents to the fourth level of conscious-ness. But what the meditator may not realize is that the interpretation of the process is based on assumptions which represent a systematic approach to Hindu theology. At the heart of this hypothesis is the mantra. Representatives of the Maharishi insist it is only a vibratory sound with "no denotive meaning." To the contrary, Hindu tradition believes that such words or syllables have supernatural powers, often invoking a deity who is believed to embody the sound.

TM as prescribed by the Maharishi requires the initiate to sit with eyes closed in a quiet, relaxed position, twenty minutes in the morning and again in the evening. All the while his mind repeats the Sanskrit word deemed to be his own personal mantra. This mantra is the means of "diving" to the depths of the mind's ocean, delving into ever subtler recesses of thought. No mental discipline is necessary. The mantra does it all. Just let the mind go out of gear and coast to its desired destiny of fulfillment.

In the process, one's deepest thoughts emerge and dissipate like tiny champagne bubbles. As the incantation progresses, the meditator is supposed to be relieving tension and disposing of stress. When the source of all thought is reached, the chanter has available "a reservoir of energy, intelligence, and happiness." Only 73,500 minutes of meditation later, the faithful have hope of absolute union with Being, provided they never meditate before bed nor after a meal.

Mantras aren't easy to acquire. The introductory fee is a mandatory requirement. Every meditator must also undergo an initiation ceremony which is distinctly idolatrous in nature. The initiate, with fruit, flowers, and a white handerchief in hand, takes off his shoes and enters a candle-lit room. Then, the instructor directs the initiate to lay these items on a flower-banked altar which features a color portrait of Guru Dev. Incense pervades the atmosphere. Finally, the teacher kneels before the altar and begins to sing in Sanskrit. The initiate may stand or kneel, too, as he listens to this ten-minute recitation.

When TM first became popular, most people didn't question this part of the ceremony. They were told it was "not a religious observance" but merely an opportunity for the teacher to "express his gratitude to the tradition from which TM comes." Apprehensive students were said to be "witnessing" the ritual, "not participating." Christian researchers weren't placated by this innocuous tale, and persisted in their attempts to uncover the truth about the proceedings. What they discovered came as no shock.

The TM initiation song is actually a devotional Hindu hymn called a *puja.* Guru Dev's picture represents a *murti,* the literal embodiment of God in corporeal form. While singing the *puja* (which means "worship") the instructor first invokes the favor and presence of the Hindu gods. Then he presents seventeen offerings to Guru Dev before finally praising him (personified by his picture-idol) as an incarnation of deity. Among the lines recited are: "To lotus-born Brahma the Creator, to Shakti, ... I bow down. At whose door the whole galaxy of gods pray ... Guru in the glory of Brahma ... Vishnu ... great Lord Shiva ... I bow down ... the teacher of the truth of the Absolute, to Shri Guru Dev, I bow down."

After this incantation, the teacher leans toward the initiate and whispers a mantra in his ear. The secret word is supposed to be his very own specialized mantra, chosen for him by a Maharishi-trained instructor. The mantra must never be divulged to an outsider, even a spouse, or it will lose its magical powers. The meditator's own particular temperament, personality, and profession have presumably been analyzed to determine *the* mantra which will produce the appropriate psychic vibrations. In fact, recent investigation has shown that only sixteen TM mantras actually exist, and these are dispensed according to age.

Does the mantra really work? Though the Maharishi's organizations publish volumes of information about research studies, most non-TM scientists are skeptical. No body of findings exists that has been subject to the proper, objective controls which would substantiate the claims of TM. The American Association for the Advancement of Science evaluated TM as to its stress-reducing capabilities. Tests concluded that the Maharishi's meditation techniques "produced no measureable change whatever in the body's basic metabolism, and further, TM did not induce a unique state of consciousness."

Evangelical critics charge that in the absence of provable positive effects, there are dangerous spiritual consequences. To begin with, TM conditions the meditator's view of reality and religion, predisposing him toward an Eastern concept of man and God. The guilt of sin can be neutralized by inducing a false sense of serenity replacing the stress caused by conviction. Demonic phenomena may result because spiritual defense mechanisms become ineffective when the mind enters a state of passivity. Some meditators report a "black-out phenomenon," waking up hours after starting to chant, unable to remember what has happened. In addition, some advanced meditators exhibit neuroses and psychoses resulting from the practice of "unstressing," the procedure of shedding karma from one's present and past lives through prolonged meditation.

To counter such criticism and to legitimize his efforts, the Maharishi has tried to further refurbish his image. God-name mantras have been dropped and the organizational entity has been subdivided. The TM empire now includes: World Plan Executive Council, Student International Meditation Society, American Foundation for Creative Intelligence, American Meditation Society, Maharishi International University (in

Fairfield, Iowa), Maharishi European Research University, Institute for Fitness and Athletic Excellence, and Affiliated Organizational Conglomerate. The Maharishi directs the activities of all these organs from his international headquarters in the Swiss village of Seelisberg.

As the number of new converts plunged to an estimated low of 4,000 per month in the late seventies, TM launched its most controversial aspect — the *Sidhi* program. (*Siddhi* is a Sanskrit term denoting supernatural, occult powers. The Maharishi has adopted the variant spelling *Sidhi* for trademark purposes.) A *Sidha* (one who has completed Sidhi training) spends from $3,000 to $5,000 to reach an enlightened state of infinite compassion. He is also supposed to have the ability to walk through walls, become invisible, and levitate.

Advanced meditators claim to have mastered dematerialization and flying, "just like Peter Pan." In mattress-filled rooms ("landings are unusually bumpy"), the Maharishi's most ardent followers say they begin by hopping, then floating, in preparation for flight. Leaders claim that nearly 4,000 have conquered the art, but offers by the press of up to $10,000 to witness a meditator on the wing have gone unclaimed. The validity of the Sidhi program is undercut by the Maharishi's preferred form of transportation — two Rolls Royces and his private helicopter which await outside his residence.

By promoting such bizarre phenomena the Maharishi may have lost his hold on mainstream America. But he seems oblivious to any indication that his welcome has been outworn. From his head office in the "International Capital of the Age of Enlightenment," a decree recently went forth: "Society will soon be characterized by harmony and happiness. Through the Science of Creative Intelligence, education will be ideal, producing fully developed citizens. Through the Transcendental Meditation programme, health will be perfect. There will be peace in the family of nations."

Whether TM's vaunted relief from tension will enhance the moral virtue claimed by this pronouncement is yet to be proven. The mantras may give meditators an improved sense of well-being. But it remains to be seen whether such positive feelings will also produce individuals who act in accordance with sound ethics.

Founder: Maharishi Mahesh Yogi, born 1911 as Mahesh Brasad Warma in Jabalpur, Madhya Pradesh, India.

Text: Hindu Vedic scriptures including the *Bhagavad-Gita* which the Maharishi views as an "indispensable" religious document.

Symbols: The Letters T and M, capitalized and appearing together (TM) as an abbreviated reference to Transcendental Meditation.

Appeal: Most seekers do not turn to TM in a search to find religious truth. They are looking for a means of attaining inner peace and cessation of stress with little involvement of time or discipline. TM claims phenomenal psychophysiological benefits as well as release from guilt feelings.

Purpose: The public posture of TM insists that the Maharishi's mantras open the mind to a state of "bliss consciousness" which unleashes creative impulses and reduces stress. In the place of suffering and salvation, TM promotes health and happiness. Once there is one TM teacher for each 1,000 citizens on Earth, social ills and conflicts will cease. The esoteric aims are to introduce the meditator to the underlying Hinduistic theological precepts (i.e., "all is one" and man is a god). As for those who do not practice TM, the Maharishi says, "There will not be a place for the unfit . . . in the Age of Enlightenment." TM practitioners who go on to advanced stages will ultimately experience a merged unity with pure Being and may possibly become unwitting mediums for familiar spirits. (Though the Maharishi acknowledges the existence of demons, he cautions any contact with them.)

Errors: The TM initiation ceremony violates the First Commandment. Matthew 6:7 denounces the chanting of mantras. Maharishi Mahesh Yogi's monist view of the universe is not compatible with the scriptural presentation of a personal God, who as Creator, is distinct from his creation. Christian meditation is an outward concentration on the Word and ways of God, whereas TM is a passive, selfish, inward withdrawal from reality. The repetitious sensory stimulation dulls the conscious mind, and makes it vulnerable to evil invasion. Christ's blood atonement is rejected in the Maharishi's statement, "[TM] is the only way to salvation and success in life: there is no other way."

Background Sources: Books by Maharishi Mahesh Yogi, including: *Science of Being and Art of Living,* 1963, New American Library, Bergenfield, NJ; *On the Bhagavad Gita: A New Translation and Commentary,* 1967, Penguin Books, Baltimore, MD; *Meditations of Maharishi Mahesh Yogi,* 1968, Bantam Books, New York; *Transcendental Meditations,* 1975, Bloomfield/Cain/Jaffe, Delacorte Press, New York; *The Mystical Maze,* 1976, Pat Means, Campus Crusade for Christ; *The Mind Benders,* 1977, Jack Sparks, Thomas Nelson Inc., Nashville, TN; *Liberty,* May/June 1979, pp. 14-15; *The Province* (Vancouver, B. C.), 10/28/78, p. 21; *The Junior Statesman* (Indian youth magazine published in Calcutta), 1/20/68 ; *Rolling Stone,* 6/3/76, p. 10; *S.C.P. Newsletter,* 11/77; *Christianity Today,* 4/9/76, p. 17; *Newsweek,* 1/7/74, pp. 73-75; *Ibid.,* 6/13/77, pp. 98-100; *Time,* 10/23/72, pp. 102-105; *Ibid.,* 10/13/75, pp. 71-74; *Ibid.,* 8/8/77, p. 75; *Right On,* 11/75, pp. 8-14; *TM Newsletter,* July/August, 1976; miscellaneous TM promotional literature.

Address/Location: TM Centers in 140 countries and approximately 400 U. S. cities. World headquarters at former Hotel Sonnenberg, Seelisberg, Switzerland.

57
UFOs

Ken Arnold could hardly believe his eyes. There, just
outside the window of the small aircraft he was piloting,
were nine metallic discs floating in the air. They darted
about with incredible speed and maneuverability. When
Arnold landed, he immediately reported the incident.
"What did they look like?" he was asked. More than
three decades later his answer is still the descriptive
preference of those who have had similar experiences —
"flying saucers."

Though observations of UFOs (unidentified flying
objects) have occurred at random times and locations, the
phenomena do bear similarities. The craft are usually
described as being circular, cylindrical, or spherical in
shape, with flashing lights and luminous brilliance. They
change color and shape, appear and disappear, and
seemingly defy the laws of thermodynamics. In just a few
seconds they can accelerate from a standing position to
speeds clocked at several thousands of miles per hour,
and then make a ninety degree turn in mid-air. In their
wake are left vile odors, mutilated animals, radiation
burns, charred landing spots, and various kinds of
electrical interference.

Dr. J. Allen Hynek, considered by some to be the

world's ranking expert on UFOs, has classified these appearances according to the following categories of "close encounters": (1) observation of a UFO within 500 feet or less; (2) physical traces left behind; (3) actual contact with the occupants; and (4) abduction or examination by these beings. The evidence concerning all four kinds of encounters is overwhelming, and in some cases, irrefutable.

With all the talk these days about UFOs and the widely circulated stories of people who claim to have communicated with the pilots of such craft, modern man is being forced to take these strange events seriously. UFO tales must either be explained, or explained away. If they are not real phenomena, then they should be dismissed without further consideration. If such occurrences are legitimate, then the nature and origin of UFOs need to be determined. Furthermore, Christians have an additional concern as to how these appearances may affect the spiritual future of mankind.

Are UFOs for real? Most are not and are easily dismissed as mistakenly identified planets, rocket launchings, weather balloons, and atmospheric phenomena. The Air Force Project Blue Book was able to provide a rationale for all but 700 out of 12,600 cases of sightings between 1947 and 1969.

Other reports are not so easy to dismiss. What of the cases where UFOs have torn off treetops, ricocheted bullets, and razed thousands of acres of forest (in the Soviet Union)? What about the hundreds of reports from responsible citizens claiming to have seen and heard unexplainable objects zooming across the sky? Why do these flying machines often hover near power lines, bodies of water, and military installations? Can such a diversity of situations with striking similarities all be dismissed as hallucinatory speculations or imaginations run wild?

If UFOs are from some unknown human source, who is responsible for them? The Russians are as puzzled as anyone. Only the industrialized nations could possibly have access to the kind of antigravitational technology necessary for such phenomena. If any advanced nation does have knowledge of such secrets, how has such information been so well hidden for so long? Supposing that such expertise does exist, only satanic influence would lead men to wreak such havoc and terror on their own unsuspecting countrymen.

The most commonly accepted theory regarding the origin of UFOs is that of ETIs (extraterrestrial intelligences). Unofficially, the U. S. government presumes that such craft must come from other planets. NASA has asked Congress for $2.1 million to begin what it calls a "Search for Extraterrestrial Intelligence." When the Voyager spacecraft rose beyond Earth's gravity, it carried aboard a twelve-inch copper LP titled, "Sounds of Earth." The record contained ninety minutes of playing time, including numerically coded explanations of our geology, chemistry, and mathematics.

Psychologist Leo Sprinkle, of the University of Wyoming Division of Counseling and Testing (he is also a consultant for the Aerial Phenomena Research Organization), claims that over the last five years he has hypnotized fifty people who say they have been aboard UFOs. Professor Sprinkle reports that these subjects are able to recall their stellar voyages in minute detail.

The accounts of ETI contacts seem to fit a pattern. The person is normally engaged in some ordinary activity when suddenly a UFO is sighted and then curiously investigated. As the humanoid occupant approaches, the contactee usually is frightened at first. Then the creature gives reassuring gestures to calm the Earthling and proceeds to give him a physical examination by passing a probe over his body. Some victims tell of sexual encounters with their captors. Contactees usually report that communication with the ETI takes place nonverbally by telepathy. The humanoids insist they are benevolent agents sent to help mankind and assist us in understanding the deeper nature of spiritual truth. A brief summary of something approximating occult philosophy is conveyed, and then the contactee may be hypnotized or placed in a trance to forget the abduction.

Accepting the existence of extraterrestrial beings necessitates subscribing to one of two explanations for their origin: the evolutionary hypothesis or a belief in other God-created stellar civilizations. The option of evolution is not available to the Christian. The simplest, single cellular organism known to man is still far too complex to have spontaneously evolved by chance anywhere in the Universe. The Bible teaches that God alone is the Creator of life, and the feasibility of conscious beings springing forth from nonorganic life is not scripturally supportable.

On the other hand, since there is no specific Bible verse prohibiting the possibility of extraterrestrial life, some argue that this omission leaves open the option that God may have created beings on other planets. Proponents of this theory insist that in the vastness of space there must surely be other races of creatures to whom God has given life. "We're so small and insignificant compared to the infinite realm of the universe," the argument goes, "how dare we be so egotistical as to assume we are alone?"

In his book, *The High Frontier: Human Colonies in Space,* Princeton physicist Gerald K. O'Neill put it this way: "The idea that we as intelligent life are unique is of course absurd. The more we learn about the origins of life, the more we realize that the conditions under which life first began on earth must have been duplicated many times over in other parts of the galaxy."

If God did choose to create intelligent beings on other planets, they too would be tainted by Adam's sin which affected the entire cosmos. They would be fallen creatures like mankind and thus have the same technological limitations that we do. If sin's retrogressive impact on man's advancement has prevented us from going to visit them, how could they possibly come to us? If for some reason sin has not invaded their race, would God permit such an unfallen civilization to contact us and thus be contaminated by our sin? The answer to both of these questions is decidedly negative. If extraterrestrial beings do exist, surely the Lord would have told us without equivocation. It seems that such a crucial matter would be discussed somewhere in the Word of God.

Since it appears likely that neither human agencies nor extraterrestrial creatures are the source of UFOs, we are left to consider whether they are of supernatural origin. Robert Achzenner (author, lecturer, and UFO expert) has put it this way: "I have come to these conclusions. The unknown objects and their manifestations are real; they are intelligently controlled; and no government authority or scientific agency knows what they are, where they are from, or why they are here."

One thing appears certain: We are not alone. Something or someone is out there. Professor Leo Sprinkle (mentioned earlier) expressed his view of the situation like this: "My guess is that they're more than just a physical phenomenon, that they're a psychic or spiritual phenomenon too."

J. Allen Hynek says these aliens may come from a "parallel reality." He concluded, "I suspect that a very advanced civilization might know something about the connections between mind and matter that we don't."

Is it possible that this "parallel reality" is angelic in origin? Such a presumption cannot be excluded since the Bible does warn us that in the end times "great signs shall there be from heaven" (Luke 21:11). Likewise, the prophet Joel declared that God would "shew wonders in the heavens." There are some committed believers who suggest that a percentage of UFOs are "chariots" of the Lord's "hosts." Others wonder if perhaps the rapture of the saints will take place when living Christians board flying saucers and are whisked away to be with the Lord. Another possibility often stated is that UFOs are evidences of God's angelic army amassing for the war in heaven prophesied for the Last Days.

To discuss whether or not UFOs are of godly origin, we need to divide the phenomena into two categories: encounters of the first kind (sightings), and encounters of the third kind (contact). Third stage encounters do not appear to be angelic. The conduct of UFO occupants (for example, sexual assaults and induced trance states) and the metaphysical message they bring is contrary to the activity that would be expected of unfallen angels. Whenever they appear in Scripture, angels of the Lord always carry out a specific, divine mission. Their purpose is to convey a glorious revelation of God's plan (for example, the announcement of Christ's birth — Luke 2:9-14) or executing the Lord's wrath and judgment (the destruction of Jehoshaphat's enemies — 2 Chron. 20:22; the overthrow of Sodom and Gomorrah — Gen. 19:22-25). Above all, as evidenced by Revelation 22:8, 9, they never draw attention to themselves. True angels of the Lord speak only when divinely commissioned to do so, with the intent of directing man's attention heavenward to God.

Having ruled out the probability of angelic encounters of the third kind, what may be said of UFO encounters of the first kind (sightings)? Obviously, if no direct, personal contact is made with the occupants of such craft, no objectively conclusive statements can be made. But inferences can be drawn from the nature of such visitations. The occurrences of poltergeist phenomena and the terror brought upon observers are indications of a demonic visitation. When God intervenes supernaturally, it is to bring comfort and peace, unless there is a clear reason for his wrath to be exhibited. What can be said of blips disappearing from radar screens, and flashing oval objects floating through distant skies? While neither God nor Satan can be positively identified as the source, the latter seems a far more likely culprit.

The descriptions given of UFO occupants usually include grotesque features and oddly shaped structures. They may have enlarged heads, slits for eyes, ethereal forms, and antennae sticking out of their skulls. Most accounts are of beings which bear a distinct resemblance to the "familiar spirits" described in classical spiritualism.

When UFO visitors speak, their message brings neither solace nor information in conformity with God's Word. They talk of cosmic awareness and transcendence to higher spiritual planes. Their discourses never glorify Christ as God and Creator. Instead, contactees are told to prepare for an age of peace that will be ushered in by these unidentified aliens. UFO occupants also encourage participation in a variety of psychic practices: astral projection, psychokinesis, automatic handwriting, clairvoyance, and levitation. Sin, judgment, and the redemptive work of Christ are never mentioned. Their words, their actions, and their appearances betray the concealed satanic origin of these beings.

If it can be concluded that the majority of UFOs are of demonic origin, then what is their ultimate purpose? Couldn't the devil just as easily accomplish his ends by another means, or do UFOs serve a unique role in the master plan of Satan to deceive mankind?

An interesting insight is provided by Jacques Vallee, a Frenchman with a master's degree in astrophysics and a doctorate in computer science. As an exponent of UFO investigations, he concluded that such phenomena are creating "a willingness to believe in extraterrestrial life." He goes on to point out that "attitudes on the subject among scientists, the media, and the public have totally changed in twenty years. We can rationalize this change or we can recognize it for what it is'— the result of a shifting of our mythological structure."

It may be that UFOs are reeducating mankind to accept a casual familiarity with paranormal activity. This conditioning process will be completed under the reign of the Antichrist. During that time an inanimate image will live and speak (Rev. 13:15), a fatal wound will be healed (Rev. 13:14), and fire will fall from heaven (Rev. 13:13). The Apostle John explains that such miracles will be used to deceive humanity into following the Antichrist (Rev. 13:14; 16:14).

Modern man would like to think he is more advanced than the primitive pagans of antiquity. But is their mythology of gods, goddesses, and superbeings really any different from the twentieth-century-mind's fascination with contacting humanoids from distant planets? The Greeks built their altar to the unknown god while we erect giant dish antennae to probe the heavens in search of some distant trace of extraterrestrial life indicated by a pulsing radio wave. Perhaps the persistent Old Testament warnings against any communication with "familiar spirits" applies to modern interest in UFOs as well.

Founder: Not applicable.

Text: Various occult and pagan writings are cited suggesting they are metaphoric references to UFOs. Some claim that Ezekiel 1 is a biblical account of UFOs.

Symbols: None.

Appeal: It is becoming increasingly obvious that mankind's dilemmas need an external solution. Those who refuse to seek a transcendent God may assume that extraterrestrials of a higher technological and spiritual state may be able to "save" humanity. Man's curiosity with the unknown gives UFOs a mystical fascination.

Purpose: Man's intent is to discover if UFO occupants are of a higher state of evolution. If so, communications with them may reap certain scientific benefits. From Satan's standpoint, UFOs may be preparing the modern mind to accept a casual familiarity with supernatural phenomena. This would facilitate the Antichrist's reign, and until then, create a milieu in which evil spirits may operate more freely.

Errors: The Bible does not give the slightest hint that extraterrestrials exist. Scripture indicates that God created only two kinds of beings — angels and men. In addition, Romans 8:19-23 indicates that Eden's fall was cosmological in its effect. Therefore, since the death of Christ at Calvary was distinctively for the sons of Adam's race, how many other times would he have needed to give his life to redeem other civilizations? Secular UFO interest fails to consider the possibility that such phenomena may be supernatural (demonic) in nature.

Background Sources: *To the Point,* 9/15/78; *Denver,* 2/78, p. 34; *Ibid.,* pp.38, 39; *Newsweek,* 11/21/77; *The Anchorage Times,* 1/1/78, p.B5; *SCP Journal,* 8/77, vol. 1, no. 2; *The UFO Experience,* 1972, J. Allen Hynek, Ballantine Books, New York.

Address/Location: CE 3K Skywatchers, P.O. Box 2300, Grand Central Station, New York 10017; Center for UFO Studies, 925 Chicago Ave., Evanston, IL 60202.

58
Urantia

When a book is described as "the finest world view of religion available to contemporary man," it stands in judgment of its own endorsement. This claim of superiority made by the members of Urantia Societies is supported by their insistence that *The Urantia Book* was personally delivered by superhuman, extraterrestrial beings. The book's 2,097 pages are said to be the "finest major divine revelation since the coming of Christ to our planet." Is it any wonder Urantia followers devoutly believe they are "custodians of the greatest message ever given to man"?

Urantia teaches that all religious concepts are outdated for our age. (In contradiction, their promotional literature insists that membership in other churches or religious organizations is compatible with membership in Urantia.) Urantia proposes to augment established religious precepts with a new understanding of man's evolutionary ascent. To accomplish this end, the organization is structured around Societies (ten or more dedicated followers who study *The Urantia Book*) chartered by the Urantia Brotherhood. The Brotherhood is described as "a voluntary and fraternal association of believers in the teachings of *The Urantia Book.*"

The Urantia Foundation is the nonprofit, tax-exempt entity that is custodian of *The Urantia Book.* Since its publication, approximately 100,000 copies have been sold at $34 each. A five-member Board of Trustees who are appointed to life terms manages the Foundation. Thirty-six members of the General Council govern the affairs of the Brotherhood. The Societies claim a domestic and foreign active membership of about 1,000. Members this author has met have been well-educated individuals of the upper socio-economic strata. Since the Brotherhood admittedly seeks quality rather than quantity it may be assumed that Urantia's scope of influence exceeds its actual numbers.

First published in 1955, *The Urantia Book* expounds a strange psychic revelation based on the cosmological view of our universe as seen from the perspective of beings from another world. The four parts of the book begin with an analysis of our Earth (Urantia, as it is known by these extraterrestrials), and its super-universe, *Havona.* In addition to descriptions of spirit entities, names of celestial designations are given which describe places such as Salvington, Nebadon, and the Isle of Paradise where the *Trinity of Trinities* dwells. There are actually three Trinities—the *Paradise Trinity,* the *Ultimate Trinity,* and the *Absolute Trinity.* The Paradise Trinity is supreme, consisting of the Universal Father, the Eternal Son, and the Infinite Spirit. The central theme of the book is a discussion of the hidden years of Christ, from age twelve to his public ministry. It purports to show the "religion of Jesus," not the "religion about Jesus."

According to Urantia, Jesus is a son of God who perfected his divinity by seven incarnations among various creatures of the Universe. His seventh incarnation on Urantia as Michael of Nebadon (p. 1323) was intended to teach us that we, too, are sons of God. He is not to be equated with *the* Eternal Son of the Paradise Trinity. Jesus is merely number 611,121 in the evolving scheme of Creator Sons who form and rule local universes. His six (not the biblical three) years of ministry ended by crucifixion, the cross being unnecessary since ". . . the Father in Paradise did not decree, demand, or require the death of his Son. All of this was man's doing, not God's" (p. 2002).

Urantia may claim to welcome Christians into its

membership, but *The Urantia Book* denies virtually every cardinal doctrine of Christianity. In *The Urantia Book* all major world religions are said to have monotheistic compatibility (pp. 1442-1454). The fall of man is dismissed as a "distorted story" (pp. 836-838), since Adam and Eve actually "carried on in the Garden for one hundred and seventeen years."

On pages 2020-2023 the bodily resurrection of Christ is refuted. ("His material or physical body was not part of the resurrected personality. . . the body of flesh in which he lived . . . was still lying there in the sepulchre" — p. 2021). Above all, the New Testament concepts of blood atonement and redemption from original sin are dismissed as the expression of a "primordial ghost fear" (p. 1005). In the place of these essential Christian beliefs, Urantia proposes a system of soul transmigration with man gradually ascending from animal-to-human-to-God.

The Urantia Book is so expansive that an exhaustive analysis is impossible. Listed below are a few more areas where the *Book* departs from Christian belief:

1. Prayer is not to be attempted until one has "exhausted the human capacity for human adjustment." In addition, "words are irrelevant to prayer" (p. 1002).
2. Paul's doctrine regarding atonement (Heb. 9:22) ". . . unnecessarily encumbered Christianity with teachings about blood and sacrifice. . ." (p. 984).
3. The home is seen as a "sociologic institution" (p. 931), and the belief that marriage is a sacred state is called "unfortunate." "Deity is not a cojoining party" in marriages which dissolve (p. 929).
4. Mankind's parents were named Andon and Fonta, who procreated the first creature born on earth, Sontad.
5. Adam, Solomon, and David were not in the direct line of ancestry of Joseph, the father of Jesus (p. 1344).
6. Jesus adopted the term "Son of Man" at age fifteen after reading a passage in the so-called Book of Enoch (p. 1390).
7. During his twenty-eighth and twenty-ninth years on Earth, Jesus toured the Roman world, accompanied by two natives from India (p. 1427).
8. The indwelling Christ is not essential to salvation, since "Jesus does not require his disciples to believe in *him* but rather to believe with him" (p. 2089). Impersonal as well as personal concepts of deity are

expounded without any acknowledgment of such an inconsistency. In some instances, both unitarian and trinitarian views seem to be considered acceptable. The only ultimate guide to faith is reliance on the "Indwelling Thought Adjuster" instead of consulting objective revelation. Thought Adjusters are said to be "undiluted . . . parts of Deity" who guide humans on the path of spiritual progress through countless lifetimes on other planets, "universe upon universe until [humans] actually attain the divine presence of [their] Paradise Father." Christians faced with such a philosophical outlook may find it difficult to present the unique claims of Christ since the Urantia member's inclusive view will seem to accept any doctrinal viewpoint. But a careful study will clearly illustrate that *The Urantia Book* contains contradictory, extrabiblical information opposing the most crucial of Christian precepts.

Founder: Dr. Bill Sadler, to whom *The Urantia Book* was delivered by seven spirit beings in 1934. A group of thirty-six people, called the Forum, studied the original manuscripts before incorporating the Urantia Foundation in 1950. John Nales is the current president.

Text: *The Urantia Book,* a 2,097-page volume said to be written by celestial beings and communicated by automatic handwriting (an occult practice). It was first published in Chicago, 1955.

Symbols: Three concentric circles.

Appeal: For those who do not accept biblical infallibility, *The Urantia Book* provides a fascinating disclosure of esoteric and cosmological information. The curious or speculative mind not rooted in Christian doctrine can easily be drawn to it.

Purpose: Urantia literature says the Foundation aims to improve man's "comprehension of Cosmology and the relation of the planet on which we live to the universe of the genesis and destiny of man and his relation to God, and of the true teachings of Jesus Christ."

Error: Urantia revelation is held to be superior to Scripture. Man is not a unique creation by God but an evolving being, descended from the animal kingdom, destined to be an angelic spirit-being, and eventually become a god. Man only needs to acknowledge that a portion of God's Spirit (the Thought Adjuster) dwells within him. Moral accountability is replaced with the Hinduistic idea of merging with God by soul transmigration. Paul's Epistle to the Colossians responds succinctly to such Gnostic-originated concepts suggesting that Jesus is only one among many spirit beings who serve as intermediaries between God and man.

Background Sources: Urantia Foundation literature including "Leavening our Religious Heritage" and "Our Task"; *The Urantia Book* and *Basic Concepts of the Urantia Book* both published by the Urantia Foundation; "The Urantia Book," 1979, Christian Research Institute Inc., Elliot Miller, Research Consultant; *The Encyclopedia of American Religions, Vol. 2,* 1978, J. Gordon Melton, p. 119; "S.P.C. Newsletter," vol 7, no. 3, 8/81.

Address/Location: The Urantia Foundation, 533 Diversey Parkway, Chicago, IL 60614.

59
Yoga

Her face is fresh and her body is incredibly slim. She looks like the model for a health food ad. The calisthenics she has just led you through are guaranteed to knock off the pounds overnight. For an exercise instructor she certainly lives what she preaches. But how does she stay in such good shape?

Almost anticipating that question she informs her students, "Now I want to show you how to *keep* those muscles toned and make sure the fat *stays* off. Sit on the floor and cross your legs. Now, put your shoulders back. Close your eyes. Take a deep breath, and as you let it out say, 'Om.' Let the *m* string out . . . like humming. This will help you to relax. Then we'll try some other yoga positions."

Yoga? Everyone thought this was a weight-loss class. Why doesn't the teacher have the students just sit in chairs to relax? Isn't yoga some kind of religion? Oh well, there's really nothing "religious" about what she wants everyone to do. Might as well go along with it. Besides, the sound of that *m* is kind of soothing. Giving it a try can't hurt . . . or can it?

Yoga as it is practiced in the Western world certainly doesn't lack for advocates. Author Erica Jong says it has spurred her creativity. Peter Max, the prince of psychedelic art, credits yoga with his success, as does Carol Burnett and gymnast Olga Korbut. Other practitioners include senators, nuns, ministers, and rock stars such as Ritchie Blackmore who wrote a song extolling its virtues. It is practiced in YWCAs and YMCAs, public schools, health spas, and churches. In an age of tranquilizers, cholesterol, cigarettes, booze, cocaine, and hypertension, yoga has become, for many, the American way to assuage neurosis and avoid physical neglect.

Most people have a naive openness to Eastern religions and have assumed yoga to be nothing more than an exotic way to achieve a beautiful body. Unfortunately, they presume that the exercises are harmless provided that they are not practiced with a spiritual intent. But yoga is much more than a series of muscular maneuvers designed to relieve tension. It is a Hindu tradition going back nearly 5,000 years and is based on mystical doctrines. Yoga, taken from the Sanskrit word *yuj* meaning "to join," literally means "union with God." Which god?

A major text on yoga states, "The aim of all yoga is realization of the Absolute Brahman." This abstract concept of God is difficult for the Western mind to understand. The Bible presents a personal, anthropomorphic God to whom we are personally, morally responsible. The God of yoga is an impersonal deity who pervades the universe as an energy force. Hindu belief teaches that God *(Brahman)* is unknowable, inexplicable, and at the same time, present in all living things. Sometimes, Brahman is referred to as the Universal Being, the Supreme Absolute, or Pure Consciousness. Whatever the name, his manifestation to men is known through the Hindu god *Shiva*. And it is Shiva, known as the Hindu godhead manifestation of destruction, who plays an integral role in the practice of yoga.

One of the basic beliefs of yoga is the dichotomous view of a material (physical) body and a so-called subtle (spiritual) body. The Bible does teach that the flesh (the physical body) and the spirit are enemies (Rom. 7:18, 19; Gal. 5:13-16). But Scripture does not say that the physical body is inherently evil. It only states that the flesh is more easily tempted to sin. Yoga, on the other hand, believes that the spiritual body is held in bondage by the physical body. Consequently, the posturing positions are intended to manipulate the skeletal and muscle structure in such a way as to release the spiritual body for its goal of yoga, union with God.

The primary concern of yoga is to heighten god-consciousness by elevating the awareness of the spiritual body. At no time does it seek to convert the spirit of man, assuming that it is intrinsically good. Christ has promised to regenerate man's spirit (John 3:1-7) and give unto him the Holy Spirit that he might have power and victory over the flesh. This promise is fulfilled by placing trust in Jesus, not by contorting limbs.

Swami Vishnudevananda, a foremost exponent of yoga and author of *The Complete Illustrated Book of Yoga,* succinctly explains the purpose of yoga. He states, "It is the duty of each developed man to train his body to the highest degree of perfection so that it may be used to pursue the spiritual purposes. The expression of the spirit increases in proportion to the development of the body and mind in which it is encased. The aim of all yoga practice is to achieve truth wherein the individual soul identifies itself with the supreme soul of God." How is this accomplished?

Swami Vishnudevananda declares ". . . the supreme power of nature" is a coiled serpent lying at the base of the spine. She is the goddess *Shakti,* whom Hindus believe is ". . . the giver of immortality and eternal happiness." But Shakti can only fulfill her promise by achieving union with Shiva, her consort. (Shiva is one member of the Hindu trinitarian godhead — Brahma, Vishnu, Shiva.) Shiva is said to reside at the center of the forehead between the eyebrows. The purpose of yoga is to arouse the serpent power of Shakti (sometimes called *kundalini)* so that she rises through the *sushumna,* a hollow canal said to be running through the spinal cord. On the ascension, Shakti passes through six *chakras,* spiritual energy centers. The seventh *chakra,* her destination, is Shiva. Once Shakti merges with Shiva, union or yoga is achieved. The next goal is permanent union to become a liberated soul and be unlimited by time and space — at one with God. The person who accomplishes this goal then possesses all powers, psychic abilities, and sinless perfection.

How does this all affect the average housewife who stands on her head to lose weight, or the business executive who contorts his muscles to placate an ulcer? There are four forms of yoga: *Karma Yoga* (spiritual union through right conduct); *Bhakti Yoga* (union with the Absolute by devotion to a guru); *Juana (Gyana)Yoga* (access to God through knowledge); and *Raja Yoga* (god-realization through mental control). Raja Yoga has three subdivisions, one of which is *Hatha Yoga,* the practice most familiar to the general public. Hatha Yoga is in turn divided into eight stages: (1) body purification; (2) postures; (3) *mudras* (postures that produce psychic energy); (4) breath control; (5) stilling the mind; 6) concentration; (7) meditation; and (8) union with god (Shiva).

Body purification, for example, can involve belching air, vomiting water, swallowing a fifteen-foot-long cloth or running a string up the nose, through the nasal cavity, and out the mouth. (These processes are known as *kriyas.*) The meditative aspects of yoga are designed to still the senses by gazing at an object without blinking (referred to as *tratak).* Some yoga meditations involve the recitation of a *mantra* (the resident name of a Hindu deity) and Hindu prayers.

Most people who begin yoga assume that the positions are mere techniques to calm the body and improve physical fitness. But yoga has distinctly religious purposes involved in every aspect. The postures *(asanas)* are sometimes designed with a devotional intent, such as the *soorya namaskar,* sun exercises. They are to be practiced by facing the rising sun and repeating the twelve names of the Lord Sun. Other positions are named after gods *(Baby Krishna, Lord Nataraja* poses) and animals (lion, scorpion, cobra, etc.). Western yoga instructors often de-emphasize these religious overtones but such departure cannot lessen the ultimate result.

Swami Vishnudevananda states, ''Hatha Yoga prescribes physical methods to begin with so that the student can manipulate the mind more easily as he advances, attaining communication with one's higher self.'' Some might argue that although Raja Yoga (the distinctly religious discipline of which Hatha Yoga is a part) has a spiritual intent, Hatha Yoga may be practiced free of these consequences. Again, the Swami warns,

"Many people think Hatha Yoga is merely physical exercise. But in reality there is no difference between Hatha Yoga and Raja Yoga."

The postures of Hatha Yoga are designed to condition the mind to experience an altered state of consciousness. Each pose is presumed to be tuning the body, glands, and psychic nervous system to a level of spiritual susceptibility and altered awareness. Hindu yoga teachers have long defined this discipline as religious both in goal and practice. Can it then be casually disassociated from its pagan origins simply because a Western teacher redefines its intent?

Once the yoga novice has learned a few basic postures, he is quickly introduced to the breathing exercises (*pranayamas*). He may be told that these are for relaxation or clearing of the lungs. However, this aspect of yoga is actually designed for the purposes of controlling what is called *prana*. This so-called "vital breath" is said to be a form of soul energy that originates with the Universal Life Force (God, Brahman) and permeates all living matter. *Prana*, sometimes called *ki*, is supposed to be the source of psychic energy and the fount of all extrasensory phenomena experienced in advanced states of yoga. *Prana* is localized in the *chakras*, the spiritual energy centers through which Shakti rises on the way to her psychosexual union with Shiva. The *chakras* regulate *prana* and thereby manipulate one's will power and all bodily functions.

Yoga's breathing exercises control *prana*, a practice claimed to be beneficial in ridding the body of diseases. *Prana* may also be transmitted as a spiritualistic healing force by the laying on of hands and connecting one's mind with "the cosmic power of god." It should be obvious that Hatha Yoga promises more than supple limbs and relief from tension. Yoga's ultimate purpose is union with Brahman and acquiring the resultant peace and harmony which Hindus believe comes from such god-realization. The supposed consequence of this achievement is the complete cessation of sickness, evil, stress, and domination of the spirit by the body. In this state, perfect souls may then unite immortally with God.

Such goals are certainly admirable. But are they attainable? The answer is no when they are compared to a Bible-based view of God, man, and the concept of union with God. Scripture teaches that a chasm of sin separates man from his Creator. This gulf can only be spanned by an act of reconciliation to God through believing on the death of his Son. Any attempt to merge or unite one's consciousness with an "Ultimate Reality" would encounter the sin barrier and thus be thwarted. It is not the human merit of ascetic disciplines that brings one harmony with God. It is by the blood of Christ that the partition of Adam's disobedience is eradicated. Faith in the saving power of that blood can bring true union with God and his will.

Yoga advocates are certainly to be admired for their devotion to healthy bodies. Many who strenuously oppose the religious overtones of yoga are themselves gluttonous specimens of the junk-food syndrome. All too many people consume inordinate amounts of coffee, sweets, and soft drinks. These individuals are certainly going to find some immediate physical benefits in yoga. Care for one's physique is important, but not at the risk of aligning oneself with pagan principles. The popularity of yoga presents a formidable challenge to Christians who ought to make their bodies a welcome place for the Holy Spirit to reside (1 Cor. 3:16, 17; 6:19, 20).

Founder: No specific person can be designated. The principles and practices of yoga developed as ascetic and physical means to achieve the spiritual purposes of Hinduism.

Text: The Hindu *Vedic* scriptures provide the theological and philosophical basis for yoga's presuppositions.

Appeal: Man has become a victim of his modern diet. Obesity and a sedentary lifestyle have become an increasing focus of concern for those who value their health and physical appearance. Yoga seems like an exotic and less strenuous way of restoring youthful vigor.

Purpose: Its original intent as a variant of Hinduism was to achieve spiritual union with the impersonal Supreme Absolute deity. It may be argued that most Westerners derive its physical benefits without entanglement in such theological premises. However, there is always the possibility that one may be drawn to experiment with the deeper stages which are distinctly religious in nature. The book *Yoga, Youth and Reincarnation* states, "Yoga is accomplished when the individual spirit merges with the Universal Spirit [God] in a spirit of oneness."

Errors: It is poor logic to assume that commitment to a religious system of approach to false gods may be excused by divorcing part of the system from its ultimate aim (i.e., doing yoga exercises for physical reasons independent of their intended integration into a methodology of spiritual merit by "works"). The Christian's concept of peace with God is based on reconciliation to the Lord, not union with a Brahmanistic pantheon. Spiritual favor and righteousness come from what Christ has done for us (Eph. 2:8, 9), not the posturing positions we do for him. Yoga ultimately strives for the deification of man and his spiritual enlightenment. It also promises release from the endless cycles of reincarnation, an unbiblical teaching.

Background Sources: *The Complete Illustrated Book of Yoga,* 1960 Swami Vishnudevananda, Bell Publishing; *Yoga, Youth and Reincarnation,* 1965, Jess Stearn, Bantam; miscellaneous texts on yoga and Hinduism.

Address/Location: None specific. Yoga centers and teachers in most major cities.

SYNOPSES
OF MINOR CULTS

60
Aetherius Society

The Aetherius Society is one of the best-known UFO groups. Founded in 1954 by Londoner Dr. George King, the Society encourages members to be willing channels of communication with extraterrestrial beings. King's involvement in Spiritualism and various forms of occultism has well suited him for leadership of this strange cult. The Society was formed when King supposedly received a message from the "cosmic brotherhood" of "space masters" — their chief spokesman being Master Aetherius of Venus. King was chosen to be the "primary terrestrial channel" for the communications these creatures desired to transmit. The purpose of this spiritistic mediumship (which includes messages from Master Jesus and Aetherius himself) is to enlist terrestrials on the side of the "space masters" in their war against certain "black magicians" living on Earth.

The Aetherius Society has U.S. centers in Detroit and Los Angeles, and publishes a periodical, *Cosmic Voice*. Society members are encouraged to maintain contact with orbiting space ships and assist the occupants of these circling saucers, whose mission it is to direct their "energy" through the minds and bodies of King's followers.

61

Alamo Christian Foundation

The year was 1970 and this author was standing at the front door of a small frame house just off Sunset Strip in Hollywood. Outside was a sign reading: *Alamo Christian Foundation*. Inside, a coed crowd of long-haired misfits mingled in a somewhat disorderly fashion. When I inquired about the nature and purpose of their crash pad, the "elder brother" in charge quickly informed me that I was sent from Satan and ordered me to leave. This small communal flophouse was the inauspicious beginning of an Alamo empire which would eventually stretch from a Saugus, California ranch to a Nashville, Tennessee clothing store.

Capitalizing upon the early seventies' Jesus Revolution, which the Alamos claim to have initiated, Tony and Susan Alamo, a flamboyant couple with extravagant tastes, fashioned an effective organization using Pentecostal-like theology and cult-control techniques. The ranks of recruits were filled with disillusioned street kids who found solace in the regimented lifestyle of the Saugus ranch complex. The deplorable living conditions were seldom questioned by the converts, though Tony and Susan lived in secluded splendor. Most Foundation members seldom saw the Alamos except when their Cadillac Fleetwood zoomed by, or when they were bused into Los Angeles to witness a taping of the Alamo TV show.

Alamo theology was bedrock, hell-fire Pentecostalism, though their practice of "speaking in tongues" appeared to be a hypnotically induced utterance. The Alamos taught that all churches were corrupt, and in spite of the members having to eat discarded foodstuffs and to labor long hours in order to crucify the flesh, they zealously believed that they were the vanguard of God's spiritual army. The press repeatedly raised charges of sensory deprivation, enslavement, and brainwashing. These allegations only served to reinforce the persecution paranoia which permeated Foundation thinking. New members were instructed to pray diligently for the healing of Susan Alamo, who was rumored to have terminal cancer. She died in 1978, and Tony has been left to guide what remains of this once-prominent (and now declining) seventies' youth cult currently centered in an Arkansas retreat location.

62

Ananda Marga Yoga Society

What Hindu-oriented group would dare consider its founder a *Maha-Guru (avatar* — incarnation of God), even after he had been sentenced to life imprisonment for murder? The Ananda Marga Yoga Society claims that distinction, though its leader, Shrii Shrii Anandamurti (also known as Prabhat Ranjan Sarkav), was later found innocent in a new trial. Still, the Indian government frowns on the organization, insisting it is fascist and teaches ritual murder. In the United States the public image is quite different, and has attracted an estimated 3,000 to 4,000 members who pursue the way of Ananda Marga ("joy"). One of its strongest followings is located in Australia.

The path of joy and bliss is laden with yogic principles and practices, including initiation by a *guru* and daily *mantric* meditation. Special emphasis is placed upon *Kiirtan* dancing, a swaying routine with raised arms. This motion is accompanied by a chant known as *Baba Nam Kevalam* ("the cosmic father is everywhere"). These choreographed steps are designed to increase spiritual vibrations and help one realize that "all of creation is a manifestation of the Lord." In addition to the *kundalini* yogic techniques employed, charitable service to society is encouraged as a way to "break down the ego-bound mind."

63

Anthroposophical Society

By reason of their inherent pragmatism and staunch
Lutheran heritage, generations of Germans have given
rise to few exotic and esoteric organized religious
movements. Rudolph Steiner's Anthroposophical Society
is a notable exception. Steiner, born in Austria in 1861,
became a Theosophist and headed the German division
of the Theosophical Society, which was chartered in 1902.
After publishing his *Spiritual Hierarchies* in 1909, Steiner
split with Theosophy over its growing emphasis on
Eastern religious philosophy. His philosophy then
became Anthroposophy (from *anthropos,* "mankind,"
plus *sophia,* "wisdom" — "the wisdom of man"), a
"spiritual science," a form of "true Christianity," which
was also called "Christian Occultism."

Borrowing heavily from a variety of mystical traditions,
Steiner theorized that man and Earth are embarked on a
progressive evolutionary journey overseen by certain
beings of the "supersensible" spirit world.
Reincarnation, *karma, chakras,* and meditation are all
concepts of his system which propose that human
perfection comes through a succession of embodiments.
Even the Earth goes through evolutionary cycles, the
current stage being its fourth reincarnation. From his
writings in more than 100 books, Steiner imaginatively

developed a complex history of mankind, including the mythology of Atlantis.

Christ, who was human until receiving the Christ-Essence at his Jordan baptism, is the only being to undergo one incarnation. His spiritual, "phantom" (not bodily) resurrection was clairvoyantly perceived by the disciples. Through Steiner's techniques of meditation, all who follow Anthroposophy may also recognize the Christ within them. Though Anthroposophists consider the Bible to be a valuable document to secret knowledge, their main focus of attention is in Steiner's works, which assume an authoritative capacity effectively superseding Scripture. By meditating on Steiner's words, the acolyte becomes capable of mediumistically communicating with initiates and departed beings of the spirit world.

Other concepts of Anthroposophy include: *Eurythmy,* a form of rhythmic movement; the founding of Waldorf Schools, institutions dedicated to awakening spiritual consciousness in children; a "fall" of humanity which has reduced man to a baser consciousness, rendering him incapable of knowing his true origin and destiny.

Dornach (near Basel), Switzerland, is the current world headquarters of Anthroposophy, coming to North America by way of German immigrants whose successors now claim thirty centers and thirteen Waldorf Schools. A sacramental branch of the Anthroposophical Society offers a liturgical form of "Christianized" Anthroposophy called the Christian Community. With its priests and ministers looking after the flock, the Christian Community maintains a separate identity with no formal ties to Anthroposophy, though it has no accommodation with orthodox Christianity. Though Steiner taught that a form of mystical Christianity replaced the outdated Eastern religions, his syncretistic result was an occult system more attuned to Spiritualism than the Good News. Rudolph Steiner was unquestionably an intelligent, articulate man whose perception of Christ as the "Lord of Karma" was clouded by his own subjective interpretation of occult phenomena.

64

Arica Institute, Inc.

What more could one ask for than "body vitality . . . mental clarity . . . a permanent higher level of awareness. . ." and a "perfect society"? Such are the promises of the Arica Institute. Arica, in Quechua (the pre-Incan language of the Andes Indians), means "open door." Arica is also the name of a Chilean town to which fifty-four Americans were lured in 1971. They had been invited by a Bolivian philosophy teacher and mystic, Oscar Ichazo.

Ichazo offered to take these seekers of truth beyond the inhibitions of their egos to "the Permanent 24," a secret name describing the mysterious state of "unity with emptiness." That original small group has now grown to an estimated 25,000 adherents (by Arica estimates) who have undergone Ichazo's training, plus some 2,500 new candidates who each year shell out $995 apiece for induction into Arica. Arica instructors practice what they call "scientific mysticism," claiming it will uncover *TOHAM KUM RAH,* "the mystical name of the radiant being" inside each person.

Arica draws from the religious philosophies of Hinduism, Zen, and Tibetan Lamaism (though Arica literature proclaims it is "not a religion"), in order to develop *psychocalisthenics.* One such exercise, the *Audicon Plantar,* teaches students to lie on the floor and absorb sound with their feet. In addition to breathing techniques, African dances, Egyptian gymnastics, Hindu mantras and incantations, the seekers engage in "mentations." This odd practice requires the student to concentrate on separate sections of his body for specified times: 8 minutes 40 seconds for the colon and kidneys, 10 minutes 45 seconds for the liver, etc.

In its offer to restore the essence of man's perfection, Arica attracts many who are emotionally disturbed or disenchanted with other self-improvement therapies, such as Esalen (discussed later in this section). Ironically, Oscar Ichazo blames the ills of humanity on society's failure to adopt his ideas wholeheartedly. Consequently, he now offers forty-day courses (the original training took three months) for universities and retirement communities.

65

Church of Armageddon
(Love Family)

Meekness, patience, and courage sound like admirable biblical qualities. But in the Church of Armageddon (sometimes called the Love Family), these virtues represent the newly adopted names of cult members. Since the Love Family considers all Christians to be descendents of the Israelites, Israel is added as a surname. Presiding over the clan is Love Israel, a former salesman named Paul Erdmann, who formed the Seattle-based cult by gathering followers to whom he expounded his visions and revelations.

Taking his cue from Revelation 16:16 in which Armageddon is mentioned, Erdmann (Love Israel) teaches his disciples that they are the true family of God. New members turn over all of their possessions to the church, cut off all communication with the outside world (including their parents and relatives unless such contacts result in donations of money and materials), and devote themselves to the goals and person of Love Israel. The disciples are also taught to adhere to some strange and unusual beliefs. Eating is considered to be a sacrament; the consumption of marijuana, hashish, and mushrooms are also sacraments; children are severely disciplined; marriage is replaced by "bonding" under Love Israel's authority; yoga is exercised; outside medical assistance is forbidden, and toluene (a solvent) vapors are inhaled as a religious rite. (After two members died from this practice, it has apparently been discontinued.)

Though Love Israel has undoubtedly "transformed" the lives of his followers, from insecure outcasts to self-confident zealots, they have paid a great price sacrificing personal freedom. Fortunately, the growth of the group has never surpassed a few hundred members, a statistic which is small consolation to anyone who has had a loved one captivated by this cult. With Love Israel as the focus of attention, the Love Family seems to be more an extension of his own personal ego rather than a "fulfilled" New Testament organ of Christ's body.

66

The Church of Bible Understanding
(Forever Family)

His usual appearance has been associated with a shaggy beard, stringy gray hair circling a bald forehead, military fatigues, Converse All-Star yellow sneakers, a chain of brown leather pouches, a dozen colored felt-tip pens in his breast pocket, and a large round pin proclaiming, "Get Smart, Get Saved." This is hardly the image one would envision for a revered spiritual leader who likens himself to Elijah and hints that he may know the exact hour of the Lord's return. But then Stewart Traill, ex-atheist and former second-hand vacuum cleaner salesman, is not a typical Messianic cult leader.

After an apparent religious conversion in Allentown, Pennsylvania, in the early seventies, Traill began teaching Bible studies and collecting a following. With his wife and new converts in tow, he formed the Forever Family. Concerned that the name lacked respectability, in 1976 it was changed to the Church of Bible Understanding (COBU). He continued to prosper until he headed a far-flung fellowship estimated to be 4,000 strong (only about 700 remain), and he amassed a fortune, including a

$2 million-a-year rug-cleaning business and three airplanes, one of them a $300,000 turboprop.

In the wake of the Jonestown debacle, Traill's prospects soured. The location of his headquarters was constantly shifted until the present Philadelphia site was selected. Although membership has dwindled to the present 700, it appears to have momentarily stabilized. Ex-members complained of being encouraged to work for a pittance (all earnings are turned over to church leaders) and being housed in rat-infested lofts. The IRS put the rug-cleaning operation out of business, and the truth of his divorce and remarriage surfaced. Traill, forty-six, and his wife had exchanged accusations of adultery in a messy divorce proceeding, after which he married his COBU secretary — half his age —only six weeks later.

An exact picture of COBU doctrine is sketchy, since few definitive statements have been published. Its communal lifestyle is regimented into categories known as "guardians" (active members who are leaders), "sheep" (advanced believers), and "lambs" (new converts). Those who have left the commune report having been intimidated by suggestions that "backsliders" may meet a tragic end. The remaining COBU members devoutly believe that they have (via Traill) the one true access to "Bible understanding." Traill contends that God deliberately secret-coded the Scriptures and that only his "figure system" and "color-coding scheme" hold the keys to the true interpretation of the Word of God.

Though the basic appeal of COBU is directed toward a "personal acceptance of Christ" with "old-time religion" terminology, Traill's denial of the Trinity, and his unsubstantiated berating of detractors ("CCs" — short for "Contentious Christians") hardly endears him to mainstream evangelicals. In addition, Traill challenges his converts to break off all familial relationships on the premise that those over thirty (excepting Traill) are too spiritually hopeless. In spite of his more recent attempt to improve his personal appearance as well as COBU's image, the prognosis for any substantial growth of the cult seems doubtful. The question of whether or not most COBU members are "genuinely saved" is open to speculation, but their coercive and rigidly methodical methods of "witnessing" are unlikely to garner many adherents, given today's skeptical anticult outlook.

67

Esalen Institute

Every summer, at least 1,500 people pass through the gates of Esalen Institute to wander naked through its groves and give vent to whatever suppressed feelings haunt their psyches. Founded in 1962, by Michael Murphy, Esalen Institute is one of the granddaddies of the so-called "human potential" movement. On its Big Sur coastal shores, some of the early experiments with encounter groups and sensitivity training first surfaced.

Though Esalen's goals purport to emphasize psychological self-help, the religious overtones are apparent to students of mystical thought. Murphy founded Esalen in 1962 (its name comes from the local Indian tribe) after studying at an *ashram* in India. His stated goal was to evoke Eastern-style spirituality by allowing participants to vent their true emotions in "the here and now...not to adjust, but to transcend." In the process, those who attend Esalen sessions may find themselves seated, facing a naked stranger and sensuously stroking his or her body. They are also encouraged to pretend they are animals in distress or to simulate the sounds of lovemaking. In an attempt to avoid phoniness, those who attend Esalen sessions are sometimes made to stare at white squares until they see visions. A former president of the American Psychological Association has been quoted as saying that Esalen is potentially "the most important educational institute in the world."

68

The Farm

Some folks in the surrounding area view this rural
Tennessee commune with alarm. Others begrudgingly
bestow kudos for its self-sufficiency and apparent
industriousness. Few really understand the historical
facts concerning The Farm, or comprehend the teachings
and practices of its leader, Stephen Gaskin. Its 1,500
members boast of a school, a health clinic, a recording
studio, an area-wide ambulance service, and
computerized typesetting facilities for a publishing
company. The Farm proudly promotes its New York Bronx
voluntary ambulance crew, and also its relief organization
PLENTY, which dispatches certain of their members to
provide aid for Third World countries. But Gaskin and his
followers are far from being the respectable band of
former hippies they have portrayed in order to earn
tax-exempt monasterial status.

In the psychedelic sixties, Stephen Gaskin was an
assistant to S. I. Hayakawa at San Francisco State College.
He dropped out to drop acid, and eventually became a
local *guru* celebrity. Gaskin held Monday night
counterculture rap sessions which were attended by as
many as 2,000 supporters. He expounded at length upon
revelations from his drug experiences, which were

enhanced through his studies in a variety of occult and Eastern practices. In the fall of 1971, he headed a ragtag caravan of sixty school buses carrying his 250 flower children. After meandering across the United States, they settled 15,000 miles later on a 1,700-acre patch of farmland sixty-five miles south of Nashville. Today, the Farm is recognized as one of the few American communes to have achieved long term success.

In the early days, commune members lived a carefree life in squalid conditions and frolicked in the effects of peyote, psilocybin, mushrooms, and marijuana (all of which Gaskin proclaimed to be sacred sacraments). The Farm was eventually raided by police and in spite of legal appeals all the way to the Supreme Court, Gaskin and three fellow members each spent a year in prison. Group marriages with full sexual privileges were tried (with Gaskin once again leading the way), but that also proved somewhat unsuccessful.

Though monogamy reigns and marijuana is no longer a Farm crop (members freely admit many of them still toke up frequently), Gaskin has not abandoned his spiritual mission. Ex-members accuse him of openly declaring to be a messenger from God. Mystical religious experiences are encouraged, along with a mixture of beliefs ranging from *tantra* (ritualistic sex), *karma,* and *mantras,* to *bodhisattvas* (incarnations of God in Buddhism), the latter fitting nicely into Gaskin's claims of spiritual leadership. His writings declare that Jesus and Buddha were incarnations of God for their age. For this modern era, another *avatar* is required. Sin is a concept which "is no longer necessary," and the crucifixion of Christ "wasn't exactly what he wanted to teach." The Farm may not be another Jonestown, but neither is its blend of Zen and agriculture the benign enigma that Summertown, Tennessee, residents view it to be.

69

Foundation of Human Understanding
(Roy Masters)

Roy Masters, the British son of a Jewish diamond cutter optimistically declares, "All of us have a natural inclination toward right action...." His self-help brand of hypnotism and meditation is heard every day on radio broadcasts. Purporting to be a "Christian mystic," Masters insists that each individual has an inherent capacity for perfection. All that's needed to commune with the inner state of intuitive innocence is to empty the mind by means of Masters' system of meditation. He claims to have initiated over 100,000 people, including hundreds of fellow inmates with whom he spent time in jail for charges of practicing medicine without a license. Little devotion to Christ is evidenced, since salvation according to Masters is not dependent on the concept of a transcendent deity. His book, *How Your Mind Can Keep You Well,* summarizes the self-sufficient principles by which Masters's meditators seek the solace of inner direction.

70

Krishnamurti Foundation of America

Annie Besant, a guiding force behind the Theosophical Society, believed him to be an incarnation of God, the divine spirit in human form. A periodical, *Herald of the Star,* was printed and an organization was formed — Order of the Star of the East — to announce his appearance to the world. Unfortunately for Annie and more than 100,000 members of the Order, Jiddu Krishnamurti wasn't interested in being worshiped. In 1929 he repudiated the ideas of his followers and commenced to travel the world proclaiming his philosophy that mankind's crises are psychological in nature. Though he was born the son of a devout Brahman, Krishnamurti declared, "Discard all theologies and all beliefs." Krishnamurti believed that all problems could be solved when human beings achieved a "right relationship" with each other. The Krishnamurti Foundation was not started by Krishnamurti himself, since his nonsectarian approach encouraged those who looked to him for spiritual wisdom to ". . . look within for the incorruptibility of self." Even as an aged "non-guru" who disdained devotees, he continued to draw large audiences in the seventies composed mostly of young people anxious to observe a mystic of "elevated consciousness." Today he travels less frequently than when he was younger, but still conducts several world tours each year. His trips to the United States are now often sponsored by New Age consciousness groups. Theosophists have not rejected him entirely and carry his literature in their bookstores. In *The New Religions* Jacob Needleman observed, "The point is that many people still think of him as the World-Teacher, even when he tells them to their faces that there is no such thing as spiritual authority, and that he is not anyone's teacher. American students, who do not know his background and reputation, often hear his talks mainly as a profound expression of their own disgust with society, its hypocrisy, its ideas of national honour, duty, race and class, its bourgeois ideals and morality."

71

Lifespring

Cult researchers familiar with est (discussed earlier in the book) are aware that some of its concepts are rooted in Mind Dynamics, a San Francisco organization which taught mind power techniques until its demise in 1975. Werner Erhard (founder of est) was a Mind Dynamics employee, as were John Hanley and Randy Revell the originators of Lifespring. Approximately 100,000 people have been trained (each at a cost of $350 – $750) by this "personal growth" movement which freely admits its similarities to est. Lifespring concepts reflect a mystical perception of reality. Even though no specific theological precepts are promoted, trainees are encouraged to indulge in parapsychology, meditation, and "guided fantasies." "Self-love" is promoted as being "the greatest love" one can experience. Such practices and teachings inherently condition the trainee to view life in a non-Christian mode. Exposés in the media and lawsuits by former participants have marred the image of Lifespring and raised serious questions about its techniques. Critics wonder if it really can aid individuals in discovering their "...core...a perfect, loving, and caring being...."

72
Mind Sciences

"If by Christian you mean that we are saved by the blood of Christ on the Cross, then we're not." That explicit admission by a Church of Religious Science minister points out the essential distinction between the mind science cults and historic Christianity. Mind science organizations include some better-known groups already discussed (Christian Science and Unity School of Christianity), as well as other entities which more specifically base their teachings on the ruminations of Ernest Holmes. They go by such names as Religious Science, Divine Science, and Science of Mind.

Drawing upon the metaphysical heritage of Charles and Myrtle Fillmore, Warren Felt Evans, Mary Baker Eddy, and Phineas Parkhurst Quimby, Holmes founded the Institute of Religious Science in 1927. *Science of Mind,* published by Holmes in 1938, is the textbook of mind science teachings, emphasizing that the law and love of God (the "Thing-in-Itself") are perfect. Applying this theory to living is a nonsupernatural process of "science." Realizing one's inherent self-worth as emanating from a divine spark is the thrust of Holmes's emphasis. "When an individual recognizes his true union with the Infinite, he automatically becomes Christ," he wrote. By using the definitive article (''the'') when referring to Christ, mind sciences distinguish between Jesus the man and the divine idea of Christ-realization attainable by all men.

Christ's incarnation and divinity are not the only orthodox doctrines denied by mind science cults. In the process of spiritualizing all biblical truth, they also relegate heaven and hell to mental states and suggest that the Resurrection did not produce a bodily risen Lord. While ignoring scriptural doctrine, mind scientists willingly accept a variety of non-Christian philosophies and sacred books, amalgamating these diverse viewpoints into a syncretistic whole. In spite of their special emphasis on the contemporary interest in healing and positive thinking, the basic presuppositions of Mind and Religious Science groups differ little from the Gnostic heretics which the Apostle Paul confronted over 1900 years ago.

73

Self-Realization Fellowship
(Paramahansa Yogananda)

If Paramahansa ("highest swan") Yogananda ("bliss through divine union") were alive today with access to the media, Guru Maharaj Ji and Maharishi Mahesh Yogi would find themselves facing some stiff competition. Had he not died in 1952 after founding the Self-Realization Fellowship (SRF), the estimated 500,000 worldwide adherents of the SRF might be part of a much larger company of devotees.

Yogananda came to the United States in 1920 to address the International Congress of Religious Liberals. His subsequent lectures across America attracted a wide following out of which in 1935 he formed the SRF (current headquarters in Los Angeles). The appeal of SRF teaching is essentially Hinduistic, with the "realization" of god coming when one achieves "cosmic consciousness." To arrive at this state one must pursue yogic disciplines, including exercises, daily meditation, and abstinence from meat and alcohol.

The foremost practice facilitating transcendence beyond the illusory material world, is *Kriya Yoga,* described as a "highly scientific technique for the control of subtle life currents." As a Hindu, Yogananda taught that "cosmic consciousness" could ordinarily be attained only after a million years of reincarnations. With Kriya Yoga, the same results can be obtained in only three years with "intelligent self-effort." As a benefit, the SRF devotee ". . . is gradually freed from *karma* or the lawful chain of cause-effects equilibriums. . . ." Yogananda boasted that thirty seconds of Kriya Yoga "equals one year of natural spiritual unfoldment." In addition, this esoteric mastery of breath control promises ". . . continuous oxygenation of the blood . . . enabling the heart to become quiet." As a testimony to the application of Kriya Yoga, SRF officials report that ". . . even 20 days after death Paramahansa Yogananda's body was apparently devoid of impurities." Whatever the state of his corpse, his teaching did not alter the finality of death.

74
Silva Mind Control

The introductory lectures certainly seem harmless enough. And the come-on is directly to the point: "In 48 hours you can learn to use your mind to do *anything* you wish." That "anything" presumably includes waking up without clocks, increasing powers of memory, improving creativity, solving problems, and developing ESP. Silva Mind Control (SMC — also called Psychorientology) is the brainchild of Jose Silva, a Laredo, Texas, hypnotist who began mental experiments in 1944. His investigations were based on the assumption that the mind can generate more energy and function more effectively at a lower "subjective" state of brain-wave frequency. Silva proposes to teach the student how to maintain alert consciousness while deriving the supposed benefits of deeper states of consciousness.

Alphagenics, the science of investigating and measuring brain waves, has classified four levels of consciousness: *beta* — the waking state of conscious actions; *alpha* — the state of relaxation and meditation; *delta* and *theta* — subtler levels of the mind which Silva Mind Control purports to unlock. At the delta level one has the capacity to achieve "cosmic awareness, enlightenment...Christ awareness," so proponents of

SMC contend. Such religious overtones are just part of the occult/mystical nature of Jose Silva's techniques.

Most people who are attracted by its glowing prospects see no harm in quietly listening to a prerecorded cassette which features a soothing voice giving instructions on how to relax. This author has had the opportunity to attend public presentations promoting SMC. These sessions make no attempt to obscure the close association that "psychorientology" has with practices such as hypnosis, yoga, TM, biofeedback, and various paranormal phenomena. At one such meeting I watched an SMC promotional film which likened Silva's techniques to the powers exercised by spiritualistic mediums. Most people are apparently more fascinated than frightened by such associations. About 2 million people have plunked down approximately $200 each to embark on the forty-hour-long course. Advanced courses offer intense involvement in occult practices.

Silva Mind Control openly courts the development of extrasensory and clairvoyant powers. Students are also taught that dilemmas in life can be solved by mentally visualizing a "laboratory." Once this fantasized room has been "furnished," the subject is told to mentally solicit "laboratory technicians (counselors)." Sometimes SMC parlance refers to these assistants as "spirit guides" or "guardian angels." The evangelical Christian can hardly feel comfortable with the close parallel such "counselors" have to the spiritistic phenomenon of demonic manifestations.

SMC also takes over where positive thinker, Norman Vincent Peale, leaves off, and adds a dash of Christian Science as the clincher. Negative thoughts are forbidden in favor of positive perceptions, which, according to Silva, actually have the power to alter reality. But these "positive beneficial phrases" may become a system of salvation by works, since the illusion of evil need only be negated by merely pronouncing it out of existence. Thus, the methodology of SMC becomes a mental exercise more suited for manipulation by visualized "counselors," rather than by a suffering Savior.

75

Swami Kriyananda

A devout former disciple of Paramahansa Yogananda, Swami Kriyananda's mystical name was conferred upon him by his spiritual mentor. It literally means "to do" *(kriya)* the way of "bliss" *(ananda)*, or "to pursue and act upon the joyful path of yoga." Kriyananda was born in Rumania of American parents and was named Donald Walters. As an eloquent spokesman for Eastern mysticism he has been called "the most respected non-Indian yoga exponent in the world."

Kriyananda was a vice-president of the Self-Realization Fellowship until he left to form his own 650-acre commune near Nevada City, California. Commune members meditate at least three times daily and refer to each other by newly-designated Indian names. Related business ventures of the commune's Yoga Fellowship, Inc. gross $2 million annually. Devotees are attracted by his Practice of Joy seminars which emphasize the attainment of outward boundless energy and inward fulfillment. "Joy," declares Kriyananda, "is the central fact of your existence." To develop the state of *ananda,* groups are coached in chanting, meditation, "energization exercises," secret sacred yoga techniques, and Kriyananda's "Songs of Divine Joy."

"Belief is no barrier," he emphasizes. "Anyone can benefit: Christian, Jew, Hindu, believer, and agnostic." A closer inspection of *THE PATH, Autobiography of a Western Yogi,* Kriyananda's definitive work, reveals that his entire system presupposes a Hinduistic interpretation of life. These pagan concepts are considered to be the "original, pure essence" of the "ancient teachings." *Raja Yoga* is emphasized as a "science" to uncover the "truth" that man is an integral part of a greater Reality: ". . . this Reality is conscious. . . infinite. . . ." Pursuing Kriyananda's path supposedly neutralizes bad *karma* and enables one to "tune-in to higher knowledge and guidance."

76

Swami Rami
**(Himalayan International Institute
of Yoga Science and Philosophy)**

Biofeedback, the psychophysiological technique of
mentally controlling body functions and responses, owes
its development to the expertise of Swami Rami.
Dr. Green of the prestigious Topeka, Kansas-based
Menninger Foundation, developed the principles of
biofeedback by observing Rami in meditative trance
states. Rami not only exhibited the ability to stop his
heartbeat for seventeen seconds, but by psychokinesis
(the supposed ability to affect physical objects by using
mental powers) he was able to move an aluminum knitting
needle while seated five feet away from it.

Five thousand students a month flock to his Himalayan
International Institute of Yoga Science and Philosophy in
Glenview, Illinois. Once there, they learn via *Raja Yoga* to
"exhale all problems" and "inhale energy" in order to
become ". . . a wave of bliss in the ocean of the universe."
Rami, who meditates eight hours a day and sleeps only
three hours each night, feels his mission is to combine
Indian religious philosophy with psychological
therapeutic techniques. As a monk of the Shankaracharya
Order, he spent the early years of his life traveling from
monasteries to caves throughout the Indian subcontinent
and living with various Sadhus. As an Americanized guru
his life has been dedicated to ". . . creating a bridge
between East and West."

77

Swami Vivekananda
(Vedanta Society)

The increasing influence of mystical thought on Western religious values owes a debt of gratitude to the first Hindu guru to be widely accepted as a legitimate spokesman for the East — Swami Vivekananda (1863-1902). In 1893 he addressed the Parliament of Religions in Chicago and took the conference by storm. His subsequent national exposure via lecture tours led to his founding of the Vedanta Society in 1894, which was the first official Hindu organization to be established in the United States. The proliferation of many current cults is but the fruition of this landmark event.

Named at the time of his birth Narendranath Datta, he later assumed the *swami* name of Vivekananda ("Bliss of Discrimination" between the real and illusory), and became a devoted disciple of the Bengali holy man, Sri Ramakrishna, who served as a priest in Calcutta's Kali Temple. Ramakrishna often experienced *samadhi* (the bliss of altered trance consciousness), and concluded that all gods and religions were but multiple manifestations of the one Absolute. He then pursued the path of *Veda-anta* (the goal of knowledge based on the *Vedas* — sacred Hindu scriptures), and developed an intellectual approach to Hinduism based in part on charitable works of mercy. Vivekananda viewed Ramakrishna as an *avatar* worthy of the kind of devotion shown Christ by his Apostles, and upon the holy man's death, he founded the Ramakrishna Mission in Calcutta.

Through the Vedanta Society, Vivekananda was able to influence favorably many prominent figures such as Aldous Huxley and Gertrude Stein. While insisting on the primacy of Hinduism, Vivekananda told them, "We accept all religions as true." Those who favorably view Vivekananda's influence on Western religious thought might do well to visit personally (as has this author) both Kali Temple and the Ramakrishna Mission in Calcutta. Kali, the blackened goddess of death, stands draped in a necklace of human skulls and holds a bloody severed head in one hand. Near the entrance of Kali Temple I witnessed bloody goat sacrifices before a phallic *lingam* (genital replica). Not far away, at the Ramakrishna Mission Temple, I watched poor peasants bow before an idol, offering the deity the little money they had. The idol's favor meant more to them than obtaining food to sustain the lives of their own children. Transporting this pagan spiritual heritage to the West is the Vedanta Society's ultimate goal. Such dehumanizing aims cannot be obscured by any intellectualized discourses regarding "existence of the One Cause" or "merging the self with Reality."

78

Swedenborgianism

His body had been laid to rest for more than 200 years in Sweden's Uppsala Cathedral, but only recently did his skull join the rest of his bones. The Swedish Royal Academy of Science paid $3,000 at Sotheby's London auction to purchase the head of Emanuel Swedenborg, an eighteenth-century mystic, scientist, and religious philosopher. Swedenborg's remains were considered so valuable that an official diplomatic pouch was dispatched to return the skull to his Swedish homeland.

Emanuel Swedenborg (1688-1772) was born the son of a pious Lutheran minister. He grew up to be a dynamic intellectual who circulated in the highest echelons of government and academia. His expertise in the field of geology earned an appointment as a college professor and membership in the Swedish Diet. Swedenborg traveled widely and gained a reputation as an expert in the field of metallurgy and crystallography. At the age of fifty-two his life changed abruptly when he answered what he felt was a divine calling to become a revelator of the symbolic meanings in Scripture.

Swedenborg developed mediumistic abilities (automatic handwriting and clairaudience) and practiced astral travel, journeying to the spirit-world to communicate with good and evil angels (deceased humans). The messages from these beings convinced him that the Bible needed special interpretation. This led him to write a commentary on the Bible and several lengthy treatises, including *Arcana Coelestia: The Earths in the Universe.* His visions included conversations with persons whom he identified as Luther, Calvin, St. Augustine, and the Apostle Paul. The latter would not have taken kindly to him because Swedenborg's theology proposed eliminating the Pauline Epistles along with much of the Old Testament.

Today, Swedenborgian ministers, who represent one of the three main branches of the Church of the New Jerusalem, generally consider Swedenborg's writings to be "divinely inspired." The "truth" he brought is said to represent "the second coming of Christ." In Swedenborg's theological system, those who die enter an intermediate state where they prepare for heaven or hell. In hell, one becomes an evil spirit, but in heaven an angelic status awaits. Either existence is a spiritual state since there is no bodily resurrection. In this life after death, each soul retains the physical appearance of early adulthood as it was lived on Earth.

The historic Christian concept of the Trinity is discarded, along with the vicarious atonement — an "abomination" and "mere human invention," according to Swedenborg. Christ's death on the Cross is described as "a climax of a life of service," not "a debt of blood." The personality of the Holy Spirit is specifically denied, and Jesus Christ is God alone, an "indivisible...Divine Essence" manifested as three principles. This unique form of spiritualism is followed by approximately 20,000 Americans and at least 100,000 others worldwide, with the largest concentrations in England. (Headquarters of the U. S. branches are: General Convention of the New Jerusalem in the U. S. A. (The Convention) — Newton, MA; General Church of the New Jerusalem — Bryn Athyn, PA.)

79
Unitarian Universalist Association

If religious movements could be classified psychologically, the label schizophrenic would certainly apply to
the Unitarian Universalist Association. Members attempt
to laud the selfless sacrifice of Christ's Crucifixion and
often quote Scripture in a feigned effort to validate its
worth. On the other hand they repudiate the virgin birth,
deity of Christ, as well as the Nicene, Chalcedonian, and
Apostles' Creeds affirming the inerrancy of the Bible.
They also reject the Trinity in favor of a Unitary God and
ascribe to the doctrine that all souls will ultimately be
saved.

In 1959 the Unitarian Church merged with the
Universalist Church, and today the combined groups
claim slightly less than 200,000 members in nearly 1,000
churches. There are no sacraments observed by the
constituents who hold Jesus to be no more than a great
prophet. Their aim, according to the charter of the
Universalist Church, is to "promote harmony among
adherents of all religious faiths, whether Christian or

otherwise." Such inclusivism has prevented the
Association from being accorded official recognition by
national Christian bodies (for example, the National
Council of Churches), though some Unitarians do belong
to local ministerial groups.

Since the truth of God is said to be revealed in the
sacred writings of all great religions, the philosophy of
Unitarians is reduced to little more than an ethical system
of morality. Heaven and hell are anathema to Unitarians
and the Atonement of Christ is said to be "offensive" and
"unbiblical." As an outgrowth of eighteenth century
Enlightenment, including rationalism and anti-
supernaturalism, Unitarian thought has historically
attracted leading intellectuals, such as poet-essayist
Ralph Waldo Emerson. Present-day members differ as to
whether they should classify themselves as being
Christian. Their adherence to universal truth as declared
in the teachings of all prophets of all ages renders the
terms "Christian" and "Unitarian" to be mutually
exclusive.

80

Yogi Bhajan
(Sikh Foundation/3HO Foundation)

He has been accused of being a womanizer who demands group massages from female attendants with whom he takes turns sleeping. The charges stem in part from his mystical view of sex, which he teaches in the *tantric* tradition. In fact, Yogi Bhajan claims to be the "only living master of *tantrism*." More than 5,000 followers (he claims 250,000) have joined his 150 Sikh Dharma U. S. *ashrams.* Bhajan's disciples arise at 3:30 A.M. for a day of meditation and to practice *Kundalini Yoga.* This system of yoga is supposed to be a simplified way of attaining spiritual enlightenment by releasing energy that travels up the spine.

Another title claimed by Bhajan is Supreme Religious and Administrative Authority of the Sikh Religion in the Western Hemisphere. Sikhism (discussed earlier in this book) is a monotheistic system of Hinduism and Islam that seeks god-realization through meditation. Indian Sikh officials aren't so certain that the once obscure Delhi airport customs officer deserves to be the leader of Western Sikhism, "the holiest man of this era." They view with suspicion his luxurious ways (over $100,000 a year in lecture fees). The manner in which the democratic principles of Sikhism are merged with the autocratic, sexually explicit style of Bhajan's 3HO (Healthy, Happy, Holy) Foundation is looked upon with equal skepticism.

In addition to indulging in nude massages and rapid breathing techniques, couples are instructed to stare into each other's eyes (or at a picture of Bhajan) while chanting *Ek Ong Kar Sat Nam Siri Wha Guru,* the repetition of God's name in a "sacred" language. Though yoga has never been an essential practice of Sikhism, Bhajan insists that in order for his disciples to experience the "infinity of God," they must position their arms and fingers in precisely patterned angles.

"The man who ties a turban on his head must live up to the purity of the whiteness and radiance of his soul," Bhajan proclaims from his forty-acre ranch near Espanola, New Mexico. The traditional Sikh symbols are uncut hair, symbolic daggers, combs, bracelets, and special chastity underwear (the "five Ks" — discussed earlier in the chapter on Hinduism). Critics wonder if Bhajan may have eliminated this special garment ensuring moral purity in his zealous pursuit of *tantrism.*

Background Sources for Minor Cults

The following notes include both quoted references as well as additional sources of research information.

Aetherius Society
1. J. Gordon Melton, *Encyclopedia of American Religions, Vol. 2,* McGrath Publishing Co., Wilmington, NC, 1978.
2. Ronald Enroth, *The Lure of the Cults,* Christian Herald Books, Chappaqua, NY, 1979.

Alamo Christian Foundation
1. Ronald Enroth, *Youth, Brainwashing and the Extremist Cults,* The Zondervan Corporation, Grand Rapids, MI, 1977.

Ananda Marga
1. Pat Means, *The Mystical Maze,* Campus Crusade for Christ, 1976.
2. *The Denver Post,* 8/15/75, p. 4BB.

Anthroposophical Society
1. *Spiritual Counterfeits Project Newsletter,* 2/77, vol. 3, no. 1, pp. 4-7.
2. J. Gordon Melton, *The Encyclopedia of American Religions, Vol. 2,* McGrath Publishing, Wilmington, NC, 1978.

Arica Institute, Inc.
1. *Time,* 5/29/72, p.88.
2. *Ibid.,* 11/9/81, p. 20.
3. *East-West Journal,* 6/76, p. 17.
4. Arica promotional advertisement, copyrighted 1973.

The Church of Armageddon (Love Family)
1. J. Gordon Melton, *The Encyclopedia of American Religions, Vol. 2,* McGrath Publishing Co., Wilmington, NC, 1978.
2. Ronald Enroth, *Youth, Brainwashing and the Extremist Cults,* The Zondervan Corporation, Grand Rapids, MI, 1977.

The Church of Bible Understanding (Forever Family)
1. *Contemporary Christianity,* Joseph Duffy, vol. 6, no. 3, March-April 1977.
2. *Philadelphia Inquirer,* "Today" Magazine, 6/24/79.
3. *Alternatives,* vol., 4, no. 6, April/May 1977.
4. *The Sunday Record,* 9/25/77.

Esalen Institute
1. John Garabedian and Orde Coombs, *Eastern Religions in the Electric Age,* Tempo Books, Workman Publishing Co., NY, 1969.

The Farm
1. *Newsweek,* 8/10/81, p. 14.
2. *San Francisco Chronicle,* 9/21/81.
3. *SCP Journal,* date unknown.
4. *East-West Journal,* 5/81, p. 11.
5. Stephen Gaskins, *Hey Beatnik!,* The Book Publishing Co., Summertown, TN, 1974.
6. Stephen Gaskins, *The Caravan,* Random House, New York, NY, 1977.

Foundation of Human Understanding
1. Walter Martin, *The New Cults,* Vision House Publishers, Santa Ana, CA, 1980.
2. Roy Masters, *How Your Mind Can Keep You Well,* Foundation Press, Los Angeles, CA, 1971.

Krishnamurti Foundation
1. *Time,* 6/7/71, p. 24.
2. *The Denver Post,* 7/23/76, p. 1BB.
3. Jacob Needleman, *The New Religions,* E. P. Dutton and Co., Inc., 1970, p. 154.

Lifespring
1. Elliot Miller, *Lifespring,* Christian Research Institute, San Juan Capistrano, CA, 1979.
2. *Forward,* "Lifespring —New-Age Danger," vol. 4, no. 1, Christian Research Institute, San Juan Capistrano, CA.

Mind Sciences
1. J. Gordon Melton, *The Encyclopedia of American Religions, Vol. 2,* McGrath Publishing Co., Wilmington, NC, 1978.
2. Todd Ehrenborg, *Religion, Science or Science of the Mind,* Christian Research Institute Inc., San Juan Capistrano, CA, 1979.

Self-Realization Fellowship
1. Paramahansa Yogananda, *Autobiography of a Yogi,* Self-Realization Fellowship, Los Angeles, CA, 1972.
2. *People,* 10/6/75, p. 70.
3. *Undreamed-of Possibilities,* Self-Realization Fellowship, Los Angeles, CA, 1971.

Silva Mind Control
1. Jose Silva and Philip Miele, *The Silva Mind Control Method,* Simon and Schuster, New York, NY, 1977.
2. Various SMC publications and promotional literature.
3. Walter Martin, *The New Cults,* Vision House Publishers, Santa Ana, CA, 1980.

Swami Kriyananda
1. Miscellaneous Ananda publications and promotional literature.

Swami Rami
1. J. Gordon Melton, *The Encyclopedia of American Religions, Vol. 2,* McGrath Publishing Co., Wilmington, NC, 1978.
2. *People,* 10/24/77.

Swami Vivekananda (Vedanta Society)
1. J. Gordon Melton, *The Encyclopedia of American Religions, Vol. 2,* McGrath Publishing Co., Wilmington, NC, 1978.
2. *Spiritual Counterfeits Project Newsletter,* vol. 5, no. 3, April-May 1979.

Swedenborgianism
1. *Eternity,* 5/81, pp. 44, 45.

2. *The Denver Post,* 1/16/76, p. 3BB.
3. Walter Martin, *Kingdom of the Cults,* Bethany Fellowship, Inc., Minneapolis, MN, 1977.
4. J. Gordon Melton, *The Encyclopedia of American Religions, Vol. 2,* McGrath Publishing Co., Wilmington, NC, 1978.

Unitarian Universalist Association
1. *Christianity Today,* 8/2/72, p. 35.
2. Walter Martin, *Kingdom of the Cults,* Bethany Fellowship, Inc., Minneapolis, MN, 1977.
3. J. Gordon Melton, *The Encyclopedia of American Religions, Vol. 2,* McGrath Publishing Co., Wilmington, NC, 1978.

Yogi Bhajan (Sikh Foundation/3HO Foundation)
1. *Newsweek,* 4/21/75, p. 65.
2. *Time,* 9/5/77, pp. 34, 35.
3. *Columbus Ohio Dispatch,* 12/12/78.
4. J. Gordon Melton, *The Encyclopedia of American Religions, Vol. 2,* McGrath Publishing Co., Wilmington, NC, 1978.

Cult Information Resources

It would be impossible for any book to cover the entire scope of cultic activity. In addition, cults are proliferating and each day brings news of another group bursting on the scene. Several evangelical organizations are dedicated to keeping watch on cult activities. These parachurch service agencies are generally very cooperative when requested to supply information regarding both newly formed and already established cults. To the knowledge of this author the organizations listed below are evangelical in theology.

Bob Larson Ministries
P. O. Box 36480
Denver, CO 80236

Christian Apologetics Project
P. O. Box 105
Absecon, NJ 08201

Christian Apologetics:
Research & Information Service (CARIS)
P. O. Box 2067
Costa Mesa, CA 92626

Christian Ministry to Cults
P. O. Box M-507
Hoboken, NJ 07030

Christian Research Institute
P. O. Box 500
San Juan Capistrano, CA 97693

Institute of Contemporary Christianity
P. O. Box A
Oakland, NJ 07436

*Spiritual Counterfeits Project
P. O. Box 2418
Berkeley, CA 94702

*Additional listings of other agencies offering anticult
information are available here. It is the author's opinion
that this organization is the most scholarly and
comprehensive source of cult information available.

Recommended Reading

The books listed below represent sources of information concerning cults for the reader who wishes to investigate more thoroughly a particular group or teaching. An asterisk indicates those volumes which are not written from a distinctly evangelical perspective. The books are listed alphabetically according to title.

1. Robert and Gretchen Passantino, *Answers to the Cultist at Your Door,* Harvest House Publishers, Eugene, OR, 1981.
2. Gordon R. Lewis, *Confronting the Cults,* The Presbyterian and Reformed Publishing Co., 1966.
3. Edmond C. Gruss, *Cults and the Occult,* Baker Book House, Grand Rapids, MI, 1974.
4. Kenneth Boa, *Cults, World Religions and You,* Victor Books, Wheaton, IL, 1977.
* 5. John H. Garabedian and Orde Coombs, *Eastern Religions in the Electric Age,* Grosset and Dunlap, Workman Publishing Co., New York, NY, 1969.
* 6. J. Gordon Melton, *(The) Encyclopedia of American Religions, Vols. 1 and 2,* McGrath Publishing Co., Wilmington, NC, 1978.

* 7. National Geographic Society, *Great Religions of the World,* 1971.
  8. Robert Morey, *How to Answer a Jehovah's Witness,* Bethany Fellowship, Inc., Minneapolis, MN, 1980.
  9. Walter Martin, *(The) Kingdom of the Cults,* Bethany Fellowship, Inc., Minneapolis, MN, 1977.
 10. David Breese, *Know the Mark of the Cults,* Victor Books, Wheaton, IL, 1980.
 11. Ronald Enroth, *(The) Lure of the Cults,* Herald Books, Chappaqua, NY, 1979.
 12. Jack Sparks, *(The) Mind Benders,* Thomas Nelson, Inc., Publishers, Nashville, TN, 1977.
 13. Pat Means, *(The) Mystical Maze,* Campus Crusade for Christ, Inc., 1976 (out of print).
 14. Walter Martin, *(The) New Cults,* Vision House, Santa Ana, CA, 1980.
 15. John Weldon and Clifford Wilson, *Occult Shock and Psychic Forces,* Master Books, San Diego, CA, 1980.
*16. James and Marcia Rudin, *Prison or Paradise?,* Fortress Press, Philadelphia, PA, 1980.
 17. Robert A. Morey, *Reincarnation and Christianity,* Bethany Fellowship, Inc., Minneapolis, MN, 1980.
*18. Gerald L. Berry, *Religions of the World,* Barnes and Noble, New York, NY, 1965.
 19. Walter Martin, *Rise of the Cults,* Vision House, Santa Ana, CA, 1980.
*20. Flo Conway and Jim Siegelman, *Snapping,* J. B. Lippincott Co., Philadelphia, PA, 1978.
 21. William J. Petersen, *Those Curious New Cults,* Keats Publishing Co., New Canaan, CT, 1975.
 22. J. L. Williams, *Victor Paul Wierwille and The Way International,* Moody Press, Chicago, IL, 1979.
 23. Ronald Enroth, *Youth, Brainwashing, and the Extremist Cults,* Zondervan Publishing House, Grand Rapids, MI, 1977.

Addenda

COERCIVE CULT TECHNIQUES

Loneliness, indecision, despair, and disappointment are the emotional characteristics cult recruiters notice. They approach the unwary with an excessively friendly invitation to a lecture, free meal, weekend workshop, or other activity offering instant solutions to overwhelming problems. Surprisingly enough, few potential cultists bother to inquire about who is extending the offer, what is behind it, and what functions will take place. Vague answers are seldom challenged, leaving the recruiter an unassailable opportunity to obscure his intentions.

Even given the current anticult climate, few targets of the cults see their future as one of involuntary slavery and physical domination. Before joining any exotic sect, one should be aware of what could result: neurosis, psychosis, suicidal tendencies, guilt, identity confusion, paranoia, hallucinations, loss of free will, intellectual sterility, and diminished capacity of judgment. It will be much easier to avoid such consequences by identifying and recognizing the following psychological forms of "cult-coercion."

1. *Absolute loyalty.* Allegiance to the sect is demanded and enforced by actual or veiled threats to one's body or eternal spiritual condition.
2. *Altered diet.* Depriving one of essential nutrients and enforcing a low-protein diet can lead to disorientation and emotional susceptibility.
3. *Chanting and meditation.* Objective intellectual input is avoided by countering anticult questions with repetitious songs and chants.

4. *Conformity.* Dress, language, names, and interests take on a sameness which erodes individuality.
5. *Doctrinal confusion.* Incomprehensible "truths" are more readily accepted when presented in a complex fashion which encourages rejection of logical thought.
6. *Exclusivity.* Those outside the cult are viewed as spiritually inferior, creating an exclusive attitude of the self-righteous "we" versus "they" mentality.
7. *Financial involvement.* All or part of one's personal assets may be donated to the cult, increasing a vested interest in sticking-with-it and lessening the chance of returning to a former vocation.
8. *Hypnotic states.* Inducing a highly susceptible state of mind may be accomplished by chanting, repetitious singing, or meditation.
9. *Isolation from outside.* Diminished perception of reality results when one is physically separated from friends, society, and the rational frame of reference in which one has previously functioned.
10. *Lack of privacy.* Reflective, critical thinking is impossible in a setting where cult members are seldom left unattended.
11. *Love bombing.* Physical affection and constant contrived attention can give a false sense of camaraderie.
12. *Megacommunication.* Long, confusing lectures can be an effective tool if the inductee is bombarded with glib rhetoric and catch phrases.
13. *New relationships.* Marriage to another cult member and the destruction of past family relationships integrates one fully into the cult "family."
14. *Nonsensical activities.* Games and other activities with no apparent purpose leave one dependent upon a group or leader to give direction and order.
15. *Pavlovian control.* Behavior modification by alternating reward and punishment leads to confusion and dependency.
16. *Peer pressure.* By exploiting one's desire for acceptance, doubts about cult practices can be overcome by offering a sense of belonging to an affirming community.
17. *Sensory deprivation.* Fatigue coupled with prolonged activity can make one vulnerable to otherwise offensive beliefs and suggestions.
18. *Surrendered privacy.* The ego's normal emotional defensive mechanisms can easily be stripped away by having the new member share personal secrets which can later be used for intimidation.
19. *Unquestioning submission.* Acceptance of cult practices is achieved by discouraging any questions or natural curiosity which may challenge what the leaders propagate.
20. *Value rejection.* As the recruit becomes more integrated into the cult, he is encouraged to denounce the values and beliefs of his former life.

ANNOTATED BIBLIOGRAPHY

1. Adair, James R. and Ted Miller, eds. *We Found our Way Out.* Grand Rapids, MI: Baker Book House, 1964. A Christian book containing testimonies of people who have come out of cults such as Mormonism, Jehovah's Witnesses, Christian Science, Armstrongism, Rosicrucianism, Humanism, Theosophy, Agnosticism, and Communism.
2. The Agency for Cultural Affairs. *Japanese Religions: A Survey.* Tokyo Kodansha International, Ltd., 1972 and 1981. A non-Christian book distributed by The Agency for Cultural Affairs in Japan discussing all of the major religions popular in Japan today. Included are the different sects of Buddhism, Hinduism, and Shintoism, as well as Christian groups which have followings in Japan. An excellent secular resource reference book.
3. Anderson, J. N. D. *Christianity and Comparative Religions.* Downers Grove, IL: Intervarsity Press, 1970. A Christian book discussing comparative religions and Christianity. It does not deal with specific religions.
4. Anderson, J. N. D. *The World's Religions.* Grand Rapids, MI: William B. Eerdmans Publishing Co., 1950 and 1975. Anderson has edited this compilation of articles on the major world religions: Judaism, Islam, Hinduism, Buddhism, Shintoism, and Confucianism. It includes religions of pre-literary society and concludes with a Christian approach to comparative religions.
5. Anderson, Einar. *The Inside Story of Mormonism.* Grand Rapids, MI: Kregel Publications, 1973. A Christian approach to Mormonism. The author shares his own testimony of how he left the Mormon Church and became a Christian. Mormon history and Mormon doctrine are discussed from a Christian perspective with biblical answers.
6. Benware, Paul N. *Ambassadors of Armstrongism.* Nutley, NJ: Presbyterian and Reformed Publishing Co., 1977. A Christian approach to Armstrongism, including a brief history of the Worldwide Church of God and a summary of the teachings of the Worldwide Church of God on Scripture, God, the Holy Spirit, Christ, angels, man, sin, salvation, the church, and eschatology.
7. Bjornstad, James. *Counterfeits at Your Door.* Ventura, CA: Gospel Light Publications, 1979. From a Christian perspective, cult expert Jim Bjornstad examines the teachings and proselytizing efforts of the Jehovah's Witnesses and the Mormons.
8. Bjornstad, James. *The Moon Is Not to the Sun.* Minneapolis, MN: Bethany Fellowship, Inc. 1976. A Christian treatment of the Unification Church of Sun Myung Moon. It contains good documentation on the major teachings of the Unification Church and some advice on how to witness to a person who is a Moonie.
9. Boa, Kenneth. *Cults, World Religions and You.* Wheaton, IL: Scripture Press Publications, 1977. A short introduction to all the major religions and cults from a Christian perspective. Discusses non-Christian religions of the East, pseudo-Christian religions of the West, occult religious systems, and new religions and cults. A brief but adequate introduction to cults and religions.
10. Burks, Thompson. *Religions of the World.* Cincinnati, OH: Standard Publishing, 1972. This book is good to use in an adult education, or

Sunday school class situation. It is divided into thirteen chapters which can be combined for a ten-week session of lessons. Includes good study outlines and discusses Judaism, Islam, Hinduism, Buddhism, and primitive religions.

11. Chang, Lit-sen. *Zen-Existentialism: The Spiritual Decline of the West.* Nutley, NJ: Presbyterian and Reformed Publishing Co., 1969. An extensive, in-depth treatment of Zen Buddhism and Christianity from a biblical perspective.

12. Cowan, Marvin W. *Mormon Claims Answered.* Salt Lake City, UT: Published by the author, 1975. A good technical treatment of the origin and history of Mormonism, its doctrines concerning God and the Bible, and a very careful study of the Book of Mormon. It also has an extensive section on salvation from the orthodox Christian point of view.

13. Dencher, Ted. *Why I Left Jehovah's Witnesses.* Fort Washington, PA: Christian Literature Crusade, 1966. An excellent book on the doctrines of Jehovah's Witnesses and the internal workings of the organization, including the testimony of Dencher who used to be a Jehovah's Witness. This is a good book for a Christian to study, but since its tone is somewhat sarcastic, it would not be wise to share it with a Jehovah's Witness.

14. Drummond, Richard H. *Gautama the Buddha: An Essay in Religious Understanding.* Grand Rapids, MI: William B. Eerdmans Publishing Co., 1974. A lengthy treatment of the life and teachings of Buddha from a Christian perspective. It also deals extensively with the general concepts of Eastern thought.

15. Duddy, Neal T. and The Spiritual Counterfeits Project. *The God-man: An Inquiry into Witness Lee and The Local Church.* Downers Grove, IL: Intervarsity Press, 1981. This is the only large single volume available covering Witness Lee and The Local Church. The sociological point of view predominates, although it does discuss doctrine from a Christian perspective.

16. Edwards, Christopher. *Crazy for God: The Nightmare of Cult Life.* Englewood Cliffs, NJ: Prentiss Hall, Inc., 1979. The testimony and life history of a young man who joined the Unification Church. He explores the time he spent as a Moonie, the deprogramming he went through, and his final release from the cult, although not necessarily from a Christian point of view.

17. Elkins, Chris. *Heavenly Deception.* Wheaton, IL: Tyndale House Publishers, Inc., 1980. The testimony of a man who was raised a Christian but joined the Unification Church. After being a Moonie for some time he was freed from the bondage he had experienced in this cult.

18. Enroth, Ronald. *Youth, Brainwashing, and the Extremist Cults.* Grand Rapids, MI: Zondervan Publishing House, 1977. An introduction to a sociologist's view of the cults. Case histories are presented along with a discussion of characteristics of cultic activity from a Christian perspective.

19. Enroth, Ronald. *The Lure of the Cults.* Chappaqua, NY: Christian Herald Books, 1979. An extension of Enroth's other book, *Youth, Brainwashing and the Extremist Cults.* Instead of dealing systematically with individual cults, he explores the sociological and psychological characteristics of cults and explains how to help someone who is in a cult.

20. Evans, Dr. Christopher. *Cults of Unreason.* New York, NY: Dell Publishing Co. Inc., 1973. A non-Christian book which deals with some of the more mystical and pseudo-scientific cults. Most of the book is devoted to a study of Scientology, and is considered to be the best current treatment of this cult from a non-Christian perspective.

21. Fraser, Gordon H. *Is Mormonism Christian?* Chicago, IL: Moody Press, 1977. An old book that has been consistently updated. It treats all the major doctrines of Mormonism from a Christian point of view, including the restoration of the church, the Mormon genealogy, Mormons and God, Mormons and Jesus Christ, Mormons and the Holy Spirit, Mormon doctrine of man, the priesthood, Mormons and baptism, Mormons and baptism for the dead, salvation, the lost tribes of Israel, and the sects of Mormonism.

22. Fraser, Gordon H. *The Sects of the Latter-Day Saints.* Eugene, OR: Industrial Litho Inc., 1978. From a Christian perspective, this book deals with the major sects of the Latter-day Saints, especially the Reorganized Church of Jesus Christ of Latter-day Saints. It also analyzes the different polygamous sects of Mormonism.

23. Griffin, Em. *The Mind-Changers: The Art of Christian Persuasion.* Wheaton, IL: Tyndale House Publishers, Inc., 1976. An excellent Christian treatment of the psychological, mental, and emotional framework conducive to cult indoctrination. Also explained are the techniques cults use to indoctrinate people and how to release someone from cult control through the power of the Holy Spirit and the renewing of his mind.

24. Gruss, Edmond Charles. *Apostles of Denial: An Examination and Expose of the History, Doctrines, and Claims of the Jehovah's Witnesses.* Grand Rapids, MI: Baker Book House, 1978. The best-documented treatment of the Jehovah's Witnesses from a Christian point of view. Gruss, who was a Jehovah's Witness himself, includes his own testimony at the end of the book.

25. Gruss, Edmond Charles. *Cults and the Occult.* Phillipsburg, NJ: Presbyterian and Reformed Publishing Co., 1980. A brief study meant to be used in an adult education or Bible class situation. It deals with Jehovah's Witnesses, Mormons, Christian Scientists, Unity, Armstrongism, Spiritualism, Astrology, Bahaism, Rosicrucianism, Ouija boards, Edgar Cayce, Unification Church, and concludes with a Christian perspective on the cults and the occult.

26. Gruss, Edmond Charles. *The Jehovah's Witnesses and Prophetic Speculation.* Nutley, NJ: Presbyterian and Reformed Publishing Co., 1972. This thoroughly documented book deals specifically with the Jehovah's Witnesses' propagation of false prophecies regarding the end of the world.

27. Gruss, Edmond Charles. *We Left the Jehovah's Witnesses — A Non-Prophet Organization.* Nutley, NJ: Presbyterian and Reformed Publishing Co., 1974. Testimonies of ex-Jehovah's Witnesses showing how to leave the Watch Tower Society and truly be born again.

28. Hefley, James C. *The Youth-Nappers.* Wheaton, IL: Scripture Press Publications, 1977. A brief Christian review of some new cults such as Unification Church, Hare Krishna, Divine Light Mission, TM, Children of God, and others.

29. Hesselgrave, David J., ed. *Dynamic Religious Movements.* Grand
Rapids, MI: Baker Book House, 1978. An excellent Christian book,
discussing cultic religions in other countries. The first section is on
Africa, the second on Europe, the third on the Far East, the fourth on
the Mideast, the fifth on North America, the sixth on South America,
and the seventh on Southeast Asia.
30. Heydt, Henry J. *A Comparison of World Religions.* Fort Washington,
PA: Christian Literature Crusade, 1967. An historical survey dealing
with Judaism, Christianity, Hinduism, Zoroastrianism, Shintoism,
Taoism, Jainism, Buddhism, Confucianism, Islam and Sikhism.
Chapter three gives a topical comparison of all these groups, and
chapter four shows the distinctive superiority of Christianity.
31. Hoekema, Anthony A. *The Four Major Cults.* Grand Rapids, MI:
William B. Eerdmans Publishing Co., 1963. A classic work on the
major cults such as Jehovah's Witnesses, Mormonism, and Christian
Science.
32. Hoekema, Anthony A. *Christian Science.* Grand Rapids, MI: William
B. Eerdmans Publishing Co., 1974. Taken from *The Four Major Cults*
and extensively updated.
33. Hoekema, Anthony A. *Jehovah's Witnesses.* Grand Rapids, MI:
William B. Eerdmans Publishing Co., 1974. Taken from *The Four
Major Cults* and extensively updated.
34. Hoekema, Anthony A. *Mormonism.* Grand Rapids, MI: William B.
Eerdmans Publishing Co., 1974. Taken from *The Four Major Cults*
and extensively updated.
35. Hopkins, Joseph. *The Armstrong Empire.* Grand Rapids, MI:
William B. Eerdmans Publishing Co., 1974. A Christian perspective
of Herbert W. Armstrong and the Worldwide Church of God. It deals
extensively with the background of Armstrong and the Church, and
includes a brief survey of WCG doctrines.
36. Hunt, Dave. *The Cult Explosion.* Eugene, OR: Harvest House
Publishers, 1980. A thoroughly scriptural, psychological, and
sociological perspective on the rise of the cults. Some of the topics
covered are: altered states of consciousness, the ultimate lie,
beyond morality, authoritarianism and responsibility, spirit
communication and the battle for the mind. This book does not deal
with cults individually or in a systematic way.
37. Kemperman, Steve. *Lord of the Second Advent: A Rare Look Inside
the Terrifying World of the Moonies.* Ventura, CA: Regal Books,
1981. An excellent testimony of a young man who joined the
Moonies. He describes his experiences of being deprogrammed
twice, and how he finally came to be released from the cult, finding
peace with Christ.
38. Lewis, Gordon R. *Confronting the Cults.* Grand Rapids, MI: Baker
Book House, 1966. A standard reference work on the major cults,
including Jehovah's Witnesses, Mormonism, Christian Science,
Unity, and Spiritualism. From a Christian perspective, Lewis
provides theological answers to cultic claims.
39. Lewis, Gordon R. *What Everyone Should Know about
Transcendental Meditation.* Ventura, CA: Regal Books, 1975. A brief
treatment of transcendental meditation from a Christian
perspective.
40. Marsh, C. R. *Share Your Faith With a Muslim.* Chicago, IL: Moody

Press, 1975. A perspective on Islam, giving its history, doctrines, and explaining how to share Christ with a Muslim.

41. Martin, Walter, ed. *Walter Martin's Cults Reference Bible.* Santa Ana, CA: Vision House Publishers, Inc., 1981. A unique volume, explaining the texts of the Old and New Testaments (King James Version) used by the major cults in support of their own teachings. Martin gives the cultic misinterpretation and the biblical Christian response to each passage. Also included are essays on all of the major cults, charts comparing the teachings of the major cults, a dictionary of terms misused by the cults, a brief essay on interpreting the Bible, and biblical helps for those witnessing to the cults.

42. Martin, Walter. *Jehovah of the Watchtower.* Minneapolis, MN: Bethany House Publishers, 1982. A re-release of Martin's classic of the Jehovah's Witnesses originally published by Moody Press. Martin deals with the history and doctrines of Jehovah's Witnesses and provides biblical responses to each of its major doctrines.

43. Martin, Walter. *Kingdom of the Cults.* Minneapolis, MN: Bethany House, 1966, and 1975. This is the classic Christian volume on the major traditional cults. A 1982 edition is completely updated with current documentation.

44. Martin, Walter. *The Maze of Mormonism.* Santa Ana, CA: Vision House Publishers, Inc. 1978. An expansive revision of Martin's 1962 classic by the same title is perhaps the best Christian treatment of the major teachings of Mormonism.

45. Martin, Walter. *The New Cults.* Santa Ana, CA: Vision House Publishers, Inc., 1980. An excellent treatment of some newer cults. The history of each cult and its leader is discussed along with each individual belief in the areas of God, Jesus Christ, man, salvation, and Scripture. Cults covered include: The Way International, Hinduism, est, the Children of God, The Ascended Masters, Silva Mind Control, Church of the Living Word, Foundation of Human Understanding, and The Local Church of Witness Lee.

46. Martin, Walter. *Rise of the Cults.* Santa Ana, CA: Vision House Publishers, Inc. 1980. A revision and update of the 1955 classic of the same title by Walter Martin. Condensed from *The Kingdom of the Cults.*

47. McElveen, Floyd C. *The Mormon Illusion.* Ventura, CA: Regal Books, 1977. A traditional Christian treatment of Mormonism, discussing Mormon history, sacred scriptures, and major doctrines.

48. Miller, Calvin. *Transcendental Hesitation.* Grand Rapids, MI: Zondervan Publishing House, 1977. An in-depth treatment of transcendental meditation, with discussion of Eastern mysticism compared to a biblical world-view.

49. Miller, William McElwee. *The Bahai Faith: Its History and Teaching.* South Pasadena, CA: William Carey Library, 1974. The best book in the English language from a Christian perspective on the Bahai Faith.

50. Miller, William McElwee. *Ten Muslims Meet Christ.* Grand Rapids, MI: William B. Eerdmans Publishing Co., 1969. Testimonies of Muslims who have accepted Christ, and a description of the persecution they have suffered in their native Muslim lands.

51. Milmine, George E. *The Life of Mary Baker G. Eddy and The History*

of Christian Science. Grand Rapids, MI: Baker Book House, 1909 and 1937. A classic biography of Mary Baker Eddy, explaining how she developed her cult by taking the teachings of Christian Science from previous writers and thinkers.

52. Morey, Robert A. *Horoscopes and the Christian.* Minneapolis, MN: Bethany House Publishers, 1981. A short booklet on the history and main tenets of astrology with a Christian response.

53. Morey, Robert A. *Reincarnation and Christianity.* Minneapolis, MN: Bethany House Publishers, 1980. An excellent treatment of reincarnation with biblical answers. Written for Morey's doctrinal treatise, it displays good scholarship and documentation.

54. Needleman, Jacob. *The New Religion.* New York, NY: E. P. Duttleman and Co., 1970. A non-Christian review of the main teachings of major religions as well as some of the new cults. The section of Zen Buddhism is particularly good.

55. Palmer, Bernard. *Understanding the Islamic Explosion.* Beaverlodge, Alberta, Canada: Horizon House Publishers, 1980. A Christian perspective on Islam, the Mideast problems (e.g. oil embargo), and how they relate to the Christian.

56. Passantino, Robert and Gretchen. *Answers to the Cultists at Your Door.* Eugene, OR: Harvest House Publishers, 1981. An excellent treatment of the five major cults Christians may encounter at the door of their homes or in public places. It deals with Jehovah's Witnesses, Mormons, Moonies, Hare Krishna, and The Way International. In addition, the book discusses the reasons for cults, characteristics of cultists and cult leaders, how to protect loved ones from the cults, and biblical responses to the major claims of each of these cults. This book is meant to help the average Christian reader.

57. Petersen, William J. *Those Curious New Cults.* New Canaan, CT: Keats Publishing, Inc., 1975. An evangelical treatment of some major new cults, as well as Spiritualism, Witchcraft, Satanism, and Astrology. A brief section on Scientology is included.

58. Rawlings, Maurice S. *Life Wish (Reincarnation: Reality or Hoax?)* Nashville, TN: Thomas Nelson Publishers, 1981. A Christian perspective on the major teachings of reincarnation contrasted with biblical truth.

59. Richardson, Don. *Eternity in Their Hearts.* Ventura, CA: Regal Books, 1981. A good perspective on the biblical view of the origin of religion including folk religions from pre-literate societies.

60. Ridenour, Fritz. *So What's the Difference?* Ventura, CA: Regal Books, 1967 and 1979. A brief introduction to some of the major religions and cults, including Buddhism, Mormonism, Unitarianism, Roman Catholicism, Christian Science, Protestantism, Jehovah's Witnesses, Islam, Hinduism, and Judaism. This book is especially compiled to work well in adult education.

61. Ringgren, Helmer. *Religions of the Ancient and Near East.* Philadelphia, PA: The Westminster Press, 1973. A discussion of Samarian, Babylonian, Syrian, and West Semitic religions and how they relate to the Book of Revelation.

62. Rosten, Leo. *Religions in America.* New York, NY: Simon and Schuster, 1963. A standard non-Christian review of the major cults and religions in the United States; however, since the articles were contributed by each group, religion, or cult concerned, the teachings represented are not necessarily objective.

63. Shah, Douglas. *The Meditators.* Plainfield, NJ: Logos International, 1975. A popular Christian treatment of Transcendental Meditation, Mysticism, Zen, Yoga, and other Eastern movements and religions.

64. Smith, Houston. *The Religions of Man.* New York, NY: Harper and Row, 1958. A classic, brief treatment of the major world religions from a non-Christian point of view.

65. Sparks, Jack. *The Mind Benders.* Nashville, TN: Thomas Nelson Publishers, 1977 and 1979. A church historian's point of view of the Unification Church, The Way, Children of God, The Local Church, Transcendental Meditation, Divine Light Mission, Hare Krishna, and The Peoples Temple. Sparks is a conservative evangelical Christian who uses the writings of the early Church and the creeds of the Church councils (along with authoritative Old and New Testament Scriptures) to refute the major teachings of these cults.

66. Spittler, Russell P. *Cults and Isms.* Grand Rapids, MI: Baker Book House, 1962. An old but still useful book on some of the major cults, including Mormonism, Spiritualism, Christian Science, Jehovah's Witnesses, Unity, Moral Rearmament (which is no longer a vital movement), Theosophy, Bahaism, Zen Buddhism, Anglo-Israelism, Astrology, Father Divine, Rosicrucianism, Swedenborgianism, Modernism, Humanism, Unitarianism, Universalism, Liberalism, and Neo-Orthodoxy.

67. Stoner, Carroll, and Jo Anne Parke. *All God's Children.* Radnor, PA: Chilton Book Co., 1977. Written by two journalists, this book is a non-Christian observation of people involved in some of the new cults. It explains the teachings of new cults and why they may be dangerous for young people.

68. Sumrall, Lester. *Where Was God When Pagan Religions Began?* Nashville, TN: Thomas Nelson Publishers, 1980. A discussion of the biblical texts related to the rise of world religions, with biblical responses to the major tenets of these faiths.

69. Tanenbaum, Marc H. and Marvin R. Wilson and A. James Rudin., eds. *Evangelicals and Jews in Conversation on Scripture, Theology, and History.* Grand Rapids, MI: Baker Book House, 1978. An objective portrayal of the differences between Judaism and Christianity, especially between modern Judaism and evangelical Christianity. This is a very good resource book using the format of a conversational interchange.

70. Weldon, John. *The Transcendental Explosion.* Irvine, CA: Harvest House Publishers, 1976. An excellent in-depth research treatment on the history and teachings of Transcendental Meditation.

71. White, Mel. *Deceived.* Old Tappan, NJ: Fleming H. Revell Co., 1979. A Christian analysis of The Peoples Temple in Guyana, explaining how such a tragedy could happen and how to watch out for other groups that may be similar.

72. Williams, J. L. *Victor Paul Wierwille and The Way International.* Chicago, IL: Moody Press, 1979. The best single volume treatment of the history and teachings of The Way International with a biblical response.

73. Yamamoto, J. Isamu. *The Puppet Master.* Downers Grove, IL: Intervarsity Press, 1977. An appraisal of the teachings of the Unification Church with a biblical response. Yamamoto especially emphasizes a sociological perspective.

Index